The Romance of
American Psychology

The Romance of American Psychology

Political Culture in the Age of Experts

Ellen Herman

UNIVERSITY OF CALIFORNIA PRESS

Berkeley / Los Angeles / London

The publisher gratefully acknowledges the contribution provided by the General Endowment Fund of the Associates of the University of California Press.

University of California Press
Berkeley and Los Angeles, California

University of California Press
London, England

Copyright © 1995 by The Regents of the University of California

Library of Congress Cataloging-in-Publication Data

Herman, Ellen.
     The romance of American psychology : political culture in the age
of experts / Ellen Herman.
         p.   cm.
     Includes bibliographical references and index.
     ISBN 0-520-08598-1 (cloth : alk. paper)
     1. Psychology—United States—History—20th century.
I. Title.
BF108.U5H47   1995
150'.973'09045—dc20   94-26930
                                                                  CIP

Printed in the United States of America

1   2   3   4   5   6   7   8   9

The paper used in this publication meets the minimum requirements of American National Standard for Information Sciences—Permanence of Paper for Printed Library Materials, ANSI Z39.48-1984

The type of oppression which threatens de-mocracies is different from anything there has ever been in the world before. . . . It likes to see the citizens enjoy themselves, pro-vided they think of nothing but enjoyment. It gladly works for their happiness but wants to be sole agent and judge of it. It provides for their security, foresees and sup-plies their necessities, facilitates their plea-sures, manages their principal concerns, di-rects their industry, makes rules for their testaments, and divides their inheritances. Why should it not entirely relieve them from the trouble of thinking and all the cares of living?

—Alexis de Tocqueville, *Democracy in America*

Contents

ABBREVIATIONS   ix

ACKNOWLEDGMENTS   xi

1
In the Name of Enlightenment   1

2
War on the Enemy Mind   17

3
The Dilemmas of Democratic Morale   48

4
Nervous in the Service   82

5
The Career of Cold War Psychology   124

6
Project Camelot and Its Aftermath   153

7
The Damaging Psychology of Race   174

8
The Kerner Commission and the Experts   208

9
The Growth Industry   238

10
The Curious Courtship of Psychology and Women's
Liberation   276

11
Toward a Larger Jurisdiction for Psychology   304

NOTES   317

INDEX   395

Abbreviations

AAA	American Anthropological Association
APA	American Psychological Association
ApA	American Psychiatric Association
ARPA	Advanced Research Projects Agency
AWP	Association for Women Psychologists (later renamed the Association for Women in Psychology)
CIA	Central Intelligence Agency
CNM	Committee for National Morale
CORE	Congress on Racial Equality
CRESS	Center for Research in Social Systems
DOD	Department of Defense
DOS	Department of State
FBI	Federal Bureau of Investigation
FCRC	Federal Contract Research Center
FEPC	Fair Employment Practices Commission
FMAD	Foreign Morale Analysis Division
GAP	Group for the Advancement of Psychiatry
HEW	Department of Health, Education and Welfare
JCMIH	Joint Commission on Mental Illness and Health
NAACP	National Association for the Advancement of Colored People
NIMH	National Institute of Mental Health
NLF	National Liberation Front
NMHA	National Mental Health Act
NRC	National Research Council

NSF	National Science Foundation
NYRW	New York Radical Women
OFF	Office of Facts and Figures
ONR	Office of Naval Research
OSS	Office of Strategic Services
OWI	Office of War Information
PHS	Public Health Service
PWD	Psychological Warfare Division
SHAEF	Supreme Headquarters, Allied Expeditionary Force
SORO	Special Operations Research Office
SPSSI	Society for the Psychological Study of Social Issues
TAT	Thematic Apperception Test
VA	Veterans Administration
VC M&M	Viet-Cong Motivation and Morale Project
WRA	War Relocation Authority

Acknowledgments

A wise person once said that it takes a whole village to raise a child. Bringing a book into being, I have discovered, is no solitary enterprise either. Without the people who graced this project with personal support, intellectual interest, and plain old curiosity, there would surely be no book at all. My heartfelt thanks to everyone who has been part of my village during the past several years, including the many who go unnamed below.

A number of individuals read large portions of the manuscript and responded with questions that invariably enriched my perspective, even though I could not always answer them well, or sometimes at all. Gerry Grob went especially far out of his way to help me, and it made all the difference. Peter Buck, Jim Capshew, Cynthia Enloe, Ben Harris, Steve Heims, Jim Kloppenberg, Jill Morawski, Sam Schweber, Andy Scull, Mark Solovey, and Steve Whitfield were kind and generous readers. Their collective breadth of knowledge sustained my search for common ground between diverse historical and social scientific fields. It goes without saying that I alone am guilty of whatever errors of fact and interpretation are to be found in the following pages.

I am also grateful to those who lifted my spirits by insisting that I had something of value to say, usually a long time before they had any reason to believe that I actually did. For their confidence, my sincerest thanks go to Betty Bayer, Larry Friedman, Laurel Furumoto, Walter Jackson, Wendy Kaminer, Jeff Masson, Henry Minton, Barbara Tischler, Fernando Vidal, and Bill Woodward.

The History of American Civilization Program at Brandeis University, and the Crown Fellowship, provided me with all-important material aid while I was a graduate student. My research was also financially supported, at the beginning, by a grant from the Rockefeller Archive Center and, at the end, by the Dibner Summer Grant for Research in History of Science. Without the vast resources of Widener Library, my task would have been much more difficult.

During the past several years, students at the University of Massachusetts at Boston and Harvard University have provided me with new appreciation for the challenge of combining critical intelligence with historical imagination. I hope that this book returns some small measure of the favor they have done me. My deepest thanks to Julie Schor, for her advocacy on my behalf, and to the Harvard Committee on Degrees in Women's Studies, for the always warm welcome and great food. I am indebted to Judy Vichniac, John McCole, and the Harvard Committee on Degrees in Social Studies for providing me with a wonderful place to hang my hat and pursue my education.

Elizabeth Knoll, editor *extraordinaire* at the University of California Press, has, from the very first, been just the sort of smart critic and enthusiastic advocate I wanted. Not only did she believe in what I was trying to accomplish; she helped me get there. For their important contributions to the bookmaking process, I would also like to thank Peter Kosenko for his meticulous copyediting, Rebecca Frazier for her varied talents in production management and scheduling, and Diana Feinberg for skilled assistance with promotion and illustrations.

My former co-workers at South End Press—especially Michael Albert, Carl Conetta, Todd Jailer, Mary Lea, Cynthia Peters, Lydia Sargent, John Schall, and Pat Walker—contributed more than they ever realized to my education. The writers whose ideas we were privileged to publish are too numerous to mention here, but their example has never ceased to inspire me.

Without a community of good friends, the time I spent on this book would have been a lot less fun than it was. For their inexhaustible reserves of good humor and willingness to endure my stubborn interest in psychology and its mysterious ways, thanks to Barbara Beltrand, Steve Birnbaum, Michael Bronski, Amy Hoffman, Carol Katz, Sue Landers, Ellen Lapowsky, and Kate Raisz. Alejandro de Avila has become a treasured member of my family as well as a dear friend. He will always have my love and profound gratitude for the door he opened several years ago.

Finally, there is no language fit to acknowledge the gift of love I have received from my immediate family. For once, words are not necessary. Lynn Stephen and Gabriel Stephen-Herman know exactly how I feel.

1

In the Name of Enlightenment

Psychological insight is the creed of our time. In the name of enlightenment, experts promise help and faith, knowledge and comfort. They devise confident formulas for happy living and ambitious plans for dissolving the knots of conflict. Psychology, according to its boosters, possesses worthwhile answers to our most difficult personal questions and practical solutions for our most intractable social problems.

In the late twentieth-century United States, we are likely to believe what psychological experts tell us. They speak with authority to a vast audience and have become familiar figures in most communities, in the media, and in virtually every corner of popular culture. Their advice is a big business. It is taken for granted that they have a right to a central place in debates about the current state and future direction of American society. From families to governments, from abuse and recovery to war and urban violence, from the mysteries of individual subjectivity to the manifest problems of our collective social life, few institutions, issues, or spheres of existence remain untouched by the progress of psychology in American society.

More important, the progress of psychology has changed American society. Americans today are likely to measure personal and civic experience according to a calculus of mental and emotional health—"self-esteem" in the current vernacular. We have been convinced that who we are and how we feel are more tangible, and probably also more relevant yardsticks, than whether our society lives up to its reputation of democracy and equality, ideals that appear increasingly abstract, difficult to grasp, and remote from the dilemmas of daily life. Many people have willingly severed the self from its social ecology, perhaps because of the need for protection against the emotionally toxic hazards of contemporary existence. Feelings of powerlessness against those conditions that shape the self—from mind-numbing corporate depersonalization to the violence ever-present on city streets—have nurtured forms of vehement individualism and elicited desperate hopes that the self can be nurtured and managed at a social distance, out of harm's way. Yet the fundamental awareness that no self exists, except in relation to others and in the context of social reality, survives at the very heart of psychological knowledge itself.

How has this happened? When did psychological experts, professions, practices, and ideas first rise to such public prominence? Why has psychology become so visible? What historical developments have inspired the "romance" of American psychology? This book begins to answer these questions by tracing psychology's rapid spread through post–World War II American society. It explains why and how psychological experts carved out a progressively larger sphere of social influence and asks what difference their success has made in our public life.

Because this book describes a wide-ranging campaign to infuse society with psychological enlightenment, it takes an equally wide-ranging view of who psychological experts were and what they did. This book is not a disciplinary history. It does not focus on professionalization, the evolution of particular theoretical schools, or the status of gatekeeping efforts between psychology and other bodies of social knowledge, even though all of these issues surface from time to time.

Who are "psychological experts"? Many of the people and organizations discussed in this book were affiliated with psychology through the usual procedures of academic and professional training. They pursued doctoral degrees in psychology or attended medical schools where they specialized in psychiatry. Between 1940 and 1970, the numbers of psychologists and psychiatrists belonging to their respective professional organizations climbed astronomically, surpassing both the growth curves in these professions prior to 1940 and those in other medical and academic fields after 1940, although the vast majority remained white and male. Membership in the American Psychological Association (APA) grew by more than 1,100 percent, from 2,739 in 1940 to 30,839 in 1970.[1] During this same period, membership in the American Psychiatric Association (ApA) rose 760 percent, from 2,423 to 18,407.[2]

In the years since 1970, the numbers of these experts have continued to skyrocket and their demographic profile—mostly white, male, and of European ancestry—has started to change as people of diverse ethnic backgrounds, and especially women, have entered the professions. As of 1993, the American Psychological Association boasted approximately 75,000 members and the American Psychiatric Association had passed the 38,000-member mark. More bachelors degrees were awarded in psychology than in most other social or natural science fields (biology and computer science still edged out psychology, but not by much) and, in 1986, there were 253,500 psychologists employed in the United States, of which approximately 22 percent held doctoral degrees. In that same year, the National Science Foundation estimated that civilian employment in psychology would increase between 27 and 39 percent by the year 2000, a far larger jobs boom than the 13 to 23 percent forecasted for all occupations. Throughout the entire postwar era, the United States has trained and employed more psychological experts, per capita, than any other country in the world.[3]

Not only were there more of them, but their careers were more varied. In addition to its traditional ties to scientific experimentation, theoretical production, and testing design and administration, psychological expertise has recently become nearly synonymous with mental health. Today, therapeutic proficiency is considered psychology's most important contribution to human understanding, happiness, and peace. This is a new development. Before World War II, professional healers and counselors were few; most individuals allied with psychology did work unrelated to "helping." After 1945 clinical occupations witnessed extraordinary growth. Today, the three largest divisions of the American Psychological Association all address the practice of psychotherapy and most of the future growth in psychological employment is projected in social and health service sectors. Clinical professionals outside of psychology and psychiatry may be especially well positioned to take advantage of future opportunities because their training is less extensive and their incomes lower. The ranks of clinical social workers alone, for example, more than tripled between 1975 and 1990, growing from 25,000 to 80,000.[4] Fields with ties to psychology's nineteenth-century past, such as physiological and philosophical psychology, on the other hand, have shrunk into numerical obscurity.

Because one of this book's goals is to document the far-flung influence of psychological ideas and practices, I also consider individuals located outside of the formal confines of psychology and psychiatry whose work was interdisciplinary in orientation or was carried out by interdisciplinary teams. Numerous anthropologists and sociologists, for example, considered themselves mental and behavioral experts, and they marched with their psychological colleagues under the banners of "culture and personality," "behavioral science," and "community mental health." This book explores why the vision of a comprehensive human science was especially tantalizing, and appeared so necessary, during the postwar decades.

That they occasionally championed similar causes does not make all of the social sciences identical to psychology, of course. Significant differences in orientation and subject matter remained between distinct professions and academic disciplines. The enthusiastic drive for unified knowledge does, however, indicate how appealing psychology was during these years to people whose concerns had little to do with the psychological (at least as "the psychological" had been understood formerly), how effectively psychological ideas were exported throughout general social-scientific ranks, and how central psychological insights were to the drive for relevant expertise. Because it illuminates why many of the geographic markers in the landscape of social knowledge appeared arbitrary to those whose ambitions included the design of social change, the history of psychological experts promises new insights into some of the most important intellectual shifts in recent years.

In the late nineteenth and early twentieth centuries, psychology's development as an academic discipline had been circumscribed for important historical reasons and experts continued to follow the upward trajectory of professionalization throughout the postwar era. After 1945, however, they clearly outgrew these bounds. What is most intriguing about psychology in recent decades—and what demands a fresh perspective on its historical evolution and social importance—is that it has flowed freely beyond customary professional domains. It no longer suffices to think of psychology as merely one category of expertise among others. Psychology in our time is a veritable worldview. As much as anything else, the romance of contemporary psychology emanates from its promise to satisfy the hunger for values and the desire for affirmation at the same time that myriad disorienting changes have demoted traditional beliefs to unsatisfying, even fallacious, platitudes.

Which leads to the obvious question: what does the term "psychology" mean? My use of the term "psychology" does not stop at the margins of an academic discipline or the boundaries of a professional job category. Rather, it indicates an emphasis on analyzing mental processes, interpersonal relationships, introspection, and behavior as a way of explaining both individual and social realities.

As an academic discipline, psychology traces its historical roots to nineteenth-century philosophy and physiology. But in the period after World War II, it has already been noted, the professions most likely to be associated with psychological expertise were those that originated in or had grown into "helping" trades: psychiatry, clinical psychology, and social work.[5] This varied and flexible history allowed psychological experts to make extremely broad claims to authority. They possessed, in turn, a technology of behavior, a science of social relations, a theory of society, and a theology of emotional healing. Psychology sometimes appeared as a social or natural science, sometimes as a source of moral, cultural, and political values that could address the meaning of human identity and existence, matters that were traditionally the exclusive province of religion or philosophy.

In the late twentieth-century United States, psychology's face is so familiar that it is tempting, but wrong, to consider it an ahistorical fact of life or an entity so amorphous and all-pervasive that it eludes definition altogether. Psychology may have seeped into virtually every facet of existence, but that does not mean that it has always been there or that what experts say has always mattered as much as it matters today.

Understanding the recent history of psychological experts is critical to understanding psychology's place in contemporary society. That history, the subject of this book, is based on an extraordinary quest for power. Enveloped in a climate of catastrophic global militarism and divisive national debate over the realization of racial and sexual equality, psychological experts shaped the direction and texture of public life deliberately, with results that were striking and unprecedented.

Because the appearance of psychological experts and their explanations in the policy-making process has been especially visible and important since 1940, this book begins with World War II. No event illustrates better how military conflict offered psychologists unprecedented opportunities to demonstrate the practical worth of their social theories, human sciences, and behavioral technologies in making and shaping public policy. While the New Deal had offered some social scientists, especially economists, the chance to exhibit the practical assistance that social experts could bring to large-scale federal operations in the years prior to 1940, it was the atmosphere of international military crisis and conflict after 1941 that permitted new varieties of social experts to outgrow their roles as private citizens and carve out niches for themselves in government, and as government advisors.

From World War II through the Vietnam era, psychological experts decisively shaped Americans' understanding of what significant public issues were and what should be done about them. How could the United States win the hearts and minds of Third World people on the battlegrounds of the Cold War? Why did bigoted attitudes and racial hatreds stubbornly persist in a society allegedly devoted to the freedom of all its citizens? What sorts of emotional adjustments would equality between men and women require? Psychological experts applied themselves to these questions, determined to understand such diverse phenomena as the appeal of revolutionary ideologies and the emotional logic of stereotyping. Their efforts were generally informed by a unified conception of behavior, a conviction that the relevant underlying variables were pretty much the same in all the most vulnerable areas of social life. Frustration and aggression, the logic of personality formation, and the gender dynamics involved in the production of healthy (or damaged) selves were legitimate sources of insight into problems at home and conflicts abroad. Why were these experts so persuasive? This is the question I have tried to answer.

This book recounts the story of psychology's rise to public power. But along the way, experts had moments of terrible disappointment and even delusion. When policy-makers rejected their research and counsel, experts seethed in frustration. On the other hand, when policy-makers embraced psychological theories as blueprints for public action and ordinary citizens espoused psychological ideas as beacons of personal understanding, experts tended to exaggerate their triumphs and imagine themselves more powerful than they actually were. In the 1940s and 1950s, few observers of the intellectual scene were able to assess these wild vacillations between despair and jubilation with any critical perspective, but maverick sociologist C. Wright Mills was such a rare critic. Marginalized within his discipline because of his radical ideas and sometimes difficult personal style, Mills was nevertheless one of the first postwar sociologists to reach a popular audience with books such as *The Causes of World War Three* (1958) and *Listen, Yankee* (1960). In *White Collar* (1951), he chastised members of his own intellectual generation for arrogant pretensions to power and pointed out that critical independence had largely given way to pathetic subservience among "intellectuals caught up in and overwhelmed by the managerial demiurge in a bureaucratic world of organized irresponsibility."[6]

Yet even Mills could see what others saw. The traumatic events of his time—the Holocaust, the ravages of world war, and a superpower rivalry that gambled the future of humanity and the planet itself—called rationality and autonomy into question. History itself was defying explanation, or even comprehension, as if warning that too much faith in the tenets of democratic theory could be a grave error. Instead, the events of midcentury drew urgent attention to a shadowy psychological underside, difficult to fathom and teeming with raw and unpredictable passions, as the likely controlling factor in human behavior. Persuaded that social developments and conflicts were hardly ever what they appeared to be, many observers (some eager, others reluctant) discarded habitual ways of studying and mediating social problems. Logical approaches, commonsense assumptions, and empirical commitments seemed shallow and inadequate in comparison with an alternative that promised insight into the irrationality and madness lurking just beneath the thin veneer of a civilized social order. "We need to characterize American society of the mid-twentieth century in more psychological terms," Mills freely acknowledged in 1951, "for now the problems that concern us most border on the psychiatric."[7]

The fact that setbacks and blunders were part of their history does not diminish the remarkable impact that psychological experts have had on postwar American society. It merely indicates that their historical progress between 1940 and 1970 was not monolithic. Nor should the central concerns of this book—efforts to bring psychological enlightenment to bear on the prosecution of war and the management of racial and gender conflict—be considered a comprehensive historical account of experts loyal to the psychological persuasion. During the postwar era, experts devoted considerable attention to other questions of social importance, from crime and education to industrial relations. Their stories remain to be told.

Not all experts agreed that psychology had a special responsibility to grease the wheels of society; countertrends existed throughout the period surveyed in this book. In psychology, there were those who drew a sharp line between science and society, kept faith with the laboratory as the only legitimate site for the production and verification of new knowledge, and viewed colleagues who testified before Congress and spoke out on public issues as alarming proof that many psychologists were prone to confusing personal politics and professional responsibilities.

B. F. Skinner, probably America's most famous psychologist, was never one to dismiss psychology's social role, but he did believe that laboratory experiments in behavioral reinforcement and conditioning held the key to even the most complicated social reforms. After the 1948 publication of *Walden Two,* a best-selling psychological utopia in which every detail was meticulously planned by wise and benevolent experts, much of Skinner's fame rested on his supreme confidence in social engineering. At the same time, he despised socially oriented psychologists who did not share his behaviorist philosophy. He did not consider them scientists, and was quick to dismiss the accumulated knowledge of the social sciences. "I don't believe we have any principles in political science or in economics that can be trusted," Skinner commented as late as 1980.[8] Whatever assistance psychology could offer society would, he felt sure, be grounded in a rigorous process of scientific discovery, and not some fuzzy-headed notion that analyzing social phenomena required insights transcending nature.

Experimentalist Edwin G. Boring of Harvard, known as "Mr. Psychology" and distinguished for his involvement in professional affairs as well as for his writing about the history of psychology, shared many of Skinner's scientific ideals but was leery of *any* psychologists who seemed too eager to put experts in charge. He made his distaste for socially oriented psychologists (his term was "sociotropes") perfectly clear on numerous occasions. "Can a sociotrope believe in democracy and work for it?" he asked skeptically in 1946. "Or does he know so much about the control of opinion that he feels contemptuous of its free expression or doubts that the word 'free' has any true meaning?" "These people," Boring concluded, "do not think they are arrogant but I think they are."[9]

Similarly, in psychiatry, those who advocated following in the footsteps of somatic medicine sought to steer clear of messy social questions. Their aim was to uncover the biological basis of mental illness and develop new drugs and surgical techniques that might move people toward health. C. C. Burlingame, for example, the psychiatrist-in-chief of the Hartford, Connecticut, Institute for Living and a staunch advocate of psychosurgery, ran for president of the American Psychiatric Association in 1948. He promised to be a leader who would "uphold the traditions of the association as a scientific medical group and not one that is trying to tell everyone else what to do and how to live."[10]

But Burlingame's campaign to defend psychiatry's historic roots from the corrupting influence of social activism was moving against the tide, and he lost his bid for professional office.

After 1945 a variety of dissidents like Boring and Burlingame stubbornly argued that psychologists and psychiatrists had no particular business involving themselves in the affairs of society, at least not as mental and behavioral experts. To do so was pronounced meddlesome, arrogant, and a serious lapse from scientific and professional obligations. Although theirs was a vision consistent with the nineteenth-century roots of psychological science and psychiatric medicine, it became more and more of a minority viewpoint during the period covered by this book. After World War II, it lost considerable ground.

In ascendance was the view that psychology demanded aggressive social intervention, not by experts acting merely as citizens, but by experts acting as an organized constituency, in the name of enlightenment. It is the rise of this outlook that I have described as the romance of American psychology. How and why it placed upon psychology awesome responsibility for its social surroundings, and endowed it with an equally awesome social authority, is documented and interpreted in the following pages.

The crusade for enlightenment proceeded rapidly after 1945. Due in some measure to their own talents and ambitions, psychological experts' rise to power was due initially to the benefits of war: world war at first, then Cold War. Military imperatives during World War II provided psychological experts with their first encounter with policymakers. Working in organizations devoted to civilian and military mobilization, and having their favorite theories applied to wartime problems, gave them their first taste of power. This formative experience advertised their ideas and earned them bountiful state patronage, both of which served to enhance their professional status. It also inspired a series of correlations that stayed with psychological experts long after 1945: between professional responsibility and patriotic service to the state; between scientific advance, national security, and domestic tranquillity; between mental health and cultural maturity; between psychological enlightenment, social welfare, and the government of a democratic society.

The alliance between psychological knowledge and power may appear ideological in retrospect, but during much of the postwar era it was considered so axiomatic as to be nearly invisible. In spite of the dramatically changed nation and world that came into view after 1945, the lessons of World War II remained at the very heart of psychology's relationship to a diversity of public issues. For two decades they resisted discussion and escaped meaningful scrutiny.

By the end of the 1960s, the general perspective nourished by World War II and the early Cold War years was finally being interrogated, quite passionately, in public. Opposition to the Vietnam War polarized the country, and frustration with the government's sluggish response to domestic movements for equality and civil rights produced a contradictory mixture of cynical demoralization and spirited activism. The crisis of the 1960s also provoked a thorough reassessment of the assumptions about knowledge and power, expertise and government, that had animated earlier decades. The war's managers, after all, were "the best and the brightest," men whose excellent educations had typically included liberal doses of up-to-date social science. Yet the conduct of the war inspired a degree of dishonesty and moral indifference in high places that shocked and sickened many Americans, casting a long shadow over the alliance between social knowledge and democracy that had been cemented during World War II. The 1960s must therefore be counted as a momentous turning point in recent political, intellectual, and cultural history. That decade's questions about the role of experts in a democratic society altered the way that policy-makers, intellectuals, and masses of ordinary citizens thought about public concerns, social responsibilities, and the various guises of modern authority. As antiwar critic Noam Chomsky put it in 1966, "It is the responsibility of intellectuals to speak the truth and to expose lies. This, at least, may seem enough of a truism to pass without comment. Not so, however. For the modern intellectual, it is not at all obvious. . . . The question 'What have I done?' is one that we may well ask ourselves . . . as we create, or mouth, or tolerate the deceptions that will be used to justify the next defense of freedom."[11]

What exactly have psychological experts done? Have they spoken the truth or manufactured deception? Have they expanded the realm of freedom or perfected the means of control? While this book suggests no simple answers to these questions, it surveys the history of psychological experts, justified at every step as an enlightening crusade, and concludes that these experts helped to transform the conceptual foundations of public life in the postwar United States.

Other writers who have commented on psychology's history have tended to produce radically divergent narratives: self-satisfied pronouncements about the inevitable goodness of scientific progress and

cranky accusations that psychology has engendered tolerance for programs of capitalist exploitation and bureaucratic depersonalization by
repackaging them as liberation. While its fans credit psychology with
being an almost magical science, its critics complain that psychology
has mainly succeeded in bringing more facets of human experience under the thumb of the market, and with more miserable results, than
was ever before the case. Writing about psychology's history and social
importance, in other words, has been as elastic as its subject, applauding
its benevolence on the one hand and denouncing its repressive capacities on the other.[12]

In this book, psychology is not fixed at one particular point on this
spectrum of moral evaluation for two important reasons. First, I wished
to recapture the meaning of social responsibility and professional ethics
among experts in the 1940s and 1950s in order to better understand
why the 1960s and post-1960s intellectual generation came to see
things in such dramatically different terms. Second, distinctions between democratic and antidemocratic uses of knowledge have changed
over time; the line separating them has a great deal more to do with
the social context of ideas than with factors intrinsic to knowledge production.

The application of psychological expertise to ends (such as racial harmony) that appear admirable today was often motivated by the very
same set of ideological assumptions that inspired episodes (such as
counterinsurgency) unlikely to attract many favorable reviews. For this
reason I do not rigidly segregate either the disparate forms or functions
of psychology. Scientific discovery or clinical practice, technological innovation or philosophical inquiry, theoretical understanding or practical application—these represented different forms of the same enterprise, at least as far as the relationship between knowledge and power
was concerned. In this book I wish to illuminate the common worldview diverse experts shared while attending to the differences in their
immediate subjects and aims. Whatever division I have imposed has
therefore been solely for the purpose of orderly discussion. (The history
of experts who thought of themselves as social and behavioral scientists
is concentrated in chapters 2 and 3 and 5 through 8; the history of their
clinical counterparts can be found mainly in chapters 4, 9, and 10.)

It may be disquieting to some readers that I neither automatically
condemn the advocacy of social engineering by some experts nor embrace the helping credo of others. But one of my goals is to demonstrate that the respective genealogies of "control" and "freedom" are

as connected as their political reputations are disconnected. To choose denunciation or celebration might seem more straightforward, but it would mislead by reassuring us that today "we" always know better than "they" did, and could surely never make similar mistakes.

Some of the experts discussed in this book treated society as a sick patient in need of cure. They attempted to control populations by administering internment camps according to psychiatric principles, tracking the vicissitudes of wartime morale, taking the pulse of Third World upheavals, and monitoring levels of racial tension in U.S. cities. Others treated individuals, seeking to induce personal adjustment and growth through a campaign of prevention and early intervention. These experts ministered to war-weary soldiers, promoted innovative mental health policies, and offered therapeutic services to ordinary citizens suffering from "normal neuroses."

Their daily chores may have been different, but all were involved in forms of human management that made the difference between unethical manipulation and enlightened facilitation appear vague—that is, when the difference was noticed at all. During and after World War II, social engineering was not a slur but a mission proudly embraced by experts active in the civil rights movement as well as by those involved in the Cold War military. Behavioral scientists who devised technologies to predict and control the behavior of populations abroad and at home were not entirely unlike clinicians who heralded the healthy personality as the basis for democracy, insisted that mental health could be mass-produced and purchased, and welcomed psychotherapy as a strategy for the manufacture of normality.

All claimed loyalty to a psychology capable of revealing universal laws about human experience, personality, social life, and subjectivity. All melded the understanding of individual and collective behavior, and in doing so, contributed significantly to the characteristic features of the postwar United States. One of the major conclusions of this book is that psychological experts have been a critical force in the recent convergence between private and public domains, cultural and political concerns. Joining the comprehension and change of self to the comprehension and change of society was their most enduring legacy.

In the end, these experts secured "a larger jurisdiction for psychology," though obstacles littered their path to power. The authority they gained was not inevitable and the forms it took were as historically conditioned as the fact and timing of psychological authority itself. In recent U.S. history, psychology has penetrated corners of politics and culture very distant from the challenges of personal adjustment usually associated with psychological healing. Psychological theory and research, as this book illustrates, became significant ingredients in public policies devoted to managing Cold War tensions abroad and racial tensions at home, while clinical theory and practice had the important, if often unintended, result of inspiring radical political critiques—feminism was one—that collapsed conventional boundaries between therapeutic and social aims by probing the relationship between the personal and the political.

Chapters 2 through 4 begin by examining World War II, a watershed in the history of psychology. Chapters 2 and 3 recount the wartime record of psychological experts in a wide range of policy-oriented occupations, from waging psychological warfare to administering internment camps and keeping tabs on fluctuating public opinion and morale. Chapter 4 discusses the efforts of clinical experts to aid the war effort by safeguarding the mental well-being of ordinary soldiers. The clinical lessons of war began a radical process of "normalizing" mental troubles, a process so comprehensive and far-reaching that it underlay the dramatic spread of clinical experience and clinicians' increasingly broad cultural appeal after 1945.

The next several chapters analyze the growing presence of psychological experts and ideas in particular areas of public policy after 1945. Chapter 5 covers the general outlines of psychology's Cold War career and describes the institutional, ideological, and theoretical developments that fueled the tight correspondence between psychology and national security during the 1950s and 1960s. Chapter 6 relates the fascinating story of Project Camelot, an ambitious, secret program built upon psychology's Cold War successes that inadvertently backfired and became an international scandal in 1965.

The benefits of war transcended military institutions, even war itself. Psychological work initiated during World War II thrived under the auspices of Cold War in the 1950s and flowed easily into domestic policy areas, such as the War on Poverty in the 1960s. Chapters 7 and 8 offer examples of this pattern in policies related to domestic racial conflict. Chapter 7 describes the evolution of psychological theories on racial identity and the sources of prejudice after World War II and explores how they were incorporated into constitutional law and social policy. Chapter 8 illustrates the ways in which these perspectives were incorporated into the research program and policy recommendations of the National Advisory Commission on Civil Disorders. Popularly known as the Kerner Commission, it was appointed by President Johnson in 1967 to investigate urban rioting and prevent future racial unrest.

The final two chapters return to the history of clinical experts, ideas, and practices first introduced in chapter 4. While policy-oriented activities made psychology's political potential explicit, clinicians became both more numerous and far more visible to the public during the postwar decades. For all intents and purposes, work associated with helping people adjust and cope constituted *the* popular reputation of psychological expertise during an era when the psychotherapeutic enterprise became, literally, a growth industry.

Associated with personal problems and anxieties, devoted to emotional adjustment and change, clinical practices at first glance appear apolitical, or at least very distant from the political questions addressed in the book's early chapters. Yet the history of clinical work has had equally fundamental consequences for U.S. public life. Although converting psychology into public culture was admittedly a less direct process than converting it into public policy, clinical developments served to alter the very definition and substance of "the political" as well as reorient the goals and styles of political participation in the postwar decades.

Chapter 9 examines the adoption of mental health as a policy priority of the federal government, the rapid popularization of psychotherapy, and the appearance of humanistic psychology, a theoretical and clinical orientation designed to move psychology away from the bizarre disturbances of a stigmatized minority and toward acceptance by the normal majority. Chapter 10 concludes with a look at the early years of the second wave of feminism, when psychology served not only to construct the female, but to construct the feminist and mobilize an agenda of "personal politics."

To this book, I bring a commitment to grasping the immediacy of lived experience with genuine interest and respect, placing subjectivity within the scope of serious inquiry, and challenging experts' fervent campaign to legitimize psychology by imitating the philosophical and methodological patterns of natural science. My perspective is shaped by the central assumption that subjective experience is real, intrinsically meaningful, and ultimately irreducible to anything outside itself. Consequently, I have made a conscious choice to consider the evidence of experience (how experts talked about war in reference to their successes and failures, for example, or why people said they sought psychothera-peutic help) as valid historical information without also turning per-sonal testimony into a type of unquestionable truth claim that obstructs critical interpretation. Good historical writing, in my view, necessarily combines the imaginative effort to represent experience with the analyt-ical ability to interpret it.[13]

The subject of this book—psychology's dramatic progress in U.S. society—is itself among the chief reasons why historians (and other ob-servers of postwar society) have been wrestling so constantly with ques-tions of identity, experience, and subjectivity in recent years. My own interest in these issues therefore marks me as a product of the very developments I document and necessarily precludes a vantage point strictly detached from the events I describe. On the other hand, if this book illustrates any single thing convincingly, I hope it illustrates how historically sensitive both subjectivity and its management have been. Psychological experts have not always existed, and during their rather brief existence, they have not converted everyone. Their rise to power and success occupies a peculiar historical niche, uniquely suited to illu-minating the recent past.

It should be obvious that I am neither a cheerleader for psychologi-cal expertise nor a disgusted detractor. I do not consider psychological enlightenment to be an unqualified good, but I also do not consider it notable exclusively as a sinister form of modern social control. Psychol-ogy, as this book shows, has been politically flexible and open to diver-gent interpretations. It has served to complicate, and often obscure, the exercise of power in recent U.S. history, but it has also legitimized innovative ideas and actions whose aim has been to personalize, and expand, the scope of liberty. On both counts, psychological experts have succeeded in large measure because they have addressed the sub-jective elements of human experience and these are both authentic and important. These are not the only important aspects of personal and social life, of course, but they cannot and must not be dismissed as peripheral matters, reduced to the status of dependent variables, or overlooked altogether.

The public consequences of psychological expertise during the pe-riod covered by this book were characteristically mixed and contradic-tory—sometimes repressive and deserving of condemnation, sometimes inspiring people to move boldly in pursuit of personal freedom and social justice. The popularization of psychological vocabulary and the public appearance of a language of subjectivity do not necessarily prove the seamlessness of elite domination or the existence of a tidal wave of false consciousness that blocks progressive social change by simultaneously corroding the self and making it the subject of almost obsessive attention. Inclinations toward personal growth, self-esteem, and pleasure can form the basis for new concepts of community and collective action even as they rationalize isolated programs of individual self-improvement.

There may be no way to prove the existence of a human impulse toward autonomy and freedom, but to deny it is to deny the deepest meaning of historical choices and the possibility of alternative futures. To believe in such an impulse is not to posit an ahistorical inner truth or a quarantined self divorced from social context; it is not to conceive of change as a stark choice forcing one to opt for social progress or personal happiness, but never both. If psychological knowledge is to mobilize people for progressive change, rather than equip them to endure new variations on old injustices, the dichotomy between internal and external transformation will have to be rejected as false and useless.

The self consists precisely of the many-faceted ties connecting the individual to the surrounding social ecology, knotting the institutional arrangement of race, gender, and class, among others, to personal identity, as it is actually experienced at particular historical moments. This is a complicated relationship, to be sure, but it is created by human beings and is subject to comprehension and change. As long as the dualism between personal and social existence stands, there are few choices but to elevate reason over emotion or emotion over reason, surrender to despair over hope or hope over despair, trust in expertise over ordinary intelligence or ordinary intelligence over expertise. And these are no alternatives at all.

This book is centrally concerned with these philosophical issues as well as with a number of the most significant historical developments of the postwar era: war, hot and cold; new social movements devoted to civil rights and social justice; government's appropriate functions and reach; experts' role in a democratic society. The romance of American psychology is important because there is something to psychological ideas, and not because psychological experts are smarter than the rest of us. This book points out what that "something" is while exploring its ramifications in public life, for better and for worse, during the postwar decades. It describes a little-noticed historical metamorphosis that deserves far greater attention, not simply because it was profound, but because our society today, and our future history, reverberate with its consequences.

2

War on the Enemy Mind

Mobilization for War

Well before the attack on Pearl Harbor, psychological experts began mobilizing to assist the war effort.[1] Their preparations, from the start, illustrated an awareness that offering patriotic assistance, earning professional advancement, and bringing psychological enlightenment to the business of government proceeded happily in unison. This link had been forged for psychologists during their first experience of world war, when they learned that war could accomplish what brilliant academic research and dedicated teaching failed to do. World War I "put the applications of psychology on the map and on the front page," fondly recalled James McKeen Cattell, a founding figure in professional psychology.[2]

Few such reminders were required. Psychology's historical debt to war was made abundantly clear by pivotal figures in World War I psychology who were still alive and professionally active in 1940.[3] Robert Yerkes, for example, had directed the military's mental testing program during World War I and became well known in the interwar period for his pioneering work in comparative psychology and primatology at Yale.[4] In preparation for World War II, he worked as a key member of the Emergency Committee in Psychology, launched in fall 1939 "to prepare the profession for a great national crisis."[5] The Emergency Committee, reorganized one year later under the auspices of the Division of Anthropology and Psychology of the National Research Council

(NRC), served as a central vehicle for mobilizing psychological experts for war work, reorganizing the profession, and planning for the postwar future. As psychology's "war cabinet," it served as the official link between many psychological professionals and the federal government.[6]

Psychological experts were early stirred to patriotic action, and they were optimistic from the outset that the war would do great things for their professions. According to Yerkes, effective mobilization would demonstrate "a large uncultivated professional area which should speedily be occupied by the psychotechnologies and related aspects of human engineering."[7] There was a gaping hole, which it was psychology's wartime mission to fill, in expert services related to "the facilitation and intelligent direction of the development and current behavior-experience of the normal person."[8] Everything from advice about childrearing and marriage to occupational counseling and education for personal happiness and adjustment would be needed. "I am looking beyond the present world conflagration," Yerkes boldly predicted in April 1941, "to a period of reconstruction during which innovations are likely to be the unescapable order of the day and the fashioning of a new civilization a necessity."[9]

Many of Yerkes's colleagues heeded this spirited call to public service and professional opportunity, confident that few experts were better suited than they for the task of designing a new social order. Before the United States had been in the war for a year, a full 25 percent of all Americans holding graduate degrees in psychology were at work on various aspects of the military crisis, most employed full-time by the federal government.[10] "This is no time for feelings of inferiority or for statistical scrupulosity," wrote prominent personality and social psychologist Gordon Allport in an effort to inspire "a bit of boldness" and calm the nerves of colleagues reluctant "to advocate policies not based upon 100 per cent scientific certainty."[11] "If the psychologist is tempted to say that he knows too little about the subject he may gain confidence by watching the inept way in which politicians, journalists, and men in public life fence with the problems of propaganda, public opinion, and morale."[12]

There were reasons to guard against overconfidence, however. In early 1941 Allport warned his colleagues: *Don't confuse lobbying for psychology with national service:*—Working for the introduction of psychologists into national and local services may be helpful to the profession, but it is not necessarily beneficial to the nation."[13] The evolving relationship between psychologists and government could, Allport thought, also pose problems. "Apparently the closer one comes to the Government," he noted, "the more complications and resistance one encounters. But after all, don't we all tend to reify 'the Government' and expect 'it' to help materialize our ideas? My experience, too, suggests that decentralized efforts are better. It is 'we, the people' who must invent and execute projects, so far as we can, by ourselves without leaning too much on Uncle Sam."[14]

By 1945 Allport and others were astounded when they compared their initial assessments of what psychology could contribute to the war effort to what had actually happened. The war ended amid a loud chorus of self-congratulations such as the following: "The application of psychology in selecting and training men, and in guiding the design of weapons so they would fit men, did more to help win this war than any other single intellectual activity."[15] Psychology's record had been impressive indeed, and as if to prove it, there were not nearly enough trained experts around to meet the rapidly increasing demand for psychological services in both the public and private sectors. The reputation of psychological experts had risen from one of lowly technicians to one of wise consultants and managers whose wartime accomplishments, especially in the military, deserved a generous payoff in public appreciation and government funds. In retrospect, it seemed clear that the war had given psychology its biggest boost ever, prodding the APA "to grow up to its responsibilities in this new world."[16]

Many psychiatrists were similarly motivated to build on the blueprint offered by their predecessors during World War I, vindicate their techniques of diagnosis and prediction, and recapture any ground that might have been lost due to psychological disarmament during the isolationist interwar period. At the outset of World War II, psychiatrists relied (just as psychologists did) on their World War I track record in testing and screening military recruits for potential emotional liabilities. Psychiatrists, however, had even older prototypes of service to the state to inspire their World War II effort, including the pioneering work of the Public Health Service's (PHS) psychiatric team, stationed on Ellis Island in 1905, for the purpose of keeping insane, and therefore undesirable, immigrants from slipping into the country.[17] The PHS psychiatric team was among the very first examples of psychological expertise being deployed by the federal government in an important area of public policy—immigration—distant from psychiatry's traditional spheres of authority: insanity and asylums.

One tremendous advantage the experts had in 1940 was that there were so many of them, at least in comparison to their numbers in 1917. Among psychiatrists, nearly 3,000 eventually participated in the World War II screening program, compared to a mere 700 in World War I. In both world wars, however, psychiatrists involved in wartime screening programs represented the vast majority of all U.S. psychiatrists: less than 1,000 at the time of World War I and more than 2,500 in 1941, when the United States entered World War II.[18] Between 1920 and 1946, membership in the American Psychiatric Association had increased more than fourfold, from 937 to 4,010, with a surge of new recruits added to the professional ranks as a result of their war experiences.[19] American Psychological Association membership had grown more than elevenfold during these same years, from 393 to 4,427.[20] At the close of World War II, around 1,700 psychologists worked directly for the World War II military, and many others had been involved in research for and consultation to war-related government agencies. A significant number—especially women—made war-related contributions in civilian areas ranging from organizing community forums for women newly employed in the war industries on how best to feed their babies to the general dispensation of "Psychological First Aid."[21] By 1945 the total numbers of psychologists and psychiatrists were running about even. Both professions would experience a historically unprecedented postwar growth curve, far outstripping general population growth or even the spectacular growth of the health-related professions.[22]

What They Did and What They Learned

The wartime psychological work detailed in this chapter and the next is nonclinical. Many practitioners who worked in areas such as "human management" and enemy morale were social psychologists or other social scientists deeply influenced by psychological theory. Social interests notwithstanding, they considered themselves as firmly committed to rigorous scientific practices as colleagues located at the more physiological end of the professional spectrum. For the most part, experimentalists who were interested in such problems as sensation and perception were involved in "man-machine" engineering problems during the war. A visible example was the Harvard Sound Control Project, which significantly improved earplug technology with a huge staff of psychologists and a $2 million government contract. Psychological scientists also conducted laboratory and field experiments designed to produce more user-friendly gunsights, improve night vision, and increase the efficiency of cargo handling, among other things. The young B. F. Skinner even spent the war years trying to prove the military value of behaviorist principles by demonstrating that living organisms—pigeons, to be precise—could be as dependable as machines when it came to guiding missiles to their targets.[23]

Clinically oriented professionals, whose activities are discussed in chapter 8, became the best known of all the wartime psychological experts for their efforts to identify and counter an epidemic of mental disturbance and incompetence. Although they entered the war years with far less professional clout than their experimentalist colleagues, the tables would turn dramatically in the postwar era, when clinical work soared to unprecedented heights of visibility, authority, and political importance.

Although the absolute numbers of experts involved in the areas of work described below were smaller than the numbers of clinicians who maintained the military's mental balance by screening recruits and administering classification tests, their work indicated more directly how psychological knowledge could be made useful to problems defined in explicitly political and military terms. How could enemy soldiers be most effectively reached with demoralizing messages? How could relocation centers for Japanese-Americans be run smoothly? How could U.S. public opinion be oriented toward supporting particular war aims and away from the powder keg of racial conflict? How could U.S. soldiers be convinced that harsh military policies were actually justified, fair, and deserving of compliance?

To these and other questions some psychological experts devoted the war years. If they felt they were advancing the causes of scientific knowledge and professional achievement (and most of them did), they also knew that their jobs existed not for these purposes, but to provide policy-makers with practical, timely, and applicable analysis and information. For each optimistic assessment that social scientists were "gradually creeping up the administrative ladder," and "see[ing] to it that many of our ideas get 'stolen' by government," there were others who glumly reported that "none of our memos were worth anything and they were the joke of Washington."[24] Dedicated throughout the war to enlarging their own sphere of influence, experts nonetheless quickly grasped that furthering a psychological science of social relations or theory of society was not the point. Winning the war was.

Although human relations advisors, specialists in psychological warfare (sometimes called "sykewarriors"), morale specialists, and opinion pollsters spent their time occupied with pressing policy matters, they drew on much the same body of psychological theory and behavioral experimentation available to clinicians. The primary wartime commitment of policy-oriented experts was to making psychology useful, but they also considered the military to be the best environment for large-scale research they had ever encountered. Figures including Eli Ginzberg, Daniel Lerner, Alexander Leighton, and Samuel Stouffer referred to the military as a "laboratory" and observed that war presented unmatched opportunities for scientific experimentation into the mysteries of human motivation, attitudes, and behavior.[25] They were usually careful, however, to keep such language to themselves, understandably nervous that their "subjects" would resist being cast as rats and guinea pigs.[26]

The work of policy-oriented experts grew out of the same intellectual roots as that of their clinical counterparts, a fact that would have profound importance to the political course and public consequences of psychological expertise in the postwar decades. Their professional training led them to adapt concepts developed initially to shed light on how individuals coped with unhealthy situations, or responded to psychopathology—frustration and aggression, for example—to analyzing social issues and designing public policy. One important result would be to blur the line between the individual and the collective, the personal and the social, and to create the potential for camouflaging clear political purposes as neutral methods of scientific discovery or therapeutic treatment. (The career of psychology during the Cold War, and its role in postwar race relations—the subjects of chapters 4 to 7—offer fascinating evidence of exactly how far this process could, and did, go.)

Psychological experts who aided in wartime administration, for example, drew on the language of health, illness, and therapeutic treatment that was the legacy of psychiatry's historic basis in medicine. Psychiatrist Alexander H. Leighton, head of the research team at the Poston Relocation Center for Japanese-Americans and later head of the Foreign Morale Analysis Division (FMAD) of the Office of War Information (OWI), encouraged those with whom he worked to adopt a "psychiatric approach in problems of community management."[27] Psychologists also tended to draw their inspiration from the biological and physical sciences. Samuel A. Stouffer, a psychologically oriented sociologist who directed the army's most ambitious in-house effort in attitude assessment, reflected constantly on the methods of scientific practice—especially controlled experimentation—that had unlocked the wonders of biology and chemistry and that he hoped would do the same for behavioral scientists, finally allowing them "to take some hypotheses of a general character, express them in precise operational terms, and devise means for crucial tests. . . . so that inferences and applications can be made from them to broad classes of concrete behavior situations."[28]

The example of World War I loomed large for these nonclinical experts. Propaganda efforts and shocking evidence of mental deficiency in the military during the Great War had done much to expose the ugly truth of public gullibility, mass emotionalism, and widespread distortions in the popular perception of important public issues. The experience turned even such democratic idealists as Walter Lippmann toward a despairing, and sometimes cynical, belief that only rational experts were in a position to understand "the world outside" and should therefore have the power to engineer public opinion, or what he called "the pictures in our heads."[29] World War I taught that representative democracy was far too emotionally unstable to safely determine the future course of U.S. society and that only those whose educations shielded them from ordinary irrationality should wield the power to make and shape public policy. Thus did science and liberal democracy diverge.[30]

No science poked more holes in democratic ideals than psychology. Many psychological experts were converted by World War I to the principles of crowd psychology, a theoretical tradition first articulated in the late nineteenth century by the aristocratic and antidemocratic French sociologist Gustave Le Bon.[31] Le Bon pointed to the unreason and intolerance of collective behavior and mass attitudes as *the* hallmark of contemporary society and as alarming threats to civilization. He called upon rulers to exert strict social controls over the emotionally explosive masses, protect the eroding powers of intellectual and governing elites, and champion the noble but rapidly evaporating ideal of the individual. During the Progressive Era, pioneers in social psychology like William McDougall (whose career had begun in Britain) and Everett Dean Martin popularized Le Bon's theories.[32] The tradition of crowd psychology also reached U.S. audiences through Freudian social theory and concepts like that of the primal horde.[33] While the elitist attacks of European intellectuals on liberal democracy were often dulled or deleted in U.S. social psychology, the analysis of crowd behavior was destined to remain a centerpiece of U.S. political criticism for a long time to come. The usefulness of crowd psychology derived from its quality of translating contentious questions of political ideology into objective axioms of social science.[34]

By the end of World War I, politicians too had embraced psychopo-litical perspectives from the Le Bon lexicon. Herbert Hoover, for exam-ple, who had provided heroic relief to the hungry masses in German-occupied Belgium before going on to manage the wartime production and marketing of food at home, spoke up for the precious American individualism he believed to be under attack by the psychology of the mob. "Acts and ideas that lead to progress are born out of the womb of the individual mind," he commented, "not out of the mind of the crowd. The crowd only feels: it has no mind of its own which can plan. The crowd is credulous, it destroys, it consumes, it hates, and it dreams—but it never builds. . . . Popular desires are no criteria to the real need; they can be determined only by deliberative consideration, by education, by constructive leadership." [35]

Political scientist Harold Lasswell, who wrote his doctoral disserta-tion on the subject of World War I propaganda, also helped to dissemi-nate crowd psychology. During the interwar period, Lasswell was in-strumental in promoting the application of psychological theories and methods—especially psychoanalysis—to political problems from his post at the University of Chicago.[36] His theoretical and practical work on the margins between psychology and politics helped to cement a notion that would become an unquestionable axiom for the World War II generation: that widespread social conflicts like war and revolution were simply examples, on a large scale to be sure, of the problems that plagued individual personalities and inharmonious interpersonal rela-tionships. Since society was nothing more than an agglomeration of many individuals, the quest for systematic laws of social and political misbehavior should be directed toward the very issues—unconscious motivation and irrational behavior—that the psychopathological ap-proach had uncovered in mentally disturbed individuals. The many di-sasters of World War I, according to Lasswell, had "led the political scientist to the door of the psychiatrist." [37]

World War II, he hoped, would lead policy-makers to the same place in time to pioneer a new "politics of prevention" before too many mis-takes occurred. Lasswell's advocacy of "prevention" came earlier than most, but before the end of World War II this code word reflected both widespread agreement and extreme optimism among psychological ex-perts about therapeutic outcomes as well as policy-oriented work. Pre-vention was a useful vehicle for the professions' ambitions because it allowed their authority to expand in new directions, offering an open invitation to psychologists, psychiatrists, and allied professionals to involve themselves in areas as distant from their traditional turf as unemployment, housing shortages, occupational health and safety, political corruption, and international relations.[38]

The mantra of prevention was, in a sense, a continuation of experts' Progressive Era love affair with efficiency and reform and it followed closely on the heels of the twin campaigns for scientific management and mental hygiene early in the century.[39] But prevention had also absorbed new justifications. No longer was it animated mainly by visions of uplift in a society coming to grips with urban culture, mass institutions, and, at least for native-born whites, an unsettling new ethnic diversity. Before the end of World War II, experts would champion prevention not primarily because it made expert talents indispensable to reform activities, but rather because conventional distinctions between positive mental health and social welfare, or proper adjustment and wise public policy, had almost entirely collapsed.

Lasswell was in the vanguard of this new, integrated understanding of psychology and politics. For him, "prevention" meant treating the issue of power as an issue of psychological management on a social level—releasing uncomfortable tensions here, adjusting sources of strain there—and transforming the exercise of power into something resembling enlightened psychiatric treatment. Straightforward conflicts of interest, consequently, need never disturb the collective peace of mind. "The politics of prevention does not depend upon a series of changes in the organization of government," he argued. "It depends upon a reorientation in the minds of those who think about society around the central problems: What are the principal factors which modify the tension level of the community? What is the specific relevance of a proposed line of action to the temporary and permanent modification of the tension level?"[40]

Human Management

Among the most straightforward examples of psychological expertise used for political purposes during World War II were researchers and analysts who used the tools of their trade to assist public administrators. They did not have to be told to subordinate the goal of knowledge production to that of human management. It was simply understood that war "forces all scientific efforts to short cuts" and that their job description involved producing tips on how to control people effectively rather than theories that might explain previously obscure aspects of social life.[41]

The Sociological Research Project, located in the Poston Relocation Center for Japanese-Americans in the Colorado River Valley, was a clear example of psychology's usefulness in this area (fig. 1).[42] Brought into existence through the forceful advocacy of War Relocation Authority (WRA) consultant Robert Redfield (dean of the Division of Social Sciences at the University of Chicago) and other believers in the administrative value of applied social analysis, the project was directed by Alexander H. Leighton, a navy psychiatrist with some previous field experience in Navajo and Eskimo communities. This innovative research effort was initiated in March 1942, shortly after the decision had been made to intern the 112,000 Japanese-Americans living on the Pacific Coast. The express intention was to experiment with techniques of human management that would prove useful to internment managers and, at the same time, prepare field workers of Japanese ancestry to help with the military occupation that was being planned for various areas of the Pacific.[43] Constructed on the model offered by the Office of Indian Affairs, which had used social scientists as administrative aides in the past, Leighton's research team brought the tools of psychological theory, psychiatric treatment, and cross-cultural research to bear on the management problems at hand. He consciously organized the effort by professional and amateur social scientists (trained in cultural anthropology, sociology, and psychiatry) along clinical lines, "but with the community rather than patients being the subject of study."[44]

Leighton's team members included anthropologists Edward H. Spicer and Elizabeth Colson as well as typists, artists, and translators drawn from among the camp's better-educated population.[45] They specifically disregarded the question of whether the evacuation itself was justified, noting only that "these questions involve matters concerning which data for forming an opinion are not available at present."[46] They did, however, dutifully apply themselves to helping administrators run the Poston Center and maintained a firm belief that their work would help to uncover the invisible laws of individual and social behavior, thereby strengthening the partnership between science and government.

The greatest promise [of the project] for men and their government, in stress and out of it, is in a fusion of administration and science to form a common body of thought and action which is not only realistic in the immediate sense

Figure 1. Aerial view of Poston Relocation Center for Japanese-Americans,
    where World War II experts aided administrators by applying "the
    psychiatric approach in problems of community management."
    Photo: National Archives.

of dealing with everyday needs, but also in the ultimate sense of moving forward in discovery and improved practice. This requires more than hiring social
scientists to make reports. It requires an administration with a scientific philosophy which employs as its frame of reference our culture's accumulated knowledge regarding the nature of man and his society.[47]

To this end, the researchers began with a "fundamental postulate"
about basic human nature: the psychological self was a universal entity
in which many cultural variations appeared. Their assumptions about
the psychological status of center residents all followed from their understanding of basic human nature and of fundamental parallels between mass and individual psychology. These assumptions can be summarized as follows: behavior was largely irrational, motivated by
emotion and past experience (especially childhood); residents' perceptions of their internment (their subjective "belief systems") were more
important than what had actually happened to them (the "objective
facts") and whether or not internment was morally justified; dangers

lurked in groups because individual fears and resentments could be kindled into hysterical and difficult-to-control crowd behavior.

Day to day, the research team conducted intensive interviewing and personality analysis and gathered general sociological data by compiling employment and education records. Staff members prepared oral and written reports that predicted reactions to an array of possible administrative moves and tried to guide management in the directions suggested by their working assumptions. "The administrator who approaches turbulent people with reason is likely to get about as much result as if he were addressing a jungle," was a typical example.[48] While team members could find themselves coping with such humdrum annoyances as unruly teenagers, they tried to concentrate on analyzing and reducing resistance to the overall relocation program as well as to particularly controversial policy suggestions, like registering each camp member for the purposes of a loyalty interrogation. In the latter case, the psychological experts' recommendations were considered important enough to be classified as confidential and circulated at very high policy-making levels.

The picture of the center that emerged from their work was of a community in psychological turmoil, cut off from previous sources of stability, anxious about what other citizens thought of Japanese-Americans, and internally divided along generational, Issei-Nisei lines. Most of all, residents needed a sense of security. Hence, providing it was the surest route to effective administration of the center. When the arrest and detention of two camp residents in a beating incident provoked a general strike at the center, the research team's recommendations helped to defuse mounting tensions quickly and peaceably. Leighton's group pointed out that some administrators' impulse to respond with force rested on a foundation of irrational, racist stereotyping and suggested instead that camp residents be granted more responsibility for maintaining order themselves. The team's recommendations for instilling security through self-government (compiled in a memo written by Conrad M. Arensberg, associate professor of sociology and anthropology at Brooklyn College) won acclaim among high-level policy-makers in the Washington office of the WRA, and resulted in the addition of a community analyst to the staff of every WRA camp in January 1943.

The general conclusions of the Poston team, summarized by Leighton in *The Governing of Men: General Principles and Recommendations Based on Experience at a Japanese Relocation Camp* (1945), were that human management techniques had to be as psychologically and emotionally oriented as their object. According to Leighton, "Societies move on the feelings of the individuals who compose them, and so do countries and nations. Very few internal policies and almost no international policies are predominantly the product of reason. . . . To blame people for being moved more by feeling than by thought is like blaming land for being covered by the sea or rivers for running down hill."[49] The best measures of social control necessarily embodied a sophisticated psychology, since managing people effectively entailed managing their feelings and attitudes, far more a question of engineering self-controls than imposing external punishments.

Enemy Morale: Warfare Waged Psychologically

Work in the fields of psychological warfare, propaganda, and intelligence fell into the sweeping, but undifferentiated category of "morale." The concern with morale that pervaded the war years represented the recognition by government officials that the human personality and its diverse and unpredictable mental states were of utmost importance in prosecuting the war. Moods, attitudes, and feelings were not simply appropriate objects of military policy; they were the *most* appropriate, and objective facts receded into the background. The naive idea that wars could be won simply by perfecting weapons technology to kill one's opponents, it was noted frequently, was incorrect. By far the most effective road to victory was to destroy enemy morale while bolstering one's own.[50] There could be no higher military priority than the control of human subjectivity.

Applied to Americans or the Allies, "morale" was used loosely to describe desirable qualities ranging from personal bravery to group spirit. It also functioned as shorthand for determination, sense of purpose, superb leadership, and occupational competence in military and civilian populations. Positive "morale" was essentially the equivalent of positive motivation, a conspicuous component of "mental hygiene" (the most common term before World War II) or "mental health," as it was increasingly called. Because it could prevent neurotic breakdown and loss of cohesion, fortifying Allied morale became a central war aim. Destroying it in the enemy was, of course, equally vital.

Early on in the war, Army Intelligence asked the NRC Division of

Anthropology and Psychology for urgent help in the area of morale since no psychological warfare program existed at the outset of the conflict.[51] As programs were constructed, "morale" came to designate activities as seemingly different as analyzing enemy communications, monitoring U.S. public opinion, gathering data on what made German and Japanese civilians tick, and keeping the spirits of U.S. GIs as high as possible.

The elasticity of morale's definition elevated the public worth of psychological experts, since if psychological experts had nothing else in common, they were at least supposed to be united in their obsession with "the mind." ("Mental processes" was much preferred by those experimentalists who resisted the metaphysical etymology of this term.) Significantly, morale also stretched the definition of war to encompass aspects of civilian social life previously considered off-limits to military policy-makers, such as influencing levels of community cohesion and confidence in political leadership. The wartime recognition that battles over hearts and minds did not stop respectfully at the edges of military institutions, that civilian minds (ours and theirs) were coequal targets, would have momentous implications for the future.

Work having anything to do with the mental state of the enemy was generally labeled "psychological warfare," and the frequency of this term's use during World War II indicated how many more elements of warfare were being considered as components of a psychological conflict. This new designation tended to replace "propaganda," the term most used during World War I. At that time, "propaganda," had denoted only that portion of psychological warfare having to do with mass communications aimed at enemy audiences. Psychological warfare, on the other hand, was much broader in meaning. The terminological shift corresponded to a shift in the concept of war itself: from a tangible battle to conquer hostile geography to an intangible battle to persuade hostile minds.

Not surprisingly, this shift sharply underlined the importance of psychological experts in determining the outcome of military conflicts. Harold Lasswell, in fact, noted that the high profile of psychological warfare in World War II came about because "the psychologists wanted 'a place in the sun'; that is, they were eager to demonstrate that their skills could be used for the national defense in time of war."[52] At the same time, the new emphasis on nonmaterial determinants of military outcomes blurred the distinction between war and peace, a confusing state of affairs that would come to feel entirely normal during the Cold War. If aspects of warfare that were not military in the conventional sense of armed conflict could make the difference between a short and relatively bloodless war and one that was long and deadly, why not consider any method of resolving conflict without resort to troops and guns a component of warfare? Effective diplomacy, Lasswell pointed out, could keep potential enemies neutral or utilize secret channels to bring war to an end, and strategically applied economic muscle could prevent enemies from gaining access to key, war-making materials.[53]

Unlike the arsenal of persuasion trained on enemy and occupied territory, work on the mental state of Americans or Allied populations (civilian and military) was never called psychological warfare, even though it did fall under the "morale" umbrella. There were, however, no important differences in the methods used to assess or persuade the two very different audiences; shared techniques included public opinion polls, attitude surveys, in-depth interviews, and personality analysis. Nor were there any differences in the professional training of those who spent the war years taking the pulse of U.S. morale rather than studying enemy minds. Not infrequently, the same people did both. And not infrequently, the policy-makers interested in enemy morale took an equal interest in its home front counterpart.[54]

The perspective that psychological experts brought to their work on enemy morale was, like that of the relocation management assistance team described above, based on a conviction that emotional appeals worked more effectively than rational ones and that chaotic irrationality infected human motivation to a much greater extent than orderly and thoughtful ideals. Similarly, those working on enemy morale did so out of a fierce conviction that behavioral insights could be powerful enough, if taken seriously, to tip the balance in the war, not to mention improve immeasurably the efficiency of military policy-making and war management. Individuals identified with this work included psychologists Leonard Doob and Edwin Guthrie and psychiatrist Alexander Leighton, among others. They worked in a range of agencies charged with understanding and influencing enemy morale, including the Office of Facts and Figures (OFF), the Office of Strategic Services (OSS), the Office of War Information (OWI), and the Psychological Warfare Division (PWD) of Supreme Headquarters, Allied Expeditionary Force (SHAEF).

Others worked outside of government, in academic institutions and community agencies, but in capacities that contributed directly to the psychological warfare effort. Typically, they coordinated their projects closely with government agencies and officials. Work in this field sometimes moved back and forth between public and private status. The

Ethnographic Board, set up by the Smithsonian Institution, the NRC, the Social Science Research Council, and the American Council of Learned Societies, compiled a central register of all U.S. social and behavioral scientists who had done foreign area research, complete with bibliographies and reports on obscure corners of the world. Harold Lasswell, whose content analysis technique inspired a tidal wave of "propanal" (short for propaganda analysis), worked initially on the Wartime Communications Research Project and then the Experimental Division for the Study of Wartime Communications. Both located in the Library of Congress, the first project was set up to afford Lasswell access to documents he could not have obtained without a governmental connection, and the second became a training ground for propaganda analysts.[55] Lasswell then moved over to the New School for Social Research, where he jointed Ernst Kris and Hans Speier in the Research Project on Totalitarian Communications.

Many psychological experts interested in systematically investigating mass communications and propaganda were brought together in the Communications Group of the Rockefeller Foundation, part of that organization's contribution to mobilizing U.S. intellectual resources for war, openly and in secret.[56] Among the many projects it supported were two at Princeton. The Princeton Listening Center, relocated in Washington in 1941, was incorporated into the Federal Communications Commission as the Foreign Broadcast Monitoring (later Intelligence) Service, where it was directed by Goodwin Watson, a social psychologist (fig. 2). The Princeton Office of Public Opinion Research was established in 1940 to analyze European radio broadcasts and diagnose Nazi psychology. Psychologist Hadley Cantril, a key figure in work on both enemy and home front morale, was its founder. In his opinion, many advantages existed in working outside of official circles, because doing so made it "possible for me to get confidential information for President Roosevelt and various other people in Washington without having to tie myself down to any government department or agency."[57]

NATIONAL CHARACTER: PERSONALITY DIAGNOSIS AND TREATMENT ON AN INTERNATIONAL SCALE

World War II underscored the real difficulties involved in distinguishing between friends and enemies. Because the war's ideological clashes made it impossible to trust such tangible indicators of loy-

Figure 2. Princeton Listening Center. Photo: Courtesy of the Rockefeller
Archive Center.

alty as what people said and how people behaved, understanding the
deep mental state of German and Japanese populations became a prerequisite to good military strategy. To this challenge, psychological experts brought the innovative concept of national character.[58] Nurtured
by the neo-Freudian movement to revise psychoanalytic orthodoxies
considered insufficiently attentive to the impact of social context on
psychological development, writings by Franz Alexander, Erich
From, Karen Horney, and Harry Stack Sullivan had already attracted
a lot of attention by the early 1940s.[59] So had similar theoretical work
by cultural anthropologists (many of them students of Franz Boas) such
as Gregory Bateson, Ruth Benedict, Geoffrey Gorer, Margaret Mead,
and Edward Sapir.

Their collective efforts to "study culture at a distance" were sometimes designated as the "cultural interpersonal school" or simply as
studies in "culture and personality."[60] A blend of psychological, sociological, and anthropological analysis was typical of this work, and at its
heart lay the conviction that microscopic questions about individual
personality and behavior and macroscopic questions about societal patterns and problems were nothing but two sides of the same coin.

"Problems of social science differ from problems of individual behavior in degree of specificity, not in kind," wrote Edward Sapir, the author of an influential series of essays explaining why cultural anthropology needed an infusion of psychological ideas.[61] Wartime research on the culture and personality model anticipated some of the most characteristic features of postwar social science: the powerful appeal of psychological insights and techniques, an adamantly interdisciplinary style, and the conviction that a unified social expertise was possible and absolutely necessary to a modern democracy.

By suggesting that psychological development and national patterns created each other, that individuals embodied their culture and cultures embodied the collective personality of their people, national character offered a way of turning psychological insight into policy directives. National groups, for example, would be classified according to the "bipolar adjectives" most familiar for their power to describe individual personality: dominance and submission, exhibitionism and spectatorship, independence and dependence, and so on.[62] Institutional vehicles of socialization, from childrearing to teacher training, could then be scrutinized for tendencies in one direction or another, and after tallying enough of these national indicators, one could hope to achieve an accurate portrait of a given country's collective personality structure.

Exploring the concept in detail and in a hurry was a military imperative, as well as an intriguing theoretical exercise, as Geoffrey Gorer, a major proponent of national character, pointed out.

The conduct of the war raised in an urgent fashion problems of exactly the nature I have been outlining—problems of national character, of understanding why certain nations were acting in the way they did, so as to understand and forestall them. Germany, and even more Japan, were acting irrationally and incomprehensibly by our standards; understanding them became an urgent military necessity, not only for psychological warfare—though that was important—but also for strategic and tactical reasons, to find out how to induce them to surrender, and having surrendered to give information; or, in the case of occupied countries, how to induce them to create and maintain a resistance movement, and so on. In an endeavour to further the war effort, a small number of anthropologists and psychiatrists were willing to risk their scientific reputations in an attempt to give an objective description of the characters of our enemies.[63]

In one neat package, the notion of national character oriented psychology toward understanding and affecting important public issues, without sacrificing the traditional language of sickness, health, and diagnosis. But it was the war that changed national character from a concept for which a daring few would "risk their scientific reputations" into a working assumption of military policy.

In a pivotal 1936 article, Lawrence K. Frank, an advocate of clinical approaches whose influential foundation posts had included the Rockefeller Foundation and the Josiah Macy Jr. Foundation, pointed out that if nations had characters, then it made sense to think of "society as the patient": "There is a growing realization among thoughtful persons that our culture is sick, mentally disordered, and in need of treatment."[64] Frank believed this perspective would move behavioral experts from the limited turf of individual adjustment to the more expansive, and therefore hopeful, terrain of social problem management. This served the dual, and entirely compatible, purposes of expanding psychology's sphere of professional influence and treating problems that stubbornly resisted piecemeal amelioration. Finally, it was practical. Since the ideology of democratic individualism and personal responsibility was obviously outmoded in an era of wholesale cultural disintegration, bringing therapeutic methods to bear on society at large promised to simplify the complicated job of social analysis by demonstrating that social forces and social organization were just as disorderly and abnormal as people analyzed one at a time.

As the news from Europe got worse, more and more experts embraced the disease metaphor. In 1940 psychiatrist Edward A. Strecker wrote that wars were nothing but "mass homicidal reactions" and ominously concluded that "unquestionably the world is sick—mentally sick."[65] But if society were a sick patient, then it could recover, especially if the right healers were consulted. Psychiatrist Richard Brickner endorsed this view in his 1943 book, appropriately titled *Is Germany Incurable?* After noting that "the national group we call Germany behaves and has long behaved startlingly like an individual involved in a dangerous mental trend," he confidently asserted that "anthropology, psychiatry and sociology are probably well enough advanced by now to make 'treatment' conceivable."[66] That treatment would involve a wholesale therapeutic strategy for postwar German society, in which citizens were inoculated against "paranoid contagion" via an artificially designed emotional atmosphere. Brickner compared this "treatment" to placing a premature newborn in an incubator.[67]

War work was a warmup for nothing less than "restructuring the culture of the world," agreed Margaret Mead.[68] The sense that responsibility was tied to power underlay all wartime work on morale. Not only could psychological experts decipher the emotional patterns of enemy propaganda to help win the war; they could also hope to become social engineers at war's end, designing a blueprint for psychological reconstruction on a mass scale that would bring the national characters of Germany and Japan back into the normal range, away from perverse dependence and toward a healthy self-reliance.[69] For the experts involved in psychological warfare, the innovative concept of national character, however rudimentary, illustrated what colleagues were learning in fields far removed from wartime activity: military usefulness and scientific progress were entirely compatible, even destined for a glorious and coordinated march into the future.[70]

The effort to scientifically systematize the basic elements of psychoanalysis, in the form of a series of concrete behavioral principles that could be empirically or experimentally validated, was another important theoretical development within psychology during the World War II era. It had a major influence on the techniques experts used both to boost and to destroy morale. Located at the Yale Institute of Human Relations, the effort to generate a "science of human behavior" was related to but distinct from the "culture and personality" studies mentioned above. Psychologists affiliated with the effort at various points in the 1930s and 1940s included John Dollard, Leonard Doob, Erik Erikson, Ernest Hilgard, Clark Hull, Neal Miller, O. H. Mowrer, Robert Sears, and Robert Yerkes.[71]

One trademark Yale product, published on the eve of war, was the collectively authored *Frustration and Aggression*.[72] Intended to test the basic notion that *"aggression is always a consequence of frustration,"* the authors' ambitious goal was to restate psychoanalytic ideas "quantitatively in the form of a connected set of postulates or behavior principles which have been confirmed by a wide range of facts drawn from laboratory experiments, clinical case studies, social statistics, and anthropological field work."[73] The authors believed this effort had both theoretical and practical value. They aimed to dispel the notion that behaviorism and psychoanalysis were conceptually incompatible and simultaneously provide a psychological framework for the analysis of sociological problems ranging from racial prejudice to political ideology itself.

War was not the least of the social phenomena they wished to explain in terms of aggression and frustration, and in doing so, the members of the Yale group were simply following Freud's clear lead. Social progress of any kind required massive efforts to repress hostility, as Freud had argued in *Civilization and Its Discontents* (1930), and the costs in personal happiness were steep enough to constantly threaten modern civilization with reversion to a state of unrestrained violence and barbarism.[74] In his famous exchange of letters with Albert Einstein, Freud equated the task of eliminating war with the challenge of advancing civilization itself. Both rested on the shaky foundation of repression.

There is no use in trying to get rid of men's aggressive inclinations. . . . For incalculable ages mankind has been passing through a process of evolution of culture. . . . We owe to that process the best of what we have become, as well as a good part of what we suffer from. . . . The psychical modifications that go along with the cultural process are striking and unambiguous. They consist in a progressive displacement of instinctual aims and a restriction of instinctual impulses. . . . Whatever fosters the growth of culture works at the same time against war.[75]

In the early years of the Yale Institute, even its sympathetic Rockefeller Foundation funders worried that such socially oriented goals as analyzing the roots of bigotry and warfare would generate storms of criticism for being insufficiently scientific.[76] Less than a decade later, following U.S. entry into World War II in 1941, Rockefeller Foundation officer Alan Gregg told Yale Institute director Mark May, "I did not see that the Institute was open to valid criticism since the psychological element in the present war was such as to make psychological studies of an importance that could not be disputed."[77]

Thus institutionally strengthened and intellectually vindicated by the outbreak of war, the Yale academics involved themselves in an ambitious Social Science Research Council plan to summarize, for the use of government policy-makers, research on the social effects of war, including studies of the family, minority groups, crime, and all varieties of morale.[78] One of the Yale Institute's projects that proved militarily useful during the war was an ambitious data bank called the Cross-Cultural Survey (later incorporated as the Human Relations Area Files). Started in 1937 by anthropologist George Peter Murdock with the aim of keeping comprehensive files on four hundred of the world's most representative "primitive" cultures, the project was greatly expanded by the navy (which gathered lots of information about Pacific societies) and the coordinator of inter-American affairs (who kept track of Latin America).[79]

Many psychologists found the formulation of Freud's frustration-aggression theory offered by John Dollard and his Yale colleagues to be a compelling, not to mention timely, explanation of international events. Gardner Murphy approvingly cited *Frustration and Aggression* and wrote, "Fighting in all its forms, from the most simple to the most complex, appears to derive from the frustration of wants. . . . Satisfied people or satisfied nations are not likely to seek war. Dissatisfied ones constitute a perennial danger."[80] What, after all, could possibly be more aggressive than war?[81]

Frustration and Aggression embodied many of the basic assumptions commonly accepted among psychologists. Even those not inclined toward Freudian theory could agree, on scientific grounds, that individual and collective behavior alike consisted of discrete adjustments that could be scrutinized methodically, if not experimentally. But *Frustration and Aggression* also represented a step toward a unified and integrated basic science of human behavior that, in expert hands, could handle with ease the complicated business of diagnosing and treating society as the patient. As John Dollard pointed out, scientific experts should be recruited for these delicate, but critically important tasks, if only because

life would be unbearable in a world where one was constantly having to choose. Uncertainty is exhausting and choice demands special psychological strengths and reserves. It is, therefore, a human necessity that the world be, to some extent, predictable. Behavior must flow along at least some of the time in golden quiet. Man needs orderly knowledge, scientific knowledge, a kind of knowledge which permits him to act most of the time without the excruciating necessity of choice.[82]

No experience illustrated better than war what could happen if behavior did not "flow along at least some of the time in golden quiet." By exposing the irrationality of motivation, the unpredictability of behavior, and the capriciousness of mass attitudes, World War II reinforced the psychological experts' faith in themselves and increased their confidence that even shaky psychological theories could guide public policy better than popular will or the conventional wisdom of diplomats. Conveniently, war also gave these experts an opportunity to operate outside the ordinary constraints of democracy. This precious and, they believed, temporary freedom was at a maximum in the military, especially in the area of psychological warfare.

THE SYKEWARRIORS ON GERMAN NATIONAL CHARACTER

The "sykewarriors" of the Psychological Warfare Division (PWD) of SHAEF (Supreme Headquarters, Allied Expeditionary Force) operated directly under the command of General Eisenhower.

Their assignment was to reach and persuade enemy minds: "to destroy the fighting morale of our enemy, both at home and on the front."[83] Not only did the overall Allied goal of unconditional surrender present endless frustrations to the sykewarriors (it severely limited their ability to persuade through positive incentives), but the PWD experts also had to live with an unsavory reputation among the military brass as a bunch of professorial "characters," "administratively irresponsible symbol-manipulators," and "unsoldierly civilians, most of them needing hair-cuts, engaged in hypnotizing the enemy."[84]

The PWD efforts to understand the German civilian and military mind relied heavily on the concept of national character and the assumption that Germany was a sick patient, experiencing a psychological episode traumatizing enough to require a thoroughgoing suppression of rational attitudes.[85] On the basis of such theorizing, Henry Dicks, a British psychiatrist associated with PWD's intelligence division, developed a questionnaire for use in POW interrogations.[86] Designed to elicit a range of attitudinal responses about National Socialism, Hitler, and so forth, the results were converted into a series of German personality types, demarcated according to different psychological responses to Nazi authority. Drawn exclusively from German men of military age, the aggregate data were generalized to German society as a whole.

1. fanatical "hard-core" Nazis (10%)
2. modified Nazis "with reservations" (25%)
3. "unpolitical" Germans (40%)
4. passive anti-Nazis (15%)
5. active anti-Nazis (10%)[87]

On the basis of this distribution, psychological warriors predicted the responses of various German groups to Allied propaganda. This particular effort to track military and political developments via analysis of individual personality was considered so successful that a U.S. psychiatrist, David M. Levy, was called in to organize a "personality screening center" even after SHAEF was dissolved.

As an example of psychology deployed for military purposes, the POW study was certainly important. It was as important, however, for its working assumptions: that political ideology was, at best, partially rational and conscious, preferably understood as an expression of deep personality structure; that the life history, and especially experience in infancy and childhood, provided the most accurate guide to individual character and social behavior; that the concept of national character was reliable enough to produce systematic ways of addressing frustrations, which in turn produced discernible national patterns in everything from childrearing to educational philosophy.[88] The many experts working on morale widely shared these hypotheses and applied them as readily to the content analysis of captured documents, print, and broadcast media as to in-depth interviews with POWs. The notion that individual personality development, political ideology, and cataclysmic social events like war could not be understood apart from one another was a characteristic feature of their theoretical approach.

The PWD experts believed that their psychological operations would shorten the war and, toward that noble end, they built a track record of genuine creativity that included artillery-fired leaflets, newspapers dropped by bombs, and a "talking tank" that made persuasion a literal element in combat. In spite of the ceremonial accolades they received at the end of the war ("Without doubt, psychological warfare has proved its right to a place of dignity in our military arsenal," wrote General Eisenhower to PWD Brigadier General Robert McClure), they were perplexed about why the real decision-makers, from FDR on down, had paid little if any attention to them in determining overall war policy.[89] Such cavalier neglect of psychological expertise, they warned, would be terribly unwise in the future. Behavioral experts, they felt sure, would shortly supplant both diplomats and soldiers in the very dangerous world to come.[90]

THE SYKEWARRIORS ON JAPANESE
NATIONAL CHARACTER

What PWD did for Germany, the Foreign Morale Analysis Division (FMAD) of the Office of War Information (OWI) did for Japan. Sponsored by the OWI in cooperation with the Military Intelligence Service of the War Department, FMAD grew directly out of the experience of the Sociological Research Project at the Poston Relocation Center for Japanese-Americans. Alexander Leighton directed both projects, and the FMAD analysis of Japanese morale was based on the very same "fundamental postulate" about human nature that had animated the earlier effort to make the "psychiatric approach in problems of community management" indispensable to administrators.

The thirty or so analysts who staffed FMAD made their first task to seek out exploitable cracks in the fighting spirit of the Japanese military, widely perceived to be unstoppable, even fanatical. Their study of Japanese national character, based on the same sorts of data used by PWD, pointed to the same soft spots in morale: powerful irrational and weak rational motives, perceptual distortions, and the likelihood that whatever individual autonomy existed would be corrupted through contact with crowd sentiment and behavior. FMAD concluded, as PWD had, that since emotional forces were of greater salience than conscious political ideals in motivating Japanese soldiers, psychological warfare strategies that rationally attacked Japanese imperialism or calmly advocated democratic ideals could have had few if any positive results. Emotional appeals had a far more dramatic effect.

Of particular importance, they found, was the emotional role of authority, and especially the image of Japanese emperor Hirohito. Direct attacks of any kind on the emperor, however cathartic they might be for Americans, were unlikely to lower Japanese morale and even threatened to backfire by rallying the Japanese military around a highly emotional symbol. "One cannot," Alexander Leighton and a colleague warned, "successfully attack with logic that which is not grounded in logic."[91] FMAD experts considered this finding, and the eventual policy decision to allow the Japanese emperor to remain on the throne, to be among the greatest political successes of wartime behavioral experts. For them, it proved that the psychological approach to policy was an extraordinary scientific advance over the dubious, if conventional, reliance by policy-makers on mere intuition or the whims of personal experience. There was, however, little evidence to show that the many confidential studies of Japanese character FMAD did for the War Department, or similar studies for the State Department, actually affected this important policy decision.[92] Indeed, had the experts been clearly heeded in this case, and had Truman announced early on a U.S. willingness to allow Hirohito to continue as emperor, it is possible that the horrors of Hiroshima and Nagasaki could have been avoided.

The foundations of Japanese civilian morale were just as emotional, with roots in distinctive childrearing, eating, and schooling habits. For example, it was suggested that "weaning trauma" frequently coincided with the arrival of siblings, fast meals recapitulated the denial of infantile needs for pleasure, and teachers smothered competition and enforced strict obedience among students—all contributing factors to an aggressive Japanese national character. Contrary to popular U.S. opinion that Japanese resolve was unwavering, FMAD research showed a sharp decline had already begun in Japanese civilian morale that would eventually lead to surrender. Reports like FMAD's "Current Psychological and Social Tensions in Japan" suggested that anger, aggression, displacement, apathy, panic, and hysteria were highly sensitive elements in Japanese national character, and ought to be as significant as food shortages and economic pressures in the calculations of military planners.[93]

The Strategic Bombing Survey on German and Japanese Morale

At the war's end, many FMAD staff participated in the Strategic Bombing Survey's Morale Division.[94] Its ambitious postwar study, designed to answer the question of whether and how aerial bombing had affected German and Japanese morale, was directed by psychologist Rensis Likert, previously head of the Division of Program Surveys, Bureau of Agricultural Economics, U.S. Department of Agriculture. In this government bureaucracy, which appeared to be located very far from the heart of military policy-making, Likert and his staff had pioneered the incorporation of intensive interviewing and research survey techniques as a routine part of large-scale government surveys intended to keep tabs on wartime public opinion.[95] The psychologists who participated in the Strategic Bombing Survey's morale study included Dorwin Cartwright, Daniel Katz, Otto Klineberg, David Krech (previously Krechevsky), Ted Newcomb, and Helen Peak. Virtually all of them were members of the Society for the Psychological Study of Social Issues (SPSSI), the most important organizational nucleus of wartime social psychology.[96]

Immediately following the German surrender, the morale experts began to collect some four thousand interviews. In Japan they conducted some three thousand interviews during the last six weeks of 1945. Plagued by familiar time and personnel shortages and faced with daunting logistical difficulties, they generated the same kinds of national character studies and collective personality profiles that outfits like PWD and FMAD had done during the war, as well as a handy, quantifiable "Morale Index" and comprehensive final reports.[97] The results generally showed that aerial bombing, while dramatic, had not had nearly the effect on morale that U.S. policy-makers had expected would be the case, a conclusion readily championed by participants, like

Alexander Leighton, who felt it vindicated the wartime predictions of FMAD and other psychological warfare think tanks that enemy morale had begun an irreversible slide toward surrender.[98]

INTELLIGENCE

Intelligence gathering comprised another critical component of work in the psychological warfare field. Intelligence did not necessarily require firsthand espionage, and the term often described the analysis of national character from a distance. The OWI's Bureau of Overseas Intelligence, for example, was headed by Leonard Doob, a psychologist affiliated with the Yale Institute of Human Relations. Its Washington research staff numbered around one hundred, with branch offices in New York and San Francisco. This outfit shared much of the general approach, already outlined, to psychological warfare. Its work disseminating "propaganda" to enemy countries and "information" to allied and neutral countries drew inspiration from national character studies and attempts to identify the strengths and weaknesses in enemy morale.[99]

The OWI Bureau of Overseas Intelligence also shared most of the headaches of other sykewarriors, especially in trying to get policymakers to appreciate the advantages of allowing psychological experts a determining role in the policy-making process. According to Doob, the work of his researchers was used when it suited the interests of policymakers and ignored when it did not, an indignity Doob attempted to remedy by spending the latter part of the war hobnobbing with high-level policy-makers and functioning as a marketer of behavioral research.[100] Although a true believer in the enlightening potential of psychological expertise, Doob admitted that he found the decision-makers as irrational as the bureau's German or Japanese research subjects.

He [Doob, referring to himself] had learned the valuable lesson, as frankness increased his frustrations, that he would be more valuable as a social scientist and happier as a human being if he treated almost every individual like a psychiatric patient who had to be understood in the gentlest possible fashion before he could be expected to swallow the pill of research. In the Overseas Branch, this meant being pleasant to what seemed to be millions of people—which, for this writer, was quite a strain.[101]

Firsthand intelligence gathering was the main job of the Office of Strategic Services (OSS), the predecessor and model for the Central Intelligence Agency (CIA), which was established by the National Security Act of 1947. The OSS Psychological Division, organized in September 1941 and directed by University of California psychologist Robert C. Tryon, was staffed by eighteen psychologists.[102] A few names have been released, but the identities of individuals affiliated with the division beyond 1942 are still considered confidential for reasons of national security.[103]

The division's own mission statement, "Role of Psychology in Defense," envisioned an ambitious morale program at home as well as abroad, supplemented by a variety of highly classified special projects. Although it had an even more top-secret image than other morale agencies, the OSS Psychological Division used the very same conceptual tools (national character) and data-gathering methods (surveys, polls, and in-depth interviews). It also called upon the same civilian consultants and professional networks for aid: officers of the APA and the Society for the Psychological Study of Social Issues (SPSSI), to mention but two examples. The OSS frequently used a farming-out method, in which key mediators, like Harvard psychologist Gordon Allport, would identify psychological experts with special skills, from foreign languages to inside knowledge about German colleagues. "The OSS interest in the problem should remain a secret," Robert MacLeod reminded Allport, "although you would be free to let it be known that your findings would be communicated to the government."[104]

The selection of intelligence agents was another critically important service provided by psychological experts to the OSS. Like many other activities in the field of psychological warfare and personnel selection, the OSS selection procedure was constructed with German psychology in mind. American experts were all too aware that their German counterparts were ahead of them. Highly effective methods of officer selection had been developed throughout the Nazi period, creating "an unprecedented type of organization for human engineering."[105] But the Americans were unwilling to be beaten at their own game. "America should have no qualms about adopting some of the best features of German military psychology," they argued, since "the Nazis have unblushingly expropriated the findings of many American scholars."[106]

The OSS assessment staff, whose driving forces included Henry Murray (an eclectic physician, psychologist, and psychoanalyst) and Donald MacKinnon (a psychologist), devised the most elaborate and thorough procedures in the entire U.S. military. The three-and-one-half-day ordeal included cover stories to disguise personal identity, simulated enemy interrogations, psychodrama improvisations, and a variety

Figure 3.   Group Rorschach used by the Office of Strategic Services for selection purposes during World War II. Photo: National Archives.

of objective and projective psychological tests (fig. 3).[107] This enormous investment of expert time and attention was certainly due in part to the perception that the stakes were very high; those selected after the lengthy ordeal would play key wartime roles. But it was also due to the fact that selection requirements for the OSS were more confusing than the measurement of particular skills or aptitudes, which was the standard requirement in most branches of the U.S. military. The personal qualities and talents necessary for a good intelligence agent were unpredictable, at least compared to those of a good aircraft mechanic, as MacKinnon admitted when he noted that "nobody knows who would make a good spy or an effective guerrilla fighter. Consequently, large numbers of misfits were recruited from the very beginning."[108] The "assessment of men" (also the title of the 1948 book which documented the work of the OSS team) "is the scientific art of arriving at sufficient conclusions from insufficient data."[109]

Like other wartime experts, the OSS assessors believed they were making a patriotic contribution and taking advantage of a golden opportunity to upgrade science at the same time. Where could they have found a more perfect place to aid the war effort and simultaneously validate personnel selection technologies? In later years, some of the OSS experts had lingering doubts about their wartime activities. Henry Murray, for example, chief of OSS Selection Station S, was transformed into a militant pacifist and peace activist after the U.S. dropped the atomic bomb on Hiroshima and Nagasaki, thought the OSS should be disbanded completely, and strenuously objected to the establishment of the CIA.[110] Donald MacKinnon, on the other hand, went on to institutionalize the OSS selection procedures at the Institute of Personality Assessment and Research at the University of California, whose goal was nothing less than "developing techniques to identity the personality characteristics which make for successful and happy adjustment to modern industrial society."[111]

For the most part, policy-makers whose own agendas did not include the scientific or professional advancement of psychology were not disturbed that the interests of nationalism and science conveniently converged during the war for their expert counselors. They were impressed by psychologists' work, content to benefit in tangible ways, and more than happy to leave the theoretical debates to the experts. In 1945, when Congressional hearings were held to determine if scientists' wartime contributions had been sufficient to win them a national foundation of their own (a process that eventually culminated in the founding of the National Science Foundation), much testimony, such as the following, was offered by military planners about the usefulness of OSS psychological activities, in personnel selection as well as in psychological warfare.

In all of the intelligence that enters into the waging of war soundly and the waging of peace soundly, it is the social scientists who make a huge contribution in the field in which they are professionals and the soldiers are the laymen. . . . The psychological and political weapons contributed significantly to the confusion, war weariness, and poor morale on the enemy's home and fighting fronts. There is no doubt that operations like these shortened the war and spared many American lives. . . . Were there to develop a dearth of social scientists, all national intelligence agencies servicing policy makers in peace or war would directly be handicapped.[112]

Such public declarations proved that psychology's accomplishments were real as well as imagined, at least insofar as reality was assessed by those in a position to further the status and funding of psychological work. There was certainly no shortage of testimonials from policy-makers that psychological experts were indispensable to the successful execution of war in the fields of human management, enemy morale, and intelligence. Experts' patriotic fervor, practical skills, soothing insights, and flair for self-promotion all convinced many policy-makers charged with military and national security planning that psychological talent would be equally necessary in future periods of war and peace. The wartime record of those psychological experts who worked on the home front, on questions ranging from U.S. public opinion and military morale to the psychology of prejudice, is examined in the next chapter.

3

The Dilemmas of
Democratic Morale

U.S. Civilian Morale

Home front morale equaled the enemy mind as an illustration of the basic doctrine that war had been reconfigured into a profoundly psychological format. The ideas and emotions of Americans were as important to winning the war as bombs and tanks. "In a democracy," Gordon Allport proclaimed, "every personality can be a citadel of resistance to tyranny. *In the co-ordination of the intelligences and wills of one hundred million 'whole' men and women lies the formula for an invincible American morale.*"[1] Policy-makers perceived their job as more than keeping tabs on what Americans were thinking and feeling; they had to skillfully engineer the appropriate U.S. outlook. Indeed, before morale ever became the unique touchstone of psychological warfare activities, it was envisioned as the glue that psychological experts could use to hold together the entire domestic war effort. The first activities to mobilize psychological experts made no distinction between the skills required to understand Germans and those needed to understand Americans. Since morale was a unifying theme among psychological experts, it ought to be a unifying theme in the war as a whole.

Organizationally too, psychological experts wanted to make morale the cornerstone of their efforts. The Committee for National Morale

(CNM), a private organization, was formed in July 1940 "in the conviction that in the present crisis Morale will probably be the decisive factor and that the United States must employ her tremendous morale resources to the fullest extent for a long time to come."[2] Chaired by Arthur Upham Pope (Gregory Bateson was secretary), the CNM sponsored committees on psychiatry, psychology, and social sciences, among others, and the CNM membership included many of the leading behavioral experts who would go on to play important wartime roles in, or in support of, a variety of public agencies: Gordon Allport, Ruth Benedict, Walter Bingham, Edwin Boring, Hadley Cantril, Leonard Doob, Erik Erikson, Erich Fromm, Geoffrey Gorer, David Levy, Kurt Lewin, Margaret Mead, Karl Menninger, Adolf Meyer, Gardner Murphy, Henry Murray, Edward Strecker, Goodwin Watson, Robert Yerkes, and countless others.[3] At first, the CNM lobbied for creating a single, comprehensive morale agency in which all federal behavioral scientists would be concentrated but this particular goal was thwarted by President Roosevelt, who supported the CNM but worried about public perceptions that such an agency would quickly push the United States into war.

The path that the CNM took would be faithfully followed, and its work replicated, by experts ensconced in agencies devoted to military propaganda and public opinion polling alike, some of which have already been described. Its first effort, the typical point of departure for most wartime psychology, was to study German strategies of psychological warfare.[4] Other efforts shortly followed. CNM consultant Erik Erikson, for example, wrote a number of memoranda analyzing Hitler's speeches and Nazi mentality with the aim of designing the most effective POW interrogation techniques and anti-Nazi propaganda. Erikson was also involved in wartime fieldwork designed to translate psychology's insights into policies that would pay off in performance efficiency for U.S. military institutions. In 1940 he wrote a memo for the CNM on the social-psychological dynamics of life on submarines after spending some time on one himself.[5] Everything Erikson wrote employed what would become standard wartime techniques of content and personality analysis, and also advanced the theory that national character could be diagnosed and treated psychologically. "It is as if the German nation as a whole could be likened to a not uncommon type of adolescent who turns delinquent."[6]

From its inception, the Emergency Committee in Psychology also committed itself to an ambitious array of morale problems, and its ambiguously named Special Subcommittee on War Experiences and Behavior was assigned the confidential task of studying the psychological resources of enemy and allied countries alike. (After the attack on Pearl Harbor, government agencies assumed responsibilities in this area.)[7] Clearly, morale and its treatment, in any and all forms, was one of the top priorities of the Emergency Committee, which sponsored a "Conference on Psychological Factors in Morale" in August 1940. As a result, the Subcommittee on Defense Seminars was formed and Gordon Allport was appointed chair. From that point on, Allport remembered, "telephone lines were hot with the inquiry, 'What do we know about civilian morale?'"[8] Although Allport also remembered that his answer to this question was "nothing," by January 1942 there were twenty-two active morale seminars functioning around the country, giving the government tips on everything from popular attitudes toward air-raid wardens to Hitler's personality.[9] Allport, who had also been president of the American Psychological Association in 1938 and chair of the APA committee on displaced foreign psychologists, eventually shifted his efforts to the SPSSI Committee on War Service and Research and the major part of his attention to the psychology of group conflict and prejudice.

In both of these cases, the intention was to spearhead a campaign that would systematically monitor morale in communities around the country, help to control wartime rumor, and line up experts to make patriotic broadcasts—all using the best in available psychological expertise. Their stated goal was to "make available to citizens, and especially to officials in a position to determine policy, the conclusions which can be drawn from scientific study of human behavior."[10]

DID AMERICANS HAVE A NATIONAL CHARACTER?

Since so much of the early morale work identified vulnerabilities in national character as the key to defeating the enemy, it did not take long before some experts were gingerly asking whether the concept of national character offered any insight into Americans themselves. Did they have an irrational national personality, as Germans and Japanese did, or was there something in U.S. history or institutions that immunized Americans against such culturewide emotional hazards? Was morale at home an asset or a liability?

Because they were convinced that the ugliness of enemy national character could be traced, at least in part, to apparently uniform aspects of human psychology—especially the propensity for behavior to express emotion rather than reason—psychological experts harbored private anxieties throughout the war about the manipulability of the characteristic U.S. personality. Their public stance, however, was resolutely optimistic. Democratic traditions and institutions, they claimed, produced a morale far superior to that of autocratic regimes, and democratic morale could not be undermined easily. Margaret Mead reassured a nervous public as follows: "Democratic procedures are not something that people have, like automobiles or hot-dog stands or a way of building roads. Democracy is not something which can be added or subtracted. . . . The way in which people behave is all of a piece, their virtues and their sins, the way they slap the baby, handle their court cases, and bury their dead. . . . We *are* our culture."[11] U.S. national character was consequently not a military soft spot but rather "the psychological equipment with which we can win the war."[12]

Margaret Mead was certain that "we are the stuff with which this war is being fought," and she was among the first to apply insights about domestic national character for practical war-related purposes.[13] Mead was already very well known before the war for her *Coming of Age in Samoa* (1925) and other studies of "primitive" cultures. She had earned bachelors and masters degrees in psychology at Barnard and Columbia before going on to study anthropology with Franz Boas at the doctoral level. Her psychological orientation was visible in her lifelong interest in patterns of child socialization and gender identity, her use of psychological testing in fieldwork, and her openness to psychoanalytic interpretations of culture. "I left psychology to live, in many ways, always within its precincts, working with psychologists and concerning myself with psychological problems," she recalled.[14]

Mead did not wait for the United States to enter the war to throw herself into public service. When she and Gregory Bateson arrived in the United States in 1939, after conducting field research in the South Seas, "we had realized that Hitler presented a terrible threat to everything we valued in the world."[15] Mead immediately wrote to Eleanor Roosevelt, "as a professional anthropologist," urging that policymakers pay serious attention to the understanding "psychiatrists and political scientists" had of the "role of Hitler's peculiar psychological make-up in European affairs."[16] But Mead's primary concern was domestic morale. In 1941 she formulated ideas for a national morale program based on her analysis of U.S. personality strengths. She stressed that policy-makers would do well to capitalize on citizens' typical anti-authoritarianism, competitiveness, and fiercely local (as opposed to national) loyalties.[17]

Published in expanded form in 1942 as *And Keep Your Powder Dry*, Mead's popular primer on morale instructed citizens about the best ways to transform their national character into a military asset and expressed an almost boundless faith in the ability of rational experts to engineer peace, freedom, national unity, orderly political participation, and a plethora of other liberal goals, including racial tolerance, which clearly contradicted the tight institutional hold that segregation had on the South.[18] "We must see this war," Mead concluded, "as a prelude to a greater job—the restructuring of the culture of the world—which we will want to do, and for which, because we are also a practical people, we must realize there are already tools half forged."[19]

The tools she referred to were the social sciences, and Mead herself was a model of social expertise mobilized in public service. In early 1942 she became the executive secretary of the NRC's Committee on Food Habits, a post she treated as "a base from which I would coordinate various kinds of anthropological input into federal programs."[20] While there, she conducted a number of studies (with the assistance of Kurt Lewin) to determine how the government could prevent hoarding, make rationing work, and feed the Allies during and after the war by enlisting characteristic U.S. personality traits.[21]

Gordon Allport was another major figure in the wartime debate on morale, and he made it his particular business to explore and promote the concept of democratic morale. He explained what it was and made it into a manageable entity by suggesting that personality theories which had evolved in order to understand individuals could and should be applied to society at large during the wartime emergency. "Morale is a condition of physical and emotional well-being residing in the individual citizen. . . . National problems . . . are nothing but personal problems shared by all citizens."[22] The hypothesis that national morale was merely individual morale multiplied by a factor of millions was very convenient. It made systematic measurement and monitoring possible through an index comprising markers like suicide and crime rates, levels of industrial strife, and patterns of mental illness and disturbance.[23] As a scientist, Allport believed empirical data of this sort to be of the utmost importance. As a democratic idealist, he was positive that a vast chasm separated the "integral" morale of Americans (based on the total personality, which included a capacity for thinking as well as feeling) from the "segmented" morale produced by fascistic regimes (based only on explosive and easily exploited emotionalism). One of the defining features of a democratic personality was the successful internalization of authority and control. In Allport's words, "the ideal of democracy calls for people to carry their backbone inside their personalities."[24]

Even as committed a champion of democracy as Allport, however, understood that U.S. morale was volatile enough to need firm management outside of public view. Even while he was busy encouraging colleagues to write speeches and articles on the topic for popular distribution in print and broadcast media (something he also frequently did himself), Allport was communicating with Washington, recommending personnel and ideas for the conduct of secret programs to measure morale and control the public psyche.[25] Throughout the war years, Allport played a mediating role between secret agencies, such as the OWI and the OSS, and professional psychologists.[26]

THE PROBLEM OF PUBLIC OPINION

The upshot of ambiguity about a distinctly democratic U.S. national character—celebrating it publicly but also behaving as if its existence were in serious doubt—seemed to be that one could not put too much faith in Americans. Allport's version of democratic morale might be accurate, and touting it in public might be just the thing to raise Americans' spirits. But what if it were not true? Policy-makers, in no mood to trust blindly that citizens at home would not behave like Germans or Japanese, believed that techniques of public opinion polling offered one of the best avenues for monitoring and shaping popular attitudes on questions of wartime importance.

Before the war, polling techniques had been developed largely in industry in the form of marketing studies. The Gallup Poll had become synonymous with the state of public opinion, and commercial organizations, like George Gallup's American Institute of Public Opinion, were already public fixtures.[27] Polling was not entirely new to the in-house operations of federal bureaucracies either, in spite of the fact that World War II is often treated as "Year One" in the history of government and behavioral expertise.[28] Washington had conducted extensive surveys on peacetime domestic issues as early as the Hoover administration's Research Committee on Social Trends. During the New Deal, the Department of Agriculture was aggressive in its use of sampling techniques to reveal agricultural trends and design its own programs. During World

War II, psychological experts used polling data to sell war bonds, implement civilian conservation programs, ease the transition to price control and rationing, and assist administrators in charge of military occupation. Much of this work was considered highly confidential.

Hadley Cantril, a Princeton social psychologist (and former student of Gordon Allport) whose work during the 1930s had ranged from theories of collective action to analysis of public response to Orson Welles's "War of the Worlds" broadcast, already moved in high-level government circles before the war, when he designed polling questions for FDR. In 1940 he founded the Princeton Office of Public Opinion Research with the scholarly goals of establishing a public opinion data bank for academics, systematically evaluating techniques of opinion measurement and studying theories about why the public thought what it did. Shortly afterwards, however, the Princeton organization began conducting war-related polling. Similar to work in the areas of psychological warfare and personnel selection, Cantril's outfit both studied and resembled its German counterpart, especially the German Psychological Institute for War and Propaganda, greatly expanded after 1933 under the Nazi regime.[29]

Perhaps because his earliest efforts showed that "most people are frightfully confused about their war opinions" and "common sense is wrong," when it came to predicting the public mood, Cantril understood how significant polling could be for the prosecution of the morale war at home, as well as abroad.[30] Throughout the war years, he operated behind the scenes, testing the murky waters of public sentiment and providing secret assistance to an impressive array of government agencies, from the OSS and the OWI to the White House and the Departments of State and Justice.[31] Not by any means confined to gathering and analyzing data about what Americans were thinking, Cantril also helped to guide the work of tricky overseas polling, which had to camouflage its purposes as a matter of course.[32] Such "disguised attitude measurement" was also practiced within U.S. borders on matters considered too delicate for truthfulness.[33]

Cantril's primary commitment was to translating psychological knowledge directly into policy rather than to maintaining the integrity of independent scientific research. One colleague described Cantril as a savvy Washington operator whose sights were set on being "Advisor to the Prince."[34] But if he spent less time worrying about psychology's scientific credentials than did some of his World War II colleagues, his belief that their collective expertise was a valuable public asset, and should be treated as such, made Cantril the very model of the new breed of policy-oriented psychological experts. He used polling results to make specific recommendations at the very highest policy-making levels: how the U.S. should explain its initial entry into the war; how to manage the opinions of problematic subgroups like union members; how postwar planning efforts should be presented to the public.[35] And he understood, along with so many of his colleagues, that advancing psychology, enlightening public policy, and contributing patriotically were all of a piece. In early 1943 he "immodestly" concluded "that perhaps more than any other research office . . . we are contributing to the war effort, to policy in high places, and to pioneering in research techniques."[36]

Of course, public opinion became a concern for psychological experts long before World War II precisely because it appeared to be a creature of the emotionalism and irrationality that was psychology's province. The Progressive Era ethos of scientific management succeeded as well as it did not only because expertise seemed so reliable but because mass opinion seemed so unreliable. The results of the World War I military intelligence testing program were shocking and widely publicized; psychologists measured the mental age of the average native-born soldier at slightly over thirteen years. This dismal news, along with the public's response to wartime propaganda, confirmed what many scientists already believed by 1920: mass opinion was dangerous as well as fickle. Scientific and psychological organizations, founded in the wake of war in order to bring order to a chaotic society, insisted that "scientific men should take the place that is theirs as masters of the modern world."[37] Skepticism, even outright disgust, at public opinion was a major motivating factor, a point aptly illustrated in the founding document of the American Society for the Dissemination of Science. "The public that we are trying to reach in the daily press is in the cultural stage when three-headed calves, Siamese twins and bearded ladies draw the crowds to the side shows."[38]

Little wonder then that the old tradition of crowd psychology, which conceived of public opinion as a latent disease state, subject to turbulent infection at unpredictable moments, was incorporated so thoroughly into psychologists' social theories in the period following World War I. Nothing that happened in the interwar years led psychological theorists to revise their view that public opinion was a real threat to rational planning, even to moral order itself. The steady progress of psychoanalytic ideas about unconscious motivation contributed to further solidifying this view.[39] In the 1930s even Gordon Allport, a vocal critic of psychoanalytic pessimism and champion of a psychology based on the possibility of consciousness and reason, participated in the expanding group of Harvard faculty and graduate students who were interested in attitudes, propaganda, and mass communication; they referred to themselves as "The Group Mind."[40]

World War II had the contradictory effect of adding to the already impressive accumulation of evidence about the dangers of public opinion at the very moment when favorable public opinion was needed as evidence that policy-makers were operating within the bounds of democratic checks and balances. Enemy ideologies, like Nazism and fascism, stubbornly defied rational explanation. They elicited countless infection metaphors and theories about collective psychopathological states as well as more traditional critiques of dictatorship. "Critical world situations, like those in which we are now immersed, stretch taut the emotions of human beings, so that self-deceptions readily occur," observed psychiatrist Edward Strecker in alarm.[41] "The cosmic indisposition seems to have involved large segments of every vital organ, and the sickness is economic, political, social, cultural, and spiritual."[42] Democratic public opinion, on the other hand, was defended as the very essence of reason and accountability. Whether or not it guided and enlightened policy-making was considered the significant difference between a just and an unjust state.

But public opinion at home was capricious too, and masses of people were shockingly ignorant of the most elementary facts about why the United States had entered the war, as Cantril and others discovered, nor did they demonstrate any inclination to obtain the type of information that democratic citizenship required.[43] One psychiatrist appraised the public's thinking as follows: "Despite the beauty of the thought, it is impossible to distill wisdom from mass opinion."[44] Attitudes related to the war certainly needed careful attention and management. And public opinion about how to conduct the war required the strictest of controls. It would be a tremendous challenge, according to public opinion experts, to "bring the public to the point where it may have its rightful voice in the choice of social objectives."[45] Experts like Richard Crossman, a high official in the PWD whose wartime occupation was shrouded in secrecy and who was elected to the British Parliament after the war, were especially concerned "to insure that an ill-informed public opinion shall not maul and mutilate the weapon of psychological warfare."[46] No sentimental fondness for open democratic procedures or accurate information, Crossman felt, could be allowed to interfere with the imperatives of victory, even though it meant shielding important policy decisions from the institutional checks of representative government. The virtues of public opinion, even for cheerleaders like Mead and Allport, were a lot clearer in theory than they were in practice.

THE PSYCHOLOGY OF PREJUDICE AND THE MORALE OF MINORITY GROUPS

Among the most glaring examples of how depraved public opinion could actually be, and therefore how much in need of expert management, was "intergroup conflict." The urgency of lessening racial tensions on the home front and in the military, and explaining Nazi racial ideology, drew the attention of psychological experts to this field and sparked an interest in the psychology of prejudice which would flourish in the postwar decades. World War II made racial and ethnic intolerance appear to be something rather more than an embarrassing blight on a democratic polity. As a manifestation of irrational psychological forces that found an outlet for personal frustration and aggression in scapegoating, racism was understood to be "unquestionably the weakest spot in our national character" and "a moral cancer that must be controlled before it kills."[47] A broad and explicit consensus developed that prejudice was a fundamental source of war and a threat to democracy. Its eradication was identified with respect for the personality, peace, mental health, and with psychological expertise itself.

Anti-Semitism emerged as the first concern not only because Nazi ideology promoted it but because morale-destroying rumors in the United States frequently featured Jews. Gordon Allport, among the many psychologists whose enduring theoretical interests in prejudice were rooted in the all-too-real turmoil of the wartime climate, succeeded in establishing a "rumor clinic" in the *Boston Traveler*. Initially activated in order to control and counter anti-Semitic accusations—that, for example, Jews were avoiding the draft through undue financial influence—the clinic became a much-imitated model in papers all over the country.[48]

As in so many other areas, World War II–era perspectives on anti-Semitism had been anticipated in the work of Harold Lasswell. In 1933 he argued that Hitler's appeal was a product of deep emotional insecurities. Nazi ideology was viable only because the German national personality structure was vulnerable to vengeful appeals. When he wrote that "emotional insecurities are reduced by hating scapegoats and adoring heroes," and "politics is a form of social therapy for potential suicides," Lasswell was fueling an analytic style which came to full flower during and after World War II: understanding political ideas (at least hostile ones) in largely psychological terms and addressing social developments with tools designed for individual psychological diagnosis and treatment.[49] By the early 1940s, social psychological perspectives on the character structure and irrational basis of fascism had been aired in the work of Wilhelm Reich, Erich Fromm, and others.[50] Drawing on an eclectic mixture of psychoanalytic and Marxist theory, sociological concern, and historical attention to detail, the approach Lasswell advocated was widely known and used by psychologists and various other social scientists who would play key roles in wartime work.[51]

Concentration camp studies dramatically confirmed that these most horrifying institutional products of German anti-Semitism were indeed built on deficits in the German national character. Further, they had a profoundly and explicitly psychological purpose: to systematically destroy the integrity of individual personalities. Bruno Bettelheim, who had just received his Ph.D. in philosophy and psychology at the University of Vienna when he was sent to Dachau and Buchenwald, wrote about the emotional realities of camp life in his famous article "Individual and Mass Behavior in Extreme Situations." It spoke eloquently of the author's desire for survival and furthered the tendency to generalize, in broad cultural and political terms, from the experience of personal dehumanization. *"It seems that what happens in an extreme fashion to the prisoners who spend several years in the concentration camp happens in less exaggerated form to the inhabitants of the big concentration camp called greater Germany."* [52] Not surprisingly, many who were moved by Bettelheim's analysis arrived at the logical conclusion that some sort of mass psychological treatment was the most appropriate response to German political history, and clinically oriented plans for postwar reeducation programs throughout Europe, to be designed and administered by psychological experts, proliferated. Reeducation would do well to treat national personalities as if they were schizophrenic, according to this line of thought, or at least symptomatic of "the postwar sickness." [53]

The high-water mark in the analysis of anti-Semitism came with the groundbreaking *The Authoritarian Personality,* which inspired a virtual flood of follow-up studies.[54] The book was a product of the Frankfurt school, a group of left-wing theorists (including Erich Fromm, Max Horkheimer, Theodor Adorno, Walter Benjamin, and Herbert Marcuse) whose trademark "critical theory" combined an abstract, philosophical Marxism with a deep interest in psychoanalysis and contemporary culture. Members of the Frankfurt school began their collective project in Frankfurt, Germany, in 1923, prior to Hitler's rise, and, because many were Jews as well as Marxists, continued their work in exile. After the war, Adorno and Horkheimer returned to Germany to reestablish the Institute for Social Research, but many of the others remained to make their names in the postwar United States.

Although not published in comprehensive book form until 1950, *The Authoritarian Personality* was a direct outgrowth of wartime insight into the emotional role authority played in enemy national characters. (Psychological warfare designed on the model of national character has already been described in the cases of the Psychological Warfare Division [PWD] of SHAEF [Supreme Headquarters, Allied Expeditionary Force] and the Foreign Morale Analysis Division [FMAD] of the Office of War Information [OWI].) Research funds made available, largely by Jewish organizations, for wartime studies of the psychology of prejudice were also central in the evolution of *The Authoritarian Personality.* A significant number of preliminary research reports, as well as articles on various aspects of morale, were published during the war years by authors Theodor Adorno, Else Frenkel-Brunswik, Daniel Levinson, and R. Nevitt Sanford. They generally shared the national character orientation of other World War II experts and were motivated, at least initially, by the desire to explain Hitler's success in Germany as well as the rise of Fascist ideologies in general.

The book reported the results of an ambitious questionnaire given to subjects ranging from college students to mental patients, prisoners, union members, and veterans. The questionnaire included (1) factual items (such as income, church membership, and political party affiliations); (2) scales designed to elicit shades of agreement or disagreement with a series of statements about anti-Semitism, ethnocentrism, and political ideology; (3) deliberately ambiguous, open-ended questions which encouraged wide-ranging emotional responses in need of interpretation, such as "What would you do if you had only six months to live, and could do anything you wanted?"[55] In addition to this written survey, psychological experts conducted numerous clinical interviews with and administered projective psychological tests (such as the Thematic Apperception Test, or TAT) to a sample of the respondents.

At the end of their study, the investigators advanced the psychoanalytically informed theory that authoritarian political regimes were built on the deep, unconscious structure of individual personalities so rigidly patterned that they were susceptible to irrational manipulation by ruthless demagogues. Democratic personalities, on the other hand, featured far less uniformity than authoritarian ones and were more likely to incorporate values like rationality and tolerance, precisely those traits that Mead and Allport had so hopefully associated with domestic national character, and which were firmly tied to the self-images of psychological experts themselves.

Conveniently, the authors offered a practical method of measuring individuals' psychopolitical inclinations: the F scale. The scale and the theory that "personality may be regarded as a *determinant* of ideological preferences" appealed to World War II–era experts and made deep impressions on diverse schools of psychological theory and far-flung areas of behavioral research.[56] *The Authoritarian Personality,* consequently, illustrated the general acceptance of those trends pioneered by Lasswell's work before World War II, especially the equation of politics and psychology and the convergence of personal and social analysis.

The fact that the research for *The Authoritarian Personality* was conducted entirely in the United States, however, raised some new and distinctly uncomfortable questions. By drawing psychologists' attention to the fact that authoritarian personalities were not an exclusively foreign phenomenon, and pointing out that plenty of them flourished uncomfortably close to home, the study painted a disturbing portrait of a potential American fascism, based on rigidly conventional and anxiously dependent personalities who were frightened of difference and change. If authoritarianism were a possibility contained within many apparently ordinary personalities, and if prejudice were a latent tendency that could be activated with a little push from the demagogue of the moment, then surely what happened in Nazi Germany could happen in the United States. This catastrophic possibility, brought to life by racial strife on the home front, made the psychology of prejudice a high priority for psychological experts long after the war was over.[57]

Anti-Semitism was not the only focus of wartime work on the psychology of prejudice. Deadly race riots in Detroit, Los Angeles, and other cities in the summer of 1943 (not to mention the internment of Japanese-Americans) were concrete proof of the explosive tensions that characterized relations between African-Americans, Mexican-Americans, and the majority of whites. If anything, they illustrated that anti-Semitism was only the tip of the iceberg, and that antiblack prejudice was even more socially acceptable and widely expressed. Attempts to analyze home front riots offer a useful illustration of how wartime efforts to comprehend German mass psychology migrated back across the Atlantic and were quickly applied to domestic developments precisely because psychological experts understood that victory abroad and stability at home were intimately, and psychologically, connected. The OWI's Bureau of Overseas Intelligence, for example, conducted a series of secret studies of black civilian morale and attitudes and concluded that policies aimed at reducing racial frustrations in both civilian and military life would be strategic steps toward military victory.[58]

That violent tensions at home were a threat to the prosecution of world war was really no secret to anyone though. Two analysts, Alfred McClung Lee and Norman Daymond Humphrey, described the 1943 Detroit riot as a "hysterical attack upon democracy and American morale" and asked "How can we keep America from dividing itself more and more with walls of intolerance into increasingly warring camps— into a psychologically Balkanized country?"[59] Maintaining the morale of minority groups may have been precarious, but it was essential.[60]

Because psychological experts understood that segregation, employment, and criminal justice practices could tip the balance of the war effort, they took it upon themselves to advise and enlighten policymakers in municipal administrations and police departments as well as in military institutions. Like the effort to give practical assistance to Japanese-American Relocation Center administrators, psychologists who took up the question of race riots typically offered clear and explicit instructions to those in power: "If These Symptoms Appear . . . Take the Following Actions."[61]

Some experts were not entirely satisfied with roles as advisors and made a commitment to using their skills in even more direct ways. Gordon Allport, for example, along with his student Leo Postman, conducted pioneering training sessions with captains in the Boston Police Department in 1944. Theirs was an attempt to reduce racial tensions in the city by exposing hostile and defensive law enforcement officials to psychology's cutting-edge reeducation techniques.[62] Allport's efforts to instill racial sensitivity in police officers through "catharsis" was another of his efforts that was much imitated in years to come.[63] According to Allport's report, he spent eight long, trying hours with a group of forty police officers who "indulged in aggressive, hostile, prejudiced discourse aimed occasionally at me, the instructor, but more

often at various minority groups (whom we were seeking to understand!), and at other scapegoats, including the public press, intellectuals, parents, and even the citizenry at large."[64] Because he resolved to
meet the racist reaction without emotion, the officers' prejudice dimin-
ished by the end of the day. Allport claimed that he had produced this
constructive effect by listening nonjudgmentally, hence allowing the
police to avoid threats to their personal status, project their guilt, and
begin restructuring their attitudes on their own, after the fashion of
Carl Rogers's nondirective counseling techniques.

Riots also presented psychological experts with the opportunity to
make good use of the tradition of crowd psychology and collective behavior that had existed long before the war and that would continue to
develop long after, when it would be expanded into an all-purpose theory of revolutionary upheaval in the Cold War era as well as a handy
explanation for urban disorder at home. The mood that made the Detroit tragedy possible, for example, was considered a result of "hysterical individual insecurity," multiplied by a factor of thousands, reaching
a point of such tension that it needed release.[65] Detroit riot analysts
Lee and Humphrey observed that rioters behaved

like a herd about to stampede. . . . *Brutalized emotions rise and are given sanc-
tion by the mob.* . . . All of this looks as though the mob is rapidly going "out of
its mind." And the generation of such mass hysteria shows the character of
insanity, except that the members of the mob are not nearly as uncontrolled,
impulsive, and depraved alone as they become under mob-suggestion. In the
race-riot mob, no rules apply, no fair play. No ethics of any kind have meaning
except the crude ones of the human-pack, even more brutal than the wolf-
pack.[66]

Many riot specialists were eager to translate such theoretical models of
collective behavior into socially useful technologies of prevention. A
psychological "Race Sentiments Barometer," according to analysts of
the Detroit riot, would be a major improvement over even such positive
measures as counteracting rumors because it would offer a "more fundamental diagnosis and more accurate prediction through determining
the power of the emotional drives at work, the significance of the societal and psychological 'ground swells.' "[67] The suggestion that psychology develop predictive indices for social managers would be repeated in later years, practically word-for-word, in reference to
predicting and controlling revolutionary upheaval around the world as
well as civil disturbance at home. In Cold War conflicts as well as during

urban riots in the late 1960s, such services were in great demand among policy-makers.

Wartime riots popularized the view that prejudice was a "general psychological condition" whose origins were to be found in early childhood experience and the treacherous steps of emotional development.[68] This view was not a rigid one and gradations were recognized. The emotional basis of intergroup conflict could range from a more or less benign neurosis to a dangerous sickness akin to insanity. The point is that the wartime environment contributed to a decidedly psychological analysis of rioting, as well as a variety of other racial and ethnic problems. The view that individual insecurities and collective emotional depravity were somehow at the heart of intergroup conflict would have lasting consequences.[69]

This was exactly what psychological experts wanted. Because they played major roles in analyzing and treating intergroup conflict during the war, they naturally assumed they would continue this occupation in the postwar era. From psychoanalytically inclined theorists who claimed riots were "violent outbreaks of infantile father hatred" to those more likely to consider sociological factors like poverty and segregation, psychological experts—clinicians, theorists, and researchers alike— emerged from World War II convinced that it was their responsibility as enlightened professionals to challenge myths of racial difference, including the myths that psychology itself had helped elevate to scientific truth earlier in the century.[70] Racism had become, for them, "America's number-one social neurosis."[71]

"Community disorders" entered the vocabulary of World War II psychiatry as a new type of diagnosis covering, among other things, racial tensions and riots.[72] Management and prevention of mental disturbance was their forté, reasoned the psychiatrists, and prejudice was clearly a deeply rooted mental disturbance. According to this line of thinking, psychiatric authority should expand into any and every sphere of social life in which frustration, fear, aggression, hatred, and insecurity were relevant factors. This argument went well beyond the treatment of racial hostility and provided a general intellectual foundation for the promotion of community psychiatry, perhaps the most significant development in that field in the postwar era.[73]

Institutional and legislative remedies for racial injustices, like the wartime Fair Employment Practices Commission (FEPC), established via executive order in order to tackle the problem of employment discrimination in the war industries, were not necessarily invalidated by this logic, and many psychological experts gladly supported such liberal means of assuring civil rights. But laws and government regulations were often relegated to secondary status, most dramatically by clinicians, whose work put them into close contact with individuals feeling the consequences of bigotry and discrimination. Such experiences, not surprisingly, bolstered the opinion that since the personal anguish surrounding matters of race was profound, personal transformation in this area could hardly be any less so. In comparison to the potential of psychological experts to help instill personal and cultural change at such deep levels, legally mandated equality was considered abstract and superficial. "The FEPC and other anti-discrimination agencies are only symptomatic and temporary therapy," commented one writer, whose final word was that "emotional growth, for the most part, is incomplete in our culture; human difference has become a liability instead of a positive factor in life experiences."[74] There could be no adequate legal solution to a fundamentally emotional problem, agreed another clinician, who explained the prevalence of racism as follows: "Quite evidently, white European man for all his boasts and his weapons did not feel secure."[75]

Gordon Allport, known for his political liberalism, distinguished between discrimination (a question of structure) and prejudice (a question of emotion).[76] If cures for discrimination and those for prejudice were not entirely distinct (Allport, for example, vigorously advocated legislative changes because he understood that legal changes would affect how people felt and behaved), it was certainly the case that Allport perceived attacking prejudice though a process of psychological reeducation as a more direct route to social change. Institutional reform may have been important, but emotional reform was clearly the tougher challenge.[77]

Ironically, but characteristically, the contents of psychology's toolbox, proposed by World War II experts as the most effective resource for combating the epidemic of intergroup conflict, had been used more frequently to fan the flames of homegrown racism in the past than it had been to put out the fire. Intelligence testing programs during World War I, in particular, had been welcomed by eugenicists, eager to prove their point about racial intelligence differences with the help of data from the military. They received prompt and solicitous attention from psychologists, who announced, as scientific dogma, that black soldiers were inferior and that there existed a mental hierarchy pegged to nationality: Anglo-Saxons were at the top while the unsavory representatives of recent immigrant groups languished far below. In 1921 Robert Yerkes, who had chaired the important World War I Committee on Methods of Psychological Examining of Recruits, wrote personally to the chairmen of congressional committees considering immigration restriction, calling their attention to the World War I army intelligence tests and suggesting, in no uncertain terms, that these products of psychological expertise could be a formidable resource in their campaign to shut off the flow of undesirable immigration. "The army tests," he claimed, "establish the relation of inferior intelligence to delinquency and crime, and justify the belief that a country which encourages, or even permits, the immigrations of simple-minded, uneducated, defective, diseased or criminalistic persons, because it needs cheap labor, seeks trouble in the shape of public expense."[78] His argument was convincing. Warnings about the mental unfitness of recent immigrants further inflamed fears, already widespread before World War I, about the increasing racial and ethnic diversity of U.S. society, especially urban centers that were magnets for newcomers. The army's testing program, and the eugenic advocacy of Yerkes and other psychologists, offered a powerful scientific foundation for the restrictions written into the Immigration Act of 1924.[79]

Yerkes, as we have already seen, went on to play a starring role in World War II psychology. He never abandoned, or even really revised, his eugenicist beliefs. His vision of a great future for psychological professionals, so crucial to early mobilization efforts, was intimately bound up with a commitment to literal life-and-death control over the "biologically unfit."[80] Nevertheless, a widespread feeling grew up among the vast majority of World War II psychological experts, who, after all, cut their professional teeth in a righteous war against racial and political tyranny, that psychological theories and applications were inextricably, dynamically linked with democratic politics. On the one hand, prevailing definitions of mental hygiene and health assumed personalities capable of making rational choices and negotiating the emotional pitfalls of freedom; these were, as we have seen, the basic elements of democratic morale. On the other hand, it was only by preserving democratic institutions that the psychological professions could ensure their futures. "We are all engaged in the same task of defending the ramparts of democracy," Edward Strecker announced to the assembled forces of the American Psychiatric Association in 1944, comparing psychiatrists to soldiers. "Our stake in the war is precious for the discipline of psychiatry can only live and flower within the framework of democracy."[81]

One large-scale, interdisciplinary research effort that powerfully embodied the marriage between liberalism and behavioral science was *An American Dilemma,* a monumental analysis of black-white race relations in the context of democratic principles, first published in 1944. Authored by Swedish-born economist and politician Gunnar Myrdal, the research for the book mobilized scores of social scientists whose wartime service made them acutely aware that domestic racial problems were an international embarrassment for the United States. *An American Dilemma* inaugurated an era of racial liberalism among academic social scientists that would endure for decades, with only very occasional dissent.[82] Whether or not psychological expertise was the essence of enlightened humanism, inherently blessed with antiracist and democratic values, would become, as we shall see, a major issue in the postwar era.

Military Morale

Monitoring and improving military morale were concerns at least as grave as unraveling the mysteries of public opinion or controlling the psychological assaults on minority groups in civilian life. "Psychological ramparts are as important as physical ramparts in modern warfare," declared public relations wizard Edward Bernays in the *Infantry Journal* several months before the attack on Pearl Harbor. "Our morale is our true first line of defense" against the hysterical manias lurking in the collective subconscious.[83]

During the war, the job of regulating the mental state of the armed forces incorporated virtually every type of civilian morale and psychological warfare activity discussed thus far: case studies of individual personality, mass surveys of soldiers' viewpoints, reports assessing policy-making options, evaluations and predictions of intergroup hostilities. Life in the military was different from life outside it, but except for combat itself, the differences were relative, not absolute.[84]

Conveniently, soldiers' attitudes were more accessible than civilians' to both measurement and manipulation. The fact that military institutions exerted much more direct control over individual behavior, and therefore offered much greater support too (at least in theory), led many morale specialists to design civilian morale programs on the basis of the military model.[85] During wartime, exerting too much control was not the biggest mistake that could be made, after all. The availability, albeit temporary, of the military total institution was yet another benefit of war, much appreciated by researchers eager to prove the scientific validity of their experimental methods and procedures.

The army institutionalized an elaborate research effort in order to stay on top of soldiers' attitudes and "to aid in practical social engineering."[86] The Research Branch of the army's Morale Division (later called the Information and Education Division) was established in October 1941 to put the most sophisticated tools of social and psychological research, especially survey techniques developed in business, at the service of the military.[87] "Its purpose," explained its director, "is to establish a clear-cut working knowledge of the American soldier, his educational background, likes and dislikes, opinions, attitudes and ambitions; and so to furnish a scientific basis either for the correction of Army maladjustments, or for explaining to the soldier the reasons back of particular policies."[88] The branch's three hundred studies and sixty thousand interviews were sometimes conducted in response to requests from policy-makers for specific information, sometimes on the branch's own initiative. The expert staff summarized findings for high-level officials and government agencies and published them in popular form for army commanders in regular periodicals (a monthly titled *What the Soldier Thinks*) and occasional pamphlets (like *Command of Negro Troops*). All of this work, even blank questionnaires, was considered highly confidential.

An impressive group of behavioral experts staffed the Research Branch, most drawn directly out of careers in academic or commercial research. Samuel Stouffer, a University of Chicago sociologist, directed the research effort. He made liberal use of civilian consultants from academia and business: John Dollard and Carl Hovland of the Yale Institute of Human Relations, Hadley Cantril of the Princeton Office of Public Opinion Research, Paul Lazarsfeld of the Columbia Bureau of Applied Social Research, Frank Stanton, director of research at CBS, to name only a few.

Like other experts, they found both opportunity and frustration in the wartime environment, which allowed them to ply their trade on a scale previously unimaginable, but also offered no guarantees that decision-makers would pay any attention to their wisdom. Samuel

Stouffer did his utmost to make the branch's research attractive to military bureaucrats. After the war he was the first to admit that "most of our time was wasted, irretrievably wasted, in so far as any contribution to social science was concerned [because] in order to help the Army, or to help 'sell' research to the Army, I had to be concerned first and foremost with what was immediately wanted or purchasable."[89] Even so, he tried to do some justice to scientific concerns by promoting an eclectic intellectual approach in the Research Branch that combined psychoanalysis, learning theory, cultural anthropology, and social systems theory, along with the latest statistical techniques in opinion polling.[90]

While this type of boundary-breaking work had begun well before the war in places like the Yale Institute of Human Relations, wartime efforts like Stouffer's advanced the prospects of an interdisciplinary and ambitious behavioral science precisely because wartime experience caused experts to dispense with many of the academic loyalties and identities they had previously cherished. In the postwar era the approach advanced by Stouffer and other like-minded experts garnered much prestige with the establishment of the Harvard Department of Social Relations (Stouffer himself became director of its Laboratory of Social Relations), the Research Center for Group Dynamics at the Massachusetts Institute of Technology, the Institute for Social Research at the University of Michigan, and the Center for Advanced Study in the Behavioral Sciences at Stanford. In each of these cases, psychological experts who had been deeply involved in war work were central figures and the Department of Defense provided most of the operating funds during their early years.

During World War II, the work of Stouffer's research staff was nothing if not varied. Their first effort measured the spirits of infantrymen the day after Pearl Harbor. Subsequent research checked up on the accuracy of the neuropsychiatric screening test, identified the factors most likely to influence good (or bad) adjustment to job assignments, and even turned its conclusions about what constituted good leaders into a training course in hopes of producing them. Among the many studies widely believed to have shaped policy directly was one that surveyed enlisted soldiers' attitudes on how demobilization should be handled, a study whose objectives were to simultaneously impress upon soldiers the significance of their input and maintain firm control over military personnel for as long as it might be necessary. The results, which tabulated soldiers' preferences, were converted into a point system that weighed length of service, combat duty, and number of dependents, among other factors. The Research Branch staff believed that such instances of turning soldiers' feelings directly into policy were evidence of a highly democratic policy-making process, largely responsible for soldiers' feeling that demobilization rules were fair. It was also clear to them that the goals of the demobilization study included keeping men in the army as long as they were needed and "overcoming the idea that the country owes soldiers a living for sacrifices they have made while in uniform."[91]

DISCOVERING UNREASONABLE ATTITUDES

Their studies were matters of great pride to Research Branch staff, and advocates of behavioral and psychological expertise in and out of government used them routinely, for many years following the war, as prime examples of socially useful science and ammunition for the argument that behavioral expertise should have a much bigger public policy-making role as well as hefty support from private foundations and universities.[92] But much of what the Research Branch turned up in the course of its research was not only far less amenable to adjustment, but even shocking in its implications. Casting doubts upon the dependability of reasoned intelligence, as so much other wartime research also did, the Research Branch effort sharply contrasted the rhetoric of democratic morale against the reality of rampant emotionalism and unconscious motivation.

Most significantly, Stouffer's organization discovered that U.S. soldiers had no meaningful understanding of why they were fighting or what the war was actually about. Worse, they did not seem to care. When soldiers were surveyed with open-ended questions about the war's aims, an astonishing 36 percent chose not to answer at all and only a handful ever mentioned fighting fascism or defending democracy. According to the Research Branch studies, the number of men who viewed the war "from a consistent and favorable intellectual position" was somewhere between 10 and 20 percent.[93] "Why we are fighting the war" was typically on the bottom of the list of things that soldiers wanted the army to teach them.[94] In dismay, Stouffer concluded that "the war was without a context . . . simply a vast detour made from the main course of life. . . . It may be said that except for a very limited number of men, *little feeling of personal commitment to the war emerged.*"[95]

Such glaring gaps between the rhetoric of democratic morale and the reality of popular ignorance and apathy spurred the Research Branch to involvement in bold efforts at direct political indoctrination. The most famous of these were the "Why We Fight" films, which the Research Branch produced with the help of filmmaking Colonel Frank Capra, but staff and consultants offered suggestions for many other training films and programs aimed at instilling the appropriate political attitudes and feelings in rank-and-file soldiers. Congress was rather touchy about making it widely known that the army was engaged in such explicit propaganda during a war directed against exactly such efforts, and only one of Capra's films was ever shown to civilians, who also knew nothing of the military's other experiments in direct indoctrination.

There were questions other than that of propriety. Did the films work? Unfortunately, not very well. When the effectiveness of the "Why We Fight" films was tested, the Research Branch found that cinematic education had succeeded in supplying soldiers with some concrete facts, but that the effect on soldiers' willingness and desire to fight passionately for U.S. political ideals was utterly "disappointing."[96]

The Research Branch went on to experiment with weekly mental conditioning sessions, hoping that active participation in group talk would be a more effective route to changing political attitudes than passively watching movies. But these met with similar failure. Psychiatrist Julius Schreiber, who eventually headed the entire Information and Education Division, was left with no positive ideas about inculcating democratic morale and capitulated to the dismal view that hatred for the enemy was easier to manufacture than genuine enthusiasm and respect for U.S. institutions. He set up a program at Camp Callan Training Center in California, using broadcast news, lectures, a weekly column, and therapy groups to inspire the maximum amount of animosity in U.S. troops toward fascism.[97] The program was later copied elsewhere. With this sort of experience behind them, it is not very surprising that Stouffer and others associated with the Research Branch emerged from the war convinced that "for the majority of individuals . . . it may be true that motivations and attitudes are generally acquired without regard to rational considerations and are practically impregnable to new rational considerations."[98]

Irrationality, however, was only the beginning of the bad news. To all appearances, U.S. soldiers were motivated by the same primitive feelings and loyalties, the same absence of conscious and reasonable motivation, the same ominous emotional attachments to authority figures, that had been identified as such alarming traits in the German and Japanese national characters. The influence of the soldier's immediate group, and the caliber of his immediate leaders, were found to be the most salient factors in soldiers' morale. From this, an unflattering portrait of the ordinary soldier gradually materialized. He was preoccupied with physical discomforts, displayed all sorts of aggression, and worried most about moving up the chain of command, making more money, and staying out of combat.[99] This was not exactly the democratic warrior the experts wanted to find.

Kurt Lewin's effort to generate a social psychology of group dynamics was tremendously influential among the experts who had to face such demoralizing facts about the pitiful psychological state of the U.S. military. Lewin's "field theory" turned personal identity into a social product and made "attitudes" a reachable halfway mark between the obscure psychic depths of individual motivation and the more comprehensible external world in which policy-makers operated. Lewin drew on the work of industrial psychologists in the interwar years who had found human relations in the corporate workplace to be emotionally charged. The Hawthorne experiments, conducted between 1924 and 1933 at the Western Electric Company, were only the most famous examples of the scientific discovery that job satisfaction and labor productivity were products of irrational attitudes, highly distorted and subjective perceptions, and group cohesiveness, rather than the specific organization of labor or authority in the workplace.[100] In the Hawthorne case, Elton Mayo and his fellow researchers from the Harvard Business School identified the personal attentions paid (or not paid) to female workers in the plant, and their immediate group environment, as the decisive factors shaping how they felt about their jobs and influencing how hard they worked. What military managers observed among World War II soldiers was really quite similar.

Lewin hypothesized that individual personality emerged from the "ground," the "life-space" of all relevant group memberships, which ranged from marriage (a small group, but a group nonetheless) to ethnic and religious communities to institutions like the military. By making individual psychology largely a matter of group psychology, Lewin did more than merge the two, which, after all, many World War II psychological experts were in the habit of doing. He held out the optimistic possibility that group management could keep soldiers' unpredictable attitudes in check *and* could be the most effective means of manufacturing democratic personalities and democratic leaders in the military.

Of course, what was applicable to the U.S. military was applicable elsewhere. Public opinion pollsters who had nothing to do with shaping soldiers' attitudes one way or another incorporated "reference group identifications" into their explanations of how and why public sentiment fluctuated on a variety of issues.[101] Many plans for postwar psychological reeducation programs—whether to reform intergroup relations at home or national character abroad—were unmistakably stamped with the imprint of Lewin's theories about the advantages of working with groups and training leaders.[102] (So too were postwar theories about the origins of revolutionary movements in the Third World, as we shall see in chapters 5 and 6.)

One of the consequences of learning all these dismal truths about Americans' lack of democratic morale and motivation, their political apathy, and their vulnerability to emotional manipulation was to strengthen psychological experts' faith in themselves and illuminate the gravity of their future choices. Simply stated, they could either become heavy-handed social engineers in charge of the future (a vision that appealed to the most pessimistic), or (for the diehard optimists) they could function as democratic guidance counselors and cheerleaders, helping an unhealthy society reach a point at which self-determination might finally become feasible. While this division was certainly significant, both personally and politically, experts at all points along the spectrum shared a commitment to serving the state through increasing and enlightening policy options related to political attitudes and participation.

INTERGROUP TENSIONS AND THE
MENTAL STATE OF BLACK SOLDIERS

As with the civilian population, the unreasonableness and emotionalism of soldiers' attitudes seemed to reach their zenith in the delicate area of intergroup tensions. The vast majority of white soldiers supported the rigidly segregated structure of the military without question. This structure not only kept black soldiers in separate units but rejected them at much higher rates than whites and restricted them to a small number of labor-intensive assignments—mainly in quartermaster, engineering, and transportation corps—if they managed to make it into the armed forces. Black soldiers were also systematically denied the opportunities for social mobility available to white soldiers, since the command of white troops was not a possibility for black officers, while many black units were led by white officers. There were, in any case, only five black officers in the entire army at the time of the Pearl Harbor attack and three of them were chaplains.

Not surprisingly, when the army's Research Branch conducted an elaborate survey about race relations in March 1943, it discovered that whites barely considered these issues, whereas black soldiers' attitudes were thoroughly shot through with resentment about military discrimination and contradictory feelings about the fairness of separating the races in a war against a racist ideology.[103] Further, the pervasive anger of black troops about racial injustices affected the way they thought and felt about everything else. Black soldiers were even less likely than whites (if that was possible) to have a reasonable grasp of war aims or be personally identified with democratic ideals. Unlike their white counterparts, however, black soldiers' uncertainty on this matter was not the product of thoughtless indifference but a pessimistic conclusion drawn from direct observation and personal experience. As one man facing imminent induction put it, "Just carve on my tombstone, 'Here lies a black man killed fighting a yellow man for the protection of a white man.'"[104]

The Research Branch was careful to note that no evidence existed that black soldiers behaved disloyally; there was no difference between draft-dodging rates among blacks and whites, for example. Clearly, black soldiers could and did respond to racial frustration in a variety of ways. Either their aggression could devolve into alienation and insistence that blacks had no reason to fight on the side of a hypocritical United States, or they could proclaim their patriotism, demand the right to serve in combat units and command positions, and hope that their wartime service would translate into racial gains at war's end. One illustration of alienated reaction was Malcolm X (then Malcolm Little), who was given a 4F after he arrived at the local induction center dressed in a zoot suit and told the psychological screeners that he either wanted to join the Japanese army or go south to organize black soldiers and kill white people.[105] Civil rights leaders and the black press, on the other hand, along with many black soldiers, agitated tirelessly against the War Department's 10.6 percent quota for blacks in the military and a selection process that counted complaints about segregation as sufficient reasons for psychiatric rejection.[106] They tried to counter the argument about frustration's negative consequences with claims that frustration made black soldiers even more determined to serve than whites. But suggesting that the gap between racial rhetoric and reality made black soldiers' patriotism especially heartfelt also depended upon the growing authority of psychological experience as a measure of political sacrifice. Just as Malcolm X understood that overt racial antagonism would likely result in rejection by the military's psychiatric gatekeepers, so too did other black soldiers wager that enduring the racism of a segregated military would eventually be seen as a badge of emotional honor, and benefit them.

The Research Branch made films and developed leadership training materials in an effort to blunt the dangerous potential for racial divisiveness in the army, just as it had done in the above-described case of addressing widespread ignorance among soldiers about the purposes of the war. In 1943 Frank Capra made a film titled *The Negro Soldier,* based, in part, on Research Branch survey data. It ritualistically celebrated a historic honor roll of black Americans who had valiantly served their country, from Crispus Attucks to the black Wacs who repaired jeeps and trucks. Capra's film was careful to mention neither slavery nor military segregation, but attempted to instill pride and solidarity in black troops through emotional identification with "the tree of liberty" and "this great country." [107] The Research Branch also put its findings to good use in publications like *Command of Negro Troops* and *Leadership and the Negro Soldier.*

Looking Toward the Future: Anxieties

Perhaps genuine patriotism or sheer persistence boosted the morale of the experts themselves and helped them stick to their tasks of making the chaos of soldiers' and civilians' attitudes orderly and manageable at points when they might otherwise have given up in despair. But the experts, in the Research Branch and elsewhere, had worries that went beyond the dismal mental state of Americans, some of these deeply rooted in the histories of their professions. Among the most constant and pressing questions were those about the efficacy of their own methods and the capacity of their psychological techniques to inform policy in ways that would stand up to the tests of rigorous science. Doubts about "validity" and "prediction" were best kept quiet, however. While they were frequently discussed within the bounds of professional networks, psychological experts steadfastly maintained a united front when it came to convincing potentially hostile customers (i.e., government policy-makers) that psychological services were worth the purchase price. If the enthusiasm of their public pronouncements and the track record of postwar psychology are any measure, they were rather successful.

But nagging questions remained. Even Samuel Stouffer, who did his utmost to produce helpful expertise for military decision-makers and whose Research Branch could point to concrete accomplishments—a number of surveys about soldiers' postwar expectations were used to plan the GI Bill, for example—worried constantly about methodological weaknesses. "If the war were to end today and if the Army should ask us what single practice General Osborn's million-dollar research operation has *proved* to be helpful to morale," he commented, "we honestly could not cite a scrap of scientific evidence. The curtain would go up on the stage and there we would stand—stark naked." [108] Toward the end of the war, Research Branch staff carefully compiled a list of "embarrassing questions" that might, in the future, tarnish the record of their work because they were scientifically unanswerable. [109] Notable for its length and detail, the list included many of the issues that advocates had insisted they could handle with ease: How do you define military morale and was it high or low? How well can you predict performance on the basis of test responses? How effectively can you change attitudes? What do you know about leadership? What did you learn about motivation?

Private consensus that such basic questions could not be answered among the very experts who had claimed the authority to do so did not stop Samuel Stouffer from singing the praises of wartime experts in public. If the work of his team was not exactly the science they wanted it to be, and had turned out to be something more like social engineering, well, that was better than nothing. "There were fires to be put out, and it was better to throw water or sand on the fires than to concentrate on studying chemistry to develop a new kind of extinguisher." [110]

What really counted was that psychological experts working in a variety of fields had cleared a path to power and their work had had an impact—more significant in some cases, less significant in others—on how the war had been conducted and won. While psychological experts were sensitive about "embarrassing questions," they were at least as proud of their public policy successes, having kept close tabs on their "hits" throughout the war.[111] The future clearly required wartime experts to continue stockpiling handy technologies and making available to policy-makers new tools of prediction and control that would ease the country's transition into an increasingly dangerous world. This was really nothing new. Predictive technologies satisfied policy-makers' demand because they capitalized on professional and disciplinary developments that, before World War II, had already been profoundly shaped by the administrative applications of measurement and testing in mass institutions: schools, prisons, corporations, armies, government organizations.[112]

One wartime idea, circulated among experts in a variety of morale agencies which had polling functions, was to develop a "Barometer of International Security," designed specifically to take the temperature of international tension and prevent the recurrence of war.[113] Alexander Leighton suggested that behavioral "weather stations" be established all over the world to constantly monitor levels of national and international aggression and hostility.[114] Ideas such as these had much in common with the "Race Sentiments Barometer" proposed by riot experts as well as the all-purpose indices developed during the war years to gauge the state of morale at home and in enemy populations. In important ways, they prefigured the outlines of Project Camelot, which came into public view almost twenty years later, similarly promising to predict tension and upheaval well enough to prevent them (see chapter 6). Whatever the future need, Stouffer predicted, persuasive "research brokers" would reap more gains for behavioral expertise than the most significant scientific breakthroughs.[115]

Their postwar future, many sensed, would be inextricably bound to the successes and failures of the World War II experience. The massive piles of data that the army's Research Branch had collected during the war, for example, were turned over to the Social Science Research Council in 1945 and eventually resulted in a four-volume study, *The American Soldier* (1949). Considering Stouffer's own views about the inability of wartime research to attain scientific standing, it is ironic that *The American Soldier* was heralded throughout the 1950s and 1960s as a major *scientific* landmark in psychological theory and research methodology. There were some psychologists who, while applauding the march of science, never quite lost sight of where such scientific opportunities had come from. Paul Lazarsfeld, a great admirer of *The*

American Soldier and a former consultant to the Research Branch, asked, "Why was a war necessary to give us the first systematic analysis of life as it really is experienced by a large sector of the population?"[116] He might have taken the next logical, if disturbing, step to ask: Where will future data for behavioral experts come from if not from future wars?

Looking Toward the Future: Hopes

Far more visible than such apprehensive undercurrents was the celebration of psychological expertise that accompanied the war's end. Proud declarations that psychology had been the key to winning the war were commonplace, and they applied equally to psychology's many faces: clinical work aimed at keeping soldiers' mental health in balance and nonclinical expertise focused on waging psychological warfare abroad and gauging public opinion at home. Occasional warnings about the dangers of overselling the skills of psychological experts were drowned out by loud cheers of self-congratulations or shoved aside by an excited mood of anticipation. Surely the government and the U.S. public would see fit to reward psychological experts for their many and varied wartime contributions. It was obvious that psychology was destined for postwar greatness.

True to form, psychological experts did not wait for government to come banging on their door, but prepared an articulate and vigorous case for important postwar roles before the war had even ended. Psychology would be at the heart of future efforts to prevent war, they claimed, but in the horrifying event of the recurrence of military conflict, psychology would also stand ready to serve the country again.

An illustrative effort on the side of war prevention was the "Psychologists' Peace Manifesto," which grew out of a suggestion by Gordon Allport at a 1943 SPSSI meeting. Formally released to the press on 5 April 1945, the statement, titled "Human Nature and the Peace," was signed by more than two thousand members of the APA (constituting a majority of the profession at the time) and summarized the lessons that socially oriented psychological experts had learned during the war, along with the important stipulation that "an enduring peace can be attained if the human sciences are utilized by our statesmen and peacemakers."[117] "Human Nature and the Peace" enumerated ten basic "principles" crucial to peace, prejudice, and democracy and warned that "neglect of them may breed new wars, no matter how well-intentioned our political leaders may be."[118]

1. War can be avoided: war is not born in men; it is built into men. . . .
2. In planning for permanent peace, the coming generation should be the primary focus of attention. Children are plastic. . . .
3. Racial, national, and group hatreds can, to a considerable degree, be controlled. . . . Prejudice is a matter of attitudes, and attitudes are to a considerable extent a matter of training and information.
4. Condescension toward "inferior" groups destroys our chances for a lasting peace. . . .
5. Liberated and enemy peoples must participate in planning their own destiny. . . .
6. The confusion of defeated people will call for clarity and consistency in the application of rewards and punishments. . . .
7. If properly administered, relief and rehabilitation can lead to self-reliance and cooperation; if improperly, to resentment and hatred. . . .
8. The root-desires of the common people of all lands are the safest guide to framing a peace. . . .
9. The trend of human relationships is toward ever wider units of collective security. . . .
10. Commitments *now* may prevent postwar apathy and reaction. . . .[119]

Although born of hopefulness, the statement began by warning that neglect of basic psychological principles was the surest route to international disaster. The psychologists involved in this effort did everything they could to ensure the statement made it into the hands of powerful people in Washington.[120]

Psychology's public face may have been turned optimistically toward peace, but wartime experts were working actively behind the scenes to ensure themselves a future in war as well. More indicative than the "Peace Manifesto" of where psychological experts were headed in the postwar era was organized activity on the side of war readiness, coordinated by Robert Yerkes. After Yerkes chaired a conference on military

psychology in July 1944, a committee drafted a set of "Recommendations Concerning Post-War Psychological Services in the Armed Services" and presented it to the Secretaries of War and Navy. Beyond
ambitious plans to train multitudes of new psychologists, institutionalize all sorts of psychological research, and promote psychologists to
important administrative and policy jobs, the Yerkes "Recommendations" took as axiomatic "the assumption that we, as a people, have
now learned the importance of preparedness and will not again risk our
existence by freezing our assets between wars."[121]

However different their goals, the "Peace Manifesto" and the "Recommendations" shared a fundamental belief about the postwar future:
it would need social engineering very badly because the "cultural lag"
that separated human control over the material world from human control over the social environment was by far the gravest threat to the
survival of the species.[122] Cultural lag encompassed an ominous, global
psychological lag that ought to be the highest postwar priority for psychological professionals. According to Eugene Lerner, one of the manifesto's supporters, "The aim of psychological reconstruction ought to
be the production of more and more democratic personalities and cultures everywhere. The various nations of the world show differential
lags in this direction."[123] Gordon Allport's preface to the "Peace Manifesto" was titled "Social Engineering," and all his faith in democracy
and psychological enlightenment could not obscure his view that the
calamity of world war had left the U.S. government and public with
few options. "The choice is clear. If we 'let nature take its course,' we
shall not have peace in our time. If we guide the process we can avoid
decades or centuries of suffering. . . . Social engineering on a world-
wide scale is a new conception, the product of the two devastating
world wars. It is an invention whose mother is grim necessity."[124] For
his part, Yerkes made it abundantly clear that World War II had shown
how essential the future of "Human Engineering" would be.

The physical sciences and technologies had gone far enough already,
and, with the atomic bomb, some thought they had gone too far.
"Man's brain lives in the twentieth century," Erich Fromm wrote in
1941, "[but] the heart of most men lives still in the Stone Age."[125] A
mere four years later, were people emotionally prepared to live in the
postwar world? Was peace a realistic possibility considering everything
the war had revealed about the perversity of national characters, the
dubiousness of democratic morale, and the irrationality of soldiers' atti-

tudes? Until psychology had progressed to a point of rough equivalence with physics, the consensus among psychological experts was that the answer to such questions would have to be negative.

Their spirits were not dampened for long. Somber warnings of future conflict, after all, seemed to guarantee psychology as big a part in a brand new world as did aspirations for peace. Who would carry the banner for democracy, reason, and peace in an irrational and frightening world if not psychologists? Harvard psychologist Edwin Boring was full of confidence. "The psychological point of view is, of course, the means of which social problems are solved and social progress is engineered. That is because it is the attitude of maturity and tolerance. It is also because engineering works by causes in a determined universe."[126]

Psychological experts emerged from World War II with their trades so firmly joined to enlightened democracy, government policy, and social order that the automatic relationship among the three became an unstated—and practically unchallenged—assumption well into the 1960s.[127] Gregory Bateson, a Cambridge-trained anthropologist who had met Margaret Mead in New Guinea, where they were both doing fieldwork, wrote excitedly to his mother in October 1940 that "democracy and psychology and anthropology [were] popping together at a great rate."[128] The war, he concluded shortly thereafter, was nothing less than "a life-or-death struggle over the role which the social sciences shall play in the ordering of human relationships."[129]

While some of their wartime efforts had clearly been more effective in shaping policy than others, and certain policy-makers continued to obstinately resist psychological counsel, most experts were secure in the knowledge that their future prospects were bright, if only because the country, and the world, looked like it might be in worse straits than ever. "Social and political psychology will become a psychology of social order and social control," Gardner Murphy predicted. "Through the agony of these years we have learned something about the problems which confront an *international social psychology.* . . . Social psychology will have to become as international as physics. . . . The internationalization of social psychology means the internationalization of the research task of war prevention."[130]

By 1945 it was clear that psychology was desperately needed and do-nothing expertise was definitely out of favor. Advancing psychological science through principled detachment from the messy business of politics and firm loyalty to the objectivity of scientific method—so characteristic of the interwar years—had been swept aside by the urgencies of war.[131] Placing scientific knowledge at the service of the state, in order to achieve important social goals, promised to help experts realize their responsibilities and increase their authority in the future. Yet neither were the perils of social engineering and control apparent in 1945. And why should they have been? Designing democratic personalities and predicting emotional surges in national and international tension levels had, in their view, not only contributed greatly to winning a good war against evil, but made the prevention of future wars a possibility at a moment when another horrifying and costly world conflict seemed unthinkable. Psychological wisdom had not yet been put to the repressive purposes that would appear such defining features of its postwar public career.

The worldview that emerged from the social movements of the 1960s and the experience of the Vietnam War would challenge virtually every fundamental commitment of the World War II generation: its equation of social responsibility with government service, democracy and tolerance with psychology, and enlightened planning with behavioral expertise. On the basis of just such assumptions, significant segments of the next generation—students opposed to the Vietnam War, for example—would accuse their predecessors of naive ignorance, at best, and, at worst, calculated criminality.

None of that, however, was apparent in 1945. Instead, the war had shown that controlling personalities, shaping attitudes and feelings, and guiding democracy through an era of emotional turbulence were major responsibilities of government. They were also the things that psychological experts did best.

4

Nervous in the Service

The benefits of World War II accrued as surely to clinicians as they did to the sykewarriors and opinion pollsters who evolved into the behavioral scientists of the postwar era. Experts who treated malfunctioning individuals and those who attempted to manage the mental state of entire populations could all claim loyalty to the practice of psychology. They pointed with pride to a common body of theoretical knowledge and insisted that its flexible application to both clinical and policy purposes validated psychology's status as a universal science. The experts surveyed in chapters 2 and 3 spent the war years guiding wartime policy around mass emotional currents that threatened to obstruct military victory and contaminate democracy by undermining the cohesiveness of civilian and military spirit. Their reward for effective service was a place in postwar public policy for themselves and their research, as we shall see in chapters 5 through 8. War brought access to policy-makers, and access to policy-makers inspired visions of altering the exercise of power.

The experts whose work is described in this chapter provided services deemed equally crucial to the war effort. Although the subject of their tasks was different, the ultimate goal was not. Clinicians were just as centrally concerned with morale, and their activities also promoted a highly subjective conception of effective warfare rather than one that emphasized, for example, superior technology. As specialists in individual treatment, they took pains to show exactly how their work furthered collective aims and, in the process, pushed work designed to instill mental hygiene and health far beyond its initial, clinical uses. According to psychiatrists Edward Strecker and Kenneth Appel, "Psychiatrists employ their skill in trying to mend broken personalities. They attempt to reassemble the fragments; fit them together; remobilize the morale. . . . A nation has a living personality. The national personality is the cross section of the personalities of all the citizens. It is a reliable barometer of the condition of the national morale."[1] Throughout the war, clinicians spent their time administering tests, formulating diagnoses, and experimenting with a range of psychotherapeutic techniques designed to help mentally anguished soldiers recover a degree of military usefulness in spite of the terrible strains of war. "Morale does not grow on trees," clinicians Strecker and Appel proclaimed just as boldly as pollsters and sykewarriors. "It must be made."[2]

Their record in "making morale" had dramatic results during the war and after. Clinical tasks multiplied, the ranks of clinical professionals surged, and clinical theories about what caused mental troubles were fundamentally reformulated, along with corresponding treatments. War on a mass scale was probably the only thing that could have made clinical treatment possible on a mass scale. It achieved what clinicians prior to World War II had never even dreamed of attempting on their own: a comprehensive "normalization" that altered the subjects and purposes of clinical work by reorienting theory and practice away from mental illness and toward mental health.

This chapter describes how the military's tangible requirements inspired such normalization and argues that it shaped clinicians' history both during World War II and long after. The normalization process was radical. In hopes of ensuring the mental stamina of the fighting forces, millions of ordinary men were brought into the orbit of clinical applications for the first time. In the short run, the outcome appeared misguided, even disastrous. Instead of improving Americans' war readiness, clinical technologies exposed an epidemic of emotional instability and betrayed the weakness of democratic resolve. In the long run, however, wartime clinical practice earned benefits for almost everyone involved. By acquainting huge numbers of ordinary people with professional healing and emotional self-management for the first time, it served as a foundation for the "growth industry" of the postwar years and lengthened the menu of services available to a rapidly expanding consumer market. War proved that more things, relationships, and experiences could alleviate mental troubles than anyone had previously imagined. And it demonstrated why taking charge of citizens' mental health was such a major obligation of a modern, democratic state.

Who They Were and What They Did

Clinicians were the war's most visible psychological experts. Not only did their numbers exceed those of their policy-oriented counterparts, but their immediate clientele—literally millions of soldiers—eclipsed the relatively small group of war managers and policymakers whose needs governed the path of experts with more conventional social scientific inclinations. One-third of the psychiatrists in the United States volunteered immediately to serve in the massive effort to screen every single one of the fifteen million recruits to the armed forces. But this amounted to a mere three thousand people, less than 2 percent of all U.S. doctors (who numbered around 180,000 in 1940) and less than 3 percent of military physicians.[3]

It was clear early on that a critical shortage of psychiatrists would hobble the effort unless a crash course in mental medicine were provided to the military's general medical personnel. Twenty-five psychiatrists comprised the military's entire psychiatric staff when the United States entered the war, but another twenty-four hundred medical officers were rapidly trained in the treatment of emotional disorders, along with a wide assortment of allied professionals, from clinical psychologists to social workers and nurses. One-quarter of the country's trained psychologists, to take only one example, served in the military by the end of the war years.[4] And the numbers of clinicians increased dramatically as a result of military requirements. In 1940 a bare 272 members of the American Psychological Association (less than 10 percent of the entire membership) had been employed in clinical capacities of any kind, and among these, very few were assigned major psychotherapeutic tasks.[5] By July 1945 seventeen hundred psychologists were working for the military, a significant number of them in clinical capacities.[6] War had offered many of them their first opportunities for clinical training and practice, persuading them that the field of individual treatment was the place to be in the future.

Because of psychiatry's medical origins, experts involved in clinical tasks appeared much less controversial at first than experts assigned to propaganda or intelligence operations, whose delicate tasks were almost always shrouded in secrecy. Indeed, before the shocking results turned information about the military's mental state into top-secret data, clinical experts proudly broadcast their plans to mount screening and treatment programs in the name of humanitarianism as well as effective management. Properly supported and implemented, clinicians argued, they could increase military efficiency by selecting out individuals who were identified, in advance, as psychological drags on the war effort and dealing quickly with cases of mental breakdown after the fact. While clinicians shared with the experts discussed in chapters 2 and 3 a commitment to advancing national security and the skillful conduct of war by the U.S. military, their historical reputations marked them as virtuous healers rather than skillful manipulators. Years spent caring for the sick and unfortunate had offered psychiatrists precious insights into the general human condition, argued Alan Gregg, director of the Rockefeller Foundation's Medical Science Division. "By showing us the common rules, the uniform limitations, and liberties all human beings live under because they are human, psychiatry gives us a sort of oneness-with-others, a kind of exquisite communion with all humanity, past, present, and future. It is a kind of scientific humanism that frees us from dogma and the tyranny of the mind, a relief from the inhuman straitjacket of rigid finality of thought."[7] According to William Menninger, who led the military's psychiatric effort during the war, Gregg's call to reveal the transcendent existential truths standing behind clinical experience was "a credo for every psychiatrist."[8]

Because of the memory that 69,394 men (around 2 percent of all those examined) had been rejected from the World War I military, the first priority was a screening program for inductees.[9] Robert Yerkes's notorious World War I intelligence testing program also came to mind as an unsettling reminder. Even though it had not been comprehensively administered, Yerkes had found a 50 percent rate of mental defectiveness among inductees and 60 to 70 percent of the rest demonstrated very low levels of intelligence: the average white, native-born soldier scored a mental age of thirteen.[10] This amounted to a virtual epidemic of feeblemindedness among the young men who were to be the country's first line of defense. In 1940 psychiatrists faulted their World War I counterparts for being insufficiently rigorous in their preemptive screening. They had relied too heavily on physical exams and symptoms, and psychiatrists were called in only on a referral basis, when some other military gatekeeper suspected the existence of a mental problem. When psychiatrists did have the chance to investigate, they

complained that military bureaucrats frequently ignored their recommendations and labeled clinicians "nutpickers" or "nutcrackers."[11]
Psychiatrists accused the World War I armed forces of harboring attitudes toward their profession that were "colored by a mixture of prejudice and ignorance."[12]

Without a doubt, the World War II screening effort would have to
be a substantial improvement, and early indications were positive. "The
Selective Service System seems to be fully awake to the importance of
psychiatric considerations," reported one professional committee with
great satisfaction.[13] Designed and run by psychiatrist Harry Stack Sullivan, director of the prestigious William Alanson White Psychiatric
Foundation, the program was incorporated into the 1940 Selective Service Act upon the express request of President Roosevelt, who was worried about the projected high costs of psychiatric hospitalization. The
screening process itself entailed a series of four to five thorough psychiatric examinations, beginning at the local draft board level. Each exam
was supposed to last fifteen to twenty minutes so as to avoid "the ridic-
ulous business of staring at people for a moment and pulling a few out
of the line for further study."[14] According to the plan, standardized
interviews would elicit detailed information about registrants' family
backgrounds and emotional profiles with such questions as "Do you
suddenly get so mad you don't know what you're doing?"[15] All screening interviews would be conducted in private.

The screening program assumed psychiatrists' ability to identify
"predisposed" individuals and thus predict mental trouble, two skills
that would, experts claimed, save the government much time and expense. It was widely publicized that psychiatric services and disability
payments to veterans had cost close to $1 billion between 1925 and
1940 and it was estimated that each psychiatric casualty during World
War II would cost at least $30,000.[16] If only screening were properly
implemented, "human values will be conserved; a great burden of unnecessary disability compensation payments, hospitalization expenses,
and pensions will be avoided—and the prestige and effectiveness of psychiatry, greatly expanded."[17] Every physician working for a local draft
board, after all, would necessarily come into enlightening contact with
psychiatry, most of them for the first time. For physicians unfamiliar
with psychiatric diagnoses, guidelines for questioning were provided,
including strict instructions that problematic candidates be immediately
referred to the psychiatric member of the nearest medical advisory
board.[18]

Predisposition was a psychiatric concept with roots in nineteenth-century medicine. By 1940 large-scale socioeconomic events like the depression had moved the concept away from a narrow, genetic meaning and neo-Freudians, including Sullivan himself, were stressing the power of culture to shape and reshape human behavior. During the interwar period, a great deal of discussion revolved around ameliorating the detrimental social conditions—childhood delinquency, sexual perversion, unemployment, and so forth—that could enhance the biological predisposition of individuals to mental troubles.

As understanding of predisposition broadened, so too did psychiatric comprehension of the condition to which it pointed: mental illness. In contrast to the narrow criteria employed during the World War I effort, psychiatric disability was defined very broadly in World War II. At the inception of the draft in November 1940, Selective Service System Medical Circular No. 1 recommended summary disqualification of individuals displaying symptoms of any one of eight types of psychiatric handicap. Stupidity, serious personality disorders, substance abuse, and organic brain disease were four of the officially sanctioned grounds for psychiatric rejection. Physicians without psychiatric training were reminded that "these conditions are likely to escape notice unless one is particularly looking for them."[19] They were also told to immediately refer individuals exhibiting the following "deviations" to the nearest psychiatrist: "instability, seclusiveness, sulkiness, sluggishness, discontent, lonesomeness, depression, shyness, suspicion, overboisterousness, timidity, sleeplessness, lack of initiative and ambition, personal uncleanliness, stupidity, dullness, resentfulness to discipline, nocturnal incontinence, sleep walking, recognized queerness, suicidal tendencies either bona fide or not, and homosexual proclivities."[20] Draftees who expressed any discomfort at all about undressing in the presence of examiners were considered potentially unsuited to the conditions of military life and were therefore subject to disqualification. "Fatigue, increase in use of alcohol or tobacco, tendency to show increasing irritability, increase in profanity, decrease in neatness, being at odds with officers, and desire for transfer" were shortly added to the long list of offenses deemed worthy of discharge.[21]

Psychiatric screening did not live up to its architects' hopes. It probably could not have done so, given the breadth of the screening criteria and the drastic shortage of trained personnel. With millions of men flooding into the military, it was simply impossible to conduct the program as it had been designed, and one or two quick exams, lasting a minute or two at most, was the rule. So overwhelming were the practical problems that psychological tests were eventually designed for use with inductees and trainees that were entirely self-administered and scored in a minute or less.[22] Questions too varied from place to place, and time pressures often reduced what was supposed to be a serious probe to yes or no answers to questions such as "Do you think you had a happy childhood?" and "Do you wet your bed?" Results too were inconsistent. One psychiatrist might judge manic-depressive candidates eminently qualified for military service while another routinely rejected all who divulged vegetarian dietary habits.[23]

Frustrated by logistical hurdles, Harry Stack Sullivan quit his Selective Service post in 1942. Others also regarded the screening effort as "little more than a farce" and concluded that the constraints under which psychiatrists were operating were likely to impair their professional reputations as well as military effectiveness.[24] "Under such circumstances psychiatric screening was bound to be a hit-or-miss affair in which the hapless psychiatrist had to spice his knowledge and experience with large sprinklings of hunches and fortune-telling."[25]

Equally serious were the disagreements that surfaced among psychiatrists themselves about the recognizability of predisposition or the qualities necessary in a good soldier. Did the military's well-known sensitivity to signs of predisposition present unexpected opportunities to malingerers, who exploited psychiatric concern to avoid military service? Could the very aggressiveness that made mental patients unmanageable prove a distinct asset in combat? Was homosexuality, surely among the most common forms of perversion in men, really such a blight on military discipline, and did it, when discovered, merit automatic discharge and criminal prosecution? Such controversial questions were responses to wartime imperatives, but they also threatened psychiatrists' hard-earned authority to predict, not to mention treat, mental trouble.

The overall results of psychiatric screening and examination were both militarily alarming and publicly contentious. A total of 1,846,000 recruits were rejected from the armed forces for "neuropsychiatric" (NP) reasons, a full 12 percent of all recruits and a full 38 percent of all rejections. (No other justifications for military rejection approached NP deficiency; only "musculo-skeletal" and "eye, ear, nose, throat" came close with 17 and 10 percent, respectively.) An additional 550,000 or so men who survived their initial exam were eventually given NP discharges, a full 49 percent of all discharges for mental and physical defects. Of these, 386,600 were "honorable" medical discharges based on a range of diagnoses, especially "psychoneurosis." Another 163,000 were "dishonorable, administrative discharges for reasons including psychopathic personality, drug addiction, alcoholism, and homosexuality. The total number of individuals formally disqualified from military service because of psychological malfunction was 2.5 million, a number dramatic enough to provide convincing evidence that rampant emotional disturbance constituted a threat to national security.[26]

More detailed statistics were just as staggering. Of the casualties severe enough to require evacuation during the major U.S. campaign in the Pacific, at Guadalcanal in summer and fall 1942, 40 percent were psychiatric. In a six-month period in 1944, combat divisions in Europe experienced a psychiatric casualty rate of 26 percent; with intensive combat, this figure jumped to 75 percent. Resentment also materialized around the disproportionately high rejection rates of Native Americans (40 percent) and black Americans (53 percent). Leaders of these communities often accused psychiatrists of racial bias and demanded easier entrance into the military. Psychiatric discharges were also 10 percent higher in the Women's Army Corps than they were among male soldiers, but no protest about gender bias was mounted. Indeed, alarm over the potential masculinization of female recruits insulated disproportionately stringent psychological screening and discharge practices from criticism. Other citizens grew impatient with all the talk about neurosis. They were convinced, as some military officials were, that perfectly capable men were using the excuse of mild or nonexistent maladjustment to remain safe at home.[27]

By 1943 the military considered such attitudes serious enough to do two things: order a major study to calm mounting objections to psychiatric screening and censor information about rejection rates and the mental state of soldiers.[28] Most clinicians believed public opinion on matters of mental health and illness was dreadfully ignorant, and they admonished that too few men were being screened out of the military, rather than too many.[29] The backlash nevertheless forced them to rethink their role. Clinicians had mobilized for the patriotic purpose of assisting the U.S. military, only to find their good intentions and diligent work overshadowed by their exposure of mental problems in millions of ordinary men.

With such grim statistics and with the military's continuing need for massive infusions of manpower, it is not surprising that the initial enthusiasm for avoiding mental troubles entirely by screening them out slid gradually into an emphasis on effectively treating men who showed signs of mental trouble. During the first two years of the war, psychiatric casualties had been summarily discharged; they were given a diagnosis, but treatment was discouraged because "the official point of view of the Army toward psychiatric illness was a mixture of fatalism and disinterest; treatment was discouraged." [30] By 1944 the army's Neuropsychiatric Consultants Division, headed by William Menninger (the first psychiatrist ever elevated to the rank of brigadier general), was downplaying the Selective Service emphasis on screening and lobbying to overturn the policy of therapeutic skepticism. Aggressive treatment programs, William Menninger argued, would allow psychiatry to display its powerful healing capabilities and shine up its tarnished image.

By March 1945 the practice of automatically discharging soldiers with NP diagnoses was terminated. Determined not to let the disappointments of the early war stand as setbacks, William Menninger pushed military clinical practices in directions ever more sensitive to social context, abandoning as unhelpful, or at least insufficient, the notion that individuals could be conclusively categorized as either predisposed to mental trouble or not. The war's progress had transformed mental troubles into transitory and relative phenomena, with a number of possible outcomes. At one extreme was descent into more or less permanent mental disturbance and incapacity of the variety familiar on the wards of state hospitals. At the other was return to normality. William Menninger suggested that, if caught early in the form of simple maladjustment, mild mental trouble would rarely lapse into severe mental illness. It was due to this belief—that prompt treatment would arrest deterioration and probably guarantee recovery—that psychotherapy came into its own.

Efforts therefore shifted from screening soldiers to educating vast numbers of military clinicians in up-to-date methods of psychiatric diagnosis and treatment. Trained psychiatrists worked in induction centers, basic training camps, and in hundreds of general military hospitals at home and overseas; ten hospitals were devoted exclusively to NP casualties. Some were assigned to combat units. Most of the people who had direct contact with soldiers, however—48,000 medical officers and 872,000 nonmedical officers—had no previous psychiatric training. Consultants, whose job it was to spread psychiatric knowledge around as liberally as possible, were in the vanguard of the treatment campaign, responsible for developing and maintaining high and consistent clinical standards throughout the military.

Personnel shortages gave psychiatrists the reason they needed to proselytize, which they did with missionary zeal. Here was an opportunity to place general psychiatric principles at the center of all medical education and practice and correct the woeful errors of doctors ignorant of psychological factors by introducing them, and impressionable medical students, to "the anatomy and the physiology of the personality."[31] Exasperated too that their fees lagged behind those of other physicians, many psychiatrists seized the opportunity war presented to raise the prestige of psychiatry within medicine. They agreed with Alan Gregg, a Rockefeller Foundation officer and one of psychiatry's biggest professional boosters, when he declared that it was high time for "radical change."[32]

[Psychiatry's task] derives in part from the incomprehension of all the rest of medicine which has gone so heavily technical and specialized that the psychiatrists are the only people left who are likely in many instances to insist upon a comprehensive view of the patient. . . . I come to the conclusion that unless psychiatry could be spread as a leaven in the lump of medicine and throwing most of its emphasis not upon madhouse material but upon the psycho-pathology of everyday life, psychoneuroses and behavior abnormalities, we would have to work in vain for any substantial improvement in the physician's comprehension of his patient.[33]

The army sponsored various efforts to shore up the numbers of military psychiatrists (including schools of military neuropsychiatry at Brooke General Hospital at Fort Sam Houston in Texas and at Lawson General Hospital in Atlanta) by offering intensive introductory courses.[34] But chronic shortages of qualified faculty brought pleas to private organizations to fund visits by civilians in order to improve the sophistication of military clinicians. The Rockefeller Foundation, which had allocated over $10 million of its medical research funds to psychiatry in the decade before the war, willingly shipped in a crew of "visiting firemen" to lecture on diagnostic procedures and demonstrate case conferences.[35] Gregg hoped they would convert their students to the messianic view that "the convergent rays of psychiatry, psychoanalysis and psychology now flood the conduct of man with light as it has never before been illuminated."[36]

The combination of advocates' enthusiasm and wartime necessity succeeded in increasing the profession's status and numbers. As of 1944, psychiatry was accorded a division of its own in the army's Office of the Surgeon General, ranking on a par with surgery and medicine. By the end of the war, twenty-four hundred physicians were working as military psychiatrists, a number equal to the total membership of the American Psychiatric Association in 1940. A majority had no prewar psychiatric training.[37] William Menninger estimated that the military trained more psychiatrists in a few short years than all U.S. medical schools could have produced in a decade.[38]

Personnel shortages also temporarily curbed rivalries between psychiatrists and nonmedical clinicians who specialized in mental troubles, especially clinical psychologists. William Menninger was a tireless advocate for clinical teamwork. He adapted the innovative models tried before the war in his family's Topeka, Kansas, clinic (which would become a national hub of interdisciplinary training after the war) and agitated for resources with which to train clinical psychologists as well as psychiatric social workers and nurses.[39] Not content with a traditional division of labor that would have left psychologists in charge of testing, he encouraged them to participate in activities limited to psychiatrists before the war: diagnosis and even the practice of psychotherapy.

If the war generated a spirit of professional cooperation, the professions nevertheless remained unequal; psychiatrists were to supervise all others who ventured into the sacred territory of individual treatment. Because their subordinate position during World War I had produced much tension and little collaboration, psychologists resisted working within the medical corps under psychiatric authority. Psychological testing, of course, remained an important—and relatively autonomous—function assigned almost exclusively to psychologists. Psychologists recalled that, more than any other single activity, military testing had paved the way for professional advances in the past. Because it "brought psychology down from the clouds" during World War I and "transformed the 'science of trivialities' into the 'science of human engineering'" in the interwar period, psychologists in World War II persuaded the military early on to locate administrative responsibility for testing in the Army Adjutant General's Office, where it was insulated from psychiatric interference.[40]

Testing programs were intended to accomplish important administrative goals; their clinical value was secondary, at least at first. By war's end, nine million men, almost 15 percent of the country's entire male population, had taken military General Classification Tests.[41] Designed as basic job placement tools and measures of trainability, these tests included exercises in reading comprehension, basic arithmetic, mechanical knowledge and aptitude, and so forth. Exercises in sentence completion included items such as:

Always _____ the salute of those under you.
1. approve   2. seek   3. appreciate   4. watch   5. return

It was clear in 1942 that victory over Japan would be an _____ victory indeed if it were coupled with a United Nations defeat in Europe at the hands of Germany.
1. important   2. appalling   3. empty   4. officious   5. indirect[42]

In 1944 alone, sixty million standardized tests were administered to twenty million individuals in the military for the purpose of efficiently sorting men into the two thousand occupational and training categories that existed in the military.[43] Military testers avoided using terms like "intelligence" and "IQ" to describe what they were doing (semantic choices such as these had drawn much controversial attention to their World War I predecessors) even though the results correlated neatly with educational background.[44]

It was exactly such unglamourous administrative personnel work that psychologists' applied roles in mass institutions before World War II had prepared them to do. Leaders of the personnel effort emphasized the significance of this brand of psychological management by calling testers "the working architects and builders of the modern Army" and their tests "war weapons, although the roar and bang of machinery is absent from the silent room in which they work."[45] But the tide was already moving away from classification and toward new areas of applied work in which tests figured prominently. The momentum of war itself swept psychologists away from administration and into the clinical picture in significant numbers, where personality inventories and projective tests become more common features of the therapeutic process, similarly valued for their time-saving attributes.[46]

The appearance of symptoms of mental trouble in countless soldiers and the serious problems these posed for the fighting efficiency of the U.S. military were the most compelling reasons why psychologists tried to make their tests promote individual healing as well as military efficiency and also took on new diagnostic and interviewing tasks previously monopolized by psychiatrists. Skyrocketing breakdown rates (NP admissions in the United States went from 31.2 per thousand per year in January 1942 to 68.9 per thousand per year in August 1943) prompted the military to set up a training program in clinical psychology at Brooke General Hospital, alongside the School of Military Neuropsychiatry.[47] Five other training centers were envisioned but never materialized. There were not enough psychiatrists to serve as teachers.

In spite of logistical obstacles to their training, psychologists rose to the challenge before them. According to a 1944 report by Robert Sears (one of the authors of the important *Frustration and Aggression*), psychologists throughout the military were quietly taking case histories or even conducting psychotherapy, learning as they went, sometimes with little or no formal training.[48] One administrator in the Veterans Administration agreed. "This was therapy and it was called 'therapy'—recourse was rarely had to the euphemism 'counseling.'"[49] They did it because it was necessary at the time, but intelligent psychologists could certainly see that individual treatment was the wave of the future. In 1946 a survey of every psychologist and psychologist-in-training who had served in the military showed a striking movement toward clinical work during the war years. Hundreds of them had practiced psychotherapy for the first time and many intended to return to school for further training in this field.[50]

Blurring the division of labor between psychiatrists and clinical psychologists did more than permanently alter the balance of power between these two professions, although it did that too. It contributed to normalization, the dramatic shift in the subject and aims of clinical expertise. Before 1940 psychological testers worked to achieve the managerial goals of mass institutions like businesses or schools, performing the administrative tasks required in the interest of scientific management, educational progress, and operational efficiency. While most psychiatrists prior to the war worked in the institutional context of state hospitals, they believed firmly that their most profound loyalty was to individual patients and the alleviation of their mental troubles. Psychology's historical bond with reformist social science and psychiatry's origins in medicine undoubtedly had much to do with this difference in disciplinary identity.

Being drawn into diagnosis and treatment during the war made psychologists appreciate and identify with the ideal of personal mental health to a greater extent than they had in the past. This in turn helped them realize that administratively useful activities like testing could double as therapeutic aids; by the end of the war, projective personality and other psychological tests were being utilized to encourage self-reflection in individuals as well as provide information to military policy-makers.

Psychiatrists, on the other hand, became more aware than ever that their roles as healers and guarantors of military efficiency might be at odds. A myriad of morale-related responsibilities and the expectation that they treat men who broke down in order to return them to duty made it clear to psychiatrists that their first duty was to the military institution—and not necessarily to the mental health of the soldiers in it. Psychiatrists, according to Harry Stack Sullivan, had to absorb the lesson that their role was similar to other wartime experts.

The Public expects a considerable human cost in war, and it hasn't much native sympathy for people who can't stand the gaff. It is the Army's business first and foremost to win the war. Considerations of needless human cost are relevant only to the extent that precaution will not hamper the war effort. Medical men are peculiarly obtuse to this. They simply have not learnt to put first things first. . . . The war calls on psychiatry to be practical. No one expects it to be perfect.[51]

Winning the war was the first priority. Humanitarian concerns were acceptable as long as they did not obstruct victory.

War and the Production of Normal Neurosis

Thus sensitized to how their own most important professional obligations were being shaped by the wartime context, clinicians were quick to see social factors at work in the production of the mental troubles they treated. Their conclusion? Individuals who became psychologically unbalanced were responding quite normally to an abnormal environment. "The situations of war, for the civilized man," reasoned psychiatrists Roy Grinker and John Spiegel, "are completely abnormal and foreign to his background. It would seem to be a more rational question to ask why the soldier does *not* succumb to anxiety, rather than why he does."[52] William Menninger went so far as to call war a "pathological outpouring of aggression and destructiveness [that] might well be regarded as a psychosis."[53]

That mental breakdown was to be expected under extreme conditions may have appeared obvious in retrospect, but it was not at first. It took time and effort to determine that men in combat units snapped in far greater numbers than did those serving in noncombat capacities and that symptoms in the air forces differed systematically from those in the ground forces. These were patterns that predisposition simply could not explain. The sheer numbers of cases seen by military clinicians— NP admissions alone totaled one million, representing 850,000 individuals—finally led them to view the typical psychiatric casualty not as an intrinsically predisposed or mentally disordered individual but as a perfectly ordinary person under incredible strain—an "Everyman."[54] "It became obvious that the question was not *who* would break down, but *when*."[55]

Psychiatrists did not discard entirely their conviction that the mental troubles of given individuals were configured in highly personal ways, conditioned especially by family background and childhood experience. They could not have done so and remained clinicians, after all. Dispensing with the study of individual mental health would have eviscerated the very basis of psychological treatment and left them no option but to become social engineers.

While few clinicians embraced this label explicitly, the movement toward an environmental understanding of wartime breakdown pushed the concerns of clinical professionals in decidedly social directions. According to William Menninger, the essence of the clinical task was to treat the whole personality in the context of the whole environment. This assignment was enormous, to say the least. Human personality consisted of "everything we are, have been, and hope to be," and environment was nothing less than "everything outside ourselves, the thing to which we have to adjust—our mates and our in-laws, the boss and the work, friends and enemies, bacteria and bullets, ease and hardship."[56]

Mental health was present when the struggles within and between personality and environment could be routinely managed through adjustment; mental disturbance occurred when this effort overwhelmed the individual. It stood to reason that unusually forceful conflicts in either the personality or the environment—such as war—could throw mental health out of balance. Psychiatric methods would therefore have to be closely coordinated with theory and research in the social and behavioral sciences. Only a socially sensitive clinical vision could encourage the type of wise policy-making that would produce a postwar environment hospitable to mental health.

Such views clearly anticipated the activist ethos of postwar clinical work and the innovative community psychology and psychiatry movements, whose leaders were World War II clinicians like William Men-

ninger (see chapter 9). In the meantime, revealing the precise causes of
mental trouble in any given case became a delicate balancing act between individual psychological patterns (determined by personal history) and changing levels of environmental hardship (in the immediate
context of war). Since war was constantly acting upon the soldier and
the soldier's circumstances, mental health and illness could no longer
be considered fixed states.

Clinical vocabulary reflected the discovery that mental troubles
could appear in the most normal of men and displayed the concomitant
etiological emphasis on social factors. "War neuroses" clearly tied neuroses to war and "stress" implied that mental pressures were largely
external. "Operational fatigue" (used in the air forces), "combat fatigue" (used in the navy), and "combat exhaustion" (used in the army)
suggested that the weariness experienced by soldiers was somehow oc-
cupationally induced. On the other hand, clinicians who prided themselves on their terminological precision often derided such terms as useless and misleading. "Operational fatigue," they complained, was not
even an accurate description. Because it had nothing to do with fatigue,
individuals suffering from it would not recover with rest. It was nothing
but a "wastebasket diagnostic term." [57]

The statistical picture that emerged from clinicians' diagnostic
choices also fostered the impression that most mental trouble was due
to the war. Ninety percent of all hospitalized cases were classified as
psychoneuroses and personality disorders, relatively minor troubles in
the world of mental disorder. Only 6 to 7 percent conformed to the
psychotic profile of the traditional mental patient.[58] The label "psycho-
neurotic" was used extensively because it functioned as a summarizing
term for a number of more specific classifications, denoting a diversity
of emotional reactions: anxiety, fear, hostility, guilt, depression, and
physical manifestations like nausea and vomiting when they appeared as
recurring psychosomatic symptoms.

Clinicians attempted to distinguish one particular "reaction" syndrome from the next with great care and the result pushed patterns of
psychiatric classification away from the neurological emphases of the
past, toward encompassing a wide variety of normal mental troubles.[59]
Several diagnoses, for example, were grouped under the category "transient personality reactions to acute or special stress," which emphasized
the immediate pressures operating on the suffering individual, the absence of past psychological problems, and the likelihood of complete
recovery in the future. Transient personality reactions were defined as

follows in the army's official Nomenclature and Method of Recording Diagnoses: "A normal personality may utilize, under conditions of great or unusual stress, established patterns of reaction to express overwhelming fear or flight reaction. The clinical picture of such reactions differs from that of neuroses or psychoses chiefly in points of a direct relationship to external precipitation and reversibility. In a great majority of such reactions, there is an essentially negative historical background."[60] A majority of more specific diagnostic labels in this and other general categories of mental disorder—from "acute situational maladjustment" to "anxiety reactions"—appeared to share a definite relationship to the individual's actual experience. War transformed clinical nomenclature.

In sum, clinicians diverged sharply from their traditional preoccupation with illness and abnormality, fixating instead on the normal. Immersed in managing the psychological symptoms of individuals, they nevertheless came to appreciate their own great potential to prevent the slide toward illness and irrationality in mass populations, exactly as nonclinical experts did. War taught them that their historical commitment to treating mental illness at the point of insanity and gross disability was terribly reactive and extremely inefficient. Why wait around for people to deteriorate into pathetic mental cases? Far more forward-looking would be a professional ideology of early intervention in cases of mental trouble, even systematic environmental design with an eye toward producing mental health—presumably so that mental illness would dissipate to a point where it required only minimal professional attention.

While it was not in clinicians' power to redesign the wartime environment so that mental trouble could be prevented entirely (i.e., end the war), they did begin to make suggestions that sounded remarkably like those of their policy-oriented counterparts. John Appel, head of the Mental Hygiene Branch in the Psychiatry Division of the army's Office of the Surgeon General, led much of the effort to reform the military's overall environment through policy changes that would have an impact on personal well-being. In the name of clinicians' twin duties to individual soldiers' mental health and military efficiency, he called for fixed tours of combat duty. Knowing exactly how much time they could expect to spend in combat would both increase soldiers' efficiency and decrease their rates of mental breakdown. The indefinite tours that were routine in the war's early years had, John Appel observed, depleted human resources to the point of utter uselessness. A policy of limiting combat to 120 days was finally adopted in the spring of 1945.[61]

Other measures geared to preventing mental trouble through environmental adjustment included improving leadership training, boosting group cohesion, establishing rest camps, and feeding soldiers good food. These reforms should sound familiar. Very little of consequence distinguished their clinical advocates, who were devoted to environmental tinkering, from the psychological experts who operated on a policy level and were examined in chapters 2 and 3. Even though the details of their daily work remained rather different, the war advanced the integration of their overall perspectives.

There were, of course, genuine differences in orientation. Clinical theories and skills were especially suited to engineering the internal, psychological environment, and it was here that clinicians excelled. For example, while clinicians were just as dismayed as nonclinical experts to learn that the average soldier did not understand the political aims of the war, their greater familiarity with the interior landscape of irrational drives and unconscious motivations allowed them to respond more hopefully to this piece of distressing news. According to William Menninger, psychiatric interviews brought military clinicians to the same unfortunate conclusion that pollsters in the Army Morale Division's Research Branch had reached. "Only a small proportion of the entire armed force was capable of feeling an emotional urge toward the real purpose of American participation in World War II."[62]

William Menninger and others involved directly in mental breakdown and recovery, however, drew on their clinical experiences and determined that there were worse things than not knowing what the war was all about. They pointed out that gut-level loyalties to buddies, automatic obedience to unit leaders, and hatred of the enemy were more important to military cohesion and the will to fight than was comprehension of the evils of fascism or the virtues of liberal democracy. "The Atlantic Charter, The Four Freedoms and postwar aims do not stir the soldier to his best efforts; only good morale within his own small group and the hope of getting home soon can do that," wrote Roy Grinker and John Spiegel, two psychiatrists who served in the Tunisian campaign in 1943.[63] "Fortunately," they added, "strong intellectual motivation has not proved to be of the first importance to good morale in combat."[64] If rational moral was weak morale, then it followed that emotion—not reason—was the source of military strength. "The will to fight must be forged out of the fiery furnaces of fear and aggressiveness; if we are to win. We have to win this war with our hearts as well as our heads and hands. Ideas alone are too pallid."[65]

The following sections briefly describe two particular areas of wartime clinical work: self-help literature designed by experts for mass consumption and the wartime practice of psychotherapy with mentally troubled soldiers. Although they employed clinical experts in different capacities, both advocated emotional management on the individual level as an indispensable element in effective military functioning and eventual victory. The process of normalizing clinical ideas and experiences, apparent in each case, provides the basis for the postwar developments that will be explored in chapters 9 and 10.

SELF-HELP: EMOTIONAL PREPAREDNESS AS MILITARY STRATEGY

The clinical drift toward prevention surfaced in preventive efforts to promote psychological self-help among normal soldiers. Advice was geared to the personal management of emotions under stress—fears and resentments, in particular—and much attention was paid to the distinction between normal and abnormal reactions in an effort to reassure soldiers that a certain amount of trepidation was to be expected as they adjusted to military life. Advice was typically packaged in the form of lectures to new recruits, short pamphlets or easy-to-read books, and popular films. In these efforts, science always gave way to simplicity. The point was to "show the men that the army was interested in their feelings" and help them adjust, not to exhibit the fine points of psychological knowledge (figs. 4–10).[66]

Edwin Boring, a prominent psychologist involved in the war effort, thought such wartime self-help literature so successful that he predicted the postwar years would expand the market for such products into radio, television, and movies and change the emphasis from controlling negative emotional states to attaining contentment and peace of mind: *Fear in Battle* (an actual example of wartime self-help literature, discussed below) would be transformed into "*How to be Happy*—at every drug store" (his prophetic fantasy of where the future might lead).[67] The dissemination of psychological knowledge through popular channels, Boring speculated, would "increase personal maturity, help social tolerance and progress, and enlarge the democratic communal base of thinking."[68]

Boring's glowing review of the genre, however typical of the period's extravagant optimism and abiding faith in the democratic consequences

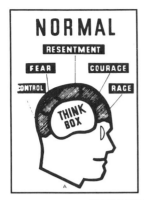

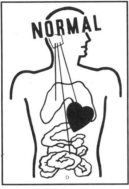
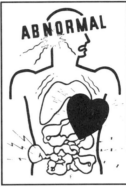

Figure 4. Graphic illustrations of normal and abnormal reactions to military life, routinely shown to soldiers as part of the war's preventive psychiatry program. Photo: Copyright American Medical Association, from *War Medicine* 5 (February 1944):85.

Panel A illustrates the normal brain, consisting of emotion and body control, which are both subordinate to reason (the "think box"). Psychiatrists stressed that it was entirely normal to experience resentment and fear. Panel B illustrates that it is also normal for resentment to increase when soldiers are first inducted and forced to leave their old lives behind. Panel C illustrates that soldiers who employ normal mental techniques, such as humor and mental toughness, can overcome these feelings.

Notice that resentment expands to fill a large part of the brain when anger and other emotions increase in panels B and C. When resentments persist through brooding and homesickness, soldiers were warned, the large area of the brain devoted to resentment takes over precious room that reason needs to function, making military training difficult or even impossible. Displacing body control also creates problems for soldiers by giving rise to physical complaints with origins in an abnormal mental attitude—too many feelings and not enough room for the "think box."

Panel D illustrates the normal body systems (heart and digestion) that accompany a normal mental attitude. Panel E illustrates how these same body systems respond to an abnormal mental attitude.

Figure 5. Graphic illustrations of normal and abnormal reactions to military life, routinely shown to soldiers. Photo: Copyright American Medical Association, from *War Medicine* 5 (February 1944):87.
    Panel A shows that when the military deprives men of their customary privacy, privileges, and opinions, soldiers respond at first with increased resentments—this is normal. Panel B shows soldiers that by letting off steam, they can shrink resentment down to size and get the brain back into a normal arrangement.

of true science, was also self-interested. He was coeditor of *Psychology for the Fighting Man,* one of the most important efforts in the self-help category. The brainchild of the Emergency Committee in Psychology, the book was part of psychologists' consciously organized effort to "sell" the notion of their professional contribution to the U.S. military.[69] Marjorie Van de Water, a professional journalist who specialized in popular science writing, was hired to turn the sometimes obscure language of experts into prose the average GI could easily read and understand.

Numerous checklists were included, for example, offering simple instructions about what to do or think in a variety of situations. Staying awake, speeding the training process, and recognizing "mental danger signals" were each considered in turn, along with other situations common in military life. The experts had numerous tips for soldiers worried about "how to fight fear" or confused about "how to win friends in foreign lands." Among them were seeking physical contact with friends, trying hard to understand strange customs, and suppressing disapproval of behavior they thought too bizarre to respect.[70] Although Boring

Figure 6. Graphic illustrations of normal and abnormal reactions to military life, routinely shown to soldiers. Photo: Copyright American Medical Association, from *War Medicine* 5 (February 1944):90.

Panel A illustrates the normal brain again. Here, reason is in the driver's seat, body control is well regulated from the main switchboard, and the emotions are chained and under rational control. Psychiatrists stressed, once again, that fear (located in the center position) was present in every normal person.

Panel B shows the normal reaction to unknown dangers: reason and body control temporarily leave their posts and fear begins to get out of control. At this point, psychiatrists stressed that soldiers' training would help them identify this situation and quickly restore reason to its normal place of control in the brain.

If soldiers neglected the lessons of preventive military psychiatry, however, panel C would result. Fear would be greatly magnified and emotion would threaten to overwhelm reason. In panel D, despair is added, and fear takes over completely. Now, it is fear that is in the driver's seat: both body control and reason have been knocked out. Soldiers were instructed that with reason out of the picture, they would "freeze," becoming pushovers for the enemy. The only hope was to use normal techniques—courage or rage—to restore the abnormal brain to its normal state.

Panel E illustrates this ultimate struggle for normalcy. Reason pulls fear out of the driver's seat and resumes its dominant mental position, while body control restores physiological equilibrium.

Figure 7. From the cartoon booklet "Story of Mack and Mike."

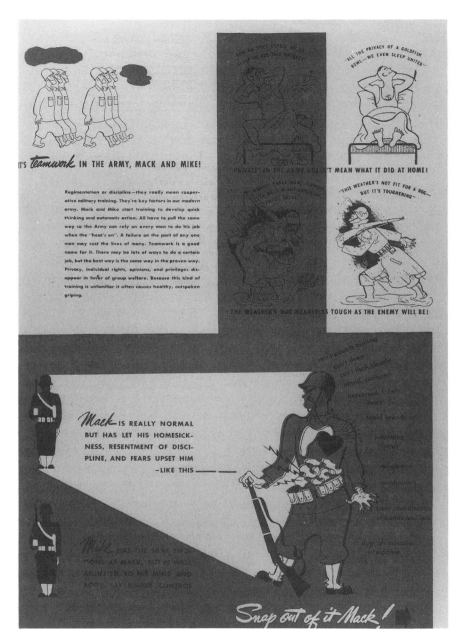

Figure 8. From the cartoon booklet "Story of Mack and Mike."

Training is Mack's life work now!

Training is Mack's life work now; he should get it well—it may mean the difference between his life or the enemy's. Remember, the duty of the American Soldier is *not* to give his life for his country, but rather to make the enemy give his life instead. If Mack is confused, troubled and physically upset, he CAN snap out of it—HERE'S HOW!

1

Be honest with yourself; figure out exactly what's worrying you.

2

remember, everyone is going through the same thing.

Figure 9. From the cartoon booklet "Story of Mack and Mike."

3

resolve to do something about it – then DO it!

4

talk your worry over with your buddy, noncoms, company commander, chaplain, doctor, or psychiatrist.

5

make yourself carry out the advice you get!

Figure 10. From the cartoon booklet "Story of Mack and Mike."

privately derided this how-to style as "soft and popular," and one reviewer dismissed the condescending "birds, bees, and flowers" tone of the book, there was no arguing with the project's success.[71] The book was published in 1943 after sections were serialized; it eventually sold around 400,000 copies at 25 cents apiece.

Authored collaboratively by fifty-nine experts and more than 450 pages long, the book covered a range of topics, including a number that were not strictly clinical. Its general purpose was to bring up-to-date psychological knowledge to the masses and explain to ordinary soldiers the challenge of ensuring satisfactory psychological resources for military purposes. "The Army has a perpetual problem of psychological logistics," the authors noted, "a problem of the supply of motives and emotions, of aptitudes and abilities, of habits and wisdom, of trained eyes and educated ears. How does it get the mental materiel to the right places at the right time?"[72] The rationale for psychological personnel testing was painstakingly explained in the book, as were the basics of vision and hearing, propaganda, and psychological warfare.

Most of the book, however, concentrated on loaded topics of great concern to individual soldiers: morale, food, sex, neurosis, panic, and personal adjustment. How to cope with sexual deprivation was a major subject and on this, as on other topics, the book's tone veered unsteadily between authoritative prescription and empathetic reassurance. If masturbation became a regular habit, or a preferred form of sexual activity, the authors counseled, "it is definitely abnormal." "If it is only resorted to as a temporary outlet," they added, it could do little mental or physical harm.[73] Prostitution could also seriously hamper military efficiency, the experts warned, and no true sexual satisfaction could be found in promiscuous contacts. But adjusting to the sexual strains of military life was no simple matter either. Everything from unusual fantasies to homosexuality could be understood as a normal response to abnormal circumstances, at least sometimes. They were inappropriate, but they were also likely to be temporary. On masturbation, prostitution, and other sexual topics, *Psychology for the Fighting Man* tried to balance clear instructions and friendly reassurance. "It is not easy for a man to get his sexual life into wise and proper adjustment."[74]

Homosexuality was a major, ongoing preoccupation for clinical experts throughout the war years, and their work on the topic was not by any means limited to the self-help literature.[75] Because homosexuality was considered a special threat to military discipline and good morale, anyone with such proclivities was automatically rejected from the armed forces. But since few homosexuals announced themselves upon induction, subsequent revelation of homosexuality was an official pretext for the psychiatric hospitalization and dishonorable discharge of thousands of soldiers and sailors.

But clinical opinion about homosexuality changed decisively during the war years and the shift bolstered the view that mental health experts were the very incarnation of modern enlightenment. The prewar consensus held that homosexuality was nothing but depraved sexual behavior in otherwise ordinary people. By 1945 clinical research made it appear that homosexuals had unique psychological profiles; in other words, they were *not* ordinary people. The military's practical response to homosexuals simply had to change, according to some clinicians. "The crude methods of the past have given way to more humane and satisfactory handling of the problems of the homosexual. No longer is it necessary to subject cases that are so definitely in the medical field to the routine of military court martial."[76] Because it involved psychological identity, homosexuality ought to be treated with compassionate psychotherapy rather than criminal penalties. Sexual deviance was no simple matter of wicked behavior; hence, punishment could not fix it. Only experts with a grasp of the personality as an integrated whole could hope to illuminate—let alone alter—the psychological processes implicated in the production of homosexuality.

Psychology for the Fighting Man managed to present both old and new views on this topic, capturing this fascinating change of attitude in progress. Soldiers were counseled that meeting heterosexual needs through homosexual behavior was understandable, even if it was also degenerate. Normal soldiers with such impulses should fight hard to control them if they could (two practical tips from the experts were praying and concentrating on killing the enemy), but, whatever happened, they would probably be just fine once they returned home. On the other hand, the experts indicated that homosexuals were a recognizable type whose perversion—if forced upon unsuspecting soldiers—deserved court martial and prompt discharge. In the first case, homosexuality was a normal response to an abnormal situation. In the second, it constituted a distinct clinical syndrome: "Attempts to reform such men are almost always futile."[77]

Belief in the possibility and desirability of reforming the self, although not necessarily applicable to sexual preferences and behaviors deemed deviant, was nevertheless at the core of most of the self-help effort. "Adjustment" was a term as likely to designate efforts to post-

pone or prevent mental breakdown through self-education and preparedness as it was the treatment of mental shock with professional
techniques such as psychotherapy.

For obvious reasons, fear was an emotion especially in need of adjustment, and its management was a major theme in *Psychology for the
Fighting Man*. The first step in the process of emotional management
was reassuring explanation. Fear, according to the experts, was entirely
natural and healthy when it was a response to actual external danger.
Moreover, it was "nature's way of meeting in an all-out way an all-out
emergency" and it was "useful in mobilizing all the body's resources."[78] Whether in combat or in anticipation of combat, all soldiers
who were honest with themselves experienced fear.

The process through which fear was normalized, it is important to
note, depended on the sex-segregated nature of the combat experience,
as well as the overwhelmingly male ranks of clinical experts themselves.
Roy Grinker was one of a number of professionals who identified wartime contact with healthy young men experiencing stress as the key to
clinicians' postwar gravitation toward normal psychology.[79] Generalized fears had, after all, long been attached to the phenomenon of hysteria in women, an unappealing, if still fascinating, syndrome marked
by extreme dependence, emotional superficiality, and a heavy dose of
melodrama. Fear of combat, however, was uniquely masculine, and
could therefore circumvent the taint of irrationality and abnormality
that marked all the terrors clinicians treated in the female gender.
Women felt "anxiety," rather than "fear," and the difference was crucial. Because the source of soldiers' combat fears was obvious and environmental, their feelings were normal and clinicians readily empathized
with their nervousness. In contrast, women's feelings could be vague,
difficult to explain, and farther from clinicians' own experience. They
tended therefore to be interpreted as abnormal anxieties with purely
intrapsychic roots. The purpose of the self-help literature, in any event,
was to help soldiers strike a balance between permitting themselves to
feel normal emotions (like fear) when it was safe to do so and strictly
regulating them when it was not. Left unmonitored, fears could grow
into anxieties, ceasing to be comprehensible emotional reactions to real
peril and becoming states of chronic inner disturbance requiring treatment.

John Dollard, a member of the Yale Institute of Human Relations
and a consultant to the Research Branch of the army's Morale Division,
authored several self-help pieces on this particular topic, including a

short pamphlet, *Fear in Battle,* and the even shorter "Twelve Rules on Meeting Battle Fear."[80] Both were intended to reassure men that fear was no cause for shame or embarrassment. Even extremely unsettling psychological experiences, Dollard advised, were perfectly ordinary amid the extraordinary circumstances soldiers faced. Emotional advice "will help any soldier with the guts to face the ordinary fact that everyone gets scared in battle."[81]

Characteristic of advice on this and other topics, and of the normalization process in general, was the insistent refrain that insight—meaning psychological self-consciousness—was the most effective method and barometer of psychological self-mastery; practiced introspection was both technique and goal. Calm, rational understanding of self was a kind of emotional armament, as necessary to the effective prosecution of war as to the goal of individual self-defense and preservation. "Keep remembering that being scared makes you a smarter soldier—and a safer one," was Dollard's rule number 3. But such comforting words were hardly an adequate guide to soldiers facing tangible horrors on the battlefield. So Dollard also prescribed specifics on suppressing fear when necessary: "Make a wisecrack when you can" and "Never show fear in battle" were two of his recommendations.[82] Nor did he neglect to remind soldiers to adopt regular habits of emotional communication. "Talk about being scared—any time you want to talk about it. Everybody gets afraid in combat. You're no exception, and neither are the rest of the men in your outfit. It's a common, every day battle experience for all normal men. It always has been—in every war in history. So there is no reason in God's world for not talking about it— during a lull in the fight, or afterward. And if you do, it helps next time—it helps every time."[83]

Wartime self-help literature attempted to communicate several different things at once. Because it provided refreshing clarity and ready sympathy to countless individuals living without much of either, its appeal was not exactly mysterious. Moreover, it highlighted the potential helpfulness of clinical expertise to ordinary people. Soldiers who absorbed the lesson that they could take steps to prevent mental breakdown themselves were living proof that the meanings of war and of mental health were both rapidly changing. Owning up to feelings like fear was defined as key to managing the military's "mental material" precisely because victory in war required the active mastery of individual subjectivity. If they agreed to strive for a state of psychological insight, experts promised soldiers that, in return, they would help them fulfill

their patriotic duty, demonstrate their emotional enlightenment, and
survive the war in body as well as in spirit.

PROFESSIONAL HELP: THE
PSYCHOTHERAPEUTIC FRONTIER EXPANDS

Not all cases of wartime mental trouble, of course, could
be efficiently managed by providing self-help literature or exhorting
soldiers to circumvent breakdown by taking responsibility for their own
emotional control. As the years wore on and psychological casualties
mounted, the challenges clinicians had initially faced in screening predisposed individuals out of the military began to pale in comparison
with treating masses of mentally troubled soldiers and returning them
to health. Clinicians turned increasingly to psychotherapeutic means of
accomplishing this task.

Before the war, psychotherapy had been associated largely with the
elite office practice of psychoanalysis (the original talking cure) or with
a range of techniques employed by psychiatrists functioning in the institutional context of state hospitals. In both cases, psychotherapy was an
unusual experience for which the prerequisites were extreme wealth,
avant-garde curiosity, or something close to insanity. Psychotherapy
was not relevant to ordinary people. If anything, it was stigmatizing.

Wartime necessity permanently altered this pattern by normalizing
psychotherapy. Clinicians' efforts to cope with anxieties and neurotic
symptoms among soldiers introduced psychotherapeutic techniques to
millions for the first time. Many of the somatic techniques used during
the war had been used before with civilian mental patients—insulin in-
jections, electroshock, and heavy sedation among them—and cases of
severe (i.e., psychotic) disorder and total collapse were usually segregated and hospitalized, much as they had been before the war.

But the time and personnel pressures endemic to wartime clinical
work, along with experts' obligations to serve the military's institutional
need for a steady supply of dependable human resources, underscored
"the necessity for therapy to adapt itself to a more or less inflexible
military framework." [84] This forced clinicians to devise a menu of creative psychotherapeutic alternatives and shortcuts "which give promise
of returning a maximum number of men to duty within a minimum of
time and with techniques which are feasible in the active theatres of
combat." [85]

For the most part, these techniques fell into the category of talking cures, even if the talking was brief and, at times, chemically facilitated by various drugs (figs. 11 and 12). Individually and in groups, soldiers discussed their feelings, combat experiences, and personal histories. The primary goal of such treatment was to help mentally troubled individuals recoup their previous level of function and return to military service, but these practices also unquestionably encouraged new levels of psychological self-exposure and self-consciousness and insinuated that these characteristics were necessarily present in healthy individuals struggling to recover from momentary mental setbacks. The result was that basic definitions of clinical practice changed. From all appearances, larger and larger numbers of normal individuals benefited from psychotherapy and many more and varied activities proved therapeutic.

Psychotherapeutic treatment for the masses placed a premium on clinicians' time and energies. Treatment was as rapid as possible. The logistics of its provision, however, changed as the war altered clinicians' views of mental distress and its causes. For example, cases of combat breakdown were initially evacuated to hospitals in the rear because they were assumed to be limited to predisposed individuals who had escaped detection at the point of screening. Early in the war, when the emphasis was still on prediction rather than treatment, clinicians believed that predisposed men were unlikely to be militarily productive, once pushed beyond their low mental thresholds. As time passed, evidence mounted that mental breakdown was normal under the pressures of war and doubt was cast on the predictive value of predisposition. "Every person, no matter how strongly integrated," noted one psychiatrist, "has his breaking point when sufficient stress is applied."[86] Brief military service was all that was required to convince most other psychiatrists. Treatment of most combat mental cases subsequently evolved from trauma-oriented procedures to something more like psychological first aid.

It was 1943 when psychiatrists were sent to combat areas for the first time.[87] Altering the geographical location of clinical work directly reflected the recognition that clinical efforts should be aimed at the normal neurosis produced in ordinary people under the abnormal conditions of combat. According to Grinker and Spiegel, psychiatrists with combat experience in North Africa, "The realities of war, including the nature of army 'society,' and traumatic stimuli, cooperate to produce a potential war neurosis in every soldier. When predisposition is combined with adequate stimuli of a certain type or degree, a neurotic breakdown is precipitated, which constitutes an illness and requires treatment."[88]

Figure 11. A military psychiatrist in the Philippines interviews a patient in his outdoor office during World War II.

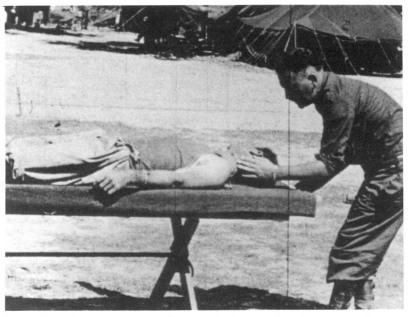

Figure 12. Hypnosis was one of the psychotherapeutic techniques used on soldiers during World War II.

After 1943 the first stop for mentally wounded soldiers was a clearing station close to the front, where they were immediately sedated so that they could sleep. After adding some good food and a bath to a decent interval of rest, 40 percent of these cases had recovered sufficiently to be returned to combat by the third day. Those who did not bounce back so quickly proceeded to the second stop for combat casualties, an "exhaustion center." Here, patients were sedated again, then offered some form of very brief psychotherapy, often in combination with drugs like sodium pentothal, which was administered for the sole purpose of speeding up the therapeutic process through "narcosynthesis."[89] Five to eight days later, another 20 percent of the men were sent back to their units.[90] Not only were these new procedures efficient from the military point of view (many of these cases would previously have been removed from active service altogether only to languish in costly and labor-intensive hospital settings), but they seemed to indicate that timely application of clinical attention to relatively mild instances of mental trouble significantly affected the outcome. Many recovered sufficient mental balance to continue military service: many in combat duty, others in noncombat capacities. The rest were evacuated (fig. 13).

Of course, important theoretical differences remained in how clinicians understood and treated war neuroses. Freudian psychology would emerge from the war as the dominant paradigm among clinicians. Partisans, like psychiatrists Roy Grinker and John Spiegel, considered predisposition (by which they meant past history, especially childhood socialization patterns and familial relationships) to be highly relevant in the precipitation of mental trouble and the determination of a given individual's neurotic symptoms. Yet they also embraced the position that the traumas present in the wartime environment had a direct bearing on mental breakdown. "Sick or well," they argued, "every combat soldier reacts to the stresses of the harsh realities of war according to how his previous psychological patterns have prepared him, and he reacts only to the proper quantities of specific stimuli to which he is sensitized. In other words, in our opinion, the *neuroses of war are psychoneuroses.*"[91] Insisting that all war neuroses were psychoneuroses was simply another way of saying that war was mentally unbalancing not in and of itself but because it mobilized old, often unconscious, emotional conflicts residing in the individual psyche, conflicts that were the most fundamental and authentic sources of mental symptoms. The ultimate point of psychotherapy was to untangle the knots tying previous psychological patterns to current psychological reactions. Clearly, the the-

Figure 13. World War II neuropsychiatric casualties in New Guinea, ready for
their evacuation to the United States.

oretical balance between psychological history and current circumstance meant that the job of delivering long-lasting psychological relief
combined a detective's investigatory zeal with a counselor's patient wisdom. Psychotherapy entailed highly disciplined effort, painstaking insight, and a lot of time.

These were luxuries unavailable during the war. Grinker and Spiegel,
along with other clinicians, sometimes regretted that the therapies they
recommended—from food and sleep to brief talking cures—were inadequate to do the job of real emotional healing. Keenly aware that wartime pressures forced them to place superficial Band-Aids over deep
mental wounds, they bemoaned their own habit of providing short-
term "covering" techniques rather than long-term "uncovering"
ones.[92] Like their policy-oriented counterparts, however, World War II
clinicians accepted without question that shortcuts were essential. The
point was not to achieve perfect mental health and insight, or scientifically validate clinical services, but fortify the military's flagging psychological resources. Clinicians agreed that temporarily interrupting the
most immediate source of neurosis—namely combat danger or fear of

it—was a first step in the process of emotional healing. Other, more ambitious steps would simply have to wait.

In the meantime, clinicians made creative use of the resources available to them. Like food and rest, everything from vocational training to good weather was eventually drafted into clinical service and relabeled "therapeutic." Clinicians could and did explain exactly why satisfying work and hot meals were psychologically beneficial and, as we have seen, they used their authority to back efforts to humanize military life in the name of preventing mental trouble. In the end, however, they knew it was not self-evident that such undertakings required their unique clinical talents. Common sense might be as much a resource as clinical expertise, and far less expensive, if the overall goal were to make the military a more hospitable place to spend time. Grossly overreaching therapeutic frontiers threatened to undermine their authority. Extending therapeutic frontiers within reason, however, could legitimate a larger sphere of operation.

In contrast to food and sleep, the practice of individual psychotherapy remained clinicians' singular contribution. Exclusively associated with clinical experts, psychotherapy claimed to alleviate mental anguish directly by establishing a helpful relationship between a troubled individual and a trained psychotherapist. The clinical theory underlying much wartime psychotherapeutic practice was Freudian in at least a rough sense, and psychodynamic approaches reached their zenith in the postwar years. Even though time and staff shortages precluded the practice of anything resembling classical psychoanalysis, clinicians held fast to an analytical version of the therapeutic relationship, however abbreviated by war. Only a deliberate professional effort, infused with insight, could successfully release whatever repressed emotions were at the root of soldiers' dysfunctional symptoms and strengthen their capacity to adjust more adeptly to the stresses of war.

Even this supposedly unique professional relationship, however, threatened at times to dissolve in the face of simple common sense. Indeed, therapists themselves were often the first to point out that empathetic attention was usually helpful to troubled people, whether offered by professionals, friends, or family members. Because so few non-psychiatric clinicians had any meaningful psychotherapeutic training before the war, military psychotherapists were generally advised to rely on intuition in their daily practice. "If [the therapist] is sincere, sensitive and open-minded in regard to himself as well as to the flier, he will instinctively take the right psychotherapeutic path," wrote Grinker and

Spiegel in an effort to reassure those with little or no previous experience in this area. But if sincerity and open-mindedness were the keys to effective psychotherapy, why limit its practice to a small number of highly paid professionals? "It is well," Grinker and Spiegel added as an afterthought, "if [the therapist] has a definite notion of precisely which path he is taking and how he means to accomplish his objective, which is to strengthen the ego in its struggle with anxiety."[93]

World War II was a moment of important professional transition for psychotherapeutic experts. It offered them the difficult challenge of proving they had something unique to offer at the same time that it offered them an unprecedented opportunity to try that something out on a new mass audience. Hampered by wartime shortages of time and staff and constrained by their own inexperience, clinicians tried to demonstrate that psychotherapy was delicate enough to require specialized skills yet not so delicate as to be confined to extreme cases of mental breakdown. Its benefits were palpable enough to merit the extension of psychotherapy to large numbers of people for many reasons in short periods of time, but only experts could achieve positive results. Amateurs, they warned, were prone to do terrible damage.

By normalizing the content and extending the subject of clinical expertise, the war redefined psychotherapy in remarkably expansive terms. According to psychiatrist Lawrence Kubie, a consultant to the Office of Scientific Research and Development and an ardent proponent of clinical emphasis on prevention, "psychotherapy embraces any effort to influence human thought or feeling or conduct, by precept or by example, by wit or humor, by exhortation or appeals to reason, by distraction or diversion, by rewards or punishments, by charity or social service, by education or by the contagion of another's spirit."[94] According to such definitions, virtually any human relationship could qualify as psychotherapeutic. It is understandable that this drastic extension of psychotherapeutic territory was confusing and failed to resolve outstanding questions about what alterations psychotherapy actually induced or who should be allowed to practice it. These controversial issues would consequently continue to be hotly debated throughout the postwar decades.

Their abilities as preventive emotional healers were matters of supreme belief among clinicians at the war's end. "As a result of our experience in the Army," William Menninger concluded with some satisfaction, "it is vividly apparent that psychiatry can and must play a much more important role in the solution of health problems of the civilian."[95] It was an article of collective faith that psychotherapeutic treatment was reliable science, not hit-or-miss art. It brought "a systematic body of knowledge" to bear on wartime mental troubles with excellent practical results that were "more a matter of training than an accident of personality."[96] In part, clinicians were simply jumping on the same scientific and technological bandwagon that had proved so auspicious for other wartime experts. In part, their extreme therapeutic optimism resulted from the genuinely novel opportunities war had offered them: to minister to mass populations under conditions that forced them to renovate the conceptual and practical tools of their trade, meeting the immediate and urgent needs of ordinary people under extraordinary pressure.

For these and other reasons, the war produced a comprehensive reassessment of clinical terms. "Normal neurosis" became a conceivable clinical category only because the concepts of mental health and illness had themselves changed drastically, from qualities inherent in or absent from individuals to a spectrum on which mental stability and instability were feats to be constantly achieved or avoided. Upbeat and hopeful, military clinicians had learned much about their own potential from their work with masses of ordinary soldiers. Not only could they treat cases of severe breakdown effectively, but they could prevent milder cases from deteriorating by intervening quickly and aggressively, nipping mental trouble in the bud. According to William Menninger, this reassessment was the war's most profound lesson, and it pointed very decidedly toward a larger jurisdiction for psychological experts.

If health *is* the concern of medicine, and if by mental health we mean satisfaction in life, efficiency, and social compatibility, then the principles of psychiatry must apply not only to each of us as individuals but to our social relationship with each other. The field of medicine must be recognized as inseparably linked to the social sciences and concerned with healthy adjustment of men, both individually and in groups.[97]

Under less strained conditions than war, he seemed to be suggesting, clinical experts could improve significantly on their very laudable military record. Psychiatrist Henry Brosin was even more explicit about what clinicians could do when the fighting ended and they applied the lessons of military experience to civilian life. "Good mental health or well-being is a commodity which *can be created* under favorable circumstances," he promised.[98]

In 1945 the mood of celebration among clinicians was the very same that animated policy-oriented experts; so too were the doubts that lurked behind it. Surely the government and the public, grateful for clinicians' tireless, patriotic service, would see fit to ensure their future with generous infusions of training and research funds. Professional advance and the national interest were, in this case, fortuitously compatible and achievable through practical means. Postwar social order and stability rested on a foundation of mental health, a goal which was also, in Henry Brosin's terms, "a commodity." "National mental health," William Menninger concurred, "could be purchased if that were our aim."[99] This consensus that augmenting clinical funding was tantamount to improving national well-being would shortly be displayed on the floor of the U.S. Congress, where government officials debated the details of a federally sponsored mental health effort that became the National Mental Health Act of 1946.

If money for mental health were not forthcoming, how would the massive social problems, just waiting to be caused by untreated veterans, be managed? Clinicians predicted that men destabilized by their wartime experiences might be mentally mutilated for life if left to their own devices, victimized by a pitiful and expensive epidemic of "pensionitis" (a syndrome of debilitating dependence upon the state allegedly caused by financially rewarding veterans' mental instability), or prone to criminal temptations.[100] According to Daniel Blain, head of psychiatry for the Veterans Administration, the "ripples that emanate from each generating unit, each veteran, must not be vicious, antisocial, discouraging, hostilely aggressive. They must be kindly, warm, invigorating ripples that unite all of us."[101] Even mild ripples of maladjustment increased the likelihood that unemployment, illiteracy, strikes, illegitimacy, and racial prejudice (to name only the most frequently mentioned scourges) would mushroom in the postwar era. With sufficient clinical infrastructure, clinicians and their advocates pledged, the country could rest assured that undesirable social conflict would be minimized and veterans would be mentally prepared to live as economically productive and law-abiding citizens. In 1944 Alan Gregg put it as follows:

There will be applications far beyond your offices and your hospitals of the further knowledge you will gain, applications not only to patients with functional and organic disease, but to the human relations of normal people—in politics, national and international, between races, between capital and labor, in government, in family life, in education, in every form of human relationship, whether between individuals or between groups. You will be concerned with optimum performance of human beings as civilized creatures.[102]

Behind this most ambitious vision of clinical responsibility for the general state of human civilization lay the same political uneasiness felt by policy-oriented experts. Clinical work, after all, had corroborated the growing body of nonclinical research demonstrating that democracy was seriously endangered by strong and unpredictable emotional currents, including ugly tendencies toward prejudice and conformity. By 1945 little or no sophisticated understanding was required to make the point psychoanalyst Franz Alexander had made ten months prior to the attack on Pearl Harbor: "It is no wonder that in the face of current world events one turns for explanation toward the psychiatrist, the specialist in irrational behavior."[103]

The course of the war had borne out the truth of Alexander's view that "the real difficulties of democracy . . . are emotional."[104] Clinicians' daily responsibilities for shoring up soldiers' morale and group cohesion had taught them that reason could never compete with emotion when human motivation and behavior were involved. Primitive fears and immediate loyalties had done far more to keep the fighting forces fighting than had campaigns (most of them miserable failures) to persuade soldiers that preserving democracy and eradicating fascism were worth the highest sacrifice.

Demoralizing as this wartime lesson was, it hardly lowered the aspirations of clinicians, the most forward-looking of whom had predicted that "the day will come when [the] Cinderella of Medicine, Psychiatry, will be honored as a wise and bountiful Social Princess dispensing a largess of culture."[105] The daunting lessons of war merely fueled their missionary vision. What were clinicians if not experts in emotional management? And was not a plan of conscious, emotional management democracy's best hope for survival? By the end of the war, most clinicians certainly thought of their professional obligations in the activist, liberal terms articulated so well by figures such as William Menninger, Harry Stack Sullivan, and Alan Gregg. They considered themselves custodians of a vital social resource—mental health—without which economic prosperity, democratic decision making, and intergroup harmony were implausible, perhaps impossible.

Although they could not have known it at the time, their future role as emotional managers was as fraught with political contradictions as was that of their counterparts who imagined themselves as the enlightened social engineers of postwar society. To champion the individual in the process of striving toward psychological insight, as they did, and to insist that the essence and future of democracy lay in this momentous struggle, as they also did, was the historic task of those experts with a unique understanding of the human personality. Lawrence K. Frank, who had proposed before the war that society be treated as a "patient," was equally prophetic when he wrote in 1940,

> We are, somewhat reluctantly, realizing that the democratic aspirations cannot be realized nor adequately expressed in and by voting and representative government; democracy, or the democratic faith, is being reformulated today in terms of the value and integrity of the individual, not as a tool or as a means, but as an end or goal for whose conservation and fulfillment social life must be reoriented. . . . Thus freedom for the personality may be viewed as the crucial issue of a democratic society, for which we must seek to develop individuals who can accept all the inhibitions and requirements necessary to group life, without these distortions and coercive, affective reactions.[106]

Ringing defenses of democracy, converted into psychological rhetoric such as "freedom for the personality," were not the inherently liberating manifestos that Frank and most other World War II–era clinicians believed them to be. They were politically ambiguous. Labeling the individual precious and dignified was certainly nothing new in U.S. history. Calling for direct control of the psychological terrain—because it was the only effective means of safeguarding democratic potential and averting a menacing epidemic of blind conformity and authoritarianism—was new, at least as an explicit public ideal and purpose of government. World War II had shown that experts would have to manufacture democratic personalities because U.S. social institutions had failed to produce people who could be trusted with democracy's future.

Thus were the clinical hopes and dreams of prevention that emerged from the war based on a collapse of faith in the rational appeal and workability of democratic ideology and behavior. Some clinicians dedicated to shoring up the emotional basis of democracy in the postwar era (humanistic theorists and practitioners, for example) did so by consecrating the individual psyche as the ultimate source of value and turning self-regulation into an act as publicly virtuous as it was personally meaningful. Others (behaviorist theorists and practitioners, for example) dismissed such psychological individualism as a foolish dream and insisted that only scientific expertise could be trusted as an incorruptible source of authority and control. Humanists wanted to actualize the perfect self. Behaviorists were more modest; they merely wanted to condition good behavior.

In spite of important tactical differences between clinical schools and tendencies, the postwar era they all envisioned was founded on the professionally unified project that emerged from World War II: to enlarge psychology's jurisdiction. As we shall see later, in chapter 9, important developments after 1945 grew out of the fundamental clinical lessons of world war. Clinical theory had to be grounded in normal psychology. Clinical services had to reach masses of ordinary people, coordinated and delivered by the state if necessary, so that normal neuroses could be treated before reaching a point that threatened social stability. And because human motivation brimmed with irrationality and resisted so stubbornly the call of reason, clinical experts would be indispensable guides in an era of social and emotional reconstruction. Democratic personalities would have to be remade from the inside out.

5

The Career of Cold War Psychology

The Cold War sustained the momentum of psychological experts' professional gains and offered numerous variations on the World War II theme that war was a struggle for national and international psyches. It reinforced the notion of psychology's intrinsic political and moral virtue, so crucial to the worldview of the World War II generation. "Psychology is perceived," wrote John Darley, an observer of Department of Defense (DOD) behavioral research in 1952, "as a vehicle that will assist in bringing about the American Creed of equality, fair play, and minimal group conflict."[1] Sentiments such at these, and correspondingly strenuous efforts to adjust always-threatening levels of international tension and reform instances of international misbehavior, flourished in the new era of uneasy peace.

The boundaries between military and civilian targets, between wartime and peacetime conflicts, already beginning to blur during World War II when examined through the lens of "sykewar," took on an eerie permanence during the Cold War. Military psychological operations experts were only stating what many Americans already felt when they pointed out that peace had lost much of its previous association with security: peace was "simply a period of less violent war in which nonmilitary means are predominantly used to achieve certain political objectives."[2] Since peace and war were no longer entirely distinguishable, the services provided by experts became a permanent military asset. "The inexorable relatedness of military and nonmilitary factors in national security policy" was a hallmark of the World War II worldview.[3]

It put psychological experts to work understanding the style of warfare (guerrilla movements in the Third World) and guiding the new kind of military mission (counterinsurgency) that the postwar decades produced.

The Cold War climate left few doubts about the appropriateness of fear or the dangerousness of the world in the aftermath of world war. It intensified the feeling that enlightened policy was not merely a factor in good government, but necessary to the very continuation of humanity. At the least, expert assistance could help U.S. foreign and military policy-makers sort out their pressing problems rationally and intelligently. At most, it held the key to survival in the atomic age.

What was the arms race, after all, if not cultural lag come true in the most terrifying of ways? From the hardware of weapons technology to the software of anti-Communist ideology, everything about the Cold War confirmed the anxieties that lurked just beneath the surface of national celebration in 1945. Wartime psychologists across the political spectrum, from the idealistic Gordon Allport to the realistic Robert Yerkes, had agreed that the combination of unchecked weapons technology and underdeveloped social technology was poisonous. Psychological expertise was among the only antidotes.

The institutional and intellectual developments that shaped psychology's Cold War trajectory are presented in this chapter. They illuminate the mechanisms of psychology's successful public career, which, by the 1960s, was flexible enough to expand well beyond the boundaries of warfare and outside the nurturing military environment, as will be evident in chapters 6 and 7 on psychology's role in the management of domestic racial conflict. The history of indebtedness to war, however, ran deep.

This history was also the prerequisite to Project Camelot, a major DOD-sponsored plan to involve behavioral experts in predicting and controlling Third World revolution and development in order to gain the upper hand in "The Minds Race."[4] Camelot had a strong psychological component, but was conceived from the start as an interdisciplinary effort on the model of World War II teamwork and in the spirit of that war's ambitious and integrated science of human behavior. Launched in 1963, it came into public view as an international scandal in July 1965, a full twenty years after the end of World War II. Camelot and its aftermath are discussed in detail in the next chapter.

In the material that follows, I argue that a combination of factors—psychology's institutional niche in the military, its theoretical explanations of Third World revolution and development, and the contours of Cold War ideology in general—contributed to securing the reputation of psychological expertise as an increasingly vital asset in the policy-making process. This step was essential to making a project like Camelot possible and provoked much of the anxiety, and many of the ethical questions, that this scandal elicited.

Psychology's Cold War career sheds light on the general progress of psychology's public career during this period. It demonstrates how intimately entangled psychology had become with military and foreign policy. It illuminates the sturdiness and persistent influence of the World War II worldview in the face of mounting challenges. In sum, it provides insight into both the building blocks and the weaknesses of psychology's rise to power and helps to explain how and why psychological experts were able to take strides toward achieving the authority they sought in the postwar decades.

Institutional Building Blocks: Defense Dollars

Between 1945 and the mid-1960s, the U.S. military was, by far, the country's major institutional sponsor of psychological research, a living illustration of what socially minded experts could accomplish, especially with a "not too gentle rain of gold."[5] Some of the reasons for the meteoric rise of military psychology were not very subtle. The military had more money than any other public institution during these years, and during the Korean War, the DOD spent more on social and behavioral science than all other federal agencies combined.[6] Projects that would have represented heavy investments for civilian bureaucracies could, on occasion, simply be ways of satisfying the military's curiosity, or appeasing psychology's overheated advocates. Although impressive, the staggering sums that were spent on military psychological services between 1945 and 1970 are not, in themselves, convincing evidence that the military establishment had been thoroughly enlightened by psychology or converted to the experts' worldview. The military spent staggering sums on many things during these years and psychology was, in relative terms at least, dirt cheap.

Many of the academic professionals who had worked in the World War II military were relieved to return home to their universities in 1945, much like the ordinary soldiers they had studied. Samuel Stouffer, who had managed the Research Branch of the army's Information and Education Division, returned briefly to the University of Chicago, then moved on to Harvard, where he became director of the new Laboratory of Social Relations. Rensis Likert, head of the Department of Agriculture's Division of Program Surveys and director of the Strategic Bombing Survey's Morale Division, went to Ann Arbor, where he headed the Institute for Social Research at the University of Michigan. Leonard Doob returned to his post at the Yale Institute of Human Relations. Even from such scattered locations in civilian academic life, however, World War II–era experts kept close tabs on the progress of military psychology (typically by serving as DOD advisors) and carefully nurtured the professional networks they had constructed during the world war, to their lasting benefit. According to Nathan Maccoby, a psychologist who worked in the Army Research Branch under the direction of Samuel Stouffer, "The Research Branch not only established one of the best old-boy (or old-girl) networks ever, but an alumnus of the Branch had an open door to most relevant jobs and career lines. We were a lucky bunch."[7]

Those who chose to stay on in the military, or young professionals who spent their entire careers in the new defense-oriented research organizations that proliferated in the postwar era, were fond of pointing out that nothing much distinguished psychology on campus from psychology administered, directly or indirectly, by the Pentagon; virtually all psychological research had military applications.[8] Further, work that was officially nonmilitary took on a military flavor, if only because association with national defense during the Cold War ensured the government's generous and sustained patronage. The National Institute of Mental Health (NIMH) and the National Science Foundation (NSF), both important civilian sources of funding for psychological and behavioral research in the postwar years, came into existence on the heels of World War II.[9] NIMH was established in 1946 as one component of the National Mental Health Act. General Louis Hershey, head of the Selective Service and one of the most vocal lobbyists for this legislation, made liberal use of the military's mental health data and warned that the psychiatric casualties of World War II were but the tip of the iceberg. The NSF was created four years later, after five years of congressional debate over twenty-one separate bills. By 1950 the Cold War climate was firmly in place and the Korean War had just begun.

NSF and NIMH were sensitive to military requirements and institutionally bound to the DOD in a number of ways in spite of their allegedly nonmilitary purposes.[10] The NSF director, for example, served on the President's Defense Science Board and was responsible for initiating and supporting military research at the request of the Secretary of Defense. Employment patterns were also quite fluid, and experts moved back and forth between military and civilian institutions. Theodore Vallance, for example, a psychologist and the director of the military research organization, the Special Operations Research Office (Camelot's sponsoring organization in the early 1960s), became Chief of the NIMH Planning Branch just a few years later. Job location changed frequently; the nature of the work did not.

During the 1950s, all the types of work that psychological experts had done in the World War II military were further institutionalized (in the DOD and on campus) with the support of military funding: psychological warfare, intelligence classification, training, clinical treatment, and "human factors" (previously called "man-machine") engineering. Even the mysteries of morale and other fields of human relations research were vigorously pursued on the theory that, however speculative in the short run, their potential military payoff was large enough to justify the investment.

In the wake of World War II, practical applications counted above all, and the patriotic rush to make psychology (and other behaviorally oriented disciplines) serviceable generated expectations that at least certain kinds of expertise would be dependable enough, and hence indispensable enough, to be called "policy sciences."[11] Lingering skeptics typically confronted the passion—and sometimes the arrogance—of true believers, such as sociologist Talcott Parsons.

> Do we have or can we develop a knowledge of human social relations that can serve as the basis of rational "engineering" control? . . . The evidence we have reviewed indicates that the answer is unequivocally affirmative. Social science is a going concern; the problem is not one of creating it, but rather of using and developing it. Those who still argue whether the scientific study of social life is possible are far behind the times. It is here, and that fact ends the argument.[12]

Such confidence drowned out whatever tentative speculation existed that the explosion of job opportunities in the military, and elsewhere in government, was turning experts into obedient servants of the state.[13] The panic set off by Sputnik in 1957 about the state of U.S. scientific and technological know-how did nothing, of course, to inspire a more critical mood; it only increased the gush of defense dollars.

By the early 1960s the DOD was spending almost all of its social science research budget on psychology, around $15 million annually, more than the *entire* budget for military research and development before World War II.[14] By the end of the 1960s the figure had almost tripled, but even the huge sums spent by the DOD had been swamped years earlier by Great Society programs wishing to direct psychological expertise toward domestic policy problems.[15] Whatever the intentions of military planners for their in-house and contract research during the Cold War, psychologists were hopeful, during the years following World War II, that "the military may serve for psychology the role that the industrial revolution served for the physical sciences."[16]

After 1945, and until the formal establishment of the NSF in 1950, the federal agency most responsible for funding psychological research was the Office of Naval Research (ONR). Established in August 1946 as the first federal agency dedicated to supporting scientific research, it took up pretty much where World War II left off. ONR inherited many wartime research contracts that employed psychologists in areas of personnel and training (test design and measurement), group dynamics (conformity, motivation, and leadership studies), human factors engineering (equipment design), and physiological psychology (sensation and perception). With a total budget for psychological research of around $2 million each year, the ONR represented a military commitment to psychological research and expertise far outstripping that of other public agencies. A decade after its establishment, the American Psychological Association (APA) celebrated the work of the ONR at an elaborate Washington banquet, "in recognition of the exceptional contributions of the Office of Naval Research to the development of American psychology and other sciences basic to the national welfare."[17]

In 1950 the Korean War confirmed the wisdom and reliability of the military-psychology combination. Widely publicized "brainwashing" of U.S. POWs by Chinese Communists gave special impetus to studies of sensory deprivation and techniques of ideological conversion, although there was a concerted effort to keep this kind of politically sensitive military research quiet.[18] Ultimately, research related to the mechanisms of mass communications and persuasion found their most eager customer in the evolving U.S. intelligence community.[19] The CIA, in particular, launched an ambitious mind control program during this period.[20] With a professional self-image that leaned heavily on psychological factors, the agency's embrace of behavioral technologies—including personality measurement and assessment—was not at all surprising. Consider the following description of an agent's primary mission by the CIA's inspector general in 1963: "The CIA case officer is first and foremost, perhaps, a practitioner of the art of assessing and exploiting human personality and motivations for ulterior purposes . . . by bringing the methods and disciplines of psychology to bear. . . . The prime objectives are control, exploitation, or neutralization. These objectives are innately anti-ethical rather than therapeutic in their intent."[21]

While the CIA's determination to train agents in the intricacies of psychological manipulation and its research into mind control were covert, not a matter of public record until decades later, the military's response to the Korean War was to reaffirm, often quite publicly, the fundamental lesson learned during World War II: war should be treated as a psychological struggle and laboratory. The Personnel Research Branch of the U.S. Army, along with several new contract research outfits (including the army's Operations Research Office of Johns Hopkins University and the air force's Human Resources Research Institute) sent psychologists to Korea to pursue the question of what exactly made a good solider. These investigations proceeded under the watchful eyes of advisors, including Samuel Stouffer, who had pioneered this sort of attitude assessment effort in World War II.[22] The army also launched Project CLEAR, an effort to check up on the slow progress of military racial integration after President Truman issued an executive order in July 1948 to desegregate the armed forces. These studies too were reminiscent of the work of the Army Research Branch during World War II. Finally, the U.S. Psychological Strategy Board, which coordinated all psychological warfare campaigns in Korea, consulted with behavioral experts including Hadley Cantril, Daniel Lerner, Harold Lasswell, Rensis Likert, Gabriel Almond, Clyde Kluckhohn, and Alexander Leighton.[23] The result was that the World War II experience was grafted onto the Cold War conflict. The commitment to psychology as a weapon continued unabated (fig. 14).

Ideological Building Blocks: Scientific Utility, Professional Gain, and National Security

In another pattern originating in World War II, military planners during the Cold War years consistently joined the lofty purposes of scientific advance to more immediate national security needs. Their notion of scientific advance, however, was a decidedly self-inter-

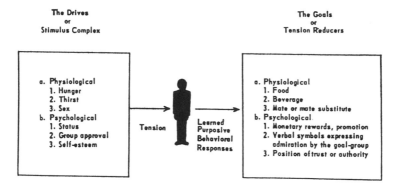

Figure 1. The individual, his drives and his goals.

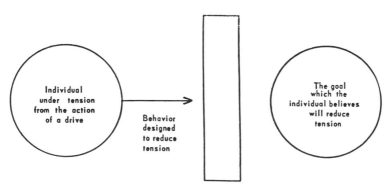

Figure 2. Frustration.

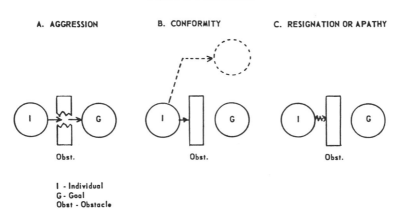

Figure 3. Three possible reactions.

Figure 14. Diagram of the individual's drives and reactions, from U.S. Army 1962 Field Manual on Psychological Operations.

ested one in which psychologists and others subordinated scientific goals to the DOD mission. In 1953 Don Price, the deputy chairman of the DOD Research and Development Board, tried to raise awareness among researchers about their properly submissive Cold War role, a role he felt they were foolishly resisting:

[The military] stands firmly on its cardinal principle: it does not make research contracts for the purpose of supporting science, but only "in order to get results that will strengthen the national defense. . . ." American scientists are still struggling to reconcile their eighteenth-century devotion to science as a system of objective and dispassionate search for knowledge and as a means for further-ing the welfare of mankind in general, with the twentieth-century necessity of using science as a means for strengthening the military power of the United States.[24]

As long as psychology could demonstrate its utility to "strengthening the military power of the United States," many military patrons were more than willing to champion it, and their record of solid support for military psychology during the Cold War years was impressive.

Psychology's conquest of the military, however, was far from com-plete. In spite of the experts' best efforts, some key policy-makers per-sisted in the old-fashioned belief that psychological knowledge was nothing but a mystified and expensive version of common sense, really a shameful waste of taxpayers' money. Others were even more hostile. Hyman Rickover, for example, the architect of the nuclear navy, "antic-ipate[d] with horror the day when the Navy is induced to place psychia-trists on board our nuclear submarines."[25] He believed that psycholog-ical experts had actually *caused* problems during World War II and *decreased* the efficiency of the military during the Cold War years. The "gauche and amateurish" antics of military psychologists, Rickover re-flected in 1968, were not merely annoying diversions. They had actually been straightforward threats to national security for almost three de-cades. According to him, psychology's silly concerns distracted soldiers from the important business at hand—beating the enemy—which had very little to do with either "morale" or "adjustment."

Rickover was not alone in feeling that military research ought to be limited to a narrow definition of winning wars and not used "to deter-mine various important human characteristics on the basis of the contents of wastepaper baskets."[26] Especially during the McCarthy years, active political suspicion was heaped onto the charge that behav-ioral expertise was stupid and irrelevant.[27] Worse, it might even be un-American. U.S. social and psychological experts, along with their foundation patrons, came under regular attack in Congress for leftist political sympathies and alleged plans "to weaken or discredit the capitalist system in the United States and to favor Marxist socialism." [28]

The constricted Cold War climate at home was likely an important factor in popularizing the new term, "behavioral science," which promised to exude hard-headed objectivity in the face of accusations that the human sciences were soft on socialism. [29] Some psychologists, Gordon Allport among them, were unhappy with the "behavioral science" label, but not too unhappy. In an address at Wellesley College, Allport mused, "Personally, I am not entirely happy with it since the science we seek is a science of feeling, of thought, of dreams and of silence, quite as much as of behavior. But philanthropic foundations seem to like the name *behavioral science,* and we shall raise no objection to it lest Cinderella miss her chance to ride in a golden coach provided by the Foundation. Up to now these sciences have been riding in a Ford model T." [30]

Suspicions about social science's socialistic inclinations never disappeared entirely, but as time went on, other concerns superseded them. [31] After the Soviet launch of Sputnik in 1957, many dedicated anti-Communists like Richard Nixon worried more about the competitive edge of U.S. social scientists than about their alleged political subversiveness. The military—along with the rest of U.S. society—came to associate psychology with sophisticated cultural and scientific understanding, a capacity that seemed not at all trivial, and certainly not optional, in a dangerous world. In January 1964 the Department of Defense reported to Congress that behavioral scientists were involved in all aspects of policy formulation, implementation, and evaluation. [32] No fuss greeted this routine announcement, and no controversial attention was paid to military behavioral science until Project Camelot came to light the next year.

The most virulent critics and the most enthusiastic proponents of military psychological expertise all based their arguments on the rhetoric of national security, a fixture of the era. While psychologists were the first to admit, to one another at least, that they actually knew appallingly little about their areas of supposed competence, they made promises to the military as a way of killing two birds with one stone: demonstrating psychology's social responsibility and advancing their own professional interests. [33] The establishment of the ONR, the National Security Act of 1947 (which reorganized all the military and national security agencies of the federal government), the Korean War, and other important developments in the wake of World War II added up to a "a dream come true" for psychological experts.[34]

If this sounds opportunistic, it was. There is no doubt that psychological experts massaged the system when they could, packaging their research plans in terms they knew would appeal to the military. Much of the debate about basic versus applied research had this quality; the distinction itself was partially created by the unprecedented sums of money available from government agencies in the period after World War II. Differences had always existed, in theory at least, between "applied" research geared toward smoothing the operations of the state and "basic" research prompted by purely scientific concerns. In practice, psychological experts worked on the assumption that their military customers always preferred the latter to the former. As one of them said, "Basic research is what I want to do, whatever that is, and whenever the mood strikes me. . . . Applied research [is] what someone else wants me to do, with some practical purpose in mind."[35] Some, undoubtedly, responded to the political economy of the research market by expediently translating their basic scientific concerns into a language filled with practical applications, thus garnering financial support under false pretenses. Many, perhaps most postwar psychological experts, however, did not have to lie, or even misrepresent their goals to military funders. They believed that defense-related work could simultaneously advance scientific knowledge and state efficiency.

Such multifaceted ambitions deepened with the Cold War because superpower hostilities created openings for projects like Camelot. If its genesis in international crisis was unfortunate, Camelot nevertheless symbolized how tantalizing the prospects were of a permanent social and psychological experiment on a very grand scale. Opportunities to study and manipulate the basic components of human motivation and behavior, and consequently to take a real shot at long-term psychological policy making, came frequently during the Cold War. The planet was still psychology's laboratory.

Most psychologists, on the other hand, were hardly crude opportunists. They were sincere in their convictions that psychology was crucial to national security and that psychologists were obligated to serve their government, perspectives deeply rooted in the World War II experience. They were certain that advancing their techniques of tension prediction and reduction could help the United States move toward an enlightened and peace-prone foreign policy rather than one crafted out of the war-prone cobwebs of intuition.

Cold war was, above all, a psychological phenomenon, just as total world war had been. While cold war presented the U.S. military with new challenges—unconventional styles of warfare against a new cast of confusing enemies—nothing could have offered clearer evidence of the World War II maxim that war was fundamentally a battle for hearts and minds. Third World upheavals were nothing if not contests for the feelings and will of people. What could have vindicated more comprehensively everything the World War II experts had said about the chaos of public opinion and morale and the need for expert management of ideology and propaganda? Military might, on its own, was simply not up to the task of winning the Cold War because victory would not go to the side with the most guns. No one was more intimately acquainted with the drift of military thinking than President Eisenhower, who proclaimed in 1954 that "the world, once divided by oceans and mountain ranges, is now split by hostile concepts of man's character and nature. . . . Two world camps . . . lie farther apart in motivation and conduct than the poles in space."[36] The Cold War was a "war for the minds of men," Eisenhower concluded.[37]

The World War II worldview was the most decisive factor shaping psychology's Cold War history, and the link between the two emerged in part from the sustained vision of a rigorous and predictive behavioral science, which lasted from 1945 well into the 1960s. The World War II sources were tangible as well as abstract. A number of individuals whose formative professional experiences had been in World War II went on to lay the plans that inspired the ill-fated Project Camelot. Charles Bray, for example, was chair of the Applied Psychology Panel of the National Defense Research Committee during World War II, which had mobilized some two hundred psychologists in twenty research projects geared to streamlining military operations and increasing proficiency. His leadership of the Smithsonian Institution's Research Group in Psychology and the Social Sciences, during the late 1950s and early 1960s, was especially important in laying the groundwork for projects like Camelot. Many other psychological experts with World War II experience involved themselves in military psychology well into the 1960s, often in important planning and advisory capacities. These included Leonard Carmichael, Leonard Doob, Frank Geldard, Daniel Lerner, Morris Janowitz, S. Smith Stevens, Samuel Stouffer, Theodore Vallance, Dael Wolfe, and others.

The most significant organizational innovation during the Cold War years was the establishment of military contract research organizations, which proliferated between 1945 and the early 1960s. Funded almost exclusively by the military, but nominally affiliated with "multiversities" and located on campuses, these new organizations (called Federal Contract Research Centers, or FCRCs) handled massive volumes of psychological and other types of scientific work for the DOD.[38] According to the NSF, the numbers of professionals of all types employed by FCRCs tripled between 1954 and 1965 and their budgets increased by 500 percent.[39]

Stationed in a kind of "twilight zone" between the clear public functions of government bureaucracies and the supposedly private concerns of universities, these FCRCs literally transferred much DOD data gathering to organizations outside of the state, furthering the mixture of military and nonmilitary, public and private, that was so characteristic of Cold War research.[40] The most famous of these hybrid organizations is undoubtedly the RAND Corporation, founded with air force aid in 1946. Another was the Special Operations Research Office (SORO), the sponsor of Project Camelot.[41]

Theoretical Building Blocks: The Psychological Basis of Development and Revolution in the Third World

DEVELOPMENT

The theoretical work of psychologists after World War II, especially in the areas of Third World development and revolution, complemented the institutional factors that were strengthening psychological research within the military and helped bring psychological perspectives to the attention of policy-makers. The notion, for example, that the roots of war were to be found in the psychological particulars of national character and the universal truth of frustration and aggression did not evaporate at the end of World War II. During the period between 1945 and 1960, psychological experts pursued questions about how to derail the development of militaristic aggressiveness, and, more ambitiously, how to construct an alternative psychology, oriented toward peaceful economic development and political stability. The fundamentals of the national character approach, although they sometimes came in for sharp methodological criticisms, gained wide currency among foreign and military policy-makers in the period following the war.[42]

Formulated as an explicit alternative to the inadequate (because they were not primarily psychological) explanations of economists and other social scientists who stressed material factors and large-scale social forces transcending the individual person, some psychologists singled out personality as the ultimate key to manipulating economic and political developments in the newly emerging states of the Third World. As early as 1946, psychologist Carl Hovland offered the following general advice to the officers of the Rockefeller Foundation, who were exploring the possibility of funding projects on the "Psychological Principles Underlying Economic Behavior": "Now it is not anticipated that it will be possible within the near future to explain all economic phenomena on the basis of psychological laws now known. But it is the writer's opinion that it is high time that a start be made."[43] Between World War II and the mid-1960s, psychologists tackled this area of theory and research. Many eventually concluded that there was little point in assisting abstractions like "developing societies" by pouring vast public sums into a process whose economic mechanisms were baffling.

Personalities, on the other hand, were concrete entities. Not only did they "develop," but they were assumed to be reachable through conscious intervention into the family's childrearing practices. Mothers, because they functioned as personality factories, became favorite subjects of expert attention and logical objects of public policy. The inner landscape, that familiar geography on which so much military conflict transpired, also turned out to be the key to unlocking peaceful economic change in far-flung corners of the world.

Leonard Doob, an important figure in World War II psychology and one of the authors of *Frustration and Aggression,* spent a number of the postwar years conducting psychological studies in African and Caribbean societies and developing a theoretical argument that posited "civilization" (by which he meant Western-style industrial and cultural development) as an outgrowth of personality change.[44] Civilization's presence or absence, in other words, had more to do with the conditions of psychological development and with the state of affairs "within people" than with such external, material realities as economic infrastructure, raw materials, population growth, or the character and extent of political institutions. *"People acquire the central goal of seeking to be-*

come more civilized," Doob argued, *"when their traditional values no longer bring them satisfaction and/or when some experience gives them a favorable view of civilization."*[45]

Although Doob held tightly to the vision of an objective and non-judgmental behavioral science, insisting, for example, that "the process of becoming more civilized is neither praised nor condemned," his conclusions told a different story.[46] His data characterized the people of "uncivilized" societies as rigid and lacking in empathy, whereas the psychological profile of civilized people included tolerance, reason, self-reflection, and a refreshing absence of dogma.[47] Doob still endorsed the psychoanalytic premise that civilization required repression, but the resulting misery seemed to fall squarely on the shoulders of those individuals who were in the process of acculturation, striving for an urbanized, industrialized society. The psychological conflicts involved in "becoming more civilized" could, according to this way of thinking, function as the basis for nationalist or revolutionary ideologies since these ideologies offered psychologically necessary safety valves for the accumulation of hostile emotions by directing those emotions toward outsiders, frequently Westerners. If residents of the Third World could be systematically aided in navigating this treacherous route toward civilized personalities, Doob suggested, they would likely find that state psychologically satisfying when they finally arrived.

His research methods, which relied heavily on projective tests like the Rorschach, were indicative of general trends in the direction of postwar social scientific research.[48] Personality measures were more and more frequently used by anthropologists, sociologists, and political scientists engaged in fieldwork in the Third World because getting illiterate or semiliterate people to draw or respond to ink blots was a practical possibility. For the many who were influenced by varieties of psychoanalytic theory, of course, exploring the levels below consciousness was also a theoretical necessity. A whole generation of postwar social scientists was routinely schooled in the use of tests like the Thematic Apperception Test (TAT), F Scale, Rorschach, and the Goodenough Drawing Test, in addition to more conventional intelligence-measuring techniques like the Stanford-Binet scale. One survey of cross-cultural research in the early 1960s concluded that "students of culture have looked to the psychologist—or at least to psychological concepts and methods—for the key to their revised scientific interest."[49]

Probably the best-known example of postwar psychological theory pushed to the limits of its explanatory power in relation to international economic development was the work of David McClelland. A personality psychologist originally interested in theories of motivation, McClelland's *The Achieving Society* (1961) aimed to illustrate that psychological determinism could be empirically sound and quantitatively rigorous when it came to explaining and predicting patterns of national economic development. McClelland, committed to methodological advance in psychology, also had in mind the practical translation of psychological theory into public policy. "The shortest way to achieve economic objectives," he wrote, "might turn out to be through changing people first. . . . The precise problem of most underdeveloped countries is that they do not have the character structure, especially the motivational structure, which would lead them to act in the ways required. The model is like a combustion engine without the gas to make it go." [50]

Individual psychology, as it turned out, was "the gas," the precious fuel of economic progress. Much as Doob had focused on the individual personality as the entity that either moved or failed to move toward a state of civilization, McClelland theorized that the personal psychological resources of a given country largely determined whether or not it would be an "achieving society." Economic development was a product of a competitive, achievement-oriented type of personality whose main sources were internal and psychological. This achieving personality (or any other kind, for that matter) was manufactured within the family. Relationships between mothers and children (in the case of McClelland's research, it was exclusively mothers and *sons*) were therefore directly implicated as likely obstacles to national economic growth and reforming motherhood emerged as possibly the clearest solution to national economic failure.

McClelland's grand theory began modestly in the early 1950s with an effort to quantitatively isolate and measure individual motives, including the one that became a central factor in his later work on economic development: the need for achievement, or what he called "*n* Achievement." Firmly committed to the most exacting experimental methods as well as to the pursuit of psychoanalytic insights, McClelland developed ingenious techniques for taking "psychic X-rays" of a given society's unconscious inclinations. These included methodical content analyses of folk stories and children's stories from around the world (in order to discern patterns of cultural fantasy and aspiration—a kind of projective test for the entire society), direct tests for *n* Achievement (via studies of mothers and sons in Germany, Japan, India, and Brazil), and observation of the actual behavior of business entrepreneurs—who were assumed to embody the achieving ideal—in the United States, Turkey, Italy, and Poland.

McClelland assumed a straightforward cause-and-effect relationship between mothers' early expectations of sons, the development of a (male) entrepreneurial class, and levels of national economic development. Although he claimed that his model was not bound to any particular economic philosophy, and would predict growth rates equally well in capitalist and socialist economies, his concept of achievement certainly assumed a fundamentally competitive and acquisitive economic drive.

His assumptions about gender merited no such self-conscious commentary. Basically, if mothers' inculcated enough *n* Achievement, the country would prosper; if they did not, it would remain impoverished or even slip backwards into underdevelopment. The fact that girls and women were central economic actors, especially in subsistence-based, agrarian societies, was entirely invisible in this model of development. Women were considered important, but for the values they instilled, as mothers, in their young sons. According to McClelland, the childrearing style that produced the highest levels of *n* Achievement balanced warmth against high expectations and exhibited just the right amount of pressure to achieve: not too much and not too little. To the extent that political or economic forces were relevant in producing national achievement levels, they operated largely on mothers and their childrearing practices. "The family as the nucleus of the social structure is a little like the nucleus of the atom; it is harder to influence by external events than one might expect."[51]

After comparing various national economic growth rates with measures of *n* Achievement in 1925 and 1950, as well as examining historical cases as divergent as Spain in the Middle Ages, the Protestant Reformation, pre-Inca Peru, and the nineteenth-century United States, McClelland found that surges in *n* Achievement levels were consistently *followed* by spurts of productive economic activity, confirming his theory that psychological change was the motor of economic history. "What people want," he concluded, "they somehow manage to get. . . . These results serve to direct our attention as social scientists away from an exclusive concern with the external events in history to the 'internal' psychological concerns that in the long run determine what happens in history."[52] At last, patterns of economic development could be reliably predicted on the basis of measurable psychological factors: "The psychologist has now developed tools for finding out what a generation wants, better than it knows itself, and *before* it has had a chance of showing by its actions what it is after."[53]

The policy implications of such awesome knowledge were very clear to Doob and McClelland. First, U.S. foreign aid geared to economic development really ought to target psychological development since the latter was both a fundamental and a measurable cause of economic growth. This simplified the policy-making process by turning it away from such elusive factors as agricultural efficiency and turning it toward those indicators with a demonstrable, empirical relationship to *n* Achievement. Second, the goal of aid should be to nurture and produce emotionally mature entrepreneurial elites who would then lead their countries toward economic growth and success. In this translation of psychology into public policy, old-fashioned development programs could still be useful, if considered in the new light of their psychological consequences. Birth control programs were, for McClelland, just one example. "One must obviously reduce the number of some kinds of people more than others, yet practically all birth-control policies ignore this problem entirely. No matter how few, the 'wrong' kind of people will not produce rapid economic development, nor will the 'right' people, no matter how many, block economic development. 'Right' and 'wrong' mean here, of course, more or less suited in motives and values to the task of economic development."[54] McClelland was more than willing to testify before Congress about the deficiencies of the country's development assistance policies, many of which, in his view, suffered from reliance on the erroneous motivational assumptions of economists. "Behavioral science knowledge about human motivation," in contrast, "could have very concrete practical implications for U.S. aid policy. . . ."[55] He recommended that all government programs of foreign assistance be carefully scrutinized for evidence of their "psychological multiplier effect" and U.S. investments restructured in favor of those which had demonstrated the biggest payoff in developing the "right" kinds of personalities and discouraging the "wrong" ones.[56]

For its part, Congress seriously explored the psychological aspects of international relationships on several occasions in the mid- and late 1960s, facilitated by J. William Fulbright (D-Ark.), chair of the Senate Committee on Foreign Relations.[57] Fulbright, who had been one of the youngest university presidents in the country (appointed to head the University of Arkansas at age thirty-four) before his entrance into electoral politics, was known for founding the program of international scholarly exchange that bears his name and also for sponsoring high-profile hearings on Vietnam, beginning in 1966, which were considered instrumental in turning public opinion against the war. He opened a 1969 hearing on "Psychological Aspects of Foreign Policy" by stating, "It is believed by many that wars begin in the minds of men. As a politician, I am inclined to view it that the mysteries of political behavior have their origin in the mysteries of the human mind, and yet an examination of the human mind in order to understand our own political behavior has not heretofore appealed to either the public or to political leaders. It may be we are frightened by the possibilities that might be revealed by some self-examination."[58] Fulbright's hearings delved into topics ranging from communism's psychological appeal to the role of unconscious projection and need for love in U.S. foreign policy; they were designed to air "unorthodox approaches."[59] Expert testimony was offered by Jerome Frank, Margaret Mead, Karl Menninger, and Charles Osgood, among others, who took advantage of the opportunities Fulbright offered to champion the usefulness of their insights but did not hesitate to scold Congress for its inadequate appreciation of mental and behavioral expertise. "Perhaps what psychiatrists have learned about establishing communication with a frightened, angry, and suspicious person may have some relevance," pointed out Jerome Frank about "Psychological Difficulties in Giving and Receiving Aid."[60] Other testimony and written reports addressed "The Effect of Natural Drives on Communism and the Changes in Communism," the "Effect of 'Face' on Rigidity of Chinese Communism," and "Is the United States Acting Rationally?"

REVOLUTION

Social psychological perspectives also pervaded the study of political upheaval in the Third World in the period after World War II, in large part because the striking pattern of interdisciplinary teamwork during World War II had left as much of a mark on many sociologists, anthropologists, political scientists, and economists as it had on those with formal psychological training. The tendency toward the study of "total societies," for example, required a patchwork of methods and theories drawn from throughout the social sciences. The new prominence of psychological research in fields conventionally associated with political science or sociology helped to push the center of gravity in research done by nonpsychologists toward the consideration of psychological variables.[61] As early as 1939, Robert Lynd had offered the following comment and advice in his critical discussion of the direction of U.S. social science: "With its field thus fortunately concentrated on the central powerhouse of culture, individuals, [psychology] is in the strategic position of having the other social sciences turn increasingly to it for the solution to realistic problems—mental health, education and child development, labor problems, advertising and market research, public opinion and propaganda. It is a safe prescription to almost any young social-scientist-in-training to 'get more psychological underpinning.'"[62]

By the early 1960s much of mainstream social science was committed to a behavioral science approach to the analysis of Third World revolution, an orientation that would significantly shape policy, as well as research, during the Vietnam era. Influential books like Walt Rostow's *The Stages of Economic Growth* (1960) made it obvious not only that societies needed to be jolted into modernization (typically by revolution), but that an appropriate psychological outlook—characterized by rationality, risk taking, and desire for growth and consumption—was a prerequisite to national "take-off."[63] A Massachusetts Institute of Technology economist during the 1950s, Rostow became a Vietnam War policy-maker and controversial advocate of counterinsurgency in the Kennedy and Johnson administrations as chairman of the Department of State Policy Planning Council and deputy to National Security Advisor McGeorge Bundy, another academic-turned-policy-maker. He testified before Congress about the advantages behavioral experts brought to "winning the Cold War" and singled out the psychologist for special mention as "a valued collaborator in penetrating the operation of the Communist mind and the attractions which communism offers certain kinds of people."[64]

By the early 1960s the analytical concept of "political culture" had also injected a new appreciation for psychology into the study of comparative politics. The very use of the term, according to its originator, Gabriel Almond, a Stanford University political scientist, indicated a *"psychological orientation toward social objects."*[65] Directly descended from World War II analyses of national character, political culture illustrated just how central a psychological orientation had become for social scientists not formally identified with psychological training, in this case political scientists interested in Third World revolution and development.[66] According to Lucian Pye,

> The concept of political culture assumes that each individual must, in his own historical context, learn and incorporate into his own personality the knowledge and feelings about the politics of his people and his community. This means in turn that the political culture of a society is limited but given firm structure by the factors basic to dynamic psychology. . . . [Political culture combines] the revolutionary findings of modern depth psychology and recent advances in the sociological techniques for measuring attitudes in mass societies.[67]

While they depended heavily on World War II–era national character studies, political culture advocates were also likely to criticize them for being biased toward the unconscious and insufficiently attentive to rational, adult motivation. They prided themselves on the theoretical flexibility with which political culture could encompass both conscious and unconscious psychological factors. This balanced emphasis, however, did not so much depart from the direction of psychological theory as conform to it. In the years after World War II, interest in conscious motivation and ego development revived, including among psychoanalytic theorists such as Heinz Hartmann.[68]

The definition of development—political and economic—that paralleled political culture made it clear too that the point was to delineate a national personality profile, but through more exhaustive and systematic comparisons than had been possible for World War II–era social psychologists. Political culture advocates included in their notion of political development precisely the kinds of findings just detailed in the work of psychologists Leonard Doob and David McClelland. They also harked back to the World War II discovery that individual subjectivity could be the key to untangling social and political processes. "Political culture does not refer to the formal or informal structures of political interaction," one key advocate remarked. "Nor does it refer to the pattern of interaction among political actors. . . . It refers not to what is happening in the world of politics, but what people believe about those happenings."[69]

The popularity of the political culture concept was fueled as much by policy-makers' immediate concerns as by the theoretical momentum of social science. Its multidisciplinary approach to the problem of nation building certainly seemed appropriate to the complicated analysis of whole political systems, a kind of bridge between the microanalysis of life histories and the macroanalysis more typical of political sociologists and historians.[70] But the concept also promised to "yield more understanding about the possibilities and limitations for consciously changing a political culture in order to facilitate national development."[71] It was partly because of the blueprint it offered for engineering political change in the Third World—a prime concern of much U.S. foreign and military policy during the Cold War years—that the political culture perspective became a dominant one by the mid-1960s.

Its advocates were concentrated in the Social Science Research Council's Committee on Comparative Politics.[72] That committee's chairman was Lucian Pye, a Massachusetts Institute of Technology political scientist and one of the DOD's many advisors on behavioral research. Pye argued that the main challenges Third World societies faced in becoming modern nation-states were psychological. "Fears of failure in the adventure of nation building create deep anxieties, which tend to inhibit effective action. . . . The dynamics of such psychological inhibitions to effective action, particularly in relation to the politics of modernization, can permeate and restrain the entire process of nation building."[73]

Like McClelland on economic development, Pye pointed out that political development would go nowhere if Third World personalities were not emotionally suited to the requirements of such a national "adventure." Referring frequently to the writing of psychoanalyst Erik Erikson, who had published the widely read *Childhood and Society* and *Young Man Luther* since his wartime studies of Hitler's psychology and Nazi mentality, Pye suggested that modernizing the political structures of Third World states would require the inculcation of new forms of identity through a revamped socialization process. Also like McClelland, personalities stood, for Pye, at a critical juncture between individual psychology and a country's political institutions. They were the critical variable and, further, they were reformable. By supporting the development of a modernizing identity among emotional elites in the Third World, the United States could promote peaceful movement toward Western models of political organization and minimize the chances of bloody, Communist-inspired revolutions.

Pye and others considered the question of national identity—whether and to what extent people developed a self-confident psychological affiliation with and sense of belonging to a nation-state—especially delicate. Instilling a clear national identity was understood to be the source of legitimacy for political institutions and elites. Patriotic service to the state during war had, after all, been the origin of their own power, and they assumed it was equally essential to stabilizing shaky Third World political systems. Analysts suggested that providing new states with assistance in building national self-identity was a task of political socialization equivalent to the family's manufacture of personal self-identity.[74] True, it occurred on the level of international relations rather than interpersonal relations, but the difference was more one of location than of kind.

Even with these new and important intellectual developments, many of the old themes of crowd psychology, which had informed psychologists' policy-oriented work during World War II and before, remained sturdy and largely unchanged, appearing at the center of behavioral schemes to understand and manipulate Third World revolution, including Camelot. In fact, Rex Hopper, the Brooklyn College sociologist who was eventually chosen to direct Project Camelot, took the crowd psychology tradition so seriously that he summarized its contributions to the literature on revolution in a 1950 article titled "The Revolutionary Process: A Frame of Reference for the Study of Revolutionary Movements."[75]

Working squarely in the tradition of Le Bon and McDougall, as well as the more recent World War II–era analysts of race rioting, Hopper laid out a series of stages through which revolutionary movements passed: "the Preliminary Stage of Mass (Individual) Excitement, the Popular Stage of Crowd (Collective) Excitement and Unrest, the Formal Stage of Formulation of Issues and Formulation of Publics, and the Institutional Stage of Legalization and Societal Organization."[76] Each stage corresponded to a particular psychological mood, to which revolutionary elements (leaders, organizations, and ideologies) had to conform. As individuals were transformed into a "psychological crowd," and as that crowd eventually became a revolutionary public and the basis for a new society, people experienced the typically painful consequences of dramatic psychological change: wish repression, oppression psychoses, motivation disturbances, and general psychological exhaustion.

Although he was a Latin America specialist himself, Hopper's summary of the literature was purely theoretical and did not single out any particular national case, or even region of the world, for examination. Nor did Hopper give any indication that the effort to predict, guide, or prevent revolution might raise ethical questions for behavioral scientists. In all likelihood, his straightforward endorsement of the notion that "a generalized description is a necessary prerequisite to any attempt to control" indicated that "the revolutionary process" he was describing was located safely on territory outside the industrialized West.[77] Years later, when he directed his attention toward dramatic shifts in the domestic social structure of the United States, his attitudes were far less neutral. With waves of cultural alienation and technologically induced unemployment becoming more frequent, "the probabilities are great that revolutionary changes will occur," he noted in dismay. "My own guess is that we shall move toward a militarized and cybernatized totalitarianism of the right."[78]

In the early 1960s, mainstream social and behavioral scientists were fully engaged with developing the kind of predictive indices that grew organically out of theoretical chronologies like Hopper's. Systematically identifying the constellation of factors that caused "internal war" was, at the time, a major effort. For example, the Princeton Symposium on Internal War, hosted in September 1961 by the Princeton Center for International Studies and funded by the Carnegie Corporation, brought together a small group of prominent social and behavioral scientists, including Gabriel Almond, Daniel Bell, Kenneth Boulding, Harold Lasswell, Seymour Martin Lipset, Talcott Parsons, Lucian Pye, and Sidney Verba.[79] For several days, they discussed the general preconditions of internal war and topics such as "The Commencement of Rebellions and the Art of Controlling Rebels." Although a purely theoretical effort on its face, the organizer of the symposium, Harry Eckstein of Princeton, presented his paper (titled "Introduction to the Study of Internal Wars: The Problem of Anticipation") to the Smithsonian Institution's Research Group in Psychology and the Social Sciences, charged with advising the DOD on the direction of military behavioral science, just a few months later.[80] Eventually, Eckstein became one of Camelot's consultants.

Edward Tiryakian, a sociologist from Duke University and another one of the participants in the Princeton symposium, later contributed his work on the prediction of Third World upheaval to a conference directly associated with the Camelot effort.[81] Tiryakian's predictive model assumed that revolutionary upheaval was necessarily destructive and endorsed political stability as the ideal state. (His hypothetical society, distinguished primarily by the absence of conflict, was called "utopia.") His "Model of Societal Change and Its Lead Indicators" developed an "index of revolutionary potential" complete with "advance warning signals" that measured increases in social pathology and instability via such indicators as the spread of sexual promiscuity and cults. Because these factors were located in the social unconscious (he called it the "social underground"), far removed from the superficial political and economic targets of revolutionary movements, they were, according to Tiryakian, by far the most reliable predictors of war's psychological preconditions.

Camelot's Organizational Background

THE SMITHSONIAN INSTITUTION'S RESEARCH GROUP IN PSYCHOLOGY AND THE SOCIAL SCIENCES

The long-term planning efforts of the Smithsonian Institution's Research Group in Psychology and the Social Sciences were the most immediate precursors of Camelot, although in significant ways this group merely updated the advice that Robert Yerkes had given to the defense establishment as early as 1944. The Smithsonian Group consisted of some of psychology's leading lights, most of whom had been deeply influenced by their experiences during World War II: Leonard Carmichael, Leonard Cottrell, Harry Harlow, Neal Miller, S. Smith Stevens, and Dael Wolfe, among others. The group's 1957 report tried to anticipate the kind of research that would be necessary to win the global struggle with the Soviet Union ten to twenty years in the future. They assumed that cold war would continue—mainly because human beings were not emotionally conditioned in such a way as to make peace very likely—and that its battleground would be primarily psychological. "The principal weapon of cold war," they asserted, "is persuasion—the persuasion of men. . . . It is assumed that persuasion is the major cold war weapon of importance in the future."[82] They concluded that "full realization of the potentialities of psychology and the social sciences in designing a fully operational Psychological Weapon System could not be expected unless that system were explicitly admitted to the arsenal of primary weapons systems of the nation."[83]

Breakthroughs in developing and countering "Psychological Weapons Systems," which the group confidently expected, would show that psychology was both militarily important and politically neutral. It could be the source of technologies devoted to manipulating motivation, designing blueprints for the "international persuasion of peoples," and gathering intelligence, techniques that could be used for good (in U.S. hands) or ill (in Communist hands). Although the Smithsonian Group predicted, with much satisfaction, that advances in these difficult areas would be realized, members also identified potential trouble spots. In particular, they noted that obstinate public opinion could be an obstacle to psychological research and development and admitted that "there will also be difficulty in finding solutions to these conflicts within the framework of democracy."[84]

Project Camelot, as it unfolded, would illustrate how accurate such anxieties were. Public perceptions and democratic institutions were, in the case of Camelot, big enough problems to cause the project's cancellation. They were not, however, big enough to stop, or even really slow, the forward momentum of Cold War psychology, based on the sturdy World War II worldview and two decades of military practice.

THE 1962 SYMPOSIUM ON "THE U.S. ARMY'S LIMITED-WAR MISSION AND SOCIAL SCIENCE RESEARCH"

A significant event, immediately preceding Camelot's launch, was a March 1962 conference, funded by the army's chief of research and development and hosted by SORO, which brought over three hundred social and behavioral scientists together in Washington, D.C. Never before had the armed forces "rolled out such a massive welcome mat for the professors."[85] There were many flattering mentions of psychological expertise and its military record, and generals and colonels repeatedly expressed much eagerness to be enlightened in the matter of counterinsurgency. "Recognition of the need for social science research within the military establishment," they assured their guests, "is quite widespread today."[86] Courses in military psychology, leadership, and human relations were, after all, on the required list at West Point; special warfare (a recently coined term for psychological warfare) had had its own school at Fort Bragg, North Carolina, since 1952; and psychologically sensitive courses in counterinsurgency were being offered all over the world, in numerous languages, by the U.S. Army.

Military planners talked at great length, leaving little room for guesswork about what kind of ammunition they were looking for: "The kind of underlying knowledge required is the *understanding and prediction of human behavior at the individual, political and social group, and society levels."* [87] Prediction and "population control" were needs at the very heart of the counterinsurgency mission, and military planners took pains to make them explicit. Methods of controlling indigenous peoples, destroying Communist-inspired guerrilla movements, exploiting national psychological vulnerabilities, and predicting the potential for internal war (one of Camelot's goals) would be terribly useful. Methods of preventing insurgencies in the first place would be even better. Could experts manage to provide these sorts of technologies? For their part, the experts spent most of the conference listening and taking notes. Even the photographic record of the conference managed to exclude them.

In spite of these indications that military planners regarded them more as dutiful technicians than as coequal partners, fervent desire to be of use was much in evidence among the behavioral scientists who attended the conference, as was the particular mood of the Smithsonian Group and its representative, Charles Bray. Conference discussion was limited to the fine points of technical assistance. No one ever questioned either the counterinsurgency mission or the appropriateness of involving social and psychological experts in it. Attendees agreed that it was their job to provide the military with an objective "technology of human behavior" and leave their own political convictions at home. Nevertheless, they did make clear assumptions about the value of the military's Cold War mission and the positive social contributions of military institutions themselves. [88]

Communism was "a malignant organism that grows and thrives on human misery—which reaches out its long tendrils in every field of human endeavor, seeking to strangle and destroy," according to Lieutenant General Arthur G. Trudeau, chief of research and development for the army. [89] On the other hand, as numerous participants pointed out, militaries around the world could—with U.S. aid—become constructive, nation-building forces. Like the benevolent railroad-building soldiers in the U.S. historical imagination, foreign militaries could become the leading edge of the modernization process in the Third World, steering new states toward the stability that U.S. national interests required. The U.S. military, it went practically without saying, was "a direct, positive instrument for human progress," and the U.S. national interest was synonymous with freedom, prosperity, and social justice all over the world. [90]

Such themes made the World War II imprint evident enough, and numerous explicit references were also made to its relevance, often by attendees—like Leonard Doob, Morris Janowitz, and Elmo Wilson—whose own experience bridged the gap between world war and cold war.[91] But the spirit of World War II expertise was also quite evident among younger scholars who came to Washington at the invitation of the military, and they had absorbed postwar trends in the analysis of development and revolution. One of them, Frederick T. C. Yu, presented a national character-type analysis of Asian identity and Chinese communism. Unlike the Germans or Japanese in 1940, Asian personality had not yet deteriorated, under the toxic influence of Communist ideology, to the point of causing global crisis. It was, however, in serious psychological trouble and needed prompt attention. "Like our young Americans in their late adolescent years," Yu analogized, "people in the developing countries [in Asia] do not really know what they want to be. They are in the process of growing up. They are searching frantically for a purpose in life and a reason in the things they do, believe, and want. But they do not really know what they should do or want, except that, in a very vague way, they want to be strong, successful, great, happy and prosperous. They are confused."[92] If psychological experts could imbue U.S. policy with therapeutic powers, then the United States could help Asian states help themselves develop clear national identities to replace the uncertainty that was causing so many problems. All the while, new states would accumulate "human motivation capital" that would be on our side in the event a counterinsurgency campaign became necessary.[93] Like wise and caring parents, "our responsibility is to help them grow, help them see and understand the meaning of things they wonder about. In short, to help them discover themselves."[94] The best therapy was a strong military. Armies represented "a sense of self-respect and self-assurance" to people who had long chafed under colonial rule and whose struggles to form independent states clearly required a psychological foundation of self-esteem.[95] The axiom that nation building was a unique military responsibility was a cornerstone of SORO director Theodore Vallance's thought as well and a position he championed long after the 1962 symposium. He always maintained that the Cold War had altered the DOD mission to the point that "the U.S. military establishment has a new functional emphasis: mediating changes in foreign cultures."[96] What could have spotlighted the importance of behavioral expertise more successfully

than the translation of military conflict into an endless series of opportunities for cultural design and mediation?

Each of the factors described in this chapter contributed something
essential to the progress of psychological expertise and to the willingness of government officials to take psychology into account when it
came to the design of U.S. foreign and military policy in the early Cold
War era. That psychological researchers found a welcome home in the
military establishment, winning financial support through the efforts of
proponents like the Smithsonian Group, was important. That psychological and political theorists had something convincing to say about
why Third World personalities were socialized into emotional and political states of underdevelopment, and how those flaws could be cor-
rected to produce "developing" people, was also important. That the
Cold War itself was so vulnerable to interpretation as a terrifying struggle for human emotional and intellectual loyalties—to be won or lost
on the battlefield of the mind—was perhaps most important of all.

Each one of these historical threads is evident in the fascinating story
of Project Camelot, which is described and analyzed in the next chapter. In Camelot's aftermath, psychology's political progress and its political consequences were clearer than ever.

6

Project Camelot and Its Aftermath

Like so many other developments in postwar psychology, Project Camelot had deep roots in World War II. During that global emergency, psychological experts gained, for the first time, a significant and growing client base among high-level policy-makers, generous financial support, and rich theoretical, methodological, and organizational experience. In return, they studied the enemy mind, designed "psyops," and predicted likely responses to various policy alternatives among civilian and military populations. In the fifteen years after 1945, psychology proceeded rapidly along the path charted by the World War II experience. The persistence of war—old-fashioned and hot in the case of Korea, new-fashioned and cold in the case of U.S.–Soviet hostilities in the Third World—sustained psychology's momentum and blessed its future. As chapter 5 illustrated, support for applied psychological research within the new bureaucracies of the national security state grew dramatically between 1945 and 1960. For their part, psychological experts promoted as inseparable the goals of national security and scientific advance and developed unique analyses of development and revolution in the emerging states of the Third World.

In all of these areas, experts were careful to maximize the practical military utility of their theoretical and research pursuits. If their functional policy orientation was less visible to the public at large than the testing or clinical work that more and more psychologists were doing during these years, it was nevertheless far more important in establishing psychology's political credentials and guaranteeing that behavioral experts would be warmly welcomed in every federal agency charged with Cold War foreign and military policy. The successful career of Cold War psychology linked psychologists' desire to serve their society even more firmly to stability-minded policy elites than had World War II and eliminated from serious consideration the possibility that work for nongovernmental organizations might be an appropriate expression of professional and social responsibility.

The story of Project Camelot and its aftermath illustrates the continuation of all of these important historical themes well into the 1960s. As a large-scale effort dedicated to translating psychological and behavioral expertise directly into the language of foreign policy and military action, Camelot shows just how far psychological experts had come since the formative years of World War II. They had come far enough so that even a major international scandal, which is what Camelot became, did not undermine their progress in the realm of public policy. Nor did it prompt severe critics like Ralph Beals (an anthropologist who conducted one of the most thorough investigations of Camelot) to reassess the fundamental loyalty to the state that was an axiom of the World War II worldview: "Social scientists have a responsibility to government even if they do not agree with government practices."[1]

Project Camelot Described

Project Camelot was initiated in 1963 by planners in the Army Office of Research and Development who were concerned about combating Soviet-inspired "wars of national liberation" in countries such as Cuba, Yemen, and the Belgian Congo. They were prepared to believe what the experts had been saying since 1945: behavioral expertise had a very important, perhaps the most important, contribution to make to Cold War victory over communism. Their goal—nothing less than the prediction and control of the social and psychological preconditions of Third World revolution—reflected the most lavish ambitions of psychological experts. In the words of its architects, "Project CAMELOT is a study whose objective is to determine the feasibility of developing a general social systems model which would make it possible to predict and influence politically significant aspects of social change in the developing nations of the world."[2] In spite of the code name (chosen to "connote the right sorts of things . . . the development of a stable society with domestic tranquility and peace and justice for all") and the ill-fated effort to disguise its military sponsorship in Chile (a lie which led to the project's exposure), Camelot was not officially classified.[3]

Camelot's mandate to "predict and influence" the process of Third World development marked it as a product of the World War II worldview. Additionally, it embodied the trend toward counterinsurgency and special operations that was so firmly identified with the Kennedy administration and its pledge to undermine the Soviet Union's support for liberation movements around the world, which Khrushchev had announced as a doctrine of Soviet policy in his famous 1960 speech "For New Victories of the World Communist Movement."

The project was funded through the Special Operations Research Organization (SORO), one of the many campus-based contract research organizations that appeared after 1945 to service the Defense Department's scientific research effort. A nonprofit organization founded in 1956, SORO existed for the purpose of conducting "nonmaterial research in support of the Department of the Army's missions in such fields as counterinsurgency, unconventional warfare, psychological operations, and military assistance."[4] SORO was so loosely affiliated with the American University that some critics retrospectively dismissed its campus setting as clever camouflage. Its director, Theodore Vallance, had been a psychological researcher during World War II, when he was an army lieutenant in charge of a field laboratory that studied B-29 gunsights and gunners at Laredo Army Air Field, in Texas.[5]

By the early 1960s Vallance was predicting a big role for "paramilitary" psychology in the "cultural engineering" of emerging Third World states, a logical outgrowth of the military's "trend away from emphasis on human components for hardware systems toward emphasis on human components of social systems."[6] Vallance was a staunch partisan of a politically neutral military psychology, very much like Charles Bray's "technology of human behavior." He was careful to describe Camelot as "an objective, nonnormative study concerned with *what is or might be* and *not* with what *ought to be*."[7] In addition to Camelot, SORO's work included providing the army with dozens of country-specific handbooks on psychological operations, case studies of Southeast Asia focusing on the exploitation of psychological vulnerabilities, and a comprehensive data bank called the Counter-Insurgency Information Analysis Center.

Camelot's projected research plan bore all the telltale traces of the World War II–era conception of an ambitious and integrated behavioral science. Psychology, cultural anthropology, and sociology were all slated to make important contributions to the final goal of the project: a model of a social system experiencing internal war accurate enough to be predictive, and therefore useful, to military policy-makers. To reach that goal, Camelot's designers anticipated moving ahead in several phases. Phase one consisted of reviewing the existing data on internal war, a largely theoretical challenge already engaging the talents of many mainstream behavioral scientists. Phase two would produce twenty-one case studies of post–World War II insurgencies and five contemporary field studies with the explicit goal of developing predictive indicators. Phase three would bring the work of the first two phases to bear on a single in-depth analysis of an undetermined country. Phase four would validate the findings of phase three, and the project as a whole, by applying the model to yet another national case.[8]

The project's focus was Latin America, and Rex Hopper, a Brooklyn College sociologist and Latin America expert, was chosen as Camelot's director. Countries in Asia and Africa, however, were also found on Camelot's list of foreign areas in need of study. Vietnam, for example, was a clear target for research and the project exploded into public view at precisely the moment when U.S. involvement in Vietnam escalated: mid-1965. "There is a general consensus that the problem [of Third World revolution] is intimately related to the social structure, culture, and behavioral patterns in the countries involved," army research and development chief Lt. Gen. W. W. Dick informed Congress. "Vietnam illustrates the problem very clearly."[9] It was also a bare two months after marines had landed in the Dominican Republic, intervening to prevent a purported Communist takeover.

Had it come to fruition, Camelot would have been the largest, and certainly the most generously funded, behavioral research project in U.S. history. With a $4–$6 million contract over a period of three years, it was considered a veritable Manhattan Project for the behavioral sciences, at least by many of the intellectuals whose services were in heavy demand.[10] Prominent behavioral scientists, including sociologists Jessie Bernard, Lewis Coser, and Neil Smelser, were among the project's consultants, and the National Academy of Sciences agreed to provide Camelot with an advisory committee.

Project Camelot Exposed

The project backfired. University of Pittsburgh anthropologist and Camelot consultant Hugo Nutini tried to promote the plan among Chilean scholars by lying to them about its fiscal sponsors; he told them it was funded by the National Science Foundation (NSF). But a concerned Norwegian sociologist, Johan Galtung, had already leaked preliminary versions of Camelot's research design, and the crucial fact of its military sponsorship, to Chilean colleagues. When they heard about it, outraged left-wing journalists in Chile decried the plan as an ominous indication that U.S. policy was shifting its sights from bananas to behavior and predicted that social science research would replace dollars as the leading edge of U.S. diplomacy.

Even though Chile had not been among those countries mentioned by Camelot's planners, the project was publicly denounced in a special session of the Chilean Senate, where politicians called it "a plan of Yankee espionage" masquerading as science.[11] Protests were lodged in Washington by the incensed U.S. ambassador to Chile, Ralph Dungan, who had never been informed about Camelot's existence. Finally, the whole project was canceled by Secretary of Defense Robert McNamara on 8 July 1965 because of all the unfavorable publicity. A subsequent memo from President Johnson, dated 2 August 1965, ordered that all future foreign area research be cleared by a new review agency, the Foreign Affairs Research Council, located in the Department of State's Bureau of Intelligence and Research. (This adjustment in the bureaucratic location of final decisions apparently had little short- or long-term effect on the nature or funding of overseas research for government agencies, but was intended to calm fears that civilian authorities had lost their grip on the direction of the U.S. military.)[12]

On the very day Camelot was canceled, the Subcommittee on International Organizations and Movements of the House Committee on Foreign Affairs convened hearings intended to get to the bottom of the scandal.[13] The testimony of army and SORO bureaucrats made it clear that they saw Camelot as a logical continuation of behavioral experts' role in World War II, Korea, and a wide spectrum of Cold War agencies, including the OSS and the CIA. They reiterated that, as far as they were concerned, "the U.S. Army has an important mission in the positive and constructive aspect of nation building as well as a responsibility to assist friendly governments in dealing with active insurgency problems."[14] Obviously, they had absorbed the mainstream social-scientific view that militaries were the leading edge of the modernization process.

Military planners readily pinned the blame for Camelot's cancellation on either Communist distortions or bureaucratic rivalries between the Department of Defense and the Department of State (DOS). While they realized that Camelot-like projects would have to be handled more discreetly in the future, they were also somewhat surprised by all the fuss. In the end, Camelot could hardly have been as consequential to its military funders, who had very deep pockets, as it was to the behavioral scientists who saw it as either the crowning achievement or failure of their careers. Camelot's fiscal sponsors had plenty of money and behavioral science was a relative bargain. Even a multimillion-dollar project, such as Camelot, was described by its military sponsors as a "feasibility study."[15] The scandal, in any case, did not put even a tiny dent in levels of DOD funding.[16]

Dante Fascell (D-Fla.), chair of the investigating subcommittee, was typical of Camelot's congressional critics. For him, the episode proved that DOS was being bypassed on key foreign policy decisions and DOD was all too willing to jeopardize foreign alliances in sensitive areas of the world. Fascell accused the DOD of inappropriately involving itself in nonmilitary business and concluded that behavioral science had not been at fault. Support for foreign area behavioral research was repeatedly expressed during the hearings; it was called "one of the vital tools in the arsenal of the free societies."[17]

The committee ended by chastising the DOS for spending such a minuscule amount of money on behavioral science—less than 1 percent of the federal government's total for foreign area research, according to Secretary of State Dean Rusk.[18] It firmly recommended that civilian foreign policy bureaucrats invest in a much bigger behavioral research program and the executive branch establish an Office of the Behavioral Science Adviser to the President. In June 1966 Dante Fascell filed House bills designed to further these goals and correct civilian policymakers' relative neglect of behavioral science.

The Intellectuals Debate Professional Ethics

Camelot's demise was also followed by much soul search-ing among intellectuals, who saw the project's significance rather differ-ently than did its military sponsors or its congressional critics.[19] Some observed that Camelot's consequences for experts were rather surpris-ing. The credibility of behavioral science, they suggested, survived the ordeal of the congressional probe not only unscathed, but strength-ened. As Robert Nisbet put it,

Let it be trumpeted far and wide: The federal government, starting with the subcommittee whose job it was to look into Camelot's coffin, and going all the way across town to Secretaries Rusk and McNamara, love the behavioral sci-ences; love them not despite but, apparently, because of their sins. . . . With the kind of luck that . . . God grants to children, fools, drunkards, and citizens of the United States of America, the behavioral sciences emerged from this poten-tially devastating hearing with their luster untarnished, their prestige, if any-thing, higher.[20]

What began as a Pandora's box may have ended as a lucky break in the coming-of-age story of behavioral experts, but intellectuals themselves were divided on Camelot's lessons. Some insisted that Camelot had been an excellent opportunity to shape policy, unforgivably squandered by incompetent operators. Others wondered about the acceptability of contracts from military agencies and compared what behavioral scien-tists were doing for the Defense Department to the huge amounts of work being conducted under the auspices of the Department of Health, Education, and Welfare (HEW) and other domestically oriented bu-reaucracies by the mid-1960s. A very few, worried that researchers were being turned into the unwitting servants of power, ventured so far as to ask whether any form of federal support could be ethical.

In the end, they reached no consensus. Few participants were naive enough to defend Camelot for its basic scientific value, but many main-tained their remarkable optimism about the potential of behavioral sci-ence in government, regarding Camelot as an example of socially en-gaged research, even a rare opportunity for science "to sublimate" the military's unfortunate tendency toward violence.[21] David Riesman, not a participant in Camelot himself, was not alone when he suggested that the episode proved "the top management of the Defense Department often seems to have a wider perspective on the world than its counterpart in State." [22] The next year, Gabriel Almond was still scolding DOS policy-makers for their backward intellectual tastes. "They believe in making policy through some kind of intuitive and antenna-like process," Almond noted testily, "which enables them to estimate what the prospects of this and that are in this or the other country. I believe they are a backward agency, as far as their relationship to science is concerned." [23]

Ithiel de Sola Pool, a political scientist who had worked with Harold Lasswell at the Library of Congress during World War II, was a key figure at the Massachusetts Institute of Technology Center for International Studies, which had been founded and supported throughout the 1950s (with Ford Foundation and secret CIA funds) "to bring to bear academic research on issues of public policy." [24] Sola Pool was probably the most enthusiastic proponent of a "humanizing" alliance between social science and government. "They [the social sciences] have the same relationship to the training of mandarins of the twentieth century that the humanities have always had to the training of mandarins in the past. . . . The only hope for humane government in the future is through the extensive use of the social sciences by government." [25] Far from considering Camelot's participants to be spies, Sola Pool went so far as to accuse critics of "a kind of neo-McCarthyism." [26]

Neither Camelot's supporters nor its detractors were politically homogeneous, and the project cannot, therefore, be easily dismissed as a perverse brainchild of rabid cold warriors. Many, perhaps even a majority, of participants were liberal anti-Communists; some were critics of U.S. involvement in Vietnam. For them, deploying the theories and techniques of behavioral science to prosecute the Cold War efficiently and nonviolently was evidence of the democratic values embedded in U.S. policy. Indeed, Camelot's critics and defenders all tended to venerate the vital and progressive role that behavioral expertise could and should play in government. Sociologist Irving Horowitz, who endorsed this position and called it the "Enlightenment Syndrome," was the most influential academic observer of the project's "life and death," "rise and fall." [27] In his own articles on the subject and in the book he edited, *The Rise and Fall of Project Camelot* (1967) (which gathered primary documents as well as critiques), Horowitz expressed the anxieties of many intellectuals when he interpreted Camelot's cancellation as a serious attack on behavioral scientists' intellectual freedom and public contribution. "The degree to which the development of the social sciences is permitted within a nation," he wrote, "operates as a twentieth-century index of freedom. . . . I do not think anyone can participate in social research and fail to see a high correlation of good social science and a good society." [28]

Unlike Horowitz's belief in the freedom-reflecting quality of behavioral expertise, Charles Bray and the Smithsonian Group (the immediate predecessors of Camelot), had at least admitted that psychotechnologies were politically neutral, capable of application to repressive as well as benevolent ends. Awareness of the negative potentials of behavioral science was never, of course, entirely absent during the period after World War II. Bray's group followed the lead of important World War II–era figures like social psychologist Kurt Lewin and sociologist and NSF administrator Harry Alpert, who, while deeply committed to a vision of behavioral scientists bringing order and enlightenment to public policy, were nevertheless alert to the ever-present danger that their wisdom could still be used for manipulative purposes. "Unfortunately there is nothing in social laws and social research which will force the practitioner toward the good. Science gives more freedom and power to both the doctor and the murderer, to democracy and Fascism," wrote Lewin in a 1946 essay. [29] Alpert restated the message more than a decade later. "Whether the atom is used for peace or destruction, whether bacteria are mobilized for purposes of health or disease, whether knowledge of human motivations is used to provide happiness or to sell soap, are alternatives which the scientist as seeker of knowledge and truth cannot determine." [30] Such warnings seemed to lose their force under the pressure of Cold War conflicts and opportunities, at least until the antiwar movement gained the loyalty of many intellectuals in the late 1960s. During the 1950s and early 1960s, few doubts surfaced that U.S. policy-makers would see fit to use behavioral expertise exclusively in the interests of freedom, just as there was correspondingly little skepticism about the repressive reach of the Soviet psychological and psychiatric professions. "Nothing in the social sciences increases the capacity to manipulate an individual against his will," insisted Daniel Lerner in 1959. "The central tendency of social science is rather to increase man's capacity to manipulate his own social environment." [31]

Horowitz was among the most thoughtful commentators on Camelot and its implications at the time. His own political views were decidedly left-wing; he was, for example, a great admirer of radical sociologist C. Wright Mills well before the New Left turned Mills into a hero.

Yet Horowitz embodied many of the assumptions of the World War II worldview, for example, that intellectuals' social responsibilities included special obligations to government, even when they opposed government policies.

In the case of Camelot, Horowitz criticized participants for their unscientific reluctance to look a gift horse in the mouth. Swallowing military objectives without question was a terrible mistake for which intellectuals should, Horowitz felt, be held responsible. But he was also convinced that contempt for social and behavioral science—rather than defective method or botched research design—was the real motive behind Camelot's termination. He regarded the whole affair as a major setback and Johnson's memo as "a gross violation of the autonomous nature of science."[32] For Horowitz, Camelot's unhappy end threatened the fragile hold that behavioral expertise had on public policy. He chose to emphasize the virtues of socially engaged intellectuals over their ideological sins. They were, after all, at least trying to survive as the voice of reason in an unreasonable political system.

Some intellectuals on the Left, like social psychologist Herbert Kelman, were more willing than Horowitz to concede that behavioral research could serve repressive ends, that "even under the most favorable conditions manipulation of the behavior of others is an ethically ambiguous act."[33] Yet Kelman too maintained that psychological expertise was a prerequisite for democratic decision making, "that social science ought to contribute to the policy process," and that it could and should be a profoundly "constructive and liberating force in society."[34] Overcoming all the negatives required ensuring that psychological research would proceed uncontaminated by mundane political considerations and that experts would be able to do their work autonomously and in the spirit of international scientific cooperation.

Horowitz and Kelman were only two of the canceled project's public critics in the social sciences and psychology. The questions they raised about the ethical values and social responsibilities of behavioral scientists, and the relationship of research to government policy, were both timely and sincere. It does not detract from the validity of their critique to point out that they were also self-interested. Few voices were heard, for example, calling for a halt to government-funded research. Dismay about Camelot did not alter the conviction, widespread among behavioral scientists across the political spectrum, that such research should be continued, and preferably expanded.

The belief that science required complete political independence in order to generate positive results was entirely compatible with insistence that whatever controls over socially useful research were needed should be retained by professionals themselves. Keeping the material and status benefits of government research contracts while expanding the authority of experts over the conditions and applications of their work was part of the ongoing, successful bargaining process that marked the public history of psychological expertise in the decades after World War II. Because experts whose political views led them to disagree about everything else (the Vietnam War, for example) could still agree about this, practically no ground was lost in the fight for government research support. Considering the international proportions of the Camelot scandal, this was a remarkable feat.

If any criticisms of Camelot questioned the very foundations of the bond between behavioral science and government, they tended to be voiced by cultural anthropologists for both historical and practical reasons. Their discipline, inextricably bound to the establishment of global empires by European states, had been shaken by espionage charges earlier in the century. In 1919 Columbia's Franz Boas accused four anthropologists of "prostitut[ing] science by using it as a cover for their activities as spies" during World War I.[35] Even though his campaign to bring sanctions against them was outvoted in the American Anthropological Association (AAA), the discipline carried the burden of its imperial heritage uncomfortably; anthropological work sensitized scholars to the impact of Western rule on the underdeveloped world. Moreover, anthropology depended more heavily than any of the other disciplines on foreign field opportunities, and these could readily evaporate if foreign authorities doubted the sincerity of researchers' scientific intentions.

After Camelot, the AAA appointed a Committee on Research Problems and Ethics, sponsored a wide-ranging inquiry into the responsibilities of social scientists, and strongly urged other behavioral science organizations to do the same. The AAA adopted a series of resolutions such as the following: "Constraint, deception, and secrecy have no place in science. . . . Academic institutions and individual members of the academic community, including students, should scrupulously avoid both involvement in clandestine intelligence activities and the use of the name of anthropology, or the title of anthropologist, as a cover for intelligence activities."[36] The anthropologists were not, however, entirely certain about how either "science" or "intelligence" should be defined. Ralph Beals, one of those most concerned with the negative consequences of Project Camelot for the profession, was also aware that the CIA extracted most of its information from civilian research. He was forced to conclude that "unfortunately today there is practically no information that may not, under some circumstances, have military significance."[37]

That this dilemma represented something more than a definitional problem was well illustrated when the alarm over Camelot in 1964 escalated into a tidal wave of shock over revelations of CIA involvement in academic life in the years that followed.[38] Advocates of an "engaged anthropology" gained momentum from news about colleagues' secret activities, as they did from the gathering strength of the antiwar movement, and young leftists formed professional groups like Anthropologists for Radical Political Action.[39] But the anthropological establishment reacted publicly too, stepping up its campaign to erect impermeable barriers between legitimate intellectual work and cloak-and-dagger intelligence gathering. The difference between the two, however, was far less obvious than caricatured images of scientists and spies would suggest, as they well knew.

As if to underscore the enduring confusion between research and espionage, antiwar activists brought evidence of counterinsurgency activities by social scientists to members of the AAA's Committee on Research Problems and Ethics in 1970, five years after Camelot had been put to rest. The Student Mobilization Committee to End the War in Vietnam documented numerous instances of cooperation between anthropologists and the U.S. military, including a counterinsurgency project in Thailand run by the American Institutes for Research, the organizational descendent of SORO and the Center for Research in Social Systems (CRESS), which superseded SORO at the American University in 1966. In spite of the AAA's formal position that an unbridgeable gulf ought to exist between covert activities and anthropological fieldwork, the two committee members who went public with this information (Eric Wolf and Joseph Jorgensen) were reprimanded by the AAA for acting outside the bounds of their authority. They finally resigned in protest.[40]

Aftermath

DIRECT CONSEQUENCES

After Camelot, Hugo Nutini, the consultant whose lie exposed Camelot in the first place, was banned from returning to Chile.

The scandal's impact, however, extended well beyond his case. Many foreign governments devised restrictions to prevent U.S. meddling and, in a few cases, even slammed the door shut entirely on U.S. researchers.[41] U.S. academics worried that "it doesn't make any difference whether you are a Ford fellow or an NSF fellow . . . the natives will all say you're working for the CIA," regardless of what the facts of research sponsorship and design actually were.[42]

Still, remarkably little about behavioral science funding or design changed after Camelot was canceled. A similar project was uncovered in Brazil less than two weeks later and others were launched in Colombia (Project Simpatico) and Peru (Operation Task), sponsored by SORO and funded by the DOD, exactly as Camelot had been.[43] Project Agile, a study of National Liberation Front (NLF) members' motivation, the attitudes of villagers, and communication patterns among South Vietnamese troops, was carried out in the years after Camelot's demise, as were studies of the "Potential for Internal Conflict in Latin America."[44] Whatever objections existed to such activities were clearly ineffective and did not interfere with the completion of the research. A confidential DOD memo written five weeks after Camelot's cancellation simply stated that counterinsurgency research involving foreign areas was "highly sensitive" and "must be treated in such a way that offense to foreign governments and propaganda advantage to the communist apparatus are avoided."[45] Four years later, the DOD admitted that not a single one of its social or behavioral science projects, or for that matter anything at all involving foreign area work, had been terminated in the years after Camelot's exposure.[46]

Two years after Camelot was canceled, the officers of most major behavioral science organizations gave their blessings to defense research in a congressional hearing on that topic. Arthur Brayfield, the director of the American Psychological Association, had this to say: "I think the military should be free to use all reasonable, ethical, and competent tools at its command to help carry out its mission, and I would say strongly that the use of behavioral science and behavioral scientists is one of those useful tools."[47] Such endorsements were qualified by warnings that it would be wise to pay closer attention to appearances in the future since it was inevitable that someone, somewhere, would always label behavioral research sensitive and accuse behavioral experts of being surreptitious manipulators.

Some visionary advocates tried to turn Camelot's negative public relations impact into a plus by arguing that the behavioral sciences deserved a federal foundation of their very own and should no longer have to rely on the largesse of the military because of their secondary status in the NSF. "Senator for Science" Fred Harris (D Okla.) led a movement in Congress in 1967 to establish a National Social Science Foundation. He agreed with Dante Fascell that foreign area research, in particular, needed to be "civilianized." Harris pointed to Camelot (and his subsequent membership on the Kerner Commission) as a turning point in his own thinking on the matter, but he often employed the shining example of World War II behavioral experts to make his case for the importance of social research in government.

Although Harris's battle for a separate foundation was ultimately lost, it is arguable that the social sciences won their war with the federal government during the 1960s.[48] In 1968 President Johnson signed a bill amending the NSF's founding legislation and granting social science the formal status it initially lacked as part of the NSF mandate. Throughout the 1960s the NSF steadily increased the proportion of its budget devoted to social science and tilted its priorities toward the applied research with which social science was commonly associated.[49]

Barely affected by Camelot's immediate fallout, the DOD nevertheless took a number of steps to shine up its tarnished image in the academic world after Camelot, and by the end of the decade such efforts were calculated as much to counteract storms of student antiwar protest as to dispel the doubts of hesitant faculty members. For example, in 1967 the DOD launched Project Themis, a program designed to encourage increasingly skeptical universities to consider the advantages of putting social and behavioral scientists to work for the DOD, and improving the caliber of those who did. In its first year alone, Themis doled out $20.5 million worth of support; the budget for its third year was projected at almost twice that.[50]

The Defense Science Board, the DOD's highest-ranking advisory group, also convened in the wake of Camelot to mend the tattered relationship between the Defense Department and academic experts. Its members, eager to bury for good the uncomfortable questions that Camelot had raised, issued a report that took as axiomatic a view that would unravel for many before the end of the war in Vietnam: that intellectuals' obligation to serve their society and work for federal government agencies were one and the same.[51] The report did not even consider the consequences, ethical or otherwise, of the specific *military* requirements and purposes of DOD behavioral science research. Instead, it concluded,

The DoD mission now embraces problems and responsibilities which have not previously been assigned to a military establishment. It has been properly stated that the DoD must now wage not only warfare but "peacefare" as well. Pacification assistance and the battle of ideas are major segments of the DoD responsibility. The social and behavioral sciences constitute the unique resource for support of these new requirements and must be vigorously pursued if our operations are to be effective.[52]

Over the next decade, the Vietnam War put great pressure on the military to wage "peacefare." Behavioral research and its operational, "psywar" counterpart were in high demand partly because that war illustrated so dramatically the failure of great military might in the absence of basic cultural and political comprehension. Vietnam "sykewarriors" simply replicated, on a grander scale, many of the techniques used during World War II. In a typical month in 1969, 713 million leaflets were dropped from the air and two thousand hours of propaganda were broadcast—all to encourage NLF defections.[53]

Other Vietnam-era studies reflected the evolution of psychological expertise since 1945. General Westmoreland demanded repeated studies of NLF psychology. He got them, pronounced them invaluable, and made them required reading for his staff.[54] The most renowned of the Vietnam motivation and morale studies, and surely among the most elaborate field studies on revolutionaries and the revolutionary process, were those conducted by the RAND Corporation between 1964 and 1969.[55] Apparently not at all affected by the Camelot scandal, the Viet-Cong Motivation and Morale Project (VC M&M) outlasted its original conception as a six-month pilot study in 1964 and became more secure and ambitious as the 1960s wore on. A classified project that studied prisoners, defectors, and refugees, sixty-two thousand pages of interviews were finally made public in 1972.

VC M&M was a classic example, during the Vietnam era, of the basic axiom about bureaucratic survival and expertise that policy-makers had learned during World War II: government uses social science the way a drunk uses a lamp post, for support rather than light.[56] Its authors' conclusions—that the enemy was near the breaking point and that heavy bombing would quickly end the conflict—told the policy-makers exactly what they wanted to hear in 1965, the precise moment of military escalation. And there is quite a bit of evidence that policy-makers were paying close attention to the findings of VC M&M, rewarding the project's researchers for their good efforts with a 100 percent increase in funding in 1966.[57]

The light-at-the-end-of-the-tunnel mentality would, of course, appear tragically misguided later on. One of the project's own staff members would go so far as to call it "a whitewash of genocide."[58] In the aftermath of Camelot, however, the RAND studies illustrated, once again, how politically useful psychological intelligence was to the policy-making process, even when it was entirely wrong.

THE PROGRESS OF COLD WAR PSYCHOLOGY

In retrospect, it seems clear that policy-oriented behavioral expertise was neither fragile at the time of Camelot nor seriously jeopardized by the outcome of the scandal. In 1966 SORO, Camelot's sponsoring organization, reconstituted itself as the Center for Research in Social Systems (CRESS) and continued, under its new name, to provide the army with detailed information about the Third World. The name change was virtually the only change. Camelot's spirit lived on. Its outlines continued to inform the work of CRESS and other research organizations long after 1965. A number of subsequent studies bore more than a passing resemblance to the shelved project.

A three-volume CRESS study, *Challenge and Response in Internal Conflict* (1968), provides some clues about what Camelot might have looked like had it been completed. Like Camelot, it was launched in 1963 under the watchful eyes of SORO director Theodore Vallance. Its purpose was to provide the army with an "institutional memory bank" that could guide counterinsurgency planning. Although its authors declined to evaluate the specific military purposes to which their research might be put because "counterinsurgency might be undertaken by either 'good' or 'bad' governments in an assorted mix of 'good' and 'bad' ways," they were quite certain that U.S. counterinsurgency efforts always assisted morally virtuous and popular regimes.[59] The finished product encompassed the work of 45 experts from 14 universities, detailed 57 cases of twentieth-century insurgencies (29 since World War II), and literally covered the globe.

In the period after Camelot, CRESS also produced a number of Camelot-like behavioral studies spotlighting the Vietnamese insurgency.[60] One, "Human Factor Considerations of Undergrounds in Insurgencies," surveyed twenty-four postwar cases, but an analysis of National Liberation Front psychology was its centerpiece. In their effort to understand why normally law-abiding individuals were drawn into the orbit of dangerous revolutionary movements, psychologists Andrew Molnar, Jerry Tinker, and John LeNoir emphasized all the basic social psychological factors that had been identified as key variables during World War II: group membership and cohesiveness, patterns of leadership, the advantage of emotional over rational appeals.[61] Like their predecessors in World War II–era psychology, they placed the individual firmly at the center of inquiries into social and political phenomena.

The study also featured a developmental stage model of the revolutionary process, based on the principles of crowd psychology, very much like the one Rex Hopper had outlined in 1950.[62] It concluded with the familiar theme that the best counterinsurgency strategy was preventive treatment. But when nipping upheavals in the bud was impossible, as was the case in Vietnam, soldiers should be trained as "agents of pacification." They should be made into admirable models of civic action, engaged in the necessary work of building roads and bridges and, at the same time, capable of coercively channeling popular frustrations into the "catharsis" provided by loyalty to the existing government.[63]

Many CRESS studies considered the frustration of personal needs a convincing explanation for revolutionary upheaval in Vietnam and elsewhere, a smooth continuation of yet another strand in World War II psychological warfare. One sophisticated 1969 survey, subcontracted by CRESS to the Princeton Center for International Studies, began by noting that "it seems evident that most riots and revolutions are made by angry men, not dispassionate ones, and that the more intense their anger, the more destructive their actions are likely to be. . . . Most human aggression occurs as a response to frustration."[64]

Ironically, Camelot's spirit was destined to have its most lethal reincarnation in Chile, the country where it had been exposed, but which had never been one of the intended targets of research. In 1973, almost a decade after Camelot was canceled, its mark could be seen in the secret, CIA-sponsored coup against the socialist government of Salvador Allende.

The connection came through Abt Associates, a research organization located in Cambridge, Massachusetts, whose president, Clark Abt, had been one of Camelot's consultants. In 1965 the DOD's Advanced Research Projects Agency (ARPA) contracted with Abt to design a computer simulation game to be used for monitoring internal war in Latin America. Except for the addition of sophisticated computer technology, Camelot's goal remained intact. Dubbed Politica, the game was first loaded with data about hundreds of social psychological variables in a given country: degree of group cohesiveness, levels of self-esteem, attitudes toward authority, and so on. Then it would "highlight those variables decisive for the description, indication, prediction, and control of internal revolutionary conflict."[65]

In the case of Chile, according to Daniel Del Solar, one of Politica's inventors, the game's results eventually gave the green light to policy-makers who favored murdering Allende in the plan to topple Chile's leftist government.[66] Politica had predicted that Chile would remain stable even after a military takeover and the president's death. Just as useful to the planners of military and covert action as the RAND study of Viet-Cong motivation and morale had been, Politica proved to be far more accurate.

Precisely because it was a fiasco, Camelot's story illustrates the stamina of the World War II worldview in the face of a significant challenge. It also helps to explain the political distance that behavioral science—psychology in particular—had traveled in twenty years, and the intimate links that had been forged between psychology's diverse public uses. By 1965 a majority of elected officials and top policy-makers thought they understood why "we have psychiatrists and psychologists running out of our ears in this Government of ours today."[67] With regular prodding from the experts, they proclaimed that behavioral scholarship was indispensable to foreign and military policy. Yet in Camelot's case the aggressive political deployment of psychological expertise was effectively obscured through psychology's old scientific and new therapeutic reputation, which made it likely that knowledge about human societies would be considered as neutral technology or impractical basic research, even when it was being paid for by military or other institutions with clear political missions.[68]

Almost two decades had passed since George Lundberg's classic formulation of social expertise as the ability "to predict with high probability the social weather, just as meteorologists predict sunshine and storm. More specifically, social scientists should be able to say what is likely to happen socially under stated conditions."[69] Yet the vision of an objective psychology whose practitioners should strive to be technically proficient social engineers, which World War II had done so much to further, remained secure. Camelot's antiseptic language often emphasized the allegedly apolitical character of behavioral science, referring, for example, to "insurgency prophylaxis" rather than counterrevolu-

tion. Even at the height of the Cold War, psychology offered a convenient way to avoid all mention of capitalism, communism, or socialism.[70]

One of Camelot's lessons was that even a significant international
scandal, which in an earlier period might have elicited much debate
about the proper relationship between knowledge and power, did not
noticeably interrupt psychology's political progress. The heated debate
among intellectuals that followed the project's cancellation revealed
more about the insecurities felt by a group of intellectuals new to power
than it did about any serious threat to their public status. Many of the
official architects of the Vietnam War, after all—policy-makers like
McGeorge Bundy, Robert McNamara, and Walt Rostow—were the
very models of the new "mandarins" Sola Pool had so hopefully proclaimed to be the vanguard of a humanistic future.[71]

They, along with the researchers put to work on Cold War projects
like Camelot, all had liberal, behaviorally oriented educational backgrounds. They had dutifully absorbed the lessons of recent war, hot
and cold: that political passions, ideas such as freedom, and military
conflicts themselves were contaminated by toxic emotions in need of
immediate treatment and firm containment. They studied the chaotic
compound known as "national character," subsequently renamed "political culture," in hopes of producing effective management techniques. For the Cold War generation, "population control," the calculated shaping of behavior at home and abroad, was both a realistic and
responsible goal. (This use of the term "population control" should not
be confused with the global family planning programs it has frequently
denoted since the 1960s.) Prediction and control via behavioral management was the enduring refrain of World War II–era experts, and it
was constantly reiterated during the years that followed 1945. According to morale specialist Rensis Likert, "The important problems of
our times concern human behaviour. . . . Problems of human behaviour underlie each of the many kinds of organized group effort on
which nations are becoming increasingly dependent. . . . The larger social problems of nations and of the world also involve human behaviour."[72] Cold War managers were, after all, charged with nothing less
than overseeing the awful dangers of superpower conflict. Because they
were involved in a global "minds race," the very future of the planet
depended on how well they could stabilize the emotional and behavioral disorder caused by aggression, fear, self-interest, primitive loyalties, and the ever-present human quest for security, which took so many

irrational forms. Is it any wonder, in the face of such imposing emotional obstacles during the postwar decades, that the most famous psychologist in the United States—B. F. Skinner—would reject individual autonomy and suggest that psychology's biggest challenge was to move "beyond freedom and dignity." Skinner defined his profession's toughest problem as follows: "to induce people not to be good but to behave well."[73]

As the years wore on, the booming postwar economy would slow and the quagmire of U.S. policy in Vietnam would become more obvious and elicit more protest. Cold War psychology, one product of the World War II worldview, would be more seriously challenged than it was at the moment of Camelot's exposure.[74] By the end of the decade, Harold Lasswell himself, the very embodiment of World War II–era faith in psychological expertise, was expressing grave doubts about the enlightening potential of scientific expertise. "If the earlier promise [of science] was that knowledge would make men free," he said, "the contemporary reality seems to be that more men are manipulated without their consent for more purposes by more techniques by fewer men than at any time in history."[75] By the time Lasswell spoke these discouraging words at the 1969 APA meetings, psychological experts had long since found secure new homes and enthusiastic new sponsors in federal bureaucracies devoted to cleaning up U.S. domestic social problems.[76] Total federal expenditures on the "psychological sciences" steadily increased throughout most of the 1960s, from $38.2 million in fiscal year 1960 to a high of $158 million in fiscal year 1967.[77] While the source of most of the funds did shift decisively from DOD to HEW early in the decade, defense-related research spending never dipped. Camelot had little if any impact on the financial resources the military made available to psychological experts.

Neither, in 1965, had intellectuals of the sort involved in Camelot been recast by the Vietnam War, and antiwar critics like linguist Noam Chomsky, as the "secular priesthood" whose job it was "to ensure that the people's voice speaks the right words."[78] Eventually, the antiwar movement would convert many Americans to views directly opposed to the World War II worldview. With a civilian population sharply divided on the merits of U.S. involvement in Vietnam, it became possible to think that psychology (and other varieties of expertise) was useful mainly because it helped the state maintain ideological control over a potentially unruly population, shield a murderous foreign policy from public view, and "manufacture consent" by insisting that U.S. motives were always pure and U.S. power always legitimate.[79]

The notion that mercenary experts were reinforcing U.S. dominance around the world in hopes of gaining power themselves was a far cry from the World War II image of exemplary citizen-intellectuals putting their social responsibility on display by going to work for the government. In 1972 Margaret Mead, compelled by the idea of a "generation gap" and exceptionally receptive to the ideas of young people, admitted as much when she reflected on what her own wartime activities had taught her: "that psychological warfare rebounded on those who perpetrated it, destroyed trust and simply prepared for later trouble—discoveries which the young radicals were to make over again in the 1960s but about which we had no doubt in the late 1940s."[80]

When Camelot unfolded, however, most of the antiwar movement's history (including the partial takeover of the 1969 APA conference by antiwar activists) still lay in the future.[81] The teach-in movement, which did so much to expose the military-industrial-*academic* complex, was just getting off the ground with novel, all-night gatherings on the campus of the University of Michigan in Ann Arbor. The ideological beliefs of the World War II generation were still, for the most part, quite solid. Momentous conflicts existed between good and evil. Democracy was infinitely superior to any political alternative. And government could be trusted to use the power of science responsibly.

In 1965 the dreams inspired by World War II had come true. Psychological experts were no longer required to prove the efficiency they brought to military functioning, nor were they pressured to defend their investments in anti-Communist foreign and military policies, tasks they had pursued avidly in earlier years. The political benefits of psychology had become, for the moment at least, entirely self-evident and, at the same time, largely invisible. Society had become the patient. Psychology had become the cure.

7

The Damaging Psychology of Race

Cold War showdowns in faraway corners of the Third World may have been dramatic examples of how psychological expertise could be drawn into the fabric of postwar U.S. foreign and military policy, but they were hardly unique. Intergroup conflict did not fade away in 1945, and the appearance of a mass-based civil rights movement in the 1950s—inspired in part by the painful contradictions black Americans had lived with during World War II—pushed race and racial conflict to the center stage of public policy more insistently than ever before. To the World War II generation, it was apparent that levels of racial tension at home were in desperate need of monitoring and control, and, if at all possible, prediction and prevention as well.

In this critical area of domestic policy, the reminders of war and its benefits were ever-present. The domestically oriented government bureaucracies that purchased expert advice and supported research on the development of racial identity and the psychology of prejudice in the years after World War II drew on the same sources of inspiration as their Cold War counterparts. They depended upon explanations for racial crises that were founded, as theories of Third World development and revolution were, on such psychological basics as personality development, the roles of frustration and aggression in motivating behavior, and the logic of identity formation. In the decades after 1945, experts recalled World War II as their touchstone as they set out to develop a "strategic guide to the war against prejudice," "community diagnosis and treatment" of this "contagious disease," and "the conquest of conflict itself."[1]

This chapter locates the origin of postwar psychological perspectives on race in the transforming experience of World War II, briefly describes a few of their characteristic features in the decades that followed, and offers a number of examples of the translation of psychology into public policy on a variety of racial matters—from educational segregation to employment. Just as chapter 5 explored some of the developments that eased the transformation of psychology into public policy in the area of Cold War military policy, the pages that follow offer a similar analysis in an important sphere of domestic politics and policy-making.

The World War II Dilemma

Fighting a global war against an oppressive racial ideology brought to the surface deep contradictions in U.S. society at home, sharply contrasting political ideals of equality and opportunity with the historic fact of slavery and the contemporary reality of segregation and discrimination. That black soldiers were called to fight racism in a segregated military and Japanese-Americans were forced by law into internment camps were only the most conspicuous manifestations of America's continuing racial dilemma.

Between 1941 and 1945 there were Americans who protested such terrible ironies, and the war reinvigorated old civil rights organizations and spurred the formation of new ones destined for a central role in the civil rights movement of the 1950s and 1960s. The Congress of Racial Equality (CORE), for example, was founded in 1942 by a small group of black and white activists who pioneered the tactic of civil disobedience that would become such a familiar feature of protest, especially during the 1960s. Many of them had been involved in the religious-pacifist Fellowship of Reconciliation and were disturbed enough by domestic racial injustice to declare themselves conscientious objectors, even during this "good war." For their part, government agencies operating in the area of race relations during the war years did what was possible to control angry outbursts of intergroup tension, thereby keeping civilian and military morale as high as possible. The tangible results ranged from the establishment of the Fair Employment Practices Commission to the desegregation of the military shortly after the war, long before the rest of U.S. society followed suit.

World war made an international issue out of U.S. race relations as well, and brought global attention as surely to the country's racial hypocrisy as it did to the nobility of those ideals, historically associated with the United States, that were being trampled in Europe. This international spotlight would remain an important factor in debates on U.S. race relations after World War II, as it would in the history of the civil rights movement, because the anticolonial revolutions that followed World War II throughout the Third World, along with the growing U.S. involvement in Indochina, underlined the chasm separating the stirring rhetoric of racial equality from the ugly reality. Racial justice and liberation, in fact, sometimes appeared as or even more likely in Southern Africa than it did in the U.S. South, a confusing and shameful development in light of many emerging states' initial identification with documents like the U.S. Declaration of Independence.

Ambitious studies of race relations and riots were conducted during the war years for the explicit purpose of morale-related policy-making. Many of these had lasting influences on the direction of postwar behavioral science. Gunnar Myrdal's *An American Dilemma: The Negro Problem and Modern Democracy,* however, funded by the Carnegie Foundation, was the landmark World War II–era study in this field.[2] Myrdal, a Swedish economist, politician, and architect of his country's welfare state during the 1930s, was chosen to head the project because its funders believed an outsider might be more objective on a subject so touchy with Americans.

Carnegie's choice of Myrdal was influenced by individuals who operated on the boundaries between intellectual life, business, and foundations. Beardsley Ruml, for example, treasurer of Macy's and a psychologist who had directed the Laura Spelman Rockefeller Memorial during the 1920s, was a vigorous proponent of behavioral research aimed at solving a multitude of social problems, a vision institutionalized in the 1923 founding of the Social Science Research Council. More than a decade later, Ruml was the first to suggest Myrdal's name. And Lawrence K. Frank, whose formulation of "society as the patient" had struck such resonant chords in World War II work on national character, heartily endorsed Myrdal for both his familiarity with psychiatry's clinical methods and his proven ability to transform theoretical expertise into public policy on a very grand scale.[3] Frank was influential in directing social and behavioral science from a series of high foundation posts: the Laura Spelman Rockefeller Memorial, the Spelman Memorial, the Rockefeller General Education Board (1923–1936), and the Josiah Macy Jr. Foundation (1936–1941). He was so dedicated to synthetic insights and practical applications in fields ranging from child guidance to psychosomatic medicine that Harvard's Henry Murray called him "the procreative Johnny Appleseed of the social sciences."[4]

Myrdal arrived in the United States to begin work on the project in the fall of 1938, long before U.S. entry into World War II. There is no doubt, however, that Myrdal's emotional and intellectual relationship to this massive research project on U.S. race relations was, from beginning to end, decisively shaped by its wartime context.[5] This was certainly the case for most, if not all, of the others who worked on the project. Samuel Stouffer, to mention but one, headed one of the most important military efforts to monitor and influence soldiers' attitudes, the army's Research Branch. During Myrdal's temporary return to Sweden in 1940–1941, he also directed the research for *An American Dilemma*.

Like Stouffer and other World War II–era social and behavioral scientists who have been discussed in earlier chapters, Myrdal considered World War II a golden opportunity to advance behavioral theories, practical applications, and patriotic service—all at the same time. Myrdal called *An American Dilemma* his "war work" and pointed out the relevance of the subject to global military conflict.[6] "In my investigation I have the world's problem in miniature: the whole aggression-complex and the circle of prejudices, violence and poverty. At the same time, the race problem is even greater than the war."[7] He also suggested that the proliferation of crises, abroad and at home, was the best argument for an accelerated program of government-supported research and rational state planning.

From the point of view of social science, this [World War II] means that social engineering will increasingly be demanded. Many things that for a long period have been predominantly a matter of individual adjustment will become more and more determined by political decision and public regulation. We are entering an era where fact-finding and scientific theories of causal relations will be seen as instrumental in planning controlled social change. The peace will bring nothing but problems, one mounting upon another, and consequently, new urgent tasks for social engineering. . . . To find the practical formulas for this never-ending reconstruction of society is the supreme task of social science.[8]

The final product, published as a 1,400-page book in 1944, was an emphatic and explicit statement of the World War II ethos. This was the same constellation of beliefs that had characterized military psychology and work on managing international diplomatic and military conflict. It included a commitment to applying behavioral theory and research to the amelioration of pressing social problems through the policy-making agencies of the state (Myrdal termed this "social engineering"); an optimistic belief that interdisciplinary research was essential to enlightened government policy; a rejection of value-free empiricism and methodological obsessions within behavioral science; and the embrace of liberal values such as racial equality and harmony.

Published in 1944, *An American Dilemma* was hailed as a monumental work of comprehensive, interdisciplinary social science. It dominated both popular and academic debates about U.S. race relations, and the status of black Americans, well into the 1960s. The incorporation of its ideas into public policy was rapid. The Truman administration's 1947 report *To Secure These Rights* was the first acknowledgment of federal responsibility for civil rights since Reconstruction; it served as ammunition for the solicitor general in cases before the Supreme Court. The report restated Myrdal's thesis, cited numerous wartime studies of intergroup conflict, and pointed to the psychological cost of racial inequality, "a kind of moral dry rot which eats away at the emotional and rational bases of democratic belief."[9]

The cost of prejudice cannot be computed in terms of markets, production, and expenditures. Perhaps the most expensive results are the least tangible ones. No nation can afford to have its component groups hostile toward one another without feeling the stress. People who live in a state of tension and suspicion cannot use their energy constructively. The frustrations of their restricted existence are translated into aggression against the dominant group. . . . It is not at all surprising that a people relegated to second-class citizenship should behave as second-class citizens. This is true, in varying degrees, of all our minorities. What we have lost in money, production, invention, citizenship, and leadership as the price for damaged, thwarted personalities—these are beyond estimate.[10]

Ironically, *An American Dilemma* was so successful, its reception so positive, that many scholars, especially from black universities, found it difficult to secure foundation funding for social scientific studies of race in the postwar era because the perception existed that the definitive statement had already been written. Even so, most, and probably all, of the postwar perspectives discussed in this chapter were indebted to its model, not infrequently through the direct involvement of their authors in this mammoth research effort.[11]

The experts whom Myrdal put to work writing reports, literature reviews, and monographs included a wide range of social scientists and an equally wide range of topics, from the structure of southern agricultural economics to the incidence of mental disorder within the black community. In *An American Dilemma*, psychological topics were sometimes addressed directly, as in sections on "Psychic Traits" and the " 'Peculiarities' of the Negro Culture and Personality." At other times, psychological concepts were imported into the analysis of historical and political developments from civil rights activism ("The Protest Motive and Negro Personality") to patterns of racial violence ("The Psychopathology of Lynching"). Myrdal's discussion of black community institutions anticipated much of the "social pathology" literature that would appear in the postwar years, suggesting that every facet of black culture, from family to personality, *"is a distorted development, or a pathological condition, of the general American culture."*[12]

Some of the material that was produced for Myrdal, in order to summarize current research in various fields, was also published separately in book form. *Characteristics of the American Negro*, edited by Columbia University social psychologist Otto Klineberg, originated in one such monograph.[13] Klineberg had dedicated his entire career to banishing racial explanations from psychology by gathering evidence that cultural determinants (educational opportunities, for instance) were responsible for social differences between groups.[14] Klineberg was also a proponent of the national character concept that informed so much wartime work on enemy morale.

Most important, the central thesis of *An American Dilemma* served to push future work and policy on matters of race in decidedly psychological directions.[15] Myrdal's main argument was that the dilemma of race for white Americans was fundamentally moral and psychological. *"The American Negro problem,"* he wrote, *"is a problem in the heart of the American. It is there that the interracial tension has its focus. It is there that the decisive struggle goes on. This is the central viewpoint of this treatise. . . . The moral struggle goes on within people and not only between them."*[16] Located safely in the United States throughout most of the war, Myrdal worried constantly about his native Sweden's delicate neutrality. Certain that the decisive European battle was for hearts and minds, he came to see U.S. race relations in similar terms: as an index of struggle within the U.S. psyche. Surely this justified a new approach to social engineering, one that would attempt to instill democracy "within" persons as well as rearrange social conditions "between them."

Myrdal's wife, Alva, also influenced his choice of a psychological approach. A brilliant intellectual, activist, and diplomat in her own right, Alva Myrdal's serious interests included child guidance, psychoanalysis, and behaviorism. Although she did not draft any of the material in *An American Dilemma,* the couple shared a long history of intellectual and political collaboration, neatly captured by the image of the desk at which they both worked, which had been designed so that they would face each other while writing.[17] Alva's role in shaping the book was no less important for being formally unacknowledged. She debated each and every point with her husband, just as she had when they were working as coauthors.[18] Her wartime activities, which included advising the OSS as well as making speeches for Swedish broadcast under OWI auspices, emphasized the strengths of U.S. democratic morale. She called for a program of spiritual and ideological preparedness much as Gordon Allport and Margaret Mead had. In her written work she drew sharp moral and psychological lines between democracy and fascism.[19]

This contrast became the centerpiece of *An American Dilemma.* At the core of Myrdal's analysis was the description of a unifying national conscience, a repository of principles like equality and democracy and a source of tremendous respect for individual dignity and the rule of law. Termed the "American Creed," it was destined eventually to triumph against the backwardness of racism and segregation, which Myrdal considered an extreme example of cultural lag. All ordinary white Americans, even the most bigoted, believed in the "American Creed," according to Myrdal, a fact which produced "a volcanic ground of doubt, disagreement, concern, and even anxiety—of moral tension and need for escape and defense."[20]

Racism and segregation, in other words, were covering up the terribly guilty conscience of the white majority. As alarming as such psychological defense mechanisms were—they provided the foundations upon which racially oppressive institutions were built and perpetuated—Myrdal was certain that psychology also held the key to undoing racism. In the final analysis, he predicted that white guilt would become the black community's best ally. Since the "American Creed" prohibited the thoroughgoing, official incorporation of racial subjugation into U.S. institutions, surely it could serve a more positive function and actually dissolve the caste barriers that comprised the American dilemma. An important task of postwar social engineering would therefore be the further investigation of white racial attitudes, so that appropriate reforms could be designed and implemented where they would count most: on the psychic interior.[21]

Theoretical Building Blocks: The Psychological Basis of Racial Identity and Prejudice

Unleashed by pressing wartime concerns about anti-Semitism and urban rioting, and stimulated by the appearance of *An American Dilemma,* a flood of studies about the psychology of racial identity and prejudice appeared during the years that followed World War II. Whereas the bulk of psychological research on racial issues prior to World War II had been limited to investigating—and frequently verifying—differences in intelligence, postwar researchers cast their net widely, grappling with new topics and promoting a decidedly environmentalist approach (culture over nature) that toppled conventional assumptions about the existence and permanence of white racial superiority. Otto Klineberg's "Tests of Negro Intelligence," a literature review written for Myrdal's project, set the postwar tone.[22] It directly repudiated biased mental testing experiments (beginning with Robert Yerkes's data from the World War I military), challenged the notion that psychological tests could even measure innate intelligence, emphasized education as a key social variable, and identified "rapport" (the racial relationship between investigator and subject) as a central methodological question.[23] It emphasized psychological experts' obligation to go beyond uncovering the facts, making the design and creation of a nonracist social environment the special responsibility of behavioral scientists.

While the scope of their ambitions widened, the subject of behavioral research on race narrowed in the postwar years. It was more concentrated on the antiblack attitudes of whites than it had been during the war or in earlier decades. Although a widely felt compulsion to make the Holocaust comprehensible was responsible for much new interest in the field, research on anti-Semitism eventually slowed to a trickle, and the attitudes of and toward a variety of other racial and ethnic minorities escaped the notice of most researchers until social movements among Native Americans and Mexican-Americans during the 1960s (to mention only two examples) made the point that the psychology of race was a diverse, even contradictory field. Between World War II and the mid-1960s, black Americans were the chief subjects for psychological investigators interested in race. Research efforts focused either on uncovering white prejudice or on measuring psychological damage and assessing social pathology among blacks. These trends were consistent with Myrdal's conclusions and illustrated the growing symbiosis between racial identity and blackness, and racial prejudice and whiteness.

The tight fit between investigations of race relations and investigations of black Americans only gained momentum in sympathy with the gathering forces of the civil rights movement during the 1950s. Although events like the 1955 Montgomery bus boycott shocked much of the country and grassroots activism among masses of poor black Americans broke the bubble of middle-class contentment and consensus, the movement demonstrated real concern with the issues of psychological freedom and healthy personality development that were, during the 1950s, becoming standard features of U.S. popular and consumer culture.[24] Until the early 1960s, movement leaders, none more so than Martin Luther King, Jr., united behind appeals to the moral conscience of white Americans. While they had taken some cues from Myrdal, their commitment to moral exhortation had other important roots: the traditions of the black church, for one.[25] The enduring impact of *An American Dilemma* was, finally, as indebted to the spiritual and psychological concerns of the movement as the movement was indebted to the work of liberal social and behavioral scientists.

Personality theory and research were increasingly foregrounded in studies of black and white racial psychology after 1945. A partial explanation, at least, can be found in the widespread influence of *The Authoritarian Personality,* which had done so much to convince so many that prejudice was determined by deep psychic structures and, conveniently, offered a practical way of measuring the personality's inclinations toward (or away from) authoritarianism. While authors of psychological perspectives on authoritarianism usually stressed the profound roots of prejudice (and the unconscious ones too, if they were psychoanalytically inclined), that did not mean they were pessimistic. Quite the contrary. If the World War II experience had shown them how social arrangements—childrearing patterns, for example—could have momentous, and sometimes lethal, consequences on the level of national character, it also taught them that bold social intervention could and should accomplish great things. They tended to believe, in Gunnar Myrdal's words, that "the social engineering of the coming epoch will be nothing but the drawing of practical conclusions from the teaching of social science that 'human nature' is changeable and that human deficiencies and unhappiness are, in large degree, preventable."[26]

Prejudice was one of those preventable "human deficiencies" because the personality was reachable, hence reformable, through social engineering. This was hopeful indeed, and echoes the confidence psychologists expressed about manipulating the personality in order to achieve any number of other public policy goals. Since the redistribution schemes of the New Deal were under sharp attack in Congress after the war, education was really the only kind of social engineering that appeared likely to succeed in a politically conservative era. Campaigns to change white attitudes by providing information about and establishing contact between otherwise segregated groups consequently became the core of a flourishing movement known as "intercultural education." These were considered the techniques most likely to eliminate ignorance and fear. The number of organizations working to reduce racial hostilities grew from approximately three hundred in 1945 to almost fourteen hundred five years later, a dramatic increase that brought the concept of prejudice into the lives of millions of Americans for the first time.[27]

If white attitudes were in need of change, black personalities were the proof that change was both mandatory and long overdue. Postwar studies that differed in other ways all agreed that racism did terrible damage to the developing self-image of the child and the mature personality of the adult. The case for psychological harm—to self, to gender identity, and to family relations—was the most effective argument that experts brought to public policy efforts in the postwar period. Gordon Allport's attempt to state this case listed the following as characteristic psychological traits in people who were targets of prejudice: ego defensiveness, insecurity, withdrawal and passivity, clowning, slyness and cunning, self-hatred, aggression, and neuroticism.[28] Minority group status and psychological victimization, in other words, were treated interchangeably, as the various examples described in this chapter will show.[29]

Black personalities, like white ones, could be tested and measured. Perhaps, psychological experts reasoned, the damage could be controlled or even reversed. This position was well intentioned and ambitious, based on the World War II doctrine that behavioral scientists had serious public obligations to enlighten policy on matters of social importance. Neither was it insignificant that many postwar intellectuals had liberal political sympathies, becoming strong supporters of the civil rights movement of the 1950s and 1960s. As early as 1934, the vast majority of "scholars in the field of racial differences" had been all but unanimous in their refusal to recognize racial superiority or inferiority as scientifically validated facts.[30] By 1948 a survey of hundreds of social psychologists, sociologists, and anthropologists found that their professional experience and scientific research had convinced almost all of them that legal segregation had detrimental psychological consequences for blacks and whites alike.[31] By the mid-1950s, support for desegregation and federal civil rights legislation had become fixtures of social scientific orthodoxy.[32]

SOCIAL CONTEXT AS THE SOURCE OF PREJUDICE

The environmentalist consensus that emerged from World War II generally prevented psychological experts from advocating crude versions of psychological reductionism and encouraged them to incorporate sociological variables into their discussions of the development of black personality or the causes of white racism. This trend was yet another instance of the abstract commitment to a comprehensive behavioral science approach during this period. It was, however, also the case that the institutional realities of race—the elaborate apparatus of legal segregation in particular, but also the legacy of slavery— were so clearly salient and so impossible to ignore. One consequence was a marked convergence between the perspectives of psychological and nonpsychological experts. Some psychologists started sounding like anthropologists, and there were many sociologists who eagerly incorporated the language of psychoanalysis into their research. Not infrequently, research involved interdisciplinary team efforts.

An example of this, which simultaneously illustrates the centrality of the war experience to postwar work in this field, was the research on racial attitudes jointly conducted by emigré psychoanalyst Bruno Bettelheim and sociologist Morris Janowitz. Both had been indelibly marked by the war. Bettelheim's first-person account of concentration camp survival had confirmed that German national character was severely disturbed and furthered the vision of postwar psychological reconstruction on a national and international scale. For his part, Janowitz had worked as an intelligence expert and "sykewarrior" during World War II. His postwar research on the political sociology of military institutions would make him a key player in Cold War behavioral science.

The Bettelheim and Janowitz study was conducted among 150 male veterans in Chicago and was published in 1950 as *Dynamics of Prejudice: A Psychological and Sociological Study of Veterans*.[33] The effort was funded by the Department of Scientific Research of the American Jewish Committee and was part of the famous "Studies in Prejudice" series that included *The Authoritarian Personality*, also published in 1950. Bettelheim's and Janowitz's own backgrounds, as well as the source of research support, undoubtedly informed their choice to study both anti-Semitic and antiblack attitudes, a choice of multiple subjects in the study of racism that would become rarer and rarer in later years, as noted above. Their use of veterans as subjects was quite deliberate. They believed that World War I veterans had been an important vehicle of anti-Semitism in Germany, and they were concerned that maladjusted U.S. veterans might contaminate the postwar domestic landscape with similar prejudices.

Their stated goal was very practical: to formulate a "diagnosis" and then "a cure for one of the major disorders in contemporary American society: ethnic discrimination and aggression."[34] This was perfectly consistent with the desire (so evident in Myrdal and in many other contemporary experts) to make behavioral expertise inform government policy and inspire social action. Bettelheim and Janowitz reached the following conclusions about the nature of prejudice. First, prejudice was an expression of fundamental hostility, anxiety, and aggression.[35] Second, it originated in past deprivations (especially in childhood) and anticipation of future deprivations (especially economic threats). Third, it resulted from an absence of ego strength and inadequately internalized controls, which caused aggression to be discharged indirectly and irrationally rather than directly and rationally. Fourth, prejudice was more likely to correlate with downward socioeconomic mobility than to be located on any particular rung on the ladder of the U.S. class structure.[36]

All of these themes were standard fare in postwar studies, with the exception of their final conclusion about class mobility, which rejected the assumption that working- and lower-class individuals were necessarily less tolerant than middle- or upper-class individuals. Equally standard was their view that such theoretical conclusions deserved direct translation into government action, even when that meant radical shifts in public policy. Bettelheim and Janowitz saw fit, for example, to call for programs of full employment, an adjusted annual wage, and a dramatic extension of social security benefits.[37] Reforms that would protect people from sliding downward, they argued, would do more than simply offer an economic safety net and insurance against poverty. They would actually insulate people from the emotional hazards and frustrations that resulted in explosions of racial intolerance and ethnic hatred.

In the end, like the experts who have been described in previous chapters, Bettelheim and Janowitz preferred prevention to even the most dramatic of social rearrangements. Because nothing appeared to have quite as much preventive potential as education, "tolerance propaganda" should begin at a very early age, guiding the release of aggression and hostility (which they assumed to be a fixed and universal feature of human psychology) in more socially acceptable directions than racial animosity.[38]

Rearranging personality structures through manipulating the process of parenting and childhood socialization held the greatest promise of all. One of the chief characteristics of the democratic personality was that it incorporated symbols of appropriate authority rather than left social control to the whims of external coercion. Bettelheim and Janowitz had contributed to the theoretical literature that implicated deep personality structures in the production of prejudice, making the manufacture of tolerant personalities the most effective route to eliminating such objectionable attitudes. The reform of childrearing was also attractive for practical reasons: it was more likely to succeed than the radical economic redistribution they had called for. "In any case," Bettelheim and Janowitz pointed out, "it seems simpler, and more feasible, to influence parental attitudes toward children, when compared with the efforts needed for assuring a stable economy free from the fear of war and unemployment."[39] David McClelland had reached similar conclusions in his quest to promote achievement-oriented personalities in developing countries as a method of heading off the violent upheavals that international inequalities and tensions were likely to produce. Mothers, everyone seemed to agree, were an appealing audience because they had an immediate impact on their young children. Moreover, they could be reached, counseled, and tested.

THE GENDER PROBLEM AND
THE BLACK FAMILY

Psychological and psychoanalytical approaches to containing and preventing prejudice leaned toward reforming childhood socialization practices, parenting patterns, and family relations of authority for reasons that were both theoretical and practical, as noted above. Given this bias, the deep concern with gender roles and their development that pervaded the postwar literature on race is not very surprising. Mothers, it was clear, were strategically positioned as cultural architects because families were personality factories. To the extent that the United States succeeded in overcoming its social problems, mothers could be credited. To the extent that social crises remained unresolved, or even worsened, mothers could be blamed. And they often were.[40]

In the case of the black family, however, the gender problem extended well beyond the willingness to identify mothers as agents of socialization and powerful sources of all sorts of attitudes—tolerant and prejudiced, achievement-oriented and fatalistic—in their (male) children. Beginning with E. Franklin Frazier's landmark study of the black family in 1939 and continuing with Abram Kardiner's and Lionel Ovesey's psychoanalytic theory and Mamie Clark's and Kenneth Clark's research in the 1950s and 1960s, "matriarchal" gender relations within the black family were analyzed and discussed as significant defects in their own right, immediate sources of personality and social problems (from warped self-esteem to juvenile delinquency to school failure), and appropriate targets for policy designed to improve race relations by enhancing masculinity and bolstering patriarchal authority.[41] By 1965 a report on the state of young urban criminals that appeared in the *New York Times Magazine* simply stated that "the welfare world of New York is a fatherless world" in which "people infect one another with the virus of failure."[42] The article continued:

The "unavailable mother"—unwed, indigent or surviving on welfare payments, socially deprived, economically deprived, intellectually deprived, often friendless, depressed, mentally disturbed, lonely, frightened, unable to supply the needs of a newborn child, already burdened with children she has rejected— the unavailable mother produces the unreachable child. This is the woman who needs the attention of the social welfare world. . . . We know that the damage to the [black] infant takes place long before he sees the dirt, the drunks, the drug addicts, the spilled garbage of the slum; the damage takes place when the unavailable mother brings her child home from the hospital and realizes she hates him for being alive.[43]

A good look at gender arrangements, in other words, showed just how deeply the black personality—especially the black male personality— had been damaged.

The emphasis on gender roles was accepted unquestioningly as an essential component of comprehensive research and policy at the time. It was, after all, completely consistent with broad cultural trends, including the widespread popularization of psychoanalysis (still associated with the scandalous yet scintillating taint of sexuality in popular perception), an avid ideology of domestic and dependent femininity in the period after 1945, and the growing interest in the history of black Americans that was sparked by the emergence of the civil rights movement. The antifeminist implications of this emphasis in the psychological literature, however, became infinitely clearer in retrospect, especially in the wake of policy controversies like the Moynihan Report and in the face of a new women's movement prepared to criticize and defy notions of essential differences between men and women, in the family and elsewhere.

E. Franklin Frazier's monumental work *The Negro Family in the United States* was a touchstone for virtually every subsequent addition to the postwar literature on the psychology of race. His thesis was that the history of marriage, family, and childrearing in the black community had been determined by external and impersonal forces since the Civil War, especially the long march of industrial capitalism. Personal and even cultural factors were, in comparison, relatively insignificant. Considering this fundamentally nonpsychological argument, which consistently attributed causal status to economic over psychological processes, Frazier's prominence in the postwar psychological literature seems puzzling. Perhaps his subject matter—the family—was such familiar territory to psychological experts, and so readily identified with them, that theorists and researchers in psychology were encouraged to claim at least Frazier's starting point as their own: that the black family was a Pandora's box that had been opened.

As a historical sociologist, Frazier emphasized long-term, macrosocial and macroeconomic developments like slavery, mass migration, and urbanization as the hinges upon which the black family's history, and future, turned. He countered the theory that the black family's peculiarities revealed its African heritage by arguing that black Americans were shaped by exactly the same historical forces as white Americans and by describing how the passage from Africa and the experience of the first several generations of black American slaves had wiped out any possibility of African cultural holdover. Frazier considered slavery to be among the most important factors shaping black families, even long after emancipation, and insisted that many contemporary features of black gender, sexual, and parenting relations could be traced to its harsh consequences.

In particular, slavery interfered with what Frazier understood to be the fundamental facts of gender, sexuality, and family economy. Women were naturally inclined toward monogamous and long-lasting emotional bonds. Male sexuality was naturally wild and terribly undiscriminating. The purpose of stable marriages and families was to tame men so that women could accomplish the necessary feats of reproduction and childrearing while being supported and protected by dependable breadwinners. Because becoming dependable breadwinners conflicted with male nature, however, incentives were required. Frazier saw those incentives in capitalist economic relations. For Frazier, ensuring patriarchal black families required an economic guarantee: that black men would be as free as white men to accumulate property, sell labor power, and otherwise function within the marketplace. In other words, Frazier assumed that capitalist patriarchy was the aspiration that made the most sense for black Americans at the moment, even while he criticized it as a historically specific social arrangement and called, at various points in his career, for nationalist and socialist alternatives.[44]

These assumptions were so profound and widespread as to merit little contemporary attention, but they defined the nature of the black family's problem nonetheless. Slavery had interfered with patriarchy by making it impossible for black men to be breadwinning husbands and devoted fathers. This had forced black women into unnatural roles of family authority and replaced the primary family relationship—between a monogamous heterosexual couple—with unusually strong mother-child bonds and little, if any, dependence on the regular economic or emotional contribution of men. Although Frazier described some slaves as heroic in their efforts to maintain loving and loyal families in spite of the inhumanities of servitude, slavery ultimately stripped men of their male prerogatives and put "motherhood in bondage."[45]

New challenges faced black families in the twentieth century, when mass migrations out of the rural South and the increasing pace of urbanization turned gender nonconformity into the kiss of death for black Americans. Frazier argued that the matriarchal family structure had been relatively benign in the rural isolation of Reconstruction, really only a matter of the "simple folkways and mores" of black peasants. Once in contact with the strong patriarchal norms of the dominant white culture, however, the black community started to disintegrate at its core. The "city of destruction" freed the corrosive forces of selfish individualism among black Americans and the result was a proliferation of "roving men and homeless women," newly equipped to destroy any hope of stable families and communities through exploitative and violent behavior.[46]

Frazier concluded that only by altering the course of those macrosocial forces that had so destabilized the black family was there any hope of encouraging more stable (i.e., more patriarchal) families in the future. Including black men in the ranks of industrial workers might be one worthwhile avenue to pursue because gains in economic power and security offered a solid basis for increasing men's power in the family and therefore the viability of the black family itself. In the long run, only the complete integration of black men into the economic life of the United States, and equal opportunities to rise or fall there, would do.

In Frazier's analysis, constructive solutions for the black family were as deeply gendered as the definition of its problems had been in the first place. In *The Negro Family in the United States,* economics and demography typically preceded psychology. For example, Frazier never suggested (as some others did later) that black families were disorganized because their men were plagued by syndromes of low self-esteem. Offering men an opportunity (such as therapy or another method of individual treatment) to sort out their feelings about themselves or their parents was not considered. Employment was. Postwar research and policy directed at black Americans consistently emphasized male employment, although in some cases psychological failures were implicated as causes where Frazier had seen them merely as painful consequences. As we shall see in the next chapter, policy planners during the 1960s hoped that getting black men into good jobs with decent pay would correct the matriarchal deviations of the black family by allowing men to function as reliable breadwinners and domestic authority figures. Supporting masculinity was, in other words, a preferred method of tackling poverty, illegitimacy, inadequate housing, poor academic achievement, and a host of other community problems, including rioting.

Abram Kardiner and Lionel Ovesey confirmed, with clinical data, the gender- and family-related damages that had been cataloged by Frazier on a sociological level. For Kardiner and Ovesey, however, personality was the primary source of institutional reform and psychology the crucible of social change. In spite of their significant departure from the direction of causation in Frazier's work, Kardiner and Ovesey's *The*

Mark of Oppression was deeply indebted to Frazier's study. They took to heart Frazier's cue about the black family and its destruction under the conditions of slavery. They incorporated his concern with the disorganizing clash between black matriarchy and the patriarchal norms of the majority white society. Finally, they showed how far explanations of U.S. racial identity and race relations had moved in psychological directions by the early 1950s, and how serious psychological experts were about seeing their theories turned into practical plans for "social engineering" in the area of race.[47]

Based on twenty-five clinical case studies and the results of their subjects' Rorschach and TAT test results, psychiatrists Abram Kardiner and Lionel Ovesey developed a psychoanalytic perspective on black personality development that displayed sensitivity to sociological factors, like class differences, which had been illuminated in the research of Bettelheim and Janowitz. They treated class differences extensively. They explained why, for example, black middle-class families were more likely to achieve patriarchal norms than their poor counterparts. Nevertheless, the case studies led them to view caste (i.e., racial barriers), rather than class, as the unifying, psychological reality that left a "mark of oppression" on all black Americans, male and female, poor and well off, rural and urban.

Kardiner and Ovesey understood gender and family as the most important vehicles through which the mark of oppression was reproduced. As critics of the looseness and superficiality with which World War II–era experts like Margaret Mead and Geoffrey Gorer had treated patterns of childrearing in their profiles of national character, Kardiner and Ovesey offered psychoanalytic principles as the preferred alternative. They substituted new terms ("basic personality" instead of "national character"), elevated the status of unconscious motivation, and applied the theory to black Americans instead of German or Japanese citizens. The result was a psychoanalytic variation on the environmental theme offered by Otto Klineberg and others during the war years. What had previously appeared to be racial differences in personality were not. If black American personality seemed different, it was a product of shared social circumstances, especially the pressures of institutionalized racism. Discrimination had constructed differences. Aggressive, antidiscriminatory policies could therefore eliminate them.

Among the social variables that produced black personality were black men's difficulties finding and keeping jobs and black women's tendency to "hold the purse-strings" and conduct their affairs independently of men.[48] Psychologically speaking, Kardiner and Ovesey noted, this type of family pattern bred disrespect, emotionally and sexually unsatisfying relationships, an unnatural dominance of "loveless [female] tyrants" exerting harsh discipline over children, and an epidemic of social disorganization that flowed outward from the domestic sphere.[49]

In addition to being impoverished, discriminated against, and ghettoized, black Americans led wretched inner lives. Hostility and aggression were, according to the projective tests administered by Kardiner and Ovesey, the most typical traits in their subjects' personalities. Considering the immense frustrations caste threw in the way of the release of black feelings, was psychological damage really such a shocking result? Instead of expressing their rage directly, it was channeled inward against the self, producing oceans of self-loathing that caused more and less severe instances of emotional incapacity. "The Negro," they concluded, "has no possible basis for a healthy self-esteem and every incentive for self-hatred."[50]

Kardiner and Ovesey were straightforward in their expression of sympathy for the plight of black Americans and direct about their antiracist intentions: "Obviously, Negro self-esteem cannot be retrieved, nor Negro self-hatred destroyed, as long as the status is quo. What is needed by the Negro is not education, but *re-integration*. It is the white man who requires the education. *There is only one way that the products of oppression can be dissolved, and that is to stop the oppression.*"[51] "Stopping the oppression" and liberating the black personality clearly involved changing the attitudes of white Americans. It did not, however, involve any reassessment of what normal gender roles or families were like in spite of the fact that Kardiner and Ovesey considered the pressure to conform to white ideals "a slow but cumulative and fatal psychological poison."[52]

It was Kenneth Clark who put the final touches on the equation between the pathology of the ghetto and the destructive "cycle of family instability" in his famous 1965 study of Harlem, *Dark Ghetto*.[53] Making the same gendered assumptions that Frazier, Kardiner, and Ovesey had made before him, Clark wrote that, because of slavery's legacy, "psychologically, the Negro male could not support his normal desire for dominance."[54] Nothing about this statement—in particular its contention that male domination was "normal"—required any explanation. As we have seen, the disabilities of black masculinity had been a constant refrain since before World War II. Attacking dismal rates of black male un- and underemployment was, for Clark, simply the obvious way to correct what was wrong with the black family.

Kenneth Clark, before and during the 1960s, was always sensitive to the many and complex aspects of ghetto life. In his concern for issues of self-image and identity, he never lost sight of the realities of institutional power, and he had only sharp words for proposals that did not include the redistribution of material wealth and political authority. His view that matriarchy had created a "distorted masculine image," damaging men far more than women, however, reinforced the rationale that men were the primary concern of psychological theory.[55] Women's psychological state was considered only secondarily, and usually as a by-product of the male experience.

By the 1960s, policy's impact on male self-esteem would become a significant and official indicator of government's success or failure, even when social welfare programs specifically targeted women and children. That self-esteem became such an important factor in policy calculations, and in such a gendered fashion, can be attributed to the persuasiveness of the postwar experts reviewed in this chapter, the progress of the civil rights movement, and a social context hospitable to turning psychology into public policy for a variety of reasons, several of which are considered below.

Policy and the Racial Politics of Self-Esteem

The truly decisive evidence of personality damage, presented accessibly and in a way that finally moved a tiny group of white Americans in a position to make a big difference, was offered by psychologists Kenneth and Mamie Clark in the early 1950s. Kenneth Clark had been a research assistant on Myrdal's project after earning his Ph.D. from Columbia University in 1940. He later moved on to found (with Mamie Clark) the Northside Center for Child Development and Harlem Youth Opportunities Unlimited, a prototypical community action program sponsored by the War on Poverty. And he was awarded numerous professional honors, including terms as president of SPSSI (in 1959) and the APA (in 1970). Mamie Clark had explored racial identification and self-esteem in all of her research since the 1930s; her masters thesis, awarded by Howard University in 1939, was titled "The Development of Consciousness of Self in Negro Pre-School Children." Two of their joint studies of black children's self-images, published in 1947 and 1950, probably did more to push theoretical treatments of self-esteem into the light of public policy than any other postwar work in the field of the psychology of race.[56] Their effectiveness was due to the Clarks' ability to personalize the consequences of racism in a vulnerable group—children—and to do so in the name of empirical, scientific research.

Their experiment consisted of giving some 160 children, ages five to seven, a coloring test. Children were asked to color objects like leaves and oranges (in order to ensure that they had a realistic sense of color relationships) before they were asked to "color this little boy (or girl) the color that you are."[57] What the Clarks found was that the children consistently portrayed themselves as distinctly lighter than the actual color of their own skin. Further, the gap between realistic and unrealistic coloring was largest among children whose skin was darkest.

Such marked preferences for light skin made the awareness of racial differences among young children, and the acceptance of racist valuations of those differences, impossible to ignore. The Clarks' accomplishment was to demonstrate that racial hierarchies were not simply a matter of abstract injustice in a society dedicated to the principle of equality, but rather a question of immediate, subjective experience: how people felt about themselves. It is hard to imagine anything that could have made this point more effectively than children's sense of who they were, damaged at such a young age. The Clarks concluded, "It is clear that the Negro child, by the age of five is aware of the fact that to be colored in contemporary American society is a mark of inferior status. . . . This apparently introduces a fundamental conflict at the very foundations of the ego structure."[58] Because the Clarks shared in the reforming zeal of their colleagues, they underlined quite explicitly the practical policy implications of their experiment.

These results seem most significant from the point of view of what is involved in the development of a positive, constructive program for more wholesome education of Negro children in the realities of race in the American culture. They would seem to point strongly to the need for a definite mental hygiene and educational program that would relieve children of the tremendous burden of feelings of inadequacy and inferiority which seem to become integrated into the very structure of the personality as it is developing.[59]

In fact, the Clarks' findings did encourage fresh strategies among civil rights advocates. Having reiterated that racial distinctions were morally and politically unjustifiable for decades, to little effect, activists turned to emphasizing how racism destroyed the developing personality of the black child, an argument destined to have tremendous success.

Even before the Clarks' work became widely known, the toll exacted by "damaged, thwarted personalities" was being seriously considered in important policy documents such as the Truman administration's *To Secure These Rights,* as we have already seen. But the Clarks wasted little time in bringing their work to policy-makers' attention. In 1950 Kenneth Clark attended the Midcentury White House Conference on Children and Youth and, as a result, a chapter on "The Effects of Prejudice and Discrimination" was included in the conference's official fact-finding report.[60] Little experimental literature existed in the early 1950s—other than the Clarks' own work—to prove that racism and segregation caused personality damage, so the chapter relied heavily on theoretical perspectives like *The Mark of Oppression* and *The Authoritarian Personality.* In spite of the scarcity of empirical research on the psychological consequences of racism, Clark suggested that an overwhelming consensus existed: psychologists knew that supporters of segregation were psychologically maladjusted and that segregation harmed the youthful and adult psyches of minority and majority group members by disturbing individuals' sense of reality and filling them with inner conflict and guilt. Clark's conclusion restated the environmental emphasis of postwar expertise, and added to it: "It is a mistake to believe that personality patterns found among Negroes indicate inherent racial tendencies. . . . As minority-group children learn the inferior status to which they are assigned and observe that they are usually segregated and isolated from the more privileged members of their society, they react with deep feelings of inferiority and with a sense of personal humiliation. Many of them become confused about their own personal worth."[61] He articulated a deep concern for the personal self-esteem of children that would prove eminently effective and influential on the level of law and public policy, as legal history would soon show.

BROWN V. BOARD OF EDUCATION: PERSONALITY DAMAGE AS A CONSTITUTIONAL ISSUE

Brown v. Board of Education, the 1954 case that overturned school segregation, and certainly one of the most important of the twentieth century, was also the first to place psychological arguments at the very heart of a Supreme Court decision. The Court's fondness for social science dated back to *Muller v. Oregon* in 1908, a case that deployed data collected by social researchers and settlement house workers to argue that the constitutionality of protective legislation limiting women's work hours should be upheld. (It was.) But *Brown* went further. It illustrated how effectively psychological perspectives on the development of racial identity, and the damage done to it by prejudice, could penetrate the public sphere as constitutional issues.

In 1951 Robert Carter and Thurgood Marshall of the NAACP Legal Defense Fund put out the call for social-scientific help in the state-level cases that preceded *Brown*. Marshall explained what was considered a chancy and extremely unorthodox legal strategy as follows.

I told the staff that we had to try this case [*Briggs v. Elliott* in South Carolina] just like any other one in which you would try to prove damages to your client. If your car ran over my client, you'd have to pay up, and my function as an attorney would be to put experts on the stand to testify to how much damage was done. We needed exactly that kind of evidence in the school cases. When Bob Carter came to me with Ken Clark's doll test, I thought it was a promising way of showing injury to these segregated youngsters.[62]

Organized by Kenneth Clark, psychologists did indeed attempt to prove damages in *Briggs v. Elliott* and the other cases that led up to *Brown*.[63] Consider, for example, Clark's own role in *Briggs*. He administered a psychological test (very similar to the coloring test described above, but employing dolls instead) to the children in whose name the suit had been brought. Then he offered the following testimony to the court, in which many of the themes of postwar psychological research and theory on racial identity can be found.

I have reached the conclusion that discrimination, prejudice and segregation have definitely detrimental effects on the personality development of the Negro child. The essence of this detrimental effect is a confusion in the child's concept of his own self-esteem—basic feelings of inferiority, conflict, confusion in the self-image, resentment, hostility towards himself, hostility towards whites . . . [or] a desire to resolve his basic conflict by sometimes escaping or withdrawing.[64]

Arguments such as these did not significantly sway the judges involved, who sided with the state, but the NAACP legal team did not abandon the strategy of showing damage. When the *Brown* case was being prepared, members of the Society for the Psychological Study of Social Issues (SPSSI) were asked to write a summary statement of the supportive testimony that social and behavioral scientists had offered in all the school segregation cases to that point. SPSSI formed a committee in order to comply with this request and eventually the statement was signed by thirty-two behavioral scientists and filed as an appendix to the appellants' brief in *Brown*.[65] The signatories comprised an honor roll of World War II–era experts; many had pioneered work on the effects of prejudice on wartime morale. They included Gordon Allport, Hadley Cantril, Kenneth Clark, Mamie Clark, Else Frenkel-Brunswik, Otto Klineberg, Alfred McClung Lee, R. Nevitt Sanford, and Samuel Stouffer.

The statement itself was titled "The Effects of Segregation and the Consequences of Desegregation: A Social Science Statement."[66] Admitting that the question of personality was located "on the frontiers of scientific knowledge," it nevertheless made a forceful case that "segregation, prejudices and discriminations, and their social concomitants potentially damage the personality of all children—the children of the majority group in a somewhat different way than the more obviously damaged children of the minority group."[67] The damage was done through a process that destroyed self-esteem (in the case of black children) and generated guilt feelings, unrealistic rationalizations, and uncritical idealization of authority (in the case of white children). The authors had been influenced by Myrdal's faith in the "American Creed" as well as by their own work in the field of race relations. While the statement was being prepared, Gordon Allport wrote to Kenneth Clark,

The one point that I hope will be made to the Supreme Court is this: People really know that segregation is un-American, even the masses in the South know it. They also have prejudices. This mental conflict is acute. . . . But, let the backbone come from the Supreme Court, and it will strengthen the moral backbone of those who now live in conflict. The decision will be accepted with only a flurry of anger, and soon subside. People do accept legislation that fortifies their inner conscience.[68]

The finished product made empirical evidence of psychological damage the focal point of the argument. Because twisted psychology could have such negative social consequences—riots and racial violence were the events most frequently cited—immediate action should be taken to desegregate schools. The statement tried to convince its audience that behavioral science, during World War II and in the years since, pointed inevitably toward this goal. It tried to reassure the Supreme Court justices that desegregation would proceed smoothly and nonviolently provided their decision was firm and united.

The statement was a huge success. The *Brown* decision argued that racial segregation in educational institutions had to be eliminated, not only because it violated the civil rights of black schoolchildren, but because it damaged the integrity of their psychological development. The opinion respectfully noted the contemporary insights of "psychological knowledge."

To separate them [black students] from others of similar age and qualifications solely because of their race generates a feeling of inferiority as to their status in the community that may affect their hearts and minds in a way unlikely ever to be undone. . . . A sense of inferiority affects the motivation of a child to learn. . . . Whatever may have been the extent of psychological knowledge at the time of *Plessy v. Ferguson,* this finding is amply supported by modern authority.[69]

Kenneth Clark's work and his impact on the Midcentury White House Conference were prominently noted in *Brown's* eleventh footnote, along with references to the work of Gunnar Myrdal, E. Franklin Frazier, and others.[70] The decision produced an unprecedented level of concerted debate about the role of such evidence and the apparent legal power of psychology's "modern authority." The decision's opponents reacted by, on the one hand, mounting McCarthyite attacks on the "socialism" of the social sciences and, on the other, by enlisting social science on the side of segregation.[71]

Brown was celebrated as well as scrutinized. Throughout the social scientific community, the decision was greeted with an outpouring of jubilation. In 1954 Senator McCarthy was censured by the Senate and the temperature of domestic anticommunism was finally starting to drop. Most experts probably thought the camouflage that racist reactionaries had found in anti-Communist rhetoric was transparent, and no real threat to their status. Apparently unconcerned, many psychologists continued to work with the NAACP, and other civil rights organizations, putting themselves at the service of legal and political strategies designed to thwart resistance to *Brown* throughout the South.[72] As had been the case during World War II, doing the right thing and advancing the causes of science and professionalization were so tightly enmeshed as to be inseparable. Experts associated with the *Brown* statement exulted in the view that the 1954 decision had been "a landmark in the development and practical significance of the social sciences."[73]

Subsequent developments would cause some of them to rethink this view. White resistance to *Brown,* which materialized immediately and sometimes took shocking and violent forms, made it plain that predictions (such as Allport's, quoted above) of orderly compliance with the "American Creed" had been overstated, to put it mildly. Desegregation efforts during the fifteen years following *Brown* offered no convincing data that the tide of psychological damage had been stemmed, either among whites or blacks. If anything, self-esteem became an increasingly public issue as time passed. After the civil rights movement's turn toward nationalism in the mid-1960s, black activists expressed great hostility toward arguments about the psychological damage wrought by segregation. Instead of repeating old maxims about the disorganizing effects of slavery, they dusted off histories of slave resistance, emphasized the cohesiveness of black families, and celebrated the resilience of black culture over time. Infused with pride, many black Americans were no longer willing to serve as exemplars of psychological debility and, as often as not, turned the tables completely. White Americans were now accused of being "sick" or "pathological."

It was after this sea change in the movement that "The Effects of Segregation and the Consequences of Desegregation" came under fire for being a premature, naive, and unrealistic contribution to public policy. The self-esteem of southern black children was, it turned out in subsequent studies, *higher* than their northern counterparts. This finding, which prompted a cautious reassessment of segregation among advocates of integration, was not lost on advocates of black separatism like Malcolm X. In defense, Stuart Cook, one of the authors of the original statement, reasserted his belief that "we must neither underestimate the potential value of social science knowledge to significant societal decisions nor overlook our obligation to make that knowledge available when and where it is needed."[74] This did not really answer the question, however, of how an allegedly scientific consensus had failed rather miserably to predict the course of desegregation and stand the test of close examination. If psychological recommendations for repairing personality damage had turned out not to be scientifically valid after all, what claims could psychological experts possibly make to influence future public policy?[75]

THE MOYNIHAN REPORT AND THE
QUESTION OF BLACK MASCULINITY

By the 1960s, concepts of self-image, self-esteem, and self-identity were commonplace in discussions of race. Pushed along by *Brown*, these themes were also advanced through the popularization of psychotherapy and the publication of a virtual flood of behavioral and clinical studies. Best-sellers like Robert Lindner's *The Fifty-Minute*

Hour (1955), a collection of psychoanalytic case studies, presented prejudice as, above all, an irrational psychological condition.[76] Explorations of racial psychology also found institutional support in new federal bureaucracies—especially the National Institute of Mental Health (NIMH)—established after World War II to support civilian behavioral research and promote mental health in the U.S. citizenry. Self-esteem was a concern that migrated from the theoretical terrain of personality development to take up residence in policy debates about black unemployment, poverty, and education in the New Frontier and the Great Society. And self-esteem typically encompassed the emphasis on gender and family issues that was so central to the work of postwar experts.[77]

The Negro Family: The Case for National Action, popularly known as the Moynihan Report, was probably the most controversial example of postwar behavioral research transformed into public policy, and its ideas have proven remarkably tenacious, outlasting the debate over social policy in the 1960s by several decades.[78] Daniel Patrick Moynihan was a young political scientist who went to Washington after Kennedy's election and upon receipt of his Ph.D. from the Fletcher School of Law and Diplomacy at Tufts University. Moynihan was representative of the new breed of "social scientist-politico" who populated military and civilian bureaucracies in the 1950s and 1960s, promoting the idea that social and behavioral science should play a much larger role in government: diagnosing problems, suggesting solutions, evaluating programs.[79]

In March 1963 Secretary of Labor W. Willard Wirtz asked Moynihan to head the new Labor Department Office of Policy Planning and Research, and Moynihan became the youngest assistant secretary in the federal government. A year earlier, Moynihan had been involved in important policy debates among psychological experts as a member of the Kennedy administration's Interagency Task Force on Mental Health. That experience exposed him to the single most important innovation in the mental health field at the time—the replacement of institutionalized treatment of mentally ill individuals with community programs to prevent and contain emotional maladjustments, a radical shift in policy that served to implicate all individuals (not just crazy ones) in the quest for psychological health. In his new job at the Department of Labor, Moynihan read Selective Service Director General Lewis Hershey's 1963 report on the dismal mental and physical state of the U.S. military, a report so shockingly reminiscent of World War II military statistics (a 50 percent rejection rate, for example) that Moynihan decided to do something about it. The something was a novel mixture of welfare and warfare. "The thought of using the Selective Service System as a national screening device came instantly to mind. To link social issues to military preparedness was, well, an idea I called Theodore C. Sorensen at the White House [about]. He liked it." [80]

Moynihan went on to contribute to a task force report, *One-Third of a Nation: A Report on Young Men Found Unqualified for Military Service,* which emphasized how effective the military might be as a social welfare program—preparing young men for jobs and offering them opportunities for education and training. Several years later, telltale traces of these recommendations showed up in Project 100,000, a Defense Department program that lowered military admissions standards with the goal of uplifting the "subterranean poor" and curing them, in the words of Secretary of Defense Robert McNamara, of the "idleness, ignorance, and apathy" that marked their lives. [81] It was not coincidental that Moynihan found inspiration and reason for hope in exactly such products of military psychology. They linked warfare to welfare, neatly illustrating an important, recurring theme in the history of psychology: the reverberation of wartime developments in distinctly nonmilitary policy spheres. In the short run, *One-Third of a Nation* functioned as a blueprint for the War on Poverty and as a model for Moynihan's next project: a report on the black family.

In writing the report, Moynihan undoubtedly drew on his own recent experience analyzing the problems of a gender-specific subject—young men unfit to serve in the military. He also drew, freely and consciously, on the insights that E. Franklin Frazier, Kenneth Clark, and others had offered into the gender dynamics of the black family. [82] The Moynihan Report thus reproduced many of the features of the postwar literature reviewed in this chapter. It blamed slavery for lowering self-esteem and increasing dependence, accepted patriarchy as normal and natural, identified black families as matriarchal and deviant, and called for the employment of responsible male breadwinners as the solution to a host of social problems in the black community. It is worth quoting the Moynihan Report at some length in order to illustrate the centrality of gender in the link Moynihan forged between welfare and warfare.

At the heart of the deterioration of the fabric of Negro society is the deterioration of the Negro family. . . . In essence, the Negro community has been forced into a matriarchal structure which, because it is so out of line with the rest of American society, seriously retards the progress of the group as a whole, and imposes a crushing burden on the Negro male and, in consequence, on a great

many Negro women as well. . . . Given the strains of the disorganized and ma-
trifocal family life in which so many Negro youth come of age, the Armed
Forces are a dramatic and desperately needed change: a world away from
women, a world run by strong men of unquestioned authority, where discipline, if harsh, is nonetheless orderly and predictable, and where rewards, if
limited, are granted on the basis of performance. The theme of a current Army
recruiting message states it as clearly as can be: "In the U.S. Army you get to
know what it means to feel like a man."[83]

Very little, if anything, that Moynihan wrote about the black family was
new, although he did pepper the report with more copious charts,
graphs, and statistical correlations than had previous writers. Moynihan
did call the black family damaged and disorganized, but hadn't Frazier
pointed out the terribly destructive consequences of slavery and urbanization twenty-five years earlier? Moynihan used the term "tangle of
pathology," but hadn't Kenneth Clark articulated a comprehensive approach to the "social pathology" of the black ghetto which had been
hinted at in *An American Dilemma?* Moynihan pointed out that the
family was a useful target of government intervention, but hadn't one
of the most appealing things about the family always been that it
seemed particularly susceptible to conscious change by outside agents?

The charges of racism that swirled around the public debate over the
Moynihan Report were especially ironic because Moynihan allowed
race far less autonomy as a factor in historical development than had
the other experts—Myrdal, Frazier, and colleagues—on whose work
the report depended. Based on his own recent study of the history of
various immigrant groups, Moynihan believed that nothing about the
black family's problems was specifically "racial."[84] One journalist even
summarized Moynihan's view as follows: "Paddy and Sambo are the
same people."[85] Like other desperately poor individuals, blacks living
in poverty needed decent jobs, educational opportunities, and the hope
of attaining some measure of security in life. What Moynihan wanted
to do was turn a ghettoized black underclass into an urban industrial
working class, hence providing the basis for an interracial economic
alliance, much as Frazier had suggested. His vision of a stable black
working class did not imply that voting rights or desegregation, the
core demands of the civil rights movement, should be rejected. Indeed,
Moynihan supported these aims. But he insisted that guaranteeing the
symbols of legal equality, while doing little to promote concrete opportunities for economic participation, was merely a way of repeating the

tragic errors of Reconstruction. Black people's basic problems, according to Moynihan, were about class, not color.[86]

Gender was implicated in either case, however. The destruction undisciplined men would wreak on a community—any community—was as evident in the histories of Irish and Italian immigrants as it was in black urban ghettos during the 1960s. Moynihan warned,

> There is one unmistakable lesson in American history: a community that allows a large number of young men to grow up in broken families, dominated by women, never acquiring any stable relationship to male authority, never acquiring any set of rational expectations about the future—that community asks for and gets chaos. Crime, violence, unrest, disorder—most particularly the furious, unrestrained lashing out at the whole social structure—that is only to be expected; it is very near to inevitable. And it is richly deserved.[87]

He had personal reasons to know. Moynihan had grown up in the poor, heavily Irish Hell's Kitchen neighborhood in Manhattan, the product of a female-headed family. During his teenage years, he worked in his mother's bar, where he and his brother frequently intervened in rough disputes between customers and got a firsthand look at the anarchy of unchecked masculinity.

The assumptions that Moynihan and his contemporaries made about gender were deep and consequential, but they went largely unquestioned at the time. There were, however, a few exceptions: women who insisted, in 1965, that female "domination" was a perverse male fantasy and that reinforcing male supremacy in the domestic sphere simply scapegoated women (like Moynihan's own mother) who were forced to earn an independent living in order to support their children. One such critic was Mary Keyserling, director of the Women's Bureau in the Department of Labor. She tried to expose and counter Moynihan's gendered assumptions about economic roles in the family by arguing that wage-earning black women were not a problem, that "our underutilization as a Nation of the great national resource which is our womanpower" is an "item of unfinished business."[88] Only men like Moynihan, Keyserling tersely pointed out, were saying that black women were "over-employed." Abandoning the workforce to become dependent wives and mothers was no solution, in Keyserling's view, because the obstacles facing black women were at least as great in the case of earning decent wages as they were in the case of finding reliable male breadwinners. She calmly noted that improving the employment status of men was a noble goal, but it should not come at women's expense. Black women, after all, were concentrated in the lowest-paid, most dead-end jobs. They needed economic advocacy as much, if not more, than others.

These were exactly the criticisms that would become standard feminist arguments just a few years later. In 1965, however, Keyserling's was a rather solitary voice. Most women active in the civil rights movement, understandably enough, would not have welcomed a choice between endorsing black women's economic dependence or abandoning the code of racial solidarity, and until the appearance of an autonomous women's movement several years later, these appeared to be the only choices. Nevertheless, research on black women's organizations has shown that the controversy over the Moynihan Report served to push many black women toward feminist consciousness several years prior to women's liberation.[89] It was only a matter of time, of course, before a chorus of feminist denunciations of Moynihan would appear.[90]

In 1965 though, the deafening silence that greeted Moynihan's gendered ideology helps to explain why Moynihan did not seem to realize, either while writing his report or afterwards, that gender, sexuality, and the family would be such hot button issues and the unacknowledged source of a great deal of the controversy. Alarm over families, and over what occurred within them—between men and women, parents and children—doubtlessly reminded the report's critics of the self-improvement approaches of psychological experts because the explosion of postwar clinical work was tied so firmly to personal difficulties and domestic adjustments. Because the women's movement had not yet turned issues like sex-role socialization into questions with legitimate public standing, it was no wonder that so many of Moynihan's critics reacted to his emphasis on sex roles and family skeptically, as a dangerous detour into the private sphere. They worried that, whatever Moynihan's intentions, policy-makers would respond to the report by endorsing counseling or therapeutic treatment because they viewed black Americans' real problem as "ego inadequacy" or "deviance" rather than an absence of equal opportunities.

After decades of performing as walking, talking examples of racism's psychological destruction, black Americans had had enough. Part of the national spasm over the Moynihan Report was surely due to the fact that it appeared during a moment of critical transition in the civil rights movement. Black Americans were no longer willing to wait patiently as experts observed their behavior, peered into their psyches, and monitored levels of social pathology in their communities. William Ryan, a psychologist and one of the most prominent of Moynihan's critics, articulated the anxiety that psychology would displace politics, and bluntly caricatured psychological experts as follows.

Writers about the Negro family dwell on the issue of sexual identification as if they had just stepped off the boat from Vienna forty years ago. They are more kosher than a rabbi, holier than a pope, more psychoanalytic than Freud himself. It sometimes appears that they worry more about the resolution of Negro Oedipus complexes than they do about black men getting decent jobs. . . . They see psychological functions, particularly sex-role induction, as far more prominent than other more important functions of the family.[91]

For many civil rights advocates who criticized the Moynihan Report, "family disorganization," "social pathology," and "the culture of poverty" were code terms. They intimated that since black Americans' problems were primarily personal and psychological, institutional racism and discrimination could be deemphasized or even eliminated as a terrain of government action. Many mainstream civil rights activists shared Moynihan's belief in the naturalness and superiority of patriarchal gender and family arrangements; even black power advocates frequently recommended a heavy dose of patriarchy as the best antidote to the poison that whites had forced on the black community. Almost all, however, emphatically objected to the notion that matriarchal families were the source of black Americans' problems. The vast majority of black families were still headed by men and, in any case, the causal relationship went in the other direction. Racial oppression produced social pathology rather than vice versa. To put the family under a microscope threatened to undermine the very foundations of the Great Society by "blaming the victim."[92]

Moynihan's goal all along had been to design a universal system of social provision to care for Americans at the bottom of the class ladder, regardless of race. His choice to promote family policy as a means to that end had more to do with practical, political considerations than anything else.[93] Families, it has been pointed out, were relatively straightforward targets of intervention and measurement. Further, family policy had a chance of winning support in a Congress dominated by a conservative majority of Republicans and southern Democrats, whereas general social welfare measures, presented as such, did not. Moynihan understood this very clearly. In later years, the War on Poverty's abandonment of class issues (for Moynihan, these were represented by jobs programs and income guarantees) and its embrace of community action programs and ideas like "maximum feasible participation" (which Moynihan rejected as an example of importing useless social-scientific concepts into government programs) was, for Moynihan, proof positive that he, and the War on Poverty, had failed.[94] Convinced that race had been overemphasized, Moynihan wrote a memo in 1970, as an advisor to the Nixon White House, urging the federal government to treat the circumstances of black Americans with "benign neglect."[95]

In 1965, when Moynihan began work on the black family report, his purpose was, quite simply, "to win the attention of those in power."[96] He wrote it "for an audience of a dozen, at most two dozen, men who in their brief authority had become accustomed to . . . making large decisions on the basis of manifestly inadequate information."[97] It was never intended to go beyond a tiny circle of high-level policy-makers, although it eventually did. Between March 1965, when the report was initially approved and printed, and July 1965, no more than eighty numbered copies had been distributed in the Department of Labor and the White House.[98] What opened the report to a firestorm of public criticism, and what made Moynihan a household name after July, was largely a fluke of timing. The Watts riot exploded on August 11, just two days after *Newsweek* had summarized the Moynihan Report. Watts was the most destructive riot in the United States since the 1943 riot in Detroit. Demand for copies of the report skyrocketed immediately; seventy thousand copies of it were eventually printed.[99]

This coincidence of timing generated a widespread perception that Moynihan's "tangle of pathology" was the Johnson administration's official explanation for the violence, arson, looting, and death that had appeared with such ferocity in Watts. The establishment news media certainly adopted this view. The *Wall Street Journal* announced that "Family Life Breakdown in Negro Slums Sows Seeds of Violence— Husbandless Homes Spawn Young Hoodlums, Impede Reforms, Sociologists Say"; the *Washington Post* reported that "the Los Angeles riots reinforce the President's feeling of the urgent need to help restore Negro families' stability."[100] Moynihan encouraged such conclusions by pointing out the dramatic rates of female-headed families and illegitimacy in Watts, and by offering his customary warnings about the dangers of unchecked masculinity. In a 1967 article, Moynihan reflected that "Watts made the report a public issue, and gave it a name."[101]

Watts also made him into an instant riot expert. Embittered by the avalanche of protest over the report, Moynihan left Washington to head the Massachusetts Institute of Technology/Harvard Joint Center for Urban Studies, where he spent the next several years designing a plan of expert first aid for the country's crisis-ridden cities. Central to his new public authority was the real desperation of federal, state, and local administrators to find anyone who might help. During the Detroit riots, in the summer of 1967, Moynihan was urgently called to that city by a mayor in need of advice. That fall, *Life* produced the following solemn headline: "A Troubled Nation Turns to Pat Moynihan." [102]

Even more than timing, the fear and angry reaction that ghetto riots provoked in white Americans seemed to vindicate Moynihan's perspective as well as erase any remaining hopes that the conscience of white America could be moved in antiracist directions. Deep reserves of feeling that black men were especially disordered in attitude and uncontrollable in behavior had been fortified by experts' emphasis on irresponsible, nonmarital sexuality, illegitimacy, and the burgeoning literature on black "matriarchy." These reserves were obviously much easier to tap than the "American Creed," if the latter even existed at all. Hadn't Moynihan at least offered a plausible explanation for this moment of crisis? What was rioting, after all, if not convincing proof that black families had twisted the masculinity of their sons to the point of extreme irrationality and violence?

Moynihan's solution, too, rang true for many. The transformation from marginal, defiant loners to integrated and responsible breadwinners would be produced by upward mobility, a move which required money but whose essence lay in wholesale changes of attitude and loyalty. As one Moynihan observer put it, "In the lower class, they don't take care of property; in the working class they do. In the lower class, the men don't work; in the working class, they're trying to get overtime. It's the difference between the rioter and the cop." [103] Just how large policy-makers thought this attitudinal gap was, and how profoundly implicated in it were postwar investigations of the sources of prejudice among whites and personality damage and gender nonconformity among blacks, can be seen in the work of the Kerner Commission, the federal government's major response to ghetto riots after 1965.

8

The Kerner Commission
and the Experts

By the mid-1960s the momentum of the civil rights movement and mounting evidence that white Americans' racial attitudes were changing with excruciating slowness had significantly altered the landscape of domestic policy-making. The intractability of white resistance and the rising tide of black anger began to undermine hope that the federal government could actually eliminate racism and poverty through dramatically expanded social welfare programs like the War on Poverty, a disheartening situation that made psychological explanations more appealing than ever. The seriousness of prejudice, personality damage, and a laundry list of social pathologies had been absorbed by policy-makers, who were convinced by landmarks like *Brown* that such maladies were profoundly consequential and therefore deserving of government attention and action, the sooner the better. And the legacy of World War II lessons about intergroup conflict and rioting—that irrational racial fears were dangerous threats to U.S. democratic morale and unity—also endured.

At the same time, evidence of psychological disorder was found to be politically expedient in new ways. The ugliness of psychic deformation offered a justification for the Great Society that was more durable, or at least fresher, than such tired old abstractions as equality and social justice. By the late 1960s, when urban riots became commonplace, Johnson's political career was in ruins and his administration's major commitments were under attack from an antiwar movement on the Left and right-wing forces increasingly alarmed about the Great Society's economic and racial reforms.

It was in such a hostile environment that a policy framework steeped in the language of psychology proved its real usefulness. Psychological arguments helped to insulate large-scale social welfare programs and shield them from political opposition by conferring upon them a new identity as "mass treatment programs" for the range of serious social problems that resulted from unchecked poverty and racism.[1] Not coincidentally, the association between mental well-being and social welfare also rebounded in new levels of psychological authority and ever-increasing government attention to psychological issues. "Freedom from mental illness has taken on a social importance somewhat equivalent to freedom from want or freedom from fear," pointed out mental health policy-makers in the 1950s, "and the right to mental health is achieving a status like that of the right to work."[2] One clear expression of the government's deepening commitment came in the form of new federal legislation and funding for clinical professions and institutions. Another, however, was the integration of psychological issues into the guts of urban, employment, and civil rights policy. The Economic Opportunity Act of 1964, for example, provided $800 million to investigate the "psychological, social and health deficits" that impaired the lives of the poor and exacted such high social costs from the society at large.

This chapter documents one case—the Kerner Commission—in which psychological expertise was employed to analyze the causes of a significant domestic problem—urban riots—and inform federal approaches to racial conflict, prejudice, and discrimination.

Beginning with the Watts riot in 1965, which coincided with the release of the controversial Moynihan Report on the black family, psychological experts relied on the major themes of postwar research and theory to explain violent civil disturbance in particular as well as the emotional turbulence of race relations in general. Riots, which brought terrible damage and death to hundreds of inner cities during the second half of the decade, also made the lessons of Cold War psychology appear as applicable in the South Bronx as they were in Southeast Asia. Even before Watts, Kenneth Clark (whose research had decisively informed the *Brown* decision and an array of Great Society programs, and whose ideas would directly influence the Kerner Commission two years later) had called for a "relevant social psychology." He identified Project Camelot, and its objective of predicting and controlling Third

World revolution, as a pertinent model for the study of riots and distur-bances at home.[3]

The National Advisory Commission on Civil Disorders (popularly known by the name of its chairman, Governor Otto Kerner of Illinois) was the federal government's major response to urban rioting during the 1960s. Because its formation was so widely publicized and its final report so widely read, it was also the best known of all the 1960s presi-dential "social issue" commissions.[4] On 27 July 1967, with the shock of the Detroit riot not even a week old, President Johnson addressed the nation solemnly, reassuring citizens that the federal government would respond swiftly and forcefully to the crisis. He announced the formation of a riot commission at the outset, but stressed that the first responsibility of officials was "not to analyze, but to end disorder."[5] Two days later, on July 29, the eleven-member body was created by executive order (fig. 15). Johnson charged it with "a tall order": investi-gating what had happened during the riots, why they had happened, and how to prevent them from ever happening again.[6]

The Kerner Commission case illustrates how indispensable psycho-logical perspectives had become in key domestic policy-making arenas. Just as Project Camelot had shown psychology's usefulness in foreign and military policy directed at Cold War counterinsurgency, the history of the Kerner Commission underlines the bond between psychological authority and government pronouncements on race and urban crisis. During its short existence, the Kerner Commission employed an army of experts to conduct large-scale research on the rioting process, invited testimony on a range of urban and racial afflictions, and received piles of unsolicited advice about what exactly had gone wrong in U.S. cities. Psychological perspectives were evident in each of these, and other, areas of the commission's work. This chapter describes the efforts of researchers to understand the causes of riots and the motivations of rioters, analyzes the relationship of experts to commission politics, and assesses the degree to which psychology informed the commission's conclusions and policy recommendations. The experience of the psy-chological experts who worked for the Kerner Commission underlines how continuous and familiar certain themes were in psychology's post-war public history. It also illuminates distinctive and changing aspects of this history in the late 1960s.

When Johnson announced the Kerner Commission's formation, his foreign and domestic policies were both already on the defensive. The pressures he faced made Johnson deny at the very outset that the com-

Figure 15. President Johnson signing the executive order that created the
National Advisory Commission on Civil Disorders (the Kerner
Commission) on 29 July 1967. Photo: Yaichi R. Okamoto,
Lyndon Baynes Johnson Library Collections.

mission's function was to prop up his administration's approach to urban policy and civil rights. He instructed the commissioners to follow
the truth freely, wherever it led. "We are looking to you, not to approve
our own notions, but to guide us and to guide the country through a
thicket of tension, conflicting evidence and extreme opinion."[7]

Seven months later, when the final report was issued, the Johnson
presidency was on the rocks. Although the commission had produced
a report that was compatible with the administration's political orientation—especially in its total disregard for how the Vietnam War was
choking the Great Society—Johnson ignored the commission's warning that extraordinary levels of new funding and political will were required to tackle poverty, racism, and urban despair. In January 1968
the beginning of the Tet Offensive had shaken Johnson's confidence
by making the depth and hopelessness of U.S. military involvement in
Vietnam clearer to the public than it had previously been. By March 1,
when the report was issued, Johnson's career was finished. On March
31 he announced his decision not to run for reelection.

The Kerner Commission may have been unusual in attempting to complete its task at the moment of ultimate political misfortune for the president who had appointed it. In its use of social and behavioral expertise, however, it was entirely typical, another in the series of postwar episodes in which science's good reputation bolstered the legitimacy of a high-level policy-making process that would otherwise have appeared thoroughly contaminated by political considerations.

To say that psychological experts were politically useful to the Kerner Commission, however, is not to say that they were mere pawns in the hands of the state, hoodwinked into supporting Johnson administration aims against their will. In a pattern very similar to Project Camelot, and World War II work before that, the Kerner Commission's experts made genuine efforts to advance scientific understanding of important public questions and fortify their own authority at the same time. They considered advising the president an important opportunity to act on their social and professional responsibilities, while pursuing the ongoing project of infusing the operations of government with psychological enlightenment. Robert Shellow, who directed the commission's research effort, reflected, "I don't believe it is enough for us to make passive offerings to decision-makers. I believe we should try to get closer to those in power and engage them actively. . . . How else can the social scientist hope to have an impact unless he is close enough to the policymakers to interpret to them his theories, to explain to them his findings and translate their implications into action?"[8]

By 1967, with scandals like Camelot behind them, experts were not at all sure how to answer such questions. Policy applications no longer appeared as unequaled opportunities for public service, scientific advance, and professional growth. Instead, they promised so many headaches and such constant compromise that researchers were often quite conscious of their contradictory position in the policy-making process and of the likelihood that their work would be used as window dressing for a policy based more on political considerations than scientific evidence. Shellow himself recalled that "a number of well-known scholars had been approached for the job [of directing the commission's research] but had declined, believing (I learned later) that the commission was destined to white-wash the crisis facing America, and was therefore too risky an enterprise with which to be associated."[9] Although he understandably defended the ultimate value of the research effort, even Shellow readily admitted that the mandate President Johnson gave to the experts was an impossible task—a social scientist's nightmare come true. . . . There was more of a preoccupation with building an argument that would hold water than with developing a reliable picture of what happened. Despite these severe constraints on the normally deliberate scientific approach, I believe that my staff and I made certain critical contributions which substantially affected the course of the commission's deliberations and its final product.[10]

Not all observers agreed with Shellow's positive assessment that the results were worth the effort. Michael Lipsky, coauthor of a book about riot commissions published several years after the Kerner Commission, concluded that its research effort had allowed the Kerner Commission "to demand changes and advocate radical reforms without calling names. . . . The problem is identified and solutions are proposed. But no one is responsible, and no one is blamed, or urged to act, as an individual, any differently."[11]

Notwithstanding such differences of opinion, psychological expertise was a standard ingredient in high-level domestic policy-making by the late 1960s. A look at the Kerner Commission's internal operations not only verifies their existence and importance but reveals the process by which almost three decades of psychological research and theory about race and rioting expanded the reach of government by defining new areas of human experience—the subjective experience of self, in particular—as appropriate and legitimate spheres of public policy. Helped along by the dramatically increased status and visibility of psychological experts in nonpolicy spheres, especially popular culture and clinical work, the Kerner Commission's experts employed all the intellectual tools that had been placed at their disposal by their World War II and Cold War predecessors: the importance of frustration and aggression, the irrationality and prejudice of public attitudes and opinion, the personality damage done to black Americans, the tradition of crowd psychology. But the commission's context in urban rioting and in the polarized social climate of the late 1960s also served to alter some of those tools, or at least shed new light on their past (and future) political importance.

THE MOVEMENT CONTEXT

Just as research on the psychology of prejudice and racial identity had been spurred on by the direction of the civil rights movement in the 1950s and early 1960s, so the work of the Kerner Commission took place in the context of that movement's turn toward black nationalism, a transition that made psychology, if anything, more prominent in the demands of activists, and certainly in analyses of them. Black power was understood, by critics and supporters alike, as a bid for self-worth and psychological independence. Alarmed observers like Erik Erikson called the departure from integrationist goals proof that black activists were moving in the direction of psychological despair, away from the "essential wholeness of experience" and toward a rigid and intolerant "totalistic world view."[12] Supporters of black nationalism expressed themselves in equally psychological terms, pointing to the analogy between black power and adolescent rebellion against "bad parents" or suggesting that long-suppressed black rage required constructive expression—in separatist forms—if the tragedy of black self-hatred and identity crisis were ever to be overcome.[13] Alvin Poussaint, for example, restated the salience of personality damage to black rage in a *New York Times Magazine* article, "A Negro Psychiatrist Explains the Negro Psyche," published just as the Kerner Commission was getting under way.[14]

Psychological analysis of this sort was not simply imposed by hostile outsiders. Civil rights activists, nationalists and integrationists alike, adopted the language and tactics of psychology as their own. A concern with black Americans' "degenerating sense of 'nobodiness'" had long been apparent in the thought of Martin Luther King, Jr., whose appeals to conscience described the terrible anguish of witnessing "ominous clouds of inferiority beginning to form" in the "little mental sky" of black children, and seeing them "begin to distort [the] personality by developing an unconscious bitterness toward white people."[15]

As they turned toward black nationalism in the mid-1960s, members of the Student Nonviolent Coordinating Committee also advanced a sharply psychological understanding that the U.S. system of race relations was permeated by inescapable, subconscious images linking blackness with evil and savagery.[16] Eldridge Cleaver, the Black Panther party's minister of information, later used the vocabulary of humanistic psychology when he titled an important essay on his personal and political development, "On Becoming."[17] And Price Cobbs, a black psychiatrist, conducted interracial encounter groups, called "Racial Confrontation as a Transcendental Experience," out of the San Francisco office of Esalen (a countercultural hub) for two years, until the effort disintegrated in a cloud of angry recriminations in 1969.[18]

Civil rights activists also tried to make psychology's insights serve their explanations of rioting and what to do about it. Black nationalist

Reverend Albert Cleage, of Detroit's Central United Church, pointed to the devastation of rioting in order to counter Moynihan's condemnation of black psychology: "His study tries to show that the black community is sick; but the black community is not as sick as the white community."[19] And a young Jesse Jackson, lieutenant to Martin Luther King and director of Chicago's Operation Breadbasket, wrote the following to Mayor Richard Daley in August 1967:

Riots are illegal, but make no mistake about it, they are not illegitimate. . . . For the victims of slum life, military suppression redirects their frustration and sets akindle a flame of passion and hate. This bottled up fear and stifled search for justice drives men to spontaneously combust and come up screaming irrationally. . . . The debate is not over the pursuit [of liberty] but over the right to be a man.[20]

The Kerner Commission Is Appointed

The Kerner Commission was established one week after the start of the Detroit riot, in which forty-three persons were killed, more than seventy-two hundred arrests were made, and approximately $40 million worth of damage was done to property. Eleven commissioners were personally named by President Johnson. As a body, the commission was weighted sharply toward the ranks of elected national officials and exuded an aura of moderation. Liberals of both parties predominated; neither southern Democrats nor black nationalists were represented; organized labor, big business, established civil rights organizations, and police departments each had some voice, and the commission included one female and two black Americans.[21] The commission's executive director, also designated by Johnson himself, was David Ginsburg, a Washington attorney. Not a single one of the commissioners was a social or behavioral scientist (although Fred Harris could certainly claim to be an advocate), and Ginsburg's credentials were obviously political rather than scientific, leading one blunt critic to dismiss him as Johnson's "chief political cadre."[22] This insensitive oversight elicited pointed criticism from the intellectual community and resulted, in the short run, in the appointment of psychiatrist W. Walter Menninger (one of William Menninger's sons) to a subsequent presidential commission.[23]

The seven months between 27 July 1967 and 1 March 1968, when the commission's final report was released, were crammed with work for commissioners, their staff, and outside consultants. The deadline for a final report, which was unrealistic in the first place, was pushed up by six months, making the already hectic pace of work almost unbearable, and even calling its quality into question. Almost no one involved believed that seven months was adequate time to methodically review all the facts about urban rioting, let alone produce a scientific explanation of its causes. But they were animated by a shared sense of terrible crisis and by the tremendous power and responsibility of telling the federal government how to cope.

In spite of the mad rush, the final report became an instant bestseller, with the result that its famous conclusion—"Our nation is moving toward two societies, one black, one white—separate and unequal"—was widely discussed even if the Johnson administration was too far gone to do anything about it.[24] The Bantam paperback press run of thirty thousand sold out in three days and another 1.6 million copies were sold between March and June 1968.[25] Marlon Brando, in a personal effort to raise the racial consciousness of his fellow citizens, even did a dramatic reading from the report on a late-night television talk show.[26]

The Experts and Their Work

The Kerner Commission's assistant deputy director for research, whose job it was to coordinate the commission's massive and hurried research program, was Robert Shellow, a social psychologist previously on the staff of the National Institute of Mental Health (NIMH). He came to the commission highly recommended by American Psychological Association Executive Officer Arthur Brayfield, who wasted no time in making staff suggestions to Fred Harris and expressing the view that the commission "must take a hard look at the psychological aspects of the problems."[27] Because of the pressure to issue an authoritative statement at the earliest possible moment, not all of the commission's research was completed in time to be included in the 1 March 1968 final report. A volume of supplemental research studies was published later on that year.[28]

The commission's data gathering and analyzing effort was vast. The in-house social science staff, although important, consisted of only a handful of researchers outside of Shellow himself, and not all of them worked full-time for the commission. David Boesel of Cornell and Louis Goldberg of Johns Hopkins were both Ph.D. candidates at the time, in political science and sociology, respectively; Gary Marx, a sociologist on the faculty of Harvard's Department of Social Relations, came to Washington three days a week; Elliot Liebow, an NIMH administrator and anthropologist, scraped together one day each week to work for the commission. Regular consultants included sociologists Ralph Turner (of the University of California, Los Angeles) and Neil Smelser (of the University of California, Berkeley).[29]

The in-house staff was tiny in part for political reasons. By 1967 many prominent social and behavioral scientists had become critics of Johnson's foreign policy, and experts with antiwar records were simply eliminated from consideration for spots on the commission staff. Administrators assumed that such individuals would be security risks.[30] There were practical reasons for the small size of the research staff as well. Lining up academic experts on very short notice proved to be a formidable logistical challenge. Few were willing to alter their immediate plans, take on a huge research project, and work at a hectic pace. A combination of politics and convenience thus determined that the number of experts engaged in contract research for the commission would far outstrip the numbers of in-house researchers. No background checks were required for contract work and it could be managed far more flexibly, without, for example, requiring that experts move to Washington, D.C. Although the vast majority of the commission's experts were not submitted to any official litmus test, the Vietnam War, a very sore spot with the administration, was not discussed anywhere in the report. Considering the war's rapid depletion of Great Society funds, this astonishing gap is difficult to explain except as a result of executive pressure.[31]

The work done by the small in-house research team was supplemented by field teams of six, who were sent out to gather information in twenty-three cities in an effort to compile accurate chronologies of urban disorders.[32] In all, team members interviewed twelve hundred people—from mayors to rioters—pored over official documents like police and fire department logs, took scores of witness depositions, and lined up confidential testimonials for the commission. Robert Shellow estimated that the final city-by-city analyses were based on 15,200 pages of raw data, excluding the teams' own voluminous research reports.[33]

Contract research that was paid for directly by the commission involved hundreds of thousands of dollars and the kinds of quasi-independent research organizations that proliferated after World War II in the rush to meet the government's new demand for expert help. For example, the University of Michigan's Survey Research Center, a branch of the Institute for Social Research, which had been a stepchild of World War II–era military expertise, handled one of the commission's supplementary studies on racial attitudes, which involved more than five thousand written surveys and personal interviews in fifteen cities.[34] Other significant pieces of research of immediate use to the Kerner Commission fell under the funding auspices of more permanent, and generously endowed, federal bureaucracies. The NIMH, for instance, cooperated fully with the Kerner Commission. It was already sponsoring more than fifty studies (at a price tag of $4 million) on "mass violence."[35] These included efforts to design accurate riot predictors by the Lemberg Center for the Study of Violence at Brandeis University and a large-scale psychiatric study in which forty NIMH staffers investigated the salience of masculinity in differences between rioters and nonrioters in Detroit.[36]

In addition to research done for, or in cooperation with, the Kerner Commission, Robert Shellow made it his business to collect and review the most recent behavioral and clinical theories. His meetings with consultants and advisors reviewed work being done by a range of academic experts on social conflict, racial attitudes, and rioting. The commission considered the feasibility of predicting individual dissatisfaction and developing phase models of revolutionary upheaval, efforts remarkably reminiscent of Project Camelot and of World War II work before that.[37] Among the consultants to the Kerner Commission were Neil Smelser (who had also been one of Project Camelot's advisors) and Ralph Turner, both important figures in the translation of crowd psychology into the sociological literature on "collective behavior." Along more clinical lines, the commission's psychiatric consultants (including Robert Coles and Charles Pinderhughes) set out to translate social problems directly into the language of psychiatry. They argued that "pathogenic" social structure should be subject to medical treatment, analyzed riots as an element in group identity, and wrote reports on various aspects of adolescent male psychology.[38]

The major accomplishment of the in-house research staff was a lengthy and controversial document, titled "The Harvest of American Racism." It concluded, in no uncertain terms, that the desperate state of U.S. cities was the fault of white racist institutions and that white—

not black—Americans were destroying the American dream. Greatly increased taxes and a multibillion-dollar assault on urban slums, far beyond anything envisioned by the Great Society, were the only possible means of preventing further riots. A shocked David Ginsburg reacted to this radical criticism of the Johnson record by firing Shellow and his immediate colleagues en masse in December 1967, along with 120 other staff members. A funding shortfall, caused by the Vietnam War, was the official reason offered for this dramatic move.[39]

In the short run, the housecleaning confirmed some experts' suspicions that they were useful only as "social science input," obediently serving a process that had been politically determined by others from the start.[40] Robert Shellow, for example, reported the following brief conversation with one of his staff superiors as evidence that the commission appreciated expertise more for its appearance than its substance.

My statement: You realize that it's going to be awfully difficult to mount a study of riots using social science methodology and compress it into four or five months.

And the reply: That's not important . . . what's important is that you've got that Ph.D.[41]

Even some experts deeply invested in the Great Society bureaucracies that "Harvest" had criticized as Band-Aid approaches reacted sharply to Ginsburg's purge of the commission staff. Research psychologist Thomas Tomlinson, of the Office of Economic Opportunity, for example, accused the commission of abandoning any and all approaches that were likely to provoke presidential wrath (either because they cost too much or pointed the finger at Vietnam), even if they were the only way to prevent future rioting.[42] Not surprisingly, Ginsburg lambasted such charges as "irresponsible and totally inaccurate."[43] Whatever the truth in this particular case, the roller-coaster relationship between expertise and public policy, which made experts feel giddy with power one moment and weak and expendable the next, was not new. It was a significant pattern in the history of policy-oriented psychological experts since 1940, as we have already seen.

MASCULINE SELF-ESTEEM REVISITED

All of the psychological experts affiliated with Kerner Commission research were steeped in the postwar literature on prejudice and personality damage, and their explorations of riot causation were marked by the characteristic themes of psychological work on race since 1945: social pathology, wounded masculinity, matriarchal families, and problematic self-esteem. Also very conspicuous in their work was the language of clinical practice. The conceptual basis of medicine and psychiatry—health, sickness, and therapeutic treatment—infused policy debates about the status of U.S. cities and the motivations of rioters, corresponding to the increased status and visibility of postwar clinical work, as well as to the innovative trends of community psychology and psychiatry. What follows is a discussion of the significance of these particular patterns, unmistakable and influential, in the testimony that was offered and the research that was done by and for the Kerner Commission.

John Gardner, the secretary of Health, Education and Welfare (HEW), was one of the very first witnesses to appear before the commission. A member of the cabinet, Gardner was the highest-ranking psychologist in the federal government. He brought to his job a perspective that had been shaped by the kinds of wartime experiences described in earlier chapters. During World War II, Gardner worked for the FCC's Foreign Broadcast Monitoring (later Intelligence) Service and the OSS. After the war, he became president of the Carnegie Corporation and consultant to government officials in the Department of Defense, the Agency for International Development, and the White House. In 1965 he brought to his job as HEW secretary a particular commitment to organizational psychology and a strong desire to champion individual potential and development in the face of mass institutions.[44]

On 1 August 1967 Gardner explained to the Kerner Commission that rioting was caused by poverty and discrimination, but he also lamented "the social evils of the ghetto," including crime, disease, and family breakdown.[45] Clearly, social pathology and gender nonconformity were on the minds of policy-makers—even cabinet secretaries—as reasons why black ghetto residents remained poor and trapped in inner cities.

Social psychologist Kenneth Clark also spoke to the commission early in its deliberations, on 13 September 1967. His pessimistic testimony made such a deep impression that a ninety-three-word excerpt was prominently featured in the conclusion of the commission's final report, a statement longer than the text of the conclusion itself.[46] Calling himself a "social diagnostician," Clark warned the commission that "the patient is suffering from a very severe and viral disease," not necessarily terminal, but with "symptoms which suggest a grave diagnosis, a serious disorder."[47] His testimony continued, full of analogies between riots and infectious disease, and he railed against the government for its unwillingness to take action beyond convening official investigating bodies. He even expressed something like regret over his own appearance before the commission. There was, he emphasized, little more to learn about rioting and human hopelessness. Psychological experts and policy-makers alike understood exactly what sort of "treatment" was needed to cure cities and turn them into environments conducive to human development rather than violence. There was, however, simply not the political will to do so; allegiance to the "American Creed" had been exposed as a myth. He even compared urban ghettos to German concentration camps and white Americans to World War II Germans who had done nothing to stop, or even acknowledge, the Holocaust while it was occurring. Finally and sadly, he pointed out that too much anxiety swirled around damage done to property. Rioting's logic was psychological, and the price to be paid for it was similarly psychological. In comparison, material destruction was trivial.

Elliot Liebow, an NIMH administrator who worked on the in-house research staff of the commission one day a week, also offered testimonial advice to the commissioners. Trained as an anthropologist, Liebow was the author of *Tally's Corner* (1967), a widely read and discussed ethnography centering on a small group of ghetto residents in Washington, D.C., who, not coincidentally, fit the accepted profile of rioters: black, male, adolescent or relatively young, under- or unemployed.[48] Liebow's fieldwork started as part of an NIMH study of childrearing among low-income families in the early 1960s, but it soon evolved into a sympathetic portrait of the men's "streetcorner society." His analysis of their emotionally impoverished lives emphasized the family; the bulk of the book described hostility between men and women and the estrangement of fathers from their children. Liebow traced the men's numerous disappointments to the gap between what the dominant culture expected them to be—reliable providers and loyal husbands—and what the men actually were—members of a "streetcorner society," an inferior friendship network in which a system of games and "public fictions" eased the pain of their failures with women and children.

In *Tally's Corner,* Liebow reiterated the view, prevalent in the postwar literature, that poor black communities were not independent subcultures, and therefore not exhibits for cultural pluralism. They were pathological variations on the white norm. The men's inability to find decent jobs and live up to the role of patriarchal breadwinner sentenced them to lifetimes of low self-esteem and dependence on an all-male version of sociability that was both shallow and pitiful. "The streetcorner," Liebow concluded, "is, among other things, a sanctuary for those who can no longer endure the experience or prospect of failure."[49] The policy implications of this point of view directly recalled the earlier work of Frazier, Myrdal, and Clark in suggesting that male wages were the key to assisting black families and communities. For Liebow, public policy had gone too far in the direction of making women and children the subjects of government social programs. Men deserved more attention.

Liebow's testimony before the commission, on 9 November 1967, began with just such a plea for the repair of masculine self-esteem. "At the heart of our family system is this husband-wife relationship and the husband is also the father. In our society we define a man as someone who is the breadwinner of the family, who supports the family and he is the head of it, and that is what it is to be a man in American society. . . . There are a lot of lower class Negro males who are not men in this sense, and why aren't they men? Why aren't they heads of families and supporters of these families? And I think that one of the things—one of the reasons that he is not, quite apart now from opportunity and quite apart from the very real conditions that he faces, is how he sees himself."[50] Liebow suggested that rioting was not the logical endpoint in a downward spiral of self-esteem but rather the behavioral response of men who were attempting to assert some form of power and control, who rejected a sense of self as lazy, incompetent, and irresponsible. This trend toward interpreting rioting in quasi-sympathetic terms—as a bid to recoup emotional or political self-esteem—was new in the late 1960s. Eventually, it helped to transform psychological and social theories of collective behavior dramatically. Beginning in the late 1960s, social movements of all sorts became far more sympathetic objects of social-scientific analysis. Theorists began turning away from the fundamentals of the crowd psychology tradition (collective action as a sort of group temper tantrum or psychotic episode), considering instead the possibility that social collectivities might act purposefully and rationally, on the basis of rising expectations and increasing material resources.

THE CITY AS PATIENT

Matthew Dumont was another NIMH administrator who offered the commission his advice in the form of a report on the positive, community-building roles of ghetto gangs, and he suggested that policy-makers would be wise to consider their potential to act as counterrioting forces.[51] His semioptimistic interpretation of civil disturbance was similar to Liebow's: "One may have to conclude that the rioter is a more mentally healthy person than the non-rioter. He is a person who still believes that action means something, that things can improve."[52] Dumont, however, did not make his special concern with black men, or masculinity, explicit. He did not really have to. Rioters, or most of them anyway, were male; therefore, his subjects were male. That rioting was a gender-specific behavior was an assumption made by most, if not all, of the Kerner Commission experts. Rarely was it considered necessary in reports or recommendations to point out that rioters were male.[53] In this sense, Dumont was not at all exceptional.

As an advocate of community psychiatry, Dumont represented one of the most innovative and significant developments in the postwar clinical professions (see chapter 9).[54] By the late 1960s, popular perception no longer tied clinicians to their historic charges: the institutionalized insane. Perfectly normal (if painfully maladjusted) individuals had become appropriate participants in clinical exchanges, and healing complex social environments had been gathered under the mantle of clinicians' ever-expanding list of therapeutic chores. Even the names of their respective movements made it evident that psychiatrists and psychologists were prepared and eager to bring diagnosis and treatment to communities at large. The working definition of community psychiatry typically covered all aspects of life, supplementing the profession's conventional commitment to clinical work with hefty chunks of research, education, urban planning, government administration, community organization, and political activism.[55] Community psychiatry and psychology implied sweeping social interventions in the name of mental health because "everything a patient does and says, including what he does and says as a participant in a social system, falls within the therapists' purview."[56]

In the case of rioting, Dumont thought it sensible to consider violence a symptom in need of immediate treatment. He was not alone.[57] To consider "the city as patient" was to acknowledge a truly remarkable expansion in the subject of psychological authority, founded on the World War II preoccupation with "prevention," expressed through massive campaigns to instill mental health in the U.S. public during the period after 1945, and finally enacted on the level of state policy through federal legislation.[58] In 1963 the Mental Retardation and Community Mental Health Centers Construction Act institutionalized psychology's progress in the form of an ambitious federal program: two thousand community centers would be built to replace the outmoded system of segregated asylums. They would be accessible to all U.S. citizens on the assumption that combating the scourge of mental disease in the community would prevent most, if not all, of the negative social consequences associated with severe psychological illness.[59]

By the time the Kerner Commission was established, their community focus made the purposes of psychiatry and psychology virtually indistinguishable at times from those of the welfare state, and advocates were quick to notice similarities between their goals and assumptions and those of the Great Society; both envisioned community participation and the enfranchisement of the poor and oppressed through deliberate improvement of damaging environments. The mission of community psychology, Robert Reiff announced in September 1967, was to "place the psychologist in the position of social interventionist, whose primary task was to intervene at the social system level to modify human behavior."[60]

Matthew Dumont stated the alliance between psychology and liberal politics even more simply: "Mental health is freedom."[61] He showed how useful a justification mental health had become for social welfare programs and how intertwined it was with language of 1960s activist politics. And he brought this perspective to the attention of the Kerner Commission, some of whose members embraced this advantageous, new way of expressing policy concerns.[62] Like Kenneth Clark's testimony, Dumont's rhetoric relied on extensive disease metaphors and called for the prompt diagnosis and treatment of social disorder. He referred frequently to "urban organisms," "painful tissue destruction," and the "sensory deprivation psychosis" experienced by ghettos. The spread of rioting convinced him that entire communities, not just individuals, were suffering the pain of poor self-esteem. "This, then, is the diagnosis. A riot is a symptomatic expression of deficits of stimulation, self esteem, a sense of community, and environmental mastery. The treatment of the condition is no secret and in inadequate dosages it has already been administered."[63]

While the parallels between socially sensitive mental health approaches and an expanded welfare state seemed obvious to Dumont, Clark, and many others by the late 1960s, some dissenting voices persisted, reminders that the application of psychological expertise to urban rioting (and social problems in general) need not result in liberal public policies. A widely discussed letter to the *Journal of the American*

Medical Association in September 1967 suggested that "brain disease" was being overlooked in the rush to stem the tide of urban violence with better jobs, housing, and education. According to two of the authors, Vernon Mark and Frank Ervin, who later expanded their controversial thesis in *Violence and the Brain* (1970), "The real lesson of the urban rioting is that, besides the need to study the social fabric that creates the riot atmosphere, we need intensive research and clinical studies of the *individuals* committing the violence. The goal of such studies would be to pinpoint, diagnose, and treat those people with low violence thresholds before they contribute to further tragedies."[64]

Complaints about the workability of expanded social programs were not limited to experts determined to unlock the biological mysteries of assaultive behavior, however. The June 1968 issue of *Psychiatric Opinion* featured a series of short pieces by psychiatrists involved in riot studies, including John Spiegel and Elliot Luby, whose work was duly considered by the Kerner Commission. All of the contributors shared a fundamental commitment to exporting psychiatric insights to the policy-making process, but Robert McMurry forcefully disagreed that extending social welfare programs was either a necessary outcome of this process or a viable solution to the ills of the city. In his view, greater permissiveness in society at large was to blame for lessening the burden of guilt for antisocial activities. This development deeply affected "riot-prone" individuals who had "no internal policing agencies in their egos."[65]

The crucial point is that many of these participants in riots are people who have little or no control over their aggressions, are largely or wholly lacking in conventional moral standards, and many are to some degree out of touch with reality. In consequence, almost none are *reasonable* people. Logic, kindness and a regard for consequences have little or no influence on their behavior. They are chronically and, in many instances, irredeemably incorrigible. They are not only misfits in society; they are threats to its integrity. . . . Like a forest fire, once ignited, this mass madness is not only contagious but is very difficult to extinguish and can lead to astronomical costs in human life, injuries and property losses.[66]

Equally determined to see urban violence addressed in a psychological fashion, McMurry nevertheless believed that aggressive surveillance, probation, and protective custody—and not employment opportunities or decent housing—would help to eliminate the problem. His argument should serve as a reminder of the political flexibility of the psychological worldview. For Dumont, the philosophy of community psychiatry implied freedom from material and spiritual impoverishment. Yet for McMurry, psychiatry held a different lesson: "Just as the criminal and the insane must be denied their freedom, so must the sociopaths, psychopathic personalities, and the emotionally immature delinquents be subjected to control. The alternative is a form of anarchy, the letting loose upon the population of a pack of potential mad dogs . . . with the capability of limitless harm."[67]

The Benefits of War, Again

Just as Cold War psychology had offered militaries a new lease on life as constructive, nation-building institutions, capable of reducing levels of national and international tension, so Dumont hoped to translate the internal policing functions of the state into a positive force for therapeutic treatment. "Law enforcement and correctional institutions may themselves be redefined as preventive and rehabilitative forces," he wrote, "with policemen functioning not as an army of occupation but as community organizers, group recreation workers, and counselors, armed with knowledge, understanding, physical prowess and self-control rather than with guns."[68] Sensitivity training for police forces had been on psychological experts' riot prevention agenda since Gordon Allport and Leo Postman first set out to reeducate Boston police during World War II and strenuous efforts had been made, in the intervening years, to "professionalize" police responses to race-related rioting through heavy doses of social psychological knowledge about frustration and aggression, childhood traumas, and the stages and types of rioting mobs.[69] Since 1964, J. Edgar Hoover informed the Kerner Commission, the FBI National Academy had run training sessions for more than seventy thousand police administrators and instructors all around the country. The curriculum included a required course on "Causative and Psychological Factors in Development and Behavior of Mobs" alongside the demonstration of riot control techniques by crack army units.[70] By August 1967, when the commission began its work, approximately sixty thousand copies of the FBI's *Prevention and Control of Mobs and Crowds* were in the hands of state and local law enforcement personnel. This standard manual, first issued in February 1965 and updated two years later, emulated the work of World War II riot experts (by defining the police role as preventive treatment and "release of tension") while also incorporating the painstaking theoretical progress that riot experts had made in the decades since. The manual carefully distinguished crowd types, crowd behavior patterns, rioters' personality profiles, and riot chronologies, among other things.[71]

By the mid-1960s the FBI was certainly more willing to accept and dispense psychological experts' advice than World War II–era police departments had been, but domestic polarization over "pacification" campaigns in Southeast Asia had begun to make optimistic analogies between law enforcement and enlightened social relations (whether applied to foreign militaries or domestic police forces) appear naive and misguided, especially to experts and observers opposed to the Vietnam War.[72] Even some professionals whose careers were based on the persuasiveness of psychological approaches ruefully agreed that equating cities with patients and law enforcement with therapy embodied terribly repressive, as well as liberating, potential.

Kenneth Keniston, well known as the author of books about generational identity such as *The Uncommitted* (1960) and *Young Radicals* (1968), penned a telling satire along these lines in 1968, "How Community Mental Health Stamped Out the Riots."[73] He warned that idealistic psychological approaches could be put to frightening purposes if they actually managed to transform public policy-making into a process of correcting individual maladjustments and community pathologies. In his article, Keniston imagined looking back on the landscape of the late 1960s from a vantage point in 1978. The Department of Defense had been renamed the Department of International Mental Health, General Westmoreland had been appointed secretary, and wars had become struggles for a mentally healthy world. On the home front, Ronald Reagan (famous during the 1960s for his law-and-order approach to campus activism and unrest in California) had directed a massive community mental health program in an effort to stem the tide of urban rioting. In 1971 laws were passed sentencing people identified as potentially violent to mandatory therapy. And since 1972 a "Total Saturation Approach" to urban problems had been used, featuring "Remote Therapy Centers" (relocating riot-prone patients to the same sites used for Japanese-Americans during World War II) and "Mobile Treatment Teams," which had been found far more effective than old-fashioned police departments. Finally, Keniston reiterated, ironically and with ominous overtones, the neat fit between mental health and social welfare. "Our long-range goal: nothing less than a society in which all men and women are guaranteed mental health by simple virtue of their citizenship. Thus, the entire community must be our target: we must insist upon *total mental health* from the womb to the grave."[74]

As the utopian hopes of postwar community psychiatry and psychology were dashed against the stubborn persistence of poverty, inequality, racism, and violence in U.S. society, Keniston's skepticism became a more common feature of progressive analysis, to the point where the sheer existence of psychological approaches to subjective experience was considered prima facie evidence of sinister schemes of social control.

Keniston sketched his negative vision in extreme and satirical terms for the purpose of dramatizing the dangers of community psychological approaches. The Kerner Commission, however, received many suggestions, completely sincere and sometimes unsolicited, that overlooked these dangers and assumed that psychological approaches were intrinsically enlightened. Therapy for rioters and modes of communication that would release unconscious fears and boost levels of self-esteem were common refrains. In letters to the Kerner Commission, citizens informed policy-makers that constructive means of preventing future riots were, among others, "reality therapy," dialogue centers, human relations councils, and in-depth clinical interviews to explore the motivations of individual rioters.[75] Given the preponderance of psychologically oriented advice from experts and ordinary citizens alike, it was little wonder that Executive Director Ginsburg identified "an entire *system of deprivation and frustration* leading to the alienation of individuals" as the commission's very first priority in developing social and economic recommendations to improve ghetto life.[76]

COLD WAR PSYCHOLOGY COMES HOME

The intimacies that transpired between Cold War psychology and policy-makers' approach to urban rioting were not figments of Kenneth Keniston's overheated imagination. The Kerner Commission made full use of resources that had been developed for the use of the military during the 1950s and 1960s, sharing with such projects as Camelot not only similar approaches to the psychology of crowds, revolutionaries, and rioters, but overlapping personnel as well.

Ted Gurr and Ithiel de Sola Pool linked the two experiences, illustrating the flexibility of policy-oriented experts and their desire to operate in diverse areas of government. Ted Gurr, a consultant to CRESS (the organizational sponsor of Project Camelot, renamed in 1966) turned his comparative studies of civil strife abroad toward more domestic topics. In 1968 he argued that sophisticated frustration-aggression theories could be applied to the circumstances of Guatemalan guerrillas, Indonesian students, and urban black Americans with roughly equal effectiveness, a view that was adopted, as noted above, by the commission's director.[77] Sola Pool, a vocal figure in military behavioral science, won a Kerner Commission contract worth $221,000 for his consulting firm, Simulmatics Inc., to track the media's contribution to urban riots.[78]

Beyond the presence of such individuals, the entire project of riot analysis was infused with the sense that the military had the most "Directly Related Experience," according to the title of a Kerner Commission memo on successful psychological warfare and counterinsurgency campaigns.[79] Much of the riot training and equipment advice sought after by municipal administrations and police departments came from the military, whose own experts sometimes derided the value of civilian knowledge on these topics.[80]

NEW VARIATIONS ON OLD
CROWD PSYCHOLOGY

The Kerner Commission experts also owed a debt to the military's patronage of expert work on the nature of social upheaval and to those elements of the crowd psychology tradition that had survived as themes in postwar theoretical models of crowd formation and revolutionary stages. By the late 1960s, crowd psychology was called by a new name, "collective behavior," and had migrated throughout the social sciences via the behavioral revolution of the 1950s, which stripped crowd psychology of its obvious antidemocratic tendencies and injected it with a heavy dose of scientific method.[81] The theoretical work of Kerner Commission consultants Neil Smelser and Ralph Turner kept alive the residue of the old psychology in the form of a sophisticated new sociology. The idea that groups were subject to unconscious social contagion remained viable, alongside the conviction that race rioting was appropriately classified with religious cults, natural disasters, and other types of social panic.[82]

The Kerner Commission experts employed phase models of urban disturbance, compiled elaborate chronologies, designed multifactored riot classification schemes, and hypothesized that rioters shared a common personality profile.[83] All of these recalled military efforts, like the failed Project Camelot, which had used these very techniques to make the explosiveness of civil unrest in the Third World at least a little bit more predictable for military and foreign policy-makers. They also all employed, sometimes almost verbatim, the theoretical jargon of social science for descriptive purposes: riots were labeled as "expressive," "suggestible," "permissive," or as prototypes of "social contagion."[84]

There were significant differences, however, having to do with the sympathy that black Americans had gained since the 1950s through the civil rights movement and the growing presence of intellectuals in a variety of 1960s social movements. The justice of civil rights demands, the slowness of racial change, and decided patterns of activism among highly educated Americans on university campuses had momentous consequences within the literature of particular social science disciplines. Also important was the movement of the psychological professions away from their preoccupations with the abnormal, a shift that decisively changed the subjects of psychological experts, beginning with World War II. All of these developments combined to make it less likely that experts in the late 1960s would view urban rioters as deviants in the grip of irrational forces. We have already considered instances of this tendency toward a more positive and rational theory of collective behavior among Kerner Commission experts, such as Elliot Liebow, who suggested that rioting was psychologically empowering for individuals whose lives were otherwise impaired by apathy and hopelessness.

Rioting was sometimes even posited as an ideological stance, a necessary, if destructive, stage in the civil rights movement, or, as it was more likely to be called in the late 1960s by advocates of this position, the black revolution. This perspective was only possible because the irrational contamination of ideological commitment, a core element of the World War II worldview, was challenged in the 1960s. The terrible destruction wrought by enemy national characters and the deep emotional appeal of fascism faded from view during a decade when the ideological commitments closest at hand—eradicating racism, poverty, and imperialism—seemed beyond reproach and the postwar "end of ideology" appeared nothing so much as an irresponsible abandonment of moral principle.

A number of Kerner Commission experts and research projects tested out this positive new assessment of ideology. Riots could appear to be purposeful, organized protests against legitimate and pressing grievances, instead of hysterical fits. That riots were taken seriously as a form of political action was sometimes indicated through the vocabulary used to describe them: "urban rebellions" competed with "mob violence" and "lawless anarchy."

Widespread consideration of riots as a rational collective activity was new, but the idea itself was not. As early as the Harlem riot of 1943, Kenneth Clark had suggested that a significant number of black Americans condoned rioting as a specific means to achieve the end of racial justice.[85] By 1965 he denied that ghetto violence was an uncontrollable force and chose instead to call it "a weird social defiance" of objective social conditions ranging from substandard housing and soaring crime and infant morality rates to impoverishment and discrimination.[86] Clark, however, sometimes reverted to the old crowd psychology themes in his observations of riots. "Such anarchy could even be a subconscious or conscious invitation to self-destruction," he noted that same year. "Those who despair in the ghetto follow their own laws— generally the laws of unreason."[87]

Gary Marx, one of the commission's in-house researchers, did not so much criticize the old crowd psychology as try to turn it upside down, by applying its principles to the behavior of police, rather than rioters. "Who controls the agents of social control?" was, Marx submitted, a major question that generally went unasked and unanswered. He went so far as to suggest that law enforcement personnel had caused urban riots, or at least intensified them, through the classic pattern of contagion, panic, and frustration usually attributed to crowd members.[88] Marx's themes found strong encouragement in the publications of the Lemberg Center for the Study of Violence at Brandeis University, a research center, established in 1965, that had blazed trails eagerly followed by Kerner Commission experts. The Lemberg Center staff insisted that rioters could be understood as reasonable actors frequently faced with "police panic." Further, they speculated, rioters were attempting to solidify a positive sense of community and masculinity. They simply could not be compared with Gustave Le Bon's primitive and herdlike crowds.[89]

The Commission's Conclusions

In retrospect, it appears that the Kerner Commission turned the expert investigation of rioting into an unprecedented executive priority. But it was hardly the first such official investigation during the 1960s. During the Johnson presidency alone, thirteen commissions were appointed at municipal and state levels.[90] Since early in the century, commissions had been among the government's favorite answers to the questions raised by riots. Between 1917 and 1943, twenty-one were established to investigate riots in East St. Louis (1917), Chicago and Washington, D.C. (1919), Detroit (1925 and 1943), Harlem (1935 and 1943), and elsewhere. According to critics, commissions offered a convenient way of "processing racial crisis" symbolically, purchasing urban stability and, at the same time, ensuring "the continuation of long-term social conflict by other means."[91] According to supporters, commissions were clear evidence of government making good on its responsibilities to maintain social order while still addressing intergroup conflict with speed and seriousness.

Following the Watts riots in the summer of 1965, California Governor Edmund G. Brown had put a state-level commission together, determined to pinpoint the causes of violence in the Los Angeles ghetto. The McCone Commission was named after its chairman, John A. McCone, a businessman who had served as CIA director. Hundreds of other riots occurred and investigating bodies formed during the two years between Watts and the Kerner Commission's formation—164 during the first nine months of 1967 alone—but the McCone Commission's work was especially important in influencing the direction that Kerner Commission experts took.[92] Because Watts had been among the largest of the riots, the McCone Commission had received wide publicity, as had its conclusions about the nature of urban disorder: that riots were "spasms" and rioters "marauding bands" who "seemed to be caught up in an insensate rage of destruction."[93] In the months and years that followed, the McCone Commission findings were used to support theories that urban riots were the handiwork of criminal "riffraff," conspiracies concocted by black nationalists, attacks of mass hysteria, or a combination of all three.

The Kerner Commission experts deliberately set out to counter these conclusions, as the final report makes clear.[94] Months of research and analysis resulted in a final report that emphasized the responsibility of white institutions and attitudes for urban rioting. "What white Americans have never fully understood—but what the Negro can never forget," the report concluded, "is that white society is deeply implicated in the ghetto. White institutions created it, white institutions maintain it, and white society condones it."[95] On the one hand, this forceful statement (which appeared in the final report's introductory summary) illustrated that the merits of the ill-fated internal document, "The Harvest of American Racism," had not been entirely lost on the commissioners. On the other hand, the final report contained evidence that led some critics to dismiss it angrily as "a white document written by white writers and aimed at a white audience—*about* black people."[96] It enumerated a long list of social pathologies and incorporated lengthy descriptions of the "culture of poverty" from which black Americans suffered, for instance. A chapter on "Unemployment, Family Structure, and Social Disorganization" reiterated all the standard themes, from the poor self-esteem of black men who could not achieve the status of patriarchal breadwinners and hence were forced to become demoralized members of a "streetcorner society" to the damaging consequences of an unnaturally high labor force participation rate among black women.[97]

The net result could be confusing. The report called "the racial attitude and behavior of white Americans" the most fundamental cause of rioting, but pronounced increased black self-esteem a crucial step in the right direction.[98] And while many of the commission's "Recommendations for National Action" were for new or reinvigorated federal programs (in the areas of jobs, education, welfare, and housing), they were sprinkled with references to the need for a new black psychology, as if to imply that institutional reforms were attractive mainly for their psychological consequences—lower levels of frustration, heightened self-esteem, and more "normal" families.[99] One month after the Kerner Commission finished its work, a parade of social experts testified before the Senate that programs geared to improving the socioeconomic status of poor black Americans were important not because they redistributed money or power, but for their psychological consequences. "We know that looting is as bad for the looter as the looted. The burning store is a statement of frustration about self as well as a criticism of a society that permitted cynicism and prejudice to grow in place of community and love."[100]

Perhaps the final report's inability to decide which came first—the unequal division of material and political power or the unequal division of psychological resources—simply mirrored the experts' ambivalence about their own position and goals. Robert Fogelson (coauthor of the commission's supplementary study "Who Riots?") was disappointed in the report's equivocation, and less than happy that his own work had been used to support what he considered muddy analysis and feeble recommendations. Because he believed that profound institutional reorganization was necessary in order to solve the problems of cities, he criticized the commission's emphasis on attitudes. He also admitted, however, that a document more to his radical taste would surely have been rejected, or even used by people in power to undermine the Great Society by blaming reformers for the problems they were trying to reform. "Its [the commission's] casual dismissal of community control and black power, not to speak of more radical proposals for social change, is particularly disappointing. But, in view of the public opinion polls, the Kerner Commission did a better job than the country deserves. . . . And had the commission abandoned its liberal perspective and submitted a more original interpretation and more radical recommendations, it would probably have been rejected outright by most Americans."[101] As if to confirm the truth of this ironic double bind, Georgia governor Lester Maddox sent the following telegram to Lyndon Johnson upon the final report's publication.

I ADVISED YOU ON NUMEROUS OCCASIONS STARTING IN EARLY 1964 THAT NATIONAL LEGISLATION OR GUIDELINES AND DIRECTIVES THAT WERE DIRECTED AT AND CONTINUED TO INSPIRE, ENCOURAGE AND OFTEN TIMES PROTECT AND FINANCE THE MISFITS, MISTAKEN, BUMS, CRIMINALS, COMMUNISTS AND OTHER LAWLESS AGITATORS WOULD BRING WAVES OF VIOLENCE, BURNING, LOOTING, INJURY AND VIOLENT DEATH TO AMERICAN CITIES SUCH AS NEVER BEFORE TO TAKE PLACE IN OUR NATION. . . . I URGE YOU . . . TO NOT ASK FOR MORE OF THE PROGRAMS THAT HAVE BROUGHT TRAGEDY TO AMERICA. PLEASE DENOUNCE THE SOCIALISTS AND FRAUDULENT RECOMMENDATIONS OF THE RIOT PROBE COMMISSION, THAT EVEN NOW ENCOURAGE INCREASED VIOLENCE.[102]

Opponents of the "socialists" on the Kerner Commission were not limited to southern Democratic power brokers like Maddox. The majority of ordinary white Americans, as the experts themselves had shown, would not change their minds under the constructive pressure of the "American Creed"; they barely recognized the prevalence of racism, let alone considered themselves a part of the rioting problem and solution. Experts' work might illustrate that radical changes were needed, but it also led to the conclusion that such changes were unlikely to be tolerated. In such a circumstance, what could experts do except complain about the uses to which their efforts had been put? Many did exactly that.[103]

Not everyone, of course, shared such a dim view of the Kerner Commission's accomplishments. Arthur Brayfield, executive officer of the

APA, was delighted with the final report. He praised it as comprehensive and deserving of support, especially for "its clear recognition of the psychological factors—the crucial role of attitudes, of feelings, and indeed of the total functioning of human personality in its social and physical environment." [104] For Brayfield, the commission had offered a positive model for government use of psychological experts because it illustrated how far government had moved in the direction of defining its responsibilities and programs in terms of their psychological consequences.

I believe that any inquiry into the development of human resources must focus on the black revolution. For the black revolution poses in its starkest form an overwhelming question: Can we design and develop a society—a set of social arrangements—a human environment—that will foster the sense of *personal worth* and *self-esteem* required to sustain the human spirit, give meaning to our lives, and provide the energizing force to forge our personal destinies and to insure the emergence and survival of a humane society? [105]

This chapter has demonstrated that the benefits of war were both flexible and far-reaching. Many of the patterns characterizing the history of psychological experts during World War II, and in Cold War military policy, were also evident in the evolution of domestic social policy. In fact, the development of the U.S. welfare and warfare states was intimately linked and mutually reinforcing, as the Kerner Commission case shows. In investigating riots at home, no less than revolutions far away, psychological experts were engaged in an ambitious, interdisciplinary project to tease apart the knotted strands of personal motivation, social context, and history, all without losing sight of political principles and realities. They came up with few, if any, new ideas that passed scientific muster, but they were remarkably successful in ways neither intended nor anticipated. In particular, psychological experts' work on the domestic policy issues tackled by the Kerner Commission made the precise relationship of psychological and social change a focal point of the policy-making process. It made individual subjectivity an ever more significant factor in policy calculations and a new and undisputed subject of government.

In the course of this process, experts and policy-makers sometimes found themselves at odds or in direct conflict. The experts typically presented the relationship between psychology and society as complex, dynamic, and confusing, a state of affairs that frustrated policy-makers' desires for unambiguous guidance and prestigious legitimation of expedient solutions. For their part, experts became increasingly conscious of the contradictions embedded in their rising status in government, a development fueled by 1960s social movements that captured their sympathy and, at the same time, pointed out how much damage uncritical intellectuals could do. Experts like Robert Shellow and his staff had tried to walk a fine line between the risks of associating with power and the risks of failing to act at all. Shellow's final thoughts about his experience with the Kerner Commission made clear just how difficult and significant a challenge that was.

It is not only possible but desirable and perhaps essential that the social scientist become more deeply involved in trying to bring about social change in a direct manner. . . . It is time . . . to get on with the job of correcting injustices rather than simply despairing of their pervasiveness or beating our breasts on the sidelines. No doubt it is best that some of us keep our distance from the unpleasantness of the arena, stick to our research craft, and content ourselves with enriching the minds of the young. But if that is all we do, the product of our efforts will be valued only among our colleagues, our theories will remain untested or untestable, and our talented and impatient youth will look elsewhere for preparation to cope with the world as they find it.[106]

During the Kerner Commission's short history, the experts and the policy-makers argued continuously about how psychological insights into rioting could best be operationalized and whether or not their consequences, in policy forms, were liberating, repressive, ineffective, or entirely irrelevant. Neither group was monolithic and neither acted on needs that were unified and clear at all times. The interests of professions were significant factors in the self-promotion campaigns of experts, but they sometimes conflicted with the political requirements of government bureaucracies. Even so, there was rarely much disagreement about psychology's fundamental relevance to matters regarding race and racial conflict, a fact that must certainly be considered a mark of great progress in the public history of psychology.

Psychology's postwar career on the level of state policy—both in the case of Cold War counterinsurgency and in the case of racial conflict at home—leaves little doubt that psychological expertise had tremendous repressive potential. It could and did, for example, assist police forces at home and in the Third World to quell legitimate protest without resort to obvious, old-fashioned mechanisms of coercion and control. On the other hand, psychology's career also illustrates that experts were increasingly aware of this negative potential as they navigated the sea change that occurred with the Vietnam War and as the old equations between psychology, democracy, and patriotism began to unravel. Experts cannot therefore be understood simply as political pawns (although they were at times), and the research and theories they developed in government service were not simply vehicles through which Washington adapted its methods according to the dictates of sophisticated, scientific obfuscation (although at times, this occurred too).

Further, psychology's politically liberating potential remained utterly convincing. For every domestic policy-maker who emerged from the 1960s convinced that black Americans needed nothing beyond vigorous self-improvement routines, there were thousands of citizens and activists who believed that the keys to mass persuasion and radical change rested within the U.S. psyche at large. For the many civil rights activists and supporters who believed their own antiracist politics had changed them psychologically and permanently, a color-blind vision of equality and opportunity could hardly be realized without a plan of truly thoroughgoing change in the psychological, as well as the material and political, spheres of social life.

This remarkable chameleonlike capacity—to serve a variety of political purposes in unpredictable ways—is perhaps the most important lesson to be learned from those facets of psychology's public history reviewed thus far. If government tended toward using psychological experts to dress up repressive public policies in enlightened disguises, it was the particular purposes that shaped the consequences, rather than anything intrinsic to psychology itself. Government, in theory at least, could as easily seek to promote as to impede social change.

The point is not to choose whether psychological experts continuously served a master of democratic progress *or* antidemocratic social control, but to see how they extended the reach of government and the purposes of public policy to include the subjective and emotional realities of power. During the postwar decades, they altered the tone of public life in a variety of ways, not by any means limited to policymaking or contained within the formal apparatus of the state. Their impact on public culture in general—on the very definition of "the political" and on the direction and style of civic participation—offers further evidence of the complexity of psychology's political history. It is to aspects of this history that we turn next.

9

The Growth Industry

Postwar psychological healers were aggressive, upbeat, and emphatically dedicated to the proposition that preventive techniques and treatment should be vigorously applied to normal people and their normal problems in normal communities. World War II, as we saw in chapter 4, had given clinicians an ominous glimpse of what could happen when healthy individual personalities were overwhelmed by unhealthy environmental stresses. Painfully aware that cures for drastic mental disturbances were flawed, if not altogether futile, they were relieved that war had presented an alternative. The agony of the desperately ill need no longer be their sole preoccupation. They could set their sights on the normal anxieties of ordinary people. And they did. In the name of prevention and mental health, clinicians pledged themselves to careers as architects of social as well as personal change.

World war ended in 1945, but the challenge of psychological adjustment endured. Combat anxieties no longer precipitated breakdown, but new social strains multiplied and spread, threatening to generate waves of civilian casualties at a moment when a country burdened by postwar reconstruction could least afford the financial and symbolic sacrifice. As if to acknowledge that unemployment, housing shortages, racial conflict, and the dawn of the nuclear age all tested the mental and emotional stamina of soldiers and citizens fatigued by years of war, the legislation that became known as the GI Bill was formally titled the Servicemen's *Readjustment* Act of 1944.

Because adjustment seemed to have such positive civic, as well as personal, overtones, maladjustment was considered a national hazard. It was this specter of incomplete or failed adjustment, and the realization that psychological and social fitness were inextricably linked in any measure of social well-being, that prompted a new mood of receptiveness to the psychological duties of national government. "Not many personalities," cautioned William Menninger in 1948, "can still be in there adjusting after a full speed head-on collision with as solid a piece of Environment as a ten-ton truck." [1]

This chapter describes how clinical experts devoted themselves to the job of keeping personality and environment in stable balance, continuing the process of normalization that began between 1941 and 1945. It shows how smoothly postwar trends paralleled clinicians' preventive credo and how quickly institutional and legislative changes helped to realize clinicians' vision of an expanded jurisdiction for psychological expertise, initially facilitated by an expanding federal government. The major outlines of clinicians' historical chronology after 1945 are quite similar to those of their colleagues in the behavioral sciences. Chapter 5, for example, described the career of policy-oriented psychological experts during the early Cold War, when grave new military priorities facilitated a flow of defense dollars to experts who promised that psychological science and technology would help manage political change in a dangerous world in exchange for continued state support and a part in determining the direction of U.S. foreign and military policy.

This convergence demonstrates, yet again, the theme that divergent types of psychological experts shared important common ground. Some worked in national security occupations trying to manage revolutionary upheaval in the Third World while others worked in local clinics trying to steer individuals toward a happier existence. Some thought they were developing social and behavioral science; others considered themselves neutral technologists; still others made unwavering commitments to professional lives delivering social service and personal aid. The particulars of their stories were distinctive. The general outlines of their histories were not.

For clinicians, the lessons of World War II were also beacons illuminating their future path, but the characteristic features of postwar U.S. society, as they emerged, were equally prominent in heightening the visibility of clinical experts and increasing the popular demand for their services. Economic affluence and an ethic of avid consumption allowed people to think of empathy and warmth as items to be purchased without recoiling from the commercialization of human connection. While the pervasive techniques of industrial psychologists contributed something to the alienation of "the organization man" (the famous William H. Whyte book by that title included an appendix on "How to Cheat on Personality Tests"), experts' promise of supportive understanding also nourished the ongoing quest for existential meaning, just as new levels of geographic mobility did by placing more people than ever out of reach of the kin and community ties with which they had grown up. Finally, an insistent ideology of patriarchal domesticity simultaneously returned civilian jobs to male veterans and sequestered women and children in a familial bubble that made private ordeals a matter of great public curiosity and untiring investigation.

It was in this context of affluence, alienation, and sharp gender distinctions that the postwar trends discussed in this chapter unfolded. Three developments in particular are described below because they illustrate the growing public influence of clinical expertise, as well as the basis of that influence in the World War II experience and the incessant militarism of the postwar years.

First, the swift acceptance by federal government of an unprecedented responsibility for the mental and emotional well-being of the entire U.S. population. With passage of the National Mental Health Act of 1946, it was apparent that the mental health of ordinary citizens would become a consequential public policy issue in its own right and the result was that more and more responsibility for its pursuit and maintenance rested with the state. Federal legislation, in turn, provided the infrastructure necessary to support a community-oriented psychology and psychiatry during the 1950s and 1960s. One of the first and most important results was the growing conviction that psychological and social change were inseparable. Political activism was as much of a social responsibility for clinical experts as personal helpfulness was.

Second, this chapter discusses the popularity and growth of psychotherapy for "the normal." Spurred in part by veterans' requests for ongoing assistance and built on the infrastructure of new federal initiatives, this development sharply altered the geographic location, professional interests, and daily responsibilities of clinical experts. The enormous new market for psychotherapy at first caused some bewilderment among clinical professionals, who were not always as confident about the services they offered the public as they would have liked to be. But for the most part, it fostered their desires for a larger territory in which to work and added the blessings of consumer demand to their arguments that psychological knowledge would increase in direct proportion to the normalization of its research, theory, and technologies. Experts allied with psychoanalysis and behaviorism alike agreed that "the study of psychotherapy, in distinction from the isolated study of abnormal behavior, is a description of the process by which *normality is created.*"[2]

Third, the emergence of humanistic perspectives within the psychological professions is examined. Presenting itself as an alternative to psychoanalysis and behaviorism, this innovative trend took wartime normalization and the postwar popularization of psychotherapy to their logical extremes. It personified the belief that an optimistic, normal psychology could provide two desperately needed prerequisites for a nation seeking renewal and revitalization—mental health and democratic behavior—neither of which had been much in evidence during World War II. Practitioners like Carl Rogers and theorists like Abraham Maslow, whose work is briefly reviewed below, advanced ideas about the inherent goodness of motivation and the primacy of subjectivity in psychology, in science, and in all human affairs. They boldly insisted on clinicians' ability to generate positive insight and mature behavior and they tirelessly popularized their own work. Humanistic approaches eventually contributed to a fundamental shift in the ideas of 1960s social movements, where "the political" was reconceptualized to encompass "the personal" and notions of social responsibility were saturated in the vocabulary of subjective experience.

The State as Healer: Mental Health as Public Policy

Taking charge of unpredictable emotions and reactions in persons and populations had not been merely, or even mainly, a humanitarian effort during the war years, nor would it be one after 1945. If at times it was presented as a matter of sheer altruism, it really was not. The job of maintaining mass emotional control was decisively taken up by the federal government in the postwar decades because it was understood that mental health was necessary to the efficacy of the armed forces in the short run and national security, domestic tranquillity, and economic competitiveness in the long run. Who could forget the shocking epidemic of emotional disorder and disability exposed during World War II? Ensuring a sufficient threshold of mental stability, because that threshold undergirded the integrity of social institutions, became a new and important sphere of federal action in the postwar decades.[3]

Prior to the war, public accountability for disturbed psychological life had rested largely with individual states, which provided an uneven patchwork of custodial services to the mentally ill in segregated institutions. After the war, federal policy-makers absorbed the lesson that it was more efficient, forward-looking, and quite possibly cheaper to take preventive action on behalf of mental health than face the demoralizing, long-term prospect of treating the chronically sick. Asylums would continue to exist, of course, and states would have to sustain and even improve them. The federal government, however, would design its new role on the basis of what clinicians believed they had learned during World War II: that mental health and illness were relative, rather than fixed states; that mental illness could be prevented with early, assertive clinical intervention; that normal adjustment to internal and external strains was a lifelong project, never permanently accomplished and always in need of vigilance.

Above all, federal mental health policy after 1945 was built on and furthered the integration of clinical and social-scientific insights, helping to merge the concerns of emotional guides and social engineers, so that by the late 1960s, movements for community mental health had effectively undermined the legitimacy of distinctions between private emotions and public policy, between clinical work and the business of politics and government.

THE ROLE OF THE VETERANS ADMINISTRATION

Even before the end of World War II, the record of the Veterans Administration (VA) clearly indicated that some federal agencies were prepared, even eager, to support vast new programs in the mental health field. The VA, of course, had little choice in the matter; next to the armed forces themselves, it was the agency whose primary job was to care for war casualties. Since huge numbers of those casualties had suffered psychiatric breakdown, the VA found itself in charge of binding more mental than physical wounds and picking up the emotional pieces of military conflict.

The number of psychiatric cases in VA hospitals almost doubled between 1940 and 1948.[4] Right after the war, in April 1946, around 60 percent of all VA patients were neuropsychiatric cases of one sort or another: forty-four thousand out of a total of seventy-four thousand.[5] Fifty percent of all disability pensions were being paid to psychiatric casualties and, by June 1947, the monthly cost of such psychiatric pensions was $20 million, with each case running the government something more than $40,000.[6] The VA's fifty-seven outpatient clinics served over one hundred thousand additional people. By the mid-1950s, half of all the hospital beds in the country were being occupied by persons with mental illness, a fact called the "greatest single problem in the nation's health picture" by the March 1955 Hoover Commission study of federal medical services.[7] The VA, alone responsible for 10 percent of the inpatient total and providing ongoing treatment to thousands upon thousands of outpatients, was making ambitious plans for new construction of hospitals and clinics.[8] Waiting lists for clinical services were long and growing rapidly.

Because personnel shortages had been so severe during the war, and psychiatrists, psychologists, and other clinicians were so scarce, professional training soon became "the most pressing medical problem" facing the agency, according to Dr. Daniel Blain, chief of psychiatry in the VA.[9] Indeed, more open positions existed in the VA at war's end for clinical psychologists than there were clinical psychologists in the entire country. In order to cope with the prospect of drastic, long-term personnel shortages, programs of professional education were swiftly put into place.

An ambitious four-year training program in clinical psychology, for example, was launched in 1946 to train two hundred individuals in twenty-two different universities.[10] Under the terms of the program, students were given free educations and prorated salaries in exchange for half-time work in a VA facility while they pursued their doctoral degrees. This instantly made the VA the single largest employer of these professionals in the entire country. In 1946, the VA's chief of clinical psychology wrote, "The significant and inevitable consequence of this development is that a large portion of the whole profession of clinical psychology will come under Governmental control. . . . The field is rapidly expanding and the opportunities for service and research are almost limitless."[11] The VA continued to produce hundreds of new clinicians each year, all of whom could expect interesting work and substantial pay in a job market where their skills were in high demand. Just three years into the clinical psychology program, it had expanded to seven hundred students in forty-one universities.[12] This pattern of steady growth, which lasted for decades, ensured that the VA would remain the source of plentiful, exciting professional opportunities and contributed to a massive shift in employment patterns within psychology away from academia and toward clinical work. The year 1962 was, R. C. Tryon noted, "a real turning point" because psychologists employed outside of universities outnumbered their academic colleagues for the first time.[13] Opportunities were not limited to clinical psychology. By the mid-1950s, the VA was employing 10 percent of all psychiatrists in its 35 psychiatric hospitals, 75 general hospitals with psychiatric services, and 62 mental health clinics; another 10 percent of psychiatrists worked as VA consultants.[14]

The VA proved a bonanza not only for clinical professionals. It was also the site of increased consumer demand. Veterans and members of veterans' families, most exposed to clinical expertise for the first time during the war, were the first to come looking for assistance with the ordinary—if still extremely difficult—problems of postwar living. It must be recalled that the vast majority of veterans who received discharges for psychiatric reasons were classified as suffering from the lower orders of mental disturbance: psychoneurosis rather than psychosis. These veterans and others tended to bring "normal" problems to the attention of VA clinicians: marital tensions and parenting difficulties were especially common.[15]

Some veterans undoubtedly remained skeptical that professional helpers could be of any practical use. If the statistics on skyrocketing numbers of VA outpatients are any indication, however, many others had received the message that had been directed at them repeatedly as soldiers: nothing was wrong with seeking psychological help; in fact, to do so was a sign of unusual strength and maturity. Quite a few clinicians who worried about the logistical headaches of servicing millions of returning soldiers reminded themselves that offering clinical assistance to the civilian masses was the logical follow-up to their earlier patriotic contributions in the military. Dispensing psychotherapy to veterans was the link connecting clinicians' past to their future.

Psychotherapy could also advance the process of social readjustment to peacetime democracy. Carl Rogers, for example, was a clinician who would become a well-known advocate of humanistic psychology in the postwar decades. In 1946 he coauthored a counseling manual, *Counseling With Returned Servicemen*, that he hoped would put simple, do-it-yourself therapeutic techniques into the hands of thousands of new clinicians so that they might ease the adjustment traumas of returning servicemen whose subjection to strict military authority had temporarily unfitted them for their postwar roles as free-thinking, independent citizens. He spelled out the social relevance of their collective task as follows: "No longer is he just another G. I. Joe. Instead he again becomes Bill Hanks or Harry Williams. In contrast to marching troops who are 'men without faces,' the client begins to resume selfhood as a specific, unique individual."[16] Not only did Rogers promise that his particular brand of sensitive, nonjudgmental clinical help could facilitate the resumption of selfhood and individuality. It could also help to recapture any democratic impulses that had been lost in the crush of wartime regimentation, and perhaps even generate attractive new styles of democratic conduct and decision making in individuals who had never previously possessed them. "All the characteristics of this type of counseling," Rogers contended, "are also tenets of democracy."[17] Surely a voluntary therapeutic relationship consciously imbued with tolerance and respect, based on confidence in individual maturity, freedom, and responsibility, might succeed in communicating some of these virtues to veterans.

THE NATIONAL MENTAL HEALTH ACT OF 1946

The most tangible evidence that citizens' mental health had been elevated to a major priority of federal government came with passage of the National Mental Health Act (NMHA) of 1946.[18] This landmark piece of legislation was inspired in large part by the dismal record of military mental health during World War II, the performance of such agencies as the VA, and vocal demands by veterans and their families for therapeutic services. Clinicians too mounted persistent advocacy efforts on their own behalf, convinced that gains in professional visibility and prestige would result from increased federal funding. For them, as for their ambitious colleagues who wished to influence postwar foreign and military policy, military experiences and mandates were both genuinely transforming and politically expedient. War had been, and would continue to be, a great persuader.

Called the National Neuropsychiatric Institute Act when it was first introduced in Congress in March 1945, the legislation's final title incorporated the term "mental health," an alteration that captured the pivotal role of World War II and its marked clinical drift toward normalization. Indeed, leading figures in wartime clinical work were conspicuous in the lobbying effort for the NMHA, and the lessons they had learned on the job, maintaining military mental health, were the most frequently heard arguments in favor of government action in this area.

Robert Felix, a psychiatrist who had been appointed director of the Public Health Service's (PHS) Division of Mental Hygiene in 1944, put most of his own energy, and his bureaucracy's muscle, into passing the bill. William Menninger, Lawrence Kubie, and others testified about how shortages of trained clinicians had sometimes thwarted military morale and how early therapeutic intervention had eventually helped the war effort by conserving personnel. They promised that federal support for professional training, research, and preventive services to the public would ease the postwar transition, humanize the face of government, and save lots of tax dollars. General Lewis Hershey, director of the Selective Service System, trotted out statistics on rejection and discharge rates from the armed services.[19] These numbers became something of a mantra during the congressional deliberations on the NMHA. It was a fact that mental illness cost a lot of money. It was simply presumed that mental health would not. The chief of Bellevue Hospital's Psychiatric Division, S. Bernard Wortis, put it as follows: "Health, sir, is a purchasable commodity, and it seems to me that if more money were put into services and brains, rather than into bricks ... much misery and much mental illness could be saved in this country."[20]

Advocating that mental health, rather than mental illness, be the centerpiece of federal policy also embodied clinicians' crusade for a larger jurisdiction for psychological expertise. That clinical insights should be applied to most or even all areas in need of government planning in the postwar era—from employment and housing to race relations—was assumed to be self-evident. Rarely did advocates offer concrete reasons why clinicians should be granted standing in such matters, but then, they were hardly ever asked to do so. A solitary dissenting voice at the congressional hearings on the NMHA illustrated the extent of expert consensus on the importance of expanding clinicians' social authority.[21] Lee Steiner, a member of the American Association of Psychiatric Social Workers, cautioned, "If we include these [diverse social policy] problems as 'preventive psychiatry,' then all problems of life and living fall into the province of the practice of medicine."[22] Her reservations, although they stand out to the contemporary reader, were buried at the time in the avalanche of certainty that clinicians could be trusted to discover the solutions to "all problems of life and living."

Almost as rare as dissenting expert testimony was nonexpert opinion. One consumer, a Marine Corps aviator, added the drama of personal witness to the congressional proceedings. Captain Robert Nystrom, who had recently recovered from manic depression, described what he had learned during his five-month hospitalization at St. Elizabeth's. He contrasted the worthless "loafer's delight" treatment he received initially with the "sort of streamlined psychoanalysis" that eventually helped him develop insight and recover function during two weekly sessions with a therapist.[23] If the NMHA were not passed, he warned, do-nothing remedies would be the awful fate of all Americans afflicted with debilitating mental troubles, and the country would be the worse for it. His story made a deep impression.[24]

The message that decisive federal action on mental health was both imperative and intelligent got through to policy-makers and politicians. According to Senator Claude Pepper (D-Fla.), the main sponsor of the legislation in the Senate, "the enormous pressures of the times, the catastrophic world war which ended in victory a few months ago, and the difficult period of reorientation and reconstruction, in which we have as yet achieved no victory, have resulted in an alarming increase in the incidence of mental disease and neuropsychiatric maladjustments among our people."[25] With "the improvement of the mental health of the people of the United States" as its stated goal, the NMHA was signed into law by President Truman on 3 July 1946. It provided financial support for research into psychological disorders, professional training, and grants to states for mental health centers and clinics. According to William Menninger, the salutary results of federal largesse were felt almost immediately. Within one year, every state had designated a state mental health authority, 42 states had submitted comprehensive mental health plans to the federal government, 59 training and 32 research grants had been awarded, and 212 students were on their way to becoming clinical professionals thanks to federal stipends.[26]

The NMHA also laid the groundwork for the National Institute of Mental Health (NIMH) and authorized funds for its construction. The NIMH, when it was formally established in 1949, replaced the Public Health Service Division of Mental Hygiene and was placed under the administrative umbrella of the National Institutes of Health. Robert Felix was named its first director. Publicly allied with reformers like Menninger and reform organizations like the Group for the Advancement of Psychiatry, Felix faithfully steered the new agency on the course that World War II and professional ambitions had specified. At the outset, he summed up his purpose as follows: "The guiding philosophy which permeates the activities of the National Institute of Mental Health is that prevention of mental illness, and the production of positive mental health, is an attainable goal."[27] This optimistic, preventive vision inspired Felix "to help the individual by helping the community"—an apt slogan for the community mental health movements that would shortly materialize on the cutting edge of clinical work.[28] By the time he retired in 1964, Felix had been widely credited with prodding the federal government out of the dark ages of indifference toward mental illness and health.

As a result of its preventive, community-sensitive orientation, the NIMH became the key institutional patron of an expansive (and expensive) mental health program during the postwar decades, one that consciously mingled the insights of clinical expertise and behavioral science. Felix appointed a panel of social science consultants as soon as the NIMH was founded and charged members with recommending ways that interdisciplinary social research could further the goal of national mental health. He named several individuals to the panel who had played key wartime roles, championing the utilization of clinical theories to achieve practical policy aims. Margaret Mead, Ronald Lippitt, and Lawrence K. Frank were among them.[29]

The abundant and ever-increasing funds that the NIMH offered to psychological professionals were an important reason for the healthy economy in mental health fields in the 1950s and 1960s. During 1950, its first year of operation, the NIMH budget was $8.7 million. Ten years later, it was over $100 million, and by 1967, it was $315 million.[30] In 1947 total federal expenditures for health-related research of all kinds had been around $27 million.[31] As the government's research program expanded in the years after World War II, far outstripping private sources of funding, the proportion devoted to mental health increased dramatically. In 1947 it was allotted a mere 1.5 percent of federal medical research dollars; just four years later, in 1951, its share had risen to almost 6.5 percent.[32] Only four other areas of medical research were granted more money than mental health in the five years after the war: general medical problems, heart disease, infectious disease, and cancer.[33] By the early 1960s, mental health had outpaced heart disease, but the precipitous rise in available dollars did little to silence critics of government spending priorities, who continued to insist that the public research investment in mental health was shortsighted and stingy when compared to the costs of mental illness.[34]

Although hardly in a position to be as generous as the Department

of Defense, the NIMH was nevertheless a major benefactor of fundamental research in the social and behavioral sciences by the late 1960s.
On the theory that any and all research related to mental health deserved support, the NIMH financed everything from anthropological
fieldwork abroad to quantitative sociological "reports on happiness" at
home.[35] Its impact was felt on research concerned with racial identity,
conflict, and violence and it gave staff and other resources to the Kerner
Commission investigations, as we have already seen.

By the early 1960s, NIMH was spending significantly more on psychological and cultural studies of behavior than it was on conventional
medical inquiries into the biological basis of mental disease.[36] In 1964,
60 percent of NIMH research funds were given to psychologists, sociologists, anthropologists, and epidemiologists; only 15 percent of the
budget went to psychiatry, with an additional 21 percent going to other
biologically oriented sciences.[37] Such conspicuously social priorities
were compatible with the community emphasis of mental health research and practice, the enhanced status of behavioral science, and the
dominance of psychodynamic perspectives among clinicians during the
1950s and early 1960s.

COMMUNITY MENTAL HEALTH AS AN
EXPRESSION OF CLINICAL SOCIAL
RESPONSIBILITY

In the years after the passage of the NMHA, several other
developments within the professions and on the federal level sustained
the forward motion of clinical experts by further institutionalizing opportunities for professional training and fostering clinicians' social influence through a process of integration with the social and behavioral
sciences. The formation of the Group for the Advancement of Psychiatry (GAP) in the spring of 1946 embodied the reforming zeal of
"young Turks" with a background in military mental health.[38] Led by
William Menninger, GAP was initially conceived as a pressure group
within the American Psychiatric Association. During the next couple of
years, GAP members captured most of the top posts in the American
Psychiatric Association, including the presidency. But GAP soon blos-
somed into an autonomous organization whose influential working
groups and published reports championed social conscience and liberal
political activism and whose professional campaigns carried the banner
of community mental health.

In July 1950 GAP's Committee on Social Issues published a manifesto, titled "The Social Responsibility of Psychiatry," which made GAP's political proclivities explicit. In draft form, the committee pledged itself to social reform: "We feel not only justified, but ethically compelled to advocate those changes in social organization which have a positive relevance to a program of mental health."[39] The final document was somewhat more moderate in tone, but its activist commitment was indisputable.

The Committee on Social Issues has the conviction that social action . . . implies a conscious and deliberate wish to foster those social developments which could promote mental health on a community-wide scale. . . . We favor the application of psychiatric principles to all those problems which have to do with family welfare, child rearing, child and adult education, social and economic factors which influence the community status of individuals and families, intergroup tensions, civil rights and personal liberty. The social crisis which confronts us today is menacing; we would surely be guilty of dereliction of duty did we not make a conscientious effort to apply whatever partial knowledge we now possess in the interests of counteracting social danger and promoting healthier being, both for individuals and groups. This, in a true sense, carries psychiatry out of the hospitals and into the community.[40]

Although there was some resistance to GAP's emphatically social interpretation of psychiatric responsibility within the profession at large, which had a long history of concern for the somatic causes of mental disorder as well as for severely ill individuals, no such resistance existed within the surging ranks of psychology.

Clinical psychology, after all, was practically a brand-new profession after World War II. It was searching for a fresh identity within a newly reorganized American Psychological Association (APA) that had defined its general purposes in unmistakably visionary terms from the very first. As Robert Yerkes put it, at the APA's Intersociety Constitutional Convention in 1943,

The world crisis, with its clash of cultures and ideologies, has created for us psychologists unique opportunity for promotive endeavor. What may be achieved through wisely-planned and well-directed professional activity will be limited only by our knowledge, faith, disinterestedness, and prophetic foresight. It is for us, primarily, to prepare the way for scientific advances and the development of welfare services which from birth to death shall guide and minister to the development and social usefulness of the individual. For beyond even our wildest dreams, knowledge of human nature may now be made to serve human needs and to multiply and increase the satisfactions of living.[41]

Clinical psychologists found that the "birth to death" ideology of the welfare state corresponded perfectly with their own aim to normalize clinical practice and expand their sphere of social authority, even when those aims—the autonomous practice of psychotherapy was perhaps the most striking—conflicted directly with the interests of organized psychiatry.

GAP's record illustrated that advocating social change in the name of improved mental health could produce both very rewarding professional and very unpredictable political results. By insisting that mental balance involved a constant state of adjustment and exchange between self and society, clinical experts could, and did, lay claim to defining what was normal in environments as well as in people. "This view of the fluidity of the interaction of the individual with society," GAP pointed out, "tends inevitably to broaden the concepts of mental illness and mental health."[42]

They did not add that it inevitably broadened the authority of psychological experts as well by giving them power to designate exactly how social institutions—economic, familial, educational, and so on— might prevent mental trouble and nourish emotional well-being. Doing so, needless to say, was extremely controversial. GAP's impeccable liberal credentials led members to endorse a social program of racial harmony, literacy, economic security, and family happiness, among other things—all founded on an expanded role for psychologically enlightened federal government. One of the best known and most widely circulated GAP reports, for example, was issued in 1957. Titled "Psychiatric Aspects of School Desegregation," there was no mistaking its immediate relevance, and support for school integration, in the face of the fierce white resistance that followed *Brown v. Board of Education.*[43]

Yet even more disagreement accompanied any definition of "normal" social structure than did the definition of "normal" individual psychology. (Whether or not racial integration qualified as one component of a normal environment was just the tip of the iceberg.) The climate of domestic anticommunism in the late 1940s and early 1950s also emboldened GAP's critics. At various points, the organization was accused of being a "radical sectarian group" full of Communist sympathizers intent on seizing control of the psychiatric profession.[44] GAP members responded to McCarthyism by dashing off a report, "Considerations Regarding the Loyalty Oath as a Manifestation of Current Social Tension and Anxiety," but political name-calling caused barely a momentary interruption in their crusade to have clinical experts act on their social responsibilities, as GAP saw them.[45]

In 1955 Congress passed the National Mental Health Study Act, paving the way for the Joint Commission on Mental Illness and Health (JCMIH). GAP members and others who shared an activist clinical philosophy believed the government had taken another decisive and enlightened step toward broadening its jurisdiction over mental health, superseding the decentralized tradition that had left policies in the hands of bungling and backward state politicians.[46] The purpose of the JCMIH (which, although a nongovernmental body, was almost entirely funded by the NIMH) was to conduct an encyclopedic survey of mental illness and health in preparation for innovative new national policy initiatives. Thirty-six participating organizations (which included the Department of Defense, the American Legion, and the American Psychiatric Association) spent several years and $1.5 million on this project and published ten scholarly monographs in addition to its final report, *Action for Mental Health.* The final report reiterated at the outset the fundamental equation between democracy and mental health that had been a constant refrain during and after World War II. Their assigned task of developing mental health policy, wrote the authors, "is our responsibility as citizens of a democratic nation founded out of faith in the uniqueness, integrity, and dignity of human life. . . . Good mental health . . . is consistent with this higher responsibility and with our professional and political ideals. It is also consistent with what the American people should want—not simply peace of mind but strength of mind."[47]

During its tenure, the JCMIH compiled a mass of data with numerous possible interpretations, but its staff and major constituencies all wished to promote the delivery of community-based services geared to prevention. According to the JCMIH studies, new, milder forms of psychotherapeutic intervention in communities across the country were worth a real try, even though intensive custodial care was in dire need of improvement. Several of its core recommendations were used by the Kennedy and Johnson administrations in the years that followed to move the federal government toward the next policy phase: establishing community mental health centers throughout the country. In this regard, an especially significant suggestion was that funding more outpatient services through community centers would result in cutting hospitalization rates (i.e., prevent at least some cases of incapacitating mental illness). The JCMIH proposed one center for every fifty thousand people.[48]

In 1963 President Kennedy (whose younger sister Rosemary had undergone psychosurgery after being diagnosed with mild retardation) became the first U.S. president to make mental illness and retardation the subjects of a special address to Congress (fig. 16). Surely this was conclusive proof that the mental and emotional status of U.S. citizens had become a pressing government concern. Kennedy's speech elated the boosters of a socially active and expansive federal policy because the president highlighted the criticisms and proposals that advocates of preventive and community mental health had been repeating for years: during World War II, in the course of passing the NMHA, and in organizations like GAP.

First, Kennedy disparaged a decentralized policy approach and accused states of neglectful reliance on "shamefully understaffed, overcrowded, unpleasant institutions from which death too often provided the only firm hope of release."[49] Then he proclaimed that "an ounce of prevention is worth more than a pound of cure."[50] Only a new federal campaign to fund research, professional training, and community-based services would replace "the cold mercy of custodial isolation" with "the open warmth of community concern and capability" and, Kennedy optimistically projected, reduce the number of institutionalized patients by 50 percent in "a decade or two."[51] Shortly afterwards, the Mental Retardation Facilities and Community Mental Health Centers Construction Act of 1963 was passed. Federal grants for the construction of community mental health centers were its main feature; a total of $150 million was appropriated for this purpose during the following three fiscal years.[52] The long-term goal (never to be realized) was to establish a national network of two thousand centers, one for each geographically defined community of 75,000 to 200,000 people. Even observers who worried that care for the most severely ill might suffer endorsed the expanded sphere of authority that the act gave to clinical professionals and pronounced it "the most significant development in recent history in the provision of services for the mentally ill."[53]

The combined efforts of policy-makers and professional advocates, and the tenor of national mental health legislation in the decades after 1945, turned the ideology of community mental health into an expression of clinical experts' social responsibility. Based on the sunny supposition that mental health could be manufactured (and illness prevented) if only the environmental conditions were favorable, clinicians marched boldly into a variety of fields—from criminal justice to education—to guarantee that they would be.[54]

Figure 16. President Kennedy addressing Congress on 5 February 1963
on the subject of mental illness and retardation. Photo: No. AR
7698A in the John F. Kennedy Library.

Claiming that all aspects of community life potentially affected individual mental health, psychiatrists redefined their clinical mission as follows: "Within our definition, all social, psychological, and biological activity affecting the mental health of the populace is of interest to the community psychiatrist, including programs for fostering social change, resolution of social problems, political involvement, community organization planning, and clinical psychiatric practice."[55] A typical formulation of community psychology simply identified it with the "optimal realization of human potential through planned social action."[56]

That something as undeniably positive as mental health could justify a process of social reform had obvious appeal during a period of dynamic grassroots and governmental activism. During the late 1950s and 1960s, an array of progressive social movements repeatedly called for equalizing changes in the distribution of political power and material resources, and the federal government responded with nothing less than the War on Poverty and the Great Society. The impetus for community mental health had, after all, come from clinicians with liberal political sympathies in the 1940s and 1950s. When the political climate shifted further to the left in the 1960s, clinicians moved a bit further to the left as well, but they continued to advance a vision that merged psychological change with social activism and responsibility. Community mental health, they were convinced, was intimately bound up with campaigns to eliminate racism, poverty, and oppression and forge a better, more humane, society. Mental health was all but synonymous with equality, prosperity, and social welfare.

It was not long, however, before radicals began to question these happy political assumptions, a process we have already seen at work in the case of psychological approaches to the problems of rioting and revolution confronted by police forces and militaries. "Sick" social environments stubbornly resisted clinicians' most well intentioned cures; ghettos remained poor and schools impoverished. How could adjustment between self and society be accomplished, or even advocated, when so many people led such wretched lives? Perhaps psychological adjustment only adjusted people to habits of powerlessness, inequality, and anguish?

By the late 1960s, the frustrating slowness of change had generated the beginnings of a skeptical, even cynical, countermovement that turned the heady idealism of the postwar years on its head. Suspicions that psychological expertise might have oppressive consequences diametrically opposed to stated intentions spread, sometimes as a result of organizing by former mental patients who bluntly denounced the treatment they had received at the hands of the mental health professionals, sometimes as a result of the advocates of "radical therapy," who aimed to merge therapeutic insight and leftist politics. Under the harsh light of this new criticism, the community mental health movement no longer appeared as an enlightening crusade, but rather as one element of a multifaceted scheme to subvert genuine democracy through a disguised program of social control. One writer, Chaim Shatan, speculated in 1969 that "the clinicians will provide emotional first aid, while the government-subsidized conveyor belt feeds manpower directly into federally sponsored operations—from the space race to community mental health itself. . . . In 1984, Big Brother may be a community psychiatrist." [57]

In March 1969 Lincoln Hospital Mental Health Services, located in the South Bronx, was taken over by its nonprofessional staff members, most of them black and Puerto Rican.[58] The center epitomized the ideals of the community mental health movement; there was a walk-in clinic for neighborhood residents, a program of consultation with community organizations, and so forth. But the protesters were fed up with the paternalism of well-intentioned white psychiatrists, as the text from their flyer made clear.

We're gonna see what you do with what you think is your center. You honkies complain that we don't respect authority and we don't want any compromise. Damn right. Your authority is no good and we've been compromising too damn long. So now you listen to what working people are saying loud and clear. And you better listen: Cause now we're not working *for* the center anymore. We and the community *are* the center.[59]

After fifteen days of occupation, during which the protesting workers appointed new department heads and issued a lengthy list of demands, the administration caved in. The center promptly changed its name, hired a new director, and severed its ties to the hospital (and the department of psychiatry at Albert Einstein College of Medicine, with which it was affiliated).

This episode, now famous as a turning point in the history of the community mental health movement, propelled forward the new spirit of negativity about the political function of clinicians and strengthened the view that community mental health was so much rhetoric plastered over an unattractive reality of domination by elites. Significantly, however, the target of the most withering criticism was the inequality between professionals and nonprofessionals. Even the Bronx protest reemphasized the liberating potential of psychological knowledge in the hands of disenfranchised people. As long as it was not monopolized by experts, community psychology "gave a voice to people who had been kept outside of history." [60] For a number of years after the 1969 takeover, the Lincoln Community Mental Health Center offered a range of alternative, largely nonprofessional mental health services to residents in the South Bronx.

Psychotherapy for the Normal as a Postwar Growth Industry

The doubts that began to cramp clinicians' high spirits by the late 1960s were somewhat removed from the concerns of the general public. During the years after 1945, ordinary people sought therapeutic attention more insistently than ever before and for more reasons than ever before. While the direction of federal policy may have helped to push clinicians out of asylums, the explosion in public interest was at least as pivotal in pulling clinicians into the lives of ordinary citizens. Gushing demand for psychotherapy was much discussed by clinicians. Even dissenters like C. C. Burlingame, the director of the Hartford, Connecticut, Institute for Living and a staunch advocate of psychosurgery, who denounced the prevalent mood of therapeutic optimism as "psychiatric nonsense," admitted that "it has come to be quite the fashion to have a psychoneurosis!"[61] Unlike Burlingame, most experts welcomed the surge in popular demand as evidence of a sort of public enlightenment "peculiar to the United States."[62] They were quick to herald it as "one of the remarkable features of our culture," whether they understood it or not.[63]

We have already seen that, in the wake of world war, new federal laws, bureaucracies, and funding embraced the changing emphasis from mental illness to health, spurred along by reenergized old and new professional pressure groups. By generating a new, publicly supported infrastructure for training, research, and service delivery in mental health fields, the federal government contributed to the migration of clinical experts out of isolated institutions devoted to insanity and into the heart of U.S. communities. A 1948 survey conducted by the American Psychiatric Association found that 35 percent of its members were already primarily engaged in private practice.[64] The 1954 introduction of the first psychoactive drug, chlorpromazine (known by the trade name Thorazine), accelerated the trend, already under way, toward emptying traditional institutions. In 1956 the total number of patients residing in public mental hospitals declined for the first time since the nineteenth century, and the deinstitutionalization process picked up speed in the mid-1960s.[65] In 1957 only 17 percent of all American Psychiatric Association members were still charged with supervising custodial care to severely and chronically ill individuals in state or VA hospitals, the sort of institutions where virtually all psychiatrists had been located prior to 1940.[66]

The new policy emphasis on deinstitutionalization was conveniently compatible with the case for normalization, delivery of preventive clinical services, and expansion of experts' authority and jurisdiction. Indeed, these factors were mutually reinforcing. The standard argument was that outmoded and ineffective institutional care would be replaced by more efficient and enlightened services delivered in a community setting. The community mental health movement, as it turned out, did not cause the numbers of institutionalized mental patients to drop.[67] Rather, changes in federal programs during the 1960s—especially the creation of Medicare and Medicaid in the 1965 amendments to the Social Security Act—shifted elderly and chronic patients out of state hospitals and into nontraditional institutions as states quickly took advantage of new funding sources.

Advocates' rhetoric notwithstanding, the movement into the community neither replaced the old system of public mental institutions, nor adequately cared for severely and chronically mentally ill individuals, most of whom were simply moved from a publicly funded custodial setting to one in the private sector, typically a nursing home. In retrospect, it appears ironic that the expansion of the welfare state, with which liberal clinical reformers identified so strongly, undermined public commitments to the mentally sick and ushered in an era during which the logic of cost containment superseded the ethic of care. Ardent critics of the policy have consequently accused reformers of "ideological camouflage" and deinstitutionalization of "allowing economy to masquerade as benevolence and neglect as tolerance."[68] Historians more sympathetic to policy reformers after World War II point to the fact of human fallibility, the impossibility of determining all consequences in advance, and the dangers of retrospective judgment and arrogance.[69]

If it failed to achieve its stated goals, community mental health did succeed in providing new services—far more psychotherapeutic in emphasis—to a new clientele—far larger, better educated, and more middle-class. This accomplishment reflected a sharp reorientation of professional interests and a decided expansion in the market for therapeutic services among normal individuals. Increases in the sheer numbers of psychiatrists were startling in the postwar decades—professional association membership grew from 3,634 in 1945, at the end of World War II, to 18,407 in 1970—and the percentage of medical school graduates choosing to specialize in psychiatry ranged from a high of 7.1 percent right after the war to 6.4 percent at the end of the 1960s, numbers two to three times greater than the 1925–1940 period.[70] Institutional care faded as the center of professional gravity it had once been. Psychiatric staff positions in public mental facilities were notoriously difficult to fill, with openings running around 25 percent nationally in the mid-1960s.[71]

By the late 1950s and 1960s, most psychiatrists were either self-employed in private office practice or worked in educational institutions, government agencies, or the growing number of community clinics that catered to a "normally neurotic" clientele. In order to help veterans adjust to student life, the VA sponsored programs that expanded counseling on the university level and in 1958, the National Defense Education Act created sixty thousand jobs for an entirely new type of professional—the school guidance counselor—making individual testing and deliberate self-inspection an ever more routine feature of young students' lives.[72] In outpatient clinics exclusively devoted to adult mental health, according to one 1955 estimate, at least 233,000 people annually were already receiving outpatient psychotherapy.[73]

Clinical psychology underwent an especially rapid process of professionalization after World War II, spurred by the popularization of psychotherapy as well as by government generosity. In 1947 the American Psychological Association gave its institutional stamp of approval to the mushrooming practice of psychotherapy when it made clinical training a mandatory element of graduate education in psychology.[74] The first effort to take stock of feverish postwar efforts to establish new training programs in clinical psychology came in August 1949 in Boulder, Colorado. Thanks to an NIMH grant, seventy-one psychologists from around the United States met to consider the future of clinical training on the graduate level. There was great excitement about future opportunities in the field, a feeling reflected in NIMH Director Robert Felix's opening comments. "The mental health program is going forward, and neither you nor I nor all of us can stop it now because the public is aware of the potentialities."[75]

Problems were nevertheless immediately apparent. Although no one present at the conference seemed to know exactly what a clinical psychologist was or what a clinical psychologist did, they quickly agreed that a doctoral degree was necessary to do it. The Ph.D. was necessary "to protect the public and to create some order out of the present confusion" because "in the public mind there is considerable confusion of the professionally trained clinical psychologist with the outright quack."[76]

What to do about the practice of psychotherapy in particular was equally baffling but probably more pressing and definitely more controversial. Conference attendees were aware of the need to balance the huge market for this service against the many unresolved questions surrounding its practice and outcomes. "Social needs, demands for service, and our own desire to serve effectively have compelled us to engage in programs of action before their validity could be adequately demonstrated."[77] Pressured to respond to public demand, they were still at a loss to describe psychotherapy or list its benefits with even minimal precision. The only definition of psychotherapy generating consensus was so general that it was of negligible use in planning training programs. According to the conference record, "psychotherapy is defined as a process involving interpersonal relationships between a therapist and one or more patients or clients by which the former employs psychological methods based on systematic knowledge of the personality in attempting to improve the mental health of the latter."[78]

Because the practice of psychotherapy was evidently as vague as it was popular, little agreement existed about the type of educational preparation required to make a good therapist, but much agreement existed that more good therapists were needed. Should therapists-in-training be required to be in psychotherapy themselves? Did students aspiring to careers as therapists really need rigorous training in scientific research methods? No one was certain. One sarcastic, unidentified conference participant summarized the muddled thinking on this question. "Psychotherapy is an undefined technique applied to unspecified problems with unpredictable outcome. For this technique we recommend rigorous training."[79]

The details governing psychotherapy and its practice remained contentious matters among the experts long after the Boulder conference. The first really damaging critique, in fact, came more than three years later from Hans Eysenck. Eysenck was a British psychologist with a reputation as a hard-nosed experimentalist whose career had taken a sharp turn toward clinical work during World War II; he eventually taught the first British course on clinical psychology. In 1952 Eysenck suggested not only that no evidence of psychotherapy's tangible benefits existed but that there was "an inverse correlation between recovery and psychotherapy."[80] Ironically, Eysenck's heresy provided psychotherapy's defenders with years' worth of work. Throughout the 1950s and 1960s, they assiduously devised ever more creative ways to define and measure psychotherapeutic outcomes and this new field of scientific research evolved into a small industry.[81]

Then there was the very delicate question of how clinicians in psychology or other professions should negotiate with psychiatrists, who had always monopolized psychotherapy and uniformly opposed its practice by other professionals.[82] The forces of organized medicine repeatedly asserted that "psychotherapy is a form of medical treatment and does not form the basis for a separate profession."[83] According to many physicians, the psychologist should have been grateful to play a limited and subordinate role similar to that played by the nurse in general medicine, who, they pointed out with some annoyance, was far more likely to understand "her" place.[84]

None of this did much to slow experts outside of psychiatry, who grew ever bolder in their claims to autonomous practice as the definition of psychotherapy stretched. To them, it was a nonmedical service "sought by people who do not think of themselves as ill but who wish to avail themselves of something they believe to be good for them, and it is offered by people who consider not that they are treating disease but that they are aiding in the realization of certain ethical values."[85] The struggle over whether psychotherapy treated the health of the body or the existential status of the soul and social welfare of humanity resulted in an ongoing professional "cold war."[86]

Outside the professions, these turf battles hardly mattered. The popularization of psychotherapy proceeded rapidly during the postwar decades, becoming a staple in drama, films, and on television.[87] Most of the cultural images were highly exaggerated. Psychological interpretation, as often as not, appeared to involve pat formulas, and portrayals of mental health professionals included malevolent abusers and incompetent fools alongside caring father figures and magical healers.[88] Aware that their talents were being put to cultural tests at least as rigorous as the scientific proofs prized within the professions, organizations like the American Psychiatric Association actively lobbied in Hollywood and elsewhere to safeguard good public relations and avert unflattering stereotypes.[89] Whatever damage the professionals feared to their collective reputation was clearly outdistanced by the almost insatiable public demand for accessible, entertaining information about who mental health experts were and what they did.

Psychotherapy was also an experience in which more and more people participated directly (fig. 17). By 1970 approximately twenty thousand psychiatrists were ministering to one million people on a purely outpatient basis.[90] Well over ten thousand psychologists were providing some type of counseling service, more than were involved in any other single area of work, and close to half of all doctoral degrees in psychology were being granted in clinical and counseling fields.[91] This was truly an extraordinary feat considering that only a tiny handful of psychologists (less than three hundred APA members) had even called themselves "clinical" thirty years earlier.[92]

In 1957, according to a major national study done for the JCMIH, ordinary people were relying more heavily than ever on clinical experts and formal help in order to deal with their routine personal problems: 14 percent of all those surveyed sought therapeutic assistance for a problem they defined in psychological terms.[93] In 1976, when the study was repeated, the percentage had almost doubled, to 26 percent, and approximately 30 percent reported consulting therapists in crisis situations.[94] More important, the highly conscious pursuit of personal and interpersonal meaning that the authors termed a "psychological revolution" had spread.[95] Activated first among better-off and better-educated sectors of the population during the 1950s, the revolution radiated outward and downward to become "common coin" by the 1970s.[96] Further, the reasons why people entered psychotherapy were changing. By the 1970s, "many people use a relationship with a professional as a way to explore and expand their personalities rather than as a way to undo painful or thoroughly negative feelings about themselves."[97] Using psychotherapy to cope with a "normal" dose of emotional anguish was no longer considered a prelude to psychiatric hospitalization or even a mark of mental abnormality.

The surge in psychotherapy's popularity was much more than a fad, and its consequences were much more than merely professional. The availability of new, government-supported services and opportunities for professional education and research did not, in themselves, generate a mass market for psychotherapy, though they helped immeasurably to do so. Psychotherapy for the normal gained momentum not only because of the formal expansion of government services but because it meshed easily with cultural trends that made therapeutic help appear acceptable, even inviting, to ordinary people at midcentury: the contin-

Figure 17. Group psychotherapy. Photo: Archives of the American
Psychiatric Association.

ued thinning of community ties; a vehement emphasis on the patriarchal nuclear family that put that institution under great pressure to satisfy the emotional needs of children and adults after World War II and
had gone so far to challenge women's conventional gender roles; a
sense of depersonalization and loss of self in huge corporate workplaces
and other mass institutions.

Clinicians, for their part, encouraged people to think of psychotherapy as a perfectly appropriate way to cope with the ups and downs of
modern existence. Because the logic of psychological development
guaranteed each and every individual the potential for neurosis, so-
called normal individuals were just as deeply affected by mental symptoms and disturbances; they were simply better at hiding them.[98] And
they went further. Just as clinicians had trumpeted psychotherapy's potential to systematically aid in postwar social adjustment, so too did
they (and their clients) proclaim in later years that the trend toward
psychotherapy for the normal illustrated promising moves toward cultural change and development. Psychotherapy, according to one sym-

pathetic observer in the late 1960s, was a noble effort to map "the country of the soul [so that] the meaning of the long-sought civilization comes into sight and may be occupied."[99] By the early 1970s, Lawrence Kubie, a psychiatrist who had opposed the involvement of nonphysicians in diagnosis and treatment prior to World War II, and who had been involved in touchy postwar discussions about clinical psychologists practicing psychotherapy independently, was offering glowing accolades to psychotherapy's popularization.

As we make therapy more widely available, an understanding in depth of the role of the neurotic process in human development will begin to permeate our culture. In fact, this is essential for the maturation of any society. . . . Insofar as the development of the new discipline [psychotherapy] will bring insight to more people than was previously possible and infuse the work of more and more of our institutions with self-knowledge in depth, we can look to this to increase each individual's freedom to change, and his freedom to use his potential skills creatively. Ultimately this state of affairs can bring the freedom to change to an entire culture.[100]

The Humanistic Tide

During the 1950s and 1960s, humanistic experts emerged as probably the most avid proponents of a psychological theory based on normality and a therapeutic practice designed to offer liberating encounters to masses of ordinary people as well as progress to U.S. culture at large. Although the majority of individuals who identified with humanistic psychology were immersed in theoretical and clinical tasks, they viewed their work as both politically and philosophically significant. In a lecture at Yale in 1954, humanistic personality theorist Gordon Allport outlined the political challenge confronting psychological professionals: "Up to now the 'behavioral sciences,' including psychology, have not provided us with a picture of man capable of creating or living in a democracy. . . . What psychology can do is to discover whether the democratic ideal is possible."[101]

By the 1960s, humanists had moved beyond trying to prove the feasibility of democracy to pointing out the congruence between a constantly evolving democratic system and their theories of psychotherapeutic change and personality development. Personhood, the goal of psychotherapy and the subject of much psychological theory, was a process, a fluid state of change, exchange, and ongoing renewal. The core imperatives of humanistic theory—to grow, to become, and to realize full human potential—were nothing less than democratic blueprints grafted onto the map of human subjectivity.

Although existentialism in its European version was too gloomy and tormented for the humanists' taste (Maslow, for one, called it "high-I.Q. whimpering on a cosmic scale"), the humanists eagerly assimilated the existentialist conviction in "the total collapse of all sources of values outside the individual." [102] Refusing to surrender to European styles of unbelief, the humanists redoubled their strenuous efforts to weave inexorable democratic promise into the fabric of normal human development. "There is no place else to turn but inward, to the self, as the locus of values." [103]

The humanists called themselves a "third force," by which they meant that they were forging a path distinct from both psychoanalysis and behaviorism.[104] Although they were scattered throughout the country and institutions devoted to perpetuating their ideas were not established until the 1960s, they operated as a self-conscious tendency within the psychological professions throughout the period after 1940. For a group accustomed to describing itself, and being described by others, as a band of rebels pounding on the walls of the psychological establishment, the humanists were unusually successful in winning conventional professional rewards as well as spreading their gospel to the popular culture in the twenty-five years after 1945. Carl Rogers and Abraham Maslow, two psychologists whose work is discussed briefly below, were each elected to the presidency of the APA, in 1947 and 1968, respectively, and both became gurulike celebrities (to Rogers's delight and Maslow's disgust) among fans of encounter, human potential, "new consciousness," and other variants of the 1960s counterculture.

Revolutionary bravado was a staple in the humanists' writing. Maslow, for example, compared the movement to the momentous work of Galileo, Darwin, Einstein, Freud, and Marx and called humanistic psychology "a new general comprehensive philosophy of life." [105] While some of their ideas were certainly original, others were borrowed from the very two "forces" against which humanistic psychology defined itself. Both Maslow and Rogers were quick to trace their own intellectual pedigrees to a variety of sources, including the neo-Freudianism of Karen Horney, Harry Stack Sullivan, and Erich Fromm, the Gestalt psychology of Kurt Goldstein, the philosophy of John Dewey and Martin Buber, and the scientific method so exalted by behaviorists.

The most important common ground between the humanists and other psychological experts was the ambition to carve out "a larger jurisdiction for psychology," an expanding sphere of social authority and influence.[106] In fact, the humanists went about the task of exploring psychology's political implications rather explicitly. In the end they proposed severely narrowing democracy's subject to "the self" and pledged that practices like psychotherapy could help make that self both autonomous and mature, capable of living up to ideals of democratic thought and action.

Proving that people were capable of reasoned behavior—and not merely victims at the mercy of strong emotional currents—was a conscious, if sometimes implicit, goal for the humanists, including Rogers and Maslow. Yet they did not think of themselves as political theorists, and certainly not as political activists. Their preferred environments were academic and clinical psychology and their professional and personal identities were shaped by desires to generate scientific personality theory and help people cope with the problems of life and living.

CARL ROGERS: INHERENT CAPACITY AS
A SCIENTIFIC BASIS FOR DEMOCRACY

Carl Rogers was a clinical psychologist who became famous after World War II for his work in developing, and then scientifically studying, an approach to psychotherapy first termed "non-directive," and later renamed "client-centered."[107] Rogers's terminology was important; he was largely responsible for the widespread adoption of the term "client" in the mental health field. "Client" gradually replaced "patient," at least outside of psychiatry, illustrating the democratization of the therapeutic relationship and the retreat from (or sometimes even outright rejection of) the medical model in which a dependent and suffering individual relied on the kindness of an omniscient doctor.[108]

After twelve years of full-time work in a child guidance clinic (the Rochester, New York, Society for the Prevention of Cruelty to Children), Rogers switched to an academic career. In 1940 he moved to Ohio State University and in later years he was affiliated with the University of Chicago, the University of Wisconsin, and the Western Behavioral Sciences Institute in La Jolla, California. Toward the end of his life, Rogers founded the Center for Studies of the Person in La Jolla. Beginning in 1940, university employment facilitated Rogers's systematic investigation of what actually occurred during counseling and psy-chotherapy. He and his colleagues were the first to use and publish unedited transcriptions of audiorecorded therapeutic encounters and they earned reputations as innovative pioneers in this new field of re-search.[109]

The client-centered approach was based on a series of hypotheses, the most fundamental of which was an almost religious belief in the inherent human capacity for growth, psychological insight, and self-regulation. Rogers, who grew up in a very religious family and studied at the Union Theological Seminary before transferring to Columbia University Teachers College to study psychology, sometimes called it a "divine spark."[110] According to Rogers, "the individual has within himself the capacity, latent if not evident, to understand those aspects of himself and of his life which are causing him dissatisfaction, anxiety, or pain and the capacity and the tendency to reorganize himself and his relationship to life in the direction of self-actualization and maturity in such a way as to bring a greater degree of internal comfort."[111] If a nurturing interpersonal environment were achieved, in psychotherapy and elsewhere, "change and constructive personal development will *in-variably* occur."[112]

The Rogerian conception of psychotherapy required a healthy self equipped with healthy psychological potential. "Therapy is not a matter of doing something *to* the individual, or of inducing him to do some-thing about himself," Rogers wrote in one early formulation. "It is in-stead a matter of freeing him for normal growth and development, and removing obstacles so that he can again move forward."[113] No longer was the therapeutic subject someone whose behavior and personality were so disordered that they needed prescriptive assistance. The thera-peutic subject may have been neurotic, but he (or she) remained a "per-son who is competent to direct himself."[114]

The humanists' concern with normality was consistent with the over-all clinical lessons of World War II. Their psychotherapeutic techniques, however, diverged sharply from those of the psychodynamic psycho-therapists who dominated the clinical professions after 1945. Simpli-fied, the theory underlying psychodynamic practice was that experts helped individuals paralyzed and helpless in the face of unconscious fears. The clinician acted simultaneously as judge, interpreter, and healer. In contrast, the Rogerian therapist was a supportive cheerleader watching the client engage in what amounted to something like delib-erate self-help. If therapists were sufficiently "permissive" (i.e., ac-cepting and empathetic), and if they made strenuous efforts never to interpret or even evaluate feelings or problems, then clients' internal capacity would inevitably move them toward self-understanding, and from there on to greater satisfaction and maturity. Robert Morison, an officer of the Rockefeller Foundation, was skeptical of Rogers's ideas about the therapeutic relationship and thought his detour from the medical model betrayed a "trace of fanaticism."[115]

Rogers frequently noted that the concept of internal capacity not only confirmed the logic of democratic social arrangements, but revealed the psychological roots of those arrangements. "If, as we think, the locus of responsible evaluation may be left with the individual, then we would have a psychology of personality and of therapy which leads in the direction of democracy, a psychology which would gradually redefine democracy in deeper and more basic terms."[116] Human nature and democracy, in other words, could be allies rather than enemies. In the following passage, Rogers approvingly quoted a student evaluation in order to make this point.

I have come to see that there may be a scientifically demonstrable basis for belief in the democratic way of life. . . . I cannot honestly say that I am now unalterably convinced of the infallibility of the democratic process, but I am encouraged and inclined to align myself with those who hold that each individual has within himself the capacity for self-direction and self-responsibility, hoping that the beginnings of research in areas such as client-centered therapy will lead to the unquestionable conclusion that the democratic way of life is most in harmony with the nature of man.[117]

The humanists were especially cognizant that their benign conception of human nature, and the fortuitous basis it provided for democratic ideas and behaviors, ran counter to much psychological theory and rather a lot of psychological data (especially notable were studies done under pressure of war). The bulk of twentieth-century psychological thought hypothesized a malignant psychological interior, an awful place where destructive instincts and monstrous terrors lurked, threatening to rip through the thin veneer of Western civilization. "There is no beast in man," Rogers wrote defensively in 1953. "There is only man in man. . . . We do not need to be afraid of being 'merely' homo sapiens."[118]

Rogers's famous 1956 dialogue with B. F. Skinner, leading behaviorist and author of the utopian novel *Walden Two*, was evidence of his deep concern not only about the political implications of various psychological theories but about the political role and direction of clinical experts and behavioral scientists themselves.[119] In his exchanges with Rogers and elsewhere, Skinner had proposed that democratic political ideology was a historical relic. He conceded that it had perhaps been necessary and important for the political tasks facing the eighteenth century (i.e., overthrowing monarchies), but Skinner believed democratic ideology was obsolete in an era of modern science. "The so-called 'democratic philosophy' of human behavior . . . is increasingly in conflict with the application of the methods of science to human affairs."[120] Science—psychological science in particular—had revealed freedom to be mythological and social control to be both necessary and inevitable. The real question, according to Skinner, was not whether social control was good or bad, but what kinds of control would be exercised, and by whom.[121]

Rogers countered with the concept of universal, inherent capacity. He forthrightly criticized the idea that experts always knew best and worried that "the growth of knowledge in the social sciences contains within itself a powerful tendency toward social control, toward control of the many by the few."[122] Giving too much power to experts could surely lead "to social dictatorship and individual loss of personhood."[123] Rogers's apprehensions, however, revolved around people like Skinner, usually behaviorists, whose calls for power and control were most candid.

Excluded from such analysis was his own brand of helping relationship, which he claimed was based on cooperative, nonauthoritarian partnerships between "equals" or "co-workers."[124] (This failed, of course, to explain why one of the "equals" was a "therapist" while the other was a "client.") Rogers thought of his politics as a logical extension of his psychology—both were intensely egalitarian projects devoted to realizing autonomy and freedom—and regretted that more of his colleagues were not aware of the intimacy of this relationship. "There are really only a few psychologists who have contributed ideas that help to set people free," Rogers complained toward the end of his life, because "it is not in fashion to believe anything."[125]

ABRAHAM MASLOW: DEMOCRACY FOR THE SELF-ACTUALIZED FEW

Abraham Maslow was an academic psychologist best known for his hierarchical theory of motivation, his description of "self-actualization," and his professional activism on behalf of humanistic psychology.[126] Initially affiliated with Brooklyn College, Maslow moved on to Brandeis University, where he spent eighteen years beginning in 1951. He lectured widely, served as a consultant to industry and government, and was a founder of the *Journal of Humanistic Psychology* in 1961 and the American Association for Humanistic Psychology in 1962.

Like Rogers, Maslow was deeply concerned with the relationship between psychology and politics. He was at least as explicit about his own political views (which were not the same as Rogers's) and wrestled constantly with the political implications of his theoretical positions, especially during the late 1960s, when he was seriously considering writing a book about "B-politics," a parallel to his "B-psychology" (*B* stood for "being"). A heart attack cut his life short in 1970 when he was only sixty-two, and Maslow never wrote the book. Consequently, his journals are often far more revealing of his politics than is the body of his published work. Begun in 1959, they were finally published nine years after his death.[127]

During the 1950s, Maslow attempted to make liberal democratic values integral to a definition of mental health and psychological maturity.[128] This was part of the general humanistic project to test the feasibility of democracy by wiring individual dignity, tolerance, freedom of choice, and similar virtues into the unfolding process of normal human development. In his explorations of self-actualizing people and their "peak experiences" during the late 1950s and 1960s, Maslow refined his understanding of the political arrangements most appropriate to normal, even exemplary, psychological functioning.

Maslow's motivational scheme consisted of a hierarchy with basic needs at the bottom and higher needs at the top. The choice of a hierarchy was not arbitrary. Maslow intended to arrange human needs from lowly to lofty, in *"a series of increasing degrees of psychological health."*[129] At the lowest level were physiological needs for food, clothing, and shelter. A bit farther up were safety needs, then needs for "belongingness" and love, and finally needs for esteem, achievement, and respect. Higher needs emerged progressively as lower needs were satisfied. Self-actualization, the inherent tendency in people to move toward becoming all they could potentially become, was located at the summit of the motivational heap. "*Very* good conditions are needed to make self-actualizing possible."[130]

Self-actualization, in other words, rested self-consciously on the type of environment that the postwar United States allegedly offered: a society of abundance. The higher reaches of human psychological experience were possible precisely because, it was assumed, poverty and material deprivation had yielded to widespread prosperity in a middle-class society. Mental health, the product of a psychic economy of plenty, resulted from economic affluence. It could be bought and sold.

The most famous part of Maslow's study was his description of individuals who had climbed the motivational heights and actualized themselves.[131] Maslow included historical figures as well as live subjects (Thomas Jefferson, Abraham Lincoln, Albert Einstein, William James, and Eleanor Roosevelt were among them) and his inventory of their characteristics became a working definition of psychological well-being. Across the board, Maslow summarized, they were perceptive, self-accepting, spontaneous, autonomous, empathetic, and creative. They always made up their own minds, displaying independence and free will, and they reported mystical states that Maslow compared to orgasms and termed "peak experiences." Capable of feeling simultaneous power and powerlessness, ecstacy, awe, and heightened awareness, Maslow's peakers were acutely self-conscious and invested in their own psychological growth and development. They exemplified psychological integration and exhibited the fullest and most admirable potential of human identity.

For these very reasons, they were the perfect psychotherapeutic subjects. Insight and the desire for personal exploration, already in place, would grease the wheels of psychotherapy, making for less resistance and more success. That self-actualizing people should be intensively studied (and not only in psychotherapy) was one of Maslow's recommendations as well as a general tenet of humanistic psychology. "It becomes more and more clear that the study of crippled, stunted, immature, and unhealthy specimens can yield only a cripple psychology and a cripple philosophy."[132] Only healthy people could be the source of a truly universal psychological knowledge with broad jurisdiction.

Because individual health and sickness were inseparable from societal health and sickness, self-actualization was a relative, dependent, and occasional goal, rather than something either present or lacking at all times in particular individuals. Maslow's vision of a good society was consequently one where social and economic arrangements expedited upward movement through the motivational hierarchy, facilitating both personal growth and the production of good citizenship.[133] "It is quite true," he noted, "that man lives by bread alone—when there is no bread."[134] "Democracy of Western sort is OK for rich & well-organized, educated society, & capitalism then can work fairly well. For people with lower basic needs satisfied, higher needs emerge & we can talk about freedom for self-fulfillment, autonomy, encouragement of growth, humanitarianism, justice, democracy, etc. . . . There is now a hierarchy of societies paralleling the hierarchy of basic needs."[135]

Maslow's "hierarchy of societies" placed authoritarianism on the bottom rung with laissez-faire capitalism higher and New Deal welfare statism highest of all. Although Maslow felt that self-actualizing people would thrive in almost any political environment, he tended to think that an antisystem of anarchic individualism made the most sense for them.[136] His portrait of Eupsychia—a utopia inhabited by psychologically healthy people—was of a society committed to democracy but opposed to laws or constitutions, united in community but devoid of any traces of nationalist passion, abounding with permissiveness but lacking such problems as crime and unemployment.[137]

Self-actualizing individuals may have been the quintessence of all that was best and most promising about human nature, but according to Maslow, they were still only a tiny minority of the population, even in the United States. Consequently, different political structures were required even within a single society. Maslow, forever coining new terms, distinguished between "jungle politics," suitable for the majority stuck on the lower end of the motivational ladder, and "specieshood politics," for the self-actualizing elite. He wrote bluntly in his journal that there should be "one [political system] for winners & one for losers."[138]

Because Maslow was much more hard-boiled than Rogers in both his political views and his political assessments, he did not shy away from the conclusion that his hierarchical scheme might support a self-actualizing ruling class and lead to a two-tiered society, a sort of psychological apartheid. Because he accepted the inevitability of inequality as scientific fact, yet was unwilling to relinquish his commitment to liberal democracy, Maslow opted for institutional arrangements that would reward the *"biological"* superiority of a natural elite, rather than one founded on aristocratic, racial, or religious prejudice.[139] I quote at some length from three separate journal entries.

I think there *are* innate superiors & inferiors. How could there not be? Everything varies from more to less. *But,* on the other hand: (1) We must make the world safe for superiors. The lower the culture & the lower people are the more likely they are to resent & hate the superiors & so to kill them off and drive them into hiding & camouflage. The more we educate the bulk of the population, the better it will be for the elite, e.g., less danger, more audience,

more disciples, protectors, financers, etc. Also the better the society & the institutional arrangements, the safer the world, the more synergic it is, the better it
is for eliteniks. . . .

It seems clear to me (I said) that the regime of freedom and self-choice
which is desirable for innovating-creative people (& which they desire) can
be ruinous for noncreative people who are too authoritarian, too passive, too
authority-ambivalent, too noncommitted, etc.—ruinous at least in the sense
that this regime permits them to fail, since it assumes resources which are not
there. . . . So I vote in favor of making life better for the ones I call "good
students,"—those who are autonomous, committed, dedicated, hard-working,
etc.—& letting the others go hang. . . .

Also, the humanistic psychology absolutely *needs* a doctrine of an elite, degrees of humanness, health & sickness, winners & losers, aggridants (whether
by heredity or by learning), good specimens, good choosers, no equal votes,
nonequal weighting. The taste or judgment of one superior can & should out-
weigh 1000 or a million blind ones.[140]

"ADJUSTED TO WHAT?"

Maslow was a self-proclaimed patriot, a supporter of the
Vietnam War, and an advocate of restrictive population and reproductive control politics whose reaction to the political mood of the 1960s
was to call his activist students and colleagues members of the "Spit-on-
Daddy Club."[141] As far as he was concerned, they were overindulged,
underdisciplined, ungrateful, and impolite. According to Maslow, even
his own beloved daughter Ellen was a naive kid who had fallen under
the spell of the demagogic leaders and "hard-bitten revolutionaries" in
the Student Nonviolent Coordinating Committee and other civil rights
organizations.[142]

It is ironic indeed that Maslow should have helped to prod an unruly
new generation into the use of psychological theory for left-wing purposes. But that is exactly what he did when he pointedly asked,

Adjusted to what? To a bad culture? To a dominating parent? What shall we
think of a well-adjusted slave? . . . Clearly what will be called personality problems depends on who is doing the calling. The slave owner? The dictator? The
patriarchal father? The husband who wants his wife to remain a child? It seems
quite clear that personality problems may sometimes be loud protests against
the crushing of one's psychological bones, of one's true inner nature. What is
sick then is *not* to protest while this crime is being committed.[143]

To interrogate the wisdom of passive self-modification, disparage equations between maturity and conformity, and speak out against injustice
in the name of one's own psychological integrity became characteristic

features of many 1960s social movements. Their inspiration came, in part, from critiques of adjustment such as Maslow's and from glowing advertisements for self-actualization, which Maslow and the other humanists had elevated to the very pinnacle of human development. Abbie Hoffman was only the most notorious individual to suggest that "Maslovian theory laid a solid foundation for launching the optimism of the sixties."[144] Hoffman, an eager student of Maslow's in the late 1950s and president of the Brandeis psychology club during his senior year, insisted that "everything Maslow wrote [was] applicable to modern revolutionary struggle in America."[145]

To be sure, Maslow protested loudly and repeatedly that his thinking had been misappropriated by Hoffman (a "pathological" publicity seeker) and other countercultural crusaders for human potential.[146] Yet he also recognized a degree of kinship with the "nuts, fringe people, and borderline characters" who were seeking the "peak experiences" he had publicized and celebrated.[147] In the end, Maslow could only clarify his intentions for the record and grudgingly admit that he had no control over the political lessons others extracted from his life work.

In contrast, Rogers did not distance himself from liberal and left-wing activists during the 1960s because he understood their goals to be identical to the goals of humanistic psychology and client-centered psychotherapy: authenticity, intimacy, nonjudgmental empathy, and trust in subjective experience, to name but a few. One of Rogers's last pieces of writing expressed his support for movements among black Americans, students, hippies, and others. "I simply say with all my heart: Power to the emerging person and the revolution he carries within."[148]

During the twenty-five years after 1945, the federal government moved toward methodically governing the mental health of ordinary U.S. citizens, those ordinary citizens moved toward enthusiastically consuming psychotherapeutic services, and psychological experts moved to solidify their authority over every aspect of individual and social life implicated in the manufacture of normality and psychological well-being. The work of theorists and clinicians affiliated with humanistic psychology, such as Rogers and Maslow, demonstrated that the durability of democratic ideas and institutions might even depend upon an intentional quest for better-than-normal psychological development. The absence of mental illness and presence of mental health were no longer sufficient. An ongoing process of conscious becoming, of self-actualization, in psychotherapy or elsewhere, was necessary to cultural as well as to personal evolution.

Each of the developments described in this chapter expanded psychology's jurisdiction by applying the theories and technologies of clinical expertise to more people in more places for more reasons than before. In so doing, psychological experts helped to stretch the definition of "the political" and alter the goals of political participation. Not only had mental health been encompassed as a legitimate sphere of public action, but subjectivity itself had been exposed as the key to maintaining social stability and attaining prosperity in communities and in the nation. Strengthening feelings of human connection and identification, struggling to adjust, gain insight, and become fully human—these were gradually transformed into important social goals as well as widespread individual preoccupations during the postwar decades.

Not only did the history of clinical experts have public repercussions; it was a significant factor in blurring the lines between culture and politics, between the immediate experience of everyday life and more abstract dialogue on matters of public power and social conflict. Especially during the 1960s, it is possible to see how profoundly clinical vocabulary influenced political thought, political action, and political change. As chapter 10 will show, psychology's cultural progress energized women's collective action during the early years of the second wave of feminism, making the public pursuit of psychological happiness more political than ever.

10

The Curious Courtship of Psychology and Women's Liberation

The rapid progress of a psychological culture touting therapeutic change and adjustment animated the spirit of the 1960s, as surely as technologies of human behavior contributed to the foreign and domestic policies of that same era. The normalization of psychotherapy and the broad reach of government-supported programs in community mental health, two of the major developments discussed in chapters 4 and 9, contributed to the political priorities and cultural sensibilities of 1960s social movements. The popular diffusion of clinical concepts and practices in the years after World War II helps to explain the appearance of movements which seemed so at odds with the ethos of the 1950s, especially its superficial veneer of consumer contentment and its penchant to prioritize private pleasures over public duties.

It is certainly true that the New Left, and other varieties of radical political activism during the 1960s, had many roots. Beat literature and bohemian subcultures, radical pacifist organizing during and after World War II, the enduring remnants of the Old Left, and the growth of an omnivorous, youth-oriented consumer culture are just some of the factors that historians have repeatedly emphasized.[1] What made the period's movements different from previous radical, or even populist, movements, however, was the extent to which they rejected an ideological emphasis on material circumstances alone. Young people (or at least young white people) who had grown up in the 1950s and whose complaints had been fashioned in an era of relative economic affluence were well positioned to develop perspectives that could challenge exclusively material understandings of what social problems were and what their solutions might be.[2]

In the culture of psychology, the period's activists saw possibilities for furthering a postmaterial agenda that could go beyond the basic requirements of food and shelter to include the emotional, cultural, and spiritual dimensions of people's lives. They were quick to appropriate psychological insights—about the perils of adjusting to pressures for conformity, for example, or the salience of "identity" to the division of power—to mobilize public pressure for civil rights and women's equality, and against the Vietnam War. The conviction that emotional experience and social organization could not ultimately be separated, that oppression and liberation alike took internal as well as external forms, was part of what made the New Left really "new." Such convictions supported and energized Martin Luther King's insistence upon the "somebodiness" of black Americans, the student movement's vision of a "participatory democracy," the counterculture's love affair with revolutionary bliss, and feminists' insistence that "the personal is political."[3]

This chapter traces the impact of the evolving psychological culture within just one of those movements—women's liberation. Like historians of the New Left, historians of feminism have left the postwar growth of the psychotherapeutic enterprise out of the explanatory picture, focusing instead upon such factors as structural changes in women's labor force participation or the contradictions women faced in the civil rights movement and the New Left, where they were simultaneously expected to seek freedom and serve coffee.[4] Yet the early years of the second wave of feminism, during the late 1960s and early 1970s, illustrate how profoundly psychology figured in the public reassessment of gender relations, a phenomenon in U.S. politics that continues unabated to this day.

Considering the publicity that surrounded investigations of sexuality during the postwar years (the Kinsey reports of 1948 and 1953 are famous examples) and the popularity of childrearing advice (millions of dog-eared copies of *Baby and Child Care* come to mind), it is hardly surprising that feminists would regard the psychological and behavioral experts who were fascinated with erotic and maternal behavior as extremely influential ideologues of sex and gender. Wartime preoccupations with "normal neurosis" in ordinary male soldiers faded after 1945 and expert attention shifted decisively toward the female gender. The new focus on women revealed a plethora of gender disorders eating away at the domestic tranquillity and national security of the country.

First in line for inspection and reprimand were soldiers' mothers. As early as 1942, Philip Wylie blamed women's increasing independence for a rash of social disasters. "Momism," an unattractive female condition caused by an overdose of freedom, had developed into "a human calamity" while men were preoccupied with war and other manly pursuits.[5] "Mom's first gracious presence at the ballot-box was roughly concomitant with the start toward a new all-time low in political scurviness, hoodlumism, gangsterism, labor strife, monopolistic thuggery, moral degeneration, civic corruption, smuggling, bribery, theft, murder, homosexuality, drunkenness, financial depression, chaos and war."[6] Wylie understood well that such extreme overstatement allowed milder forms of antifeminism to attract the loyalty of experts, as he pointed out almost thirty years later. "After my somewhat ribald exposition of 'momism' a great many psychologists got up the nerve to produce books on the same subject, using my brashness as their icebreaker."[7]

And so they did. It was Edward Strecker, chair of the Department of Psychiatry at the University of Pennsylvania Medical School, former president of the American Psychiatric Association, and an initial appointee to the NIMH National Advisory Mental Health Council, who gave "momism" psychiatry's stamp of approval as a pathological syndrome. He recalled with dismay the epidemic of psychoneurosis he had witnessed as a consultant to the World War II military, accused mothers of producing immaturity in their sons by failing to "untie the emotional apron string," and concluded that momism was "the product of a social system veering toward a matriarchy":[8] "Our war experiences—the alarming number of so-called 'psychoneurotic' young Americans— point to and emphasize this threat to our survival. No one could view this huge test tube of man power, tried and found wanting, without realizing that an extremely important factor was the inability or unwillingness of the American mom and her surrogates to grant the boon of emotional emancipation during childhood. Already we have incurred a large penalty. The threat to our security must not be allowed to go farther."[9] In 1947 an influential book by Ferdinand Lundberg (a sociologist) and Marynia Farnham (a psychoanalyst), *Modern Woman: The Lost Sex,* argued that feminism was "a deep illness" infecting "the highly disturbed psychobiological organism: the mother."[10] The government would be wise, the authors advised, to launch a massive psychotherapy campaign aimed at controlling the outbreak of female independence and ensuring compliant maternalism in the future.[11] Lundberg and Farnham championed psychological solutions while adding sociological fuel to the antifeminist fire.

Blaming women for everything from children's misbehavior to the alarming state of Western civilization became a public ritual among experts during the postwar years, and it was not confined to the worlds of academia or professional exchange, though scholarly legitimacy certainly eased the wider expression of antifeminist sentiments. Clearly visible in the popular media was the message that feminism, "as quaint as linen dusters and high button shoes," had yielded one terribly damaging product: the working woman.[12] A 1956 *Life* special issue devoted to American women, for example, surveyed four psychiatrists on the question of changing roles within marriage. Glumly, the experts agreed that an epidemic of gender ambiguity was trickling downward from the top of society, producing a wave of masculinized women, feminized men, and confused children so emotionally unstable that the very future of the country was placed in jeopardy. Careers spelled an irreparable loss of feminine identity, warned New York psychiatrist John Cotton in no uncertain terms: "She may find satisfactions in her job, but the chances are that she, her husband and her children will suffer psychological damage, and that she will be basically an unhappy woman. . . . If they are feminine women, with truly feminine attitudes, they will— without self-conscious exhortations about the delights of domesticity— accept their wifely functions with good humor and pleasure."[13] Only in the embrace of an avid domesticity, and in the sharply increasing reproductive output of educated, middle-class women, did the experts see any signs of hope.

Considering the postwar consensus that female independence was likely to poison marriage and harm children, it is hardly surprising that feminists in the late 1960s, especially feminists within the psychological professions, accused psychological theories and practices of contributing more than their fair share to the creation and maintenance of sexual inequality. During contemporary feminism's formative period, psychological experts and organizations functioned as frequent targets of angry protest. In the eyes of many feminists, psychology was little more than sexism masquerading as science. Even Dr. Spock, admired on the left for his peace activism, was unceremoniously called a "counterrevolutionary" for his authorship of the baby boom's childrearing bible and its presumption that mothers belonged at home with their children.[14]

Some psychologists dutifully lived up to their role as enemies of feminism by updating the antifeminist rhetoric of earlier decades. They dismissed the new movement as an unfortunate by-product of overpermissive childrearing practices or called it a pathological symptom of young women's collective inability to come to terms with adult gender identity. To which feminists responded in kind, with withering insults of their own. Perhaps because the dialogue between feminists and psychological experts was so acrimonious, feminist criticisms of psychological expertise and challenges to the psychological establishment are relatively well known.

The authority of psychological experts was best known to feminists early in the second wave as a burden limiting their humanity and an obstacle in their way. What I hope to show is that while psychology helped to "construct the female," it also helped to construct the feminist.[15] It offered resources with which to support the ideas and actions of the women's movement: to resist the separation of private and public, to bridge the yawning chasms between the psychic and the social, the self and the other.

Finally, by inspiring a climate attuned to the nuances of subjectivity and identity, the culture of psychology supported a chorus of dissident voices within feminism itself, perhaps even more conspicuous in recent years than during the late 1960s and early 1970s. Monolithic understandings of "woman" and "gender" were discredited and eventually discarded not because feminists' analyses of gender were wrongheaded, but because their blindness to race, class, sexual orientation, and other differences among women had not done justice to the full truth of female experience.

Psychology Constructs the Female

THE CRITIQUE IS FORMULATED

In 1968 Naomi Weisstein boldly declared that "psychology constructs the female."[16] This was not a compliment. Hers was the opening salvo in a battle that pitted the accumulated wisdom of psychological experts against the growing number of young women who took up the banner of women's liberation.

Weisstein was a Harvard-trained experimental psychologist who decided to investigate the evidence used to support psychological theories of gender development and difference. Like other women who received academic and professional training in the late 1950s and early 1960s, she had been intensely frustrated by her own educational and professional experience in psychology. A graduate of Wellesley College, where, she recalled later, the all-female student body "retarded my discovery that women were supposed to be stupid and incompetent," Weisstein went on to study psychology at Harvard.[17] Denied the use of equipment she needed for her doctoral research (because she might break it), she somehow managed to graduate first in her class in 1964.[18] Prospective employers asked: "How can a little girl like you teach a great big class of men?" and "Who did the research for you?"[19] Even in a booming academic market, Weisstein received no job offers. Disappointed and outraged, she found support, and a feasible explanation for her own experience, in the emergence of feminism. She became a founding member of the Chicago Women's Liberation Union. An organized women's movement, she came to believe, was more likely to "change this man's world and this man's science" than were the empiricism and scientific reasoning she had cherished and nurtured for years.[20]

Her 1968 manifesto combined a belief in women's equality with a thorough investigation of the psychological literature, including the work of Erik Erikson, Bruno Bettelheim, Joseph Rheingold, and others. What she discovered was that "psychology has nothing to say about what women are really like, what they need and what they want, essentially because psychology does not know."[21] Because they relied on subjective assessment and not empirical evidence, Weisstein argued, the explanations personality theorists and clinicians offered for gender differences were not what they appeared to be. They falsely embraced the mantle of science when psychology was actually a repository for cultural myths about men and women. Sex differences were ideological, not scientific, constructions, propped up by "psychosexual incantation and biological ritual curses."[22] Significantly, Weisstein remained an advocate for what "real" science could accomplish and pointed out that "psychologists must realize that it is they who are limiting discovery of human potential."[23]

An authentically scientific psychology, in other words, could reveal the truth about gender, according to Weisstein, and would aid the cause of sexual equality by subverting ossified notions of subordination and difference. In order to do so, it would have to cease its futile quest for inner traits and set its sights on social context, which was "the true signal which can predict behavior."[24] After citing the famous experiments of Yale psychologist Stanley Milgram, and other social psychological research directed at understanding conformity and obedience to authority, Weisstein noted that "it is obvious that a study of human behavior requires, first and foremost, a study of the social context within which people move, the expectations as to how they will behave, and the authority which tells them who they are and what they are supposed to do."[25]

In the following years, a steady stream of feminist scholars and activists echoed Weisstein's accusation that psychological experts manufactured gender difference and created "ideological pollution" aimed at maintaining women's second-class status (fig. 18).[26] One by one, they exposed the sexist expectations underlying patriarchal authority. Clinicians were often singled out for especially harsh rebuke. Pauline Bart, a sociologist who had written a dissertation about depression in middle-aged women and who would later become a leading early expert on rape, was a vocal critic of psychotherapists, going so far as to suggest "demanding reparations from the psychotherapists for all the years that so many women have wasted and all the money that so many women have spent in psychotherapy, a psychotherapy based on false assumptions about the nature of women."[27]

Psychologist Phyllis Chesler's work on women, madness, and psychiatric institutionalization was even better known. Not only did she condemn psychological experts for false assumptions about women; she theorized that marriage and psychiatry were two institutions closely implicated in women's subordination: each similarly presented male domination as women's salvation.[28] Further, she wrote, *"What we consider 'madness,' whether it appears in women or in men, is either the acting out of the devalued female role or the total or partial rejection of one's sex-role stereotype."*[29] Women were categorized as mentally unstable whether they conformed to the dictates of femininity or rebelled against them and femininity defined the territory of abnormality in which clinicians operated. "Madness and asylums generally function as mirror images of the female experience, and as penalties for *being* 'female,' as well as for desiring or daring *not* to be."[30] Unwilling to call for a total ban on therapeutic practice because she believed women's unhappiness was genuine, Chesler opposed the treatment of women by male profession-

Figure 18. Feminist cartoon lampooning psychological (in this case psycho-analytical) sexism.

als ("even their sympathy is damaging and oppressive") and supported the development of "all-female therapeutic communities" and other separatist alternatives.[31]

By the late 1970s the effort to eliminate gender bias from psychological theories and practices and establish feminist beachheads in psychotherapy, child guidance, mental testing, psychoanalysis, and other fields had gained ground. Real steps had been taken toward showing exactly how psychology constructed the female: through distinctly male-centered theories of human development, psychiatric diagnoses that pathologized femininity, experimental methods that recapitulated gender dualisms, psychological tests that incorporated biases against women's ways of knowing, and so forth.[32] The faith Weisstein had expressed in the power of science was fading fast, however, as was the conviction that women could ever be legitimately discussed as a unitary group.[33]

Weisstein, who had been active in the Congress of Racial Equality and who also helped form a women's caucus within Students for a Democratic Society, relayed important elements of the New Left's general critique of expertise as she demolished the foundations of psychological knowledge about women and gender. This pattern of multiple political loyalties, of affiliation with a comprehensive "movement," was not unique to Weisstein. Ongoing exchange and influence between social movements was evident in the overall theoretical and organizational direction of feminism, and the new women's movement was deeply indebted to the ideas and strategies that had been forged by civil rights, student, and countercultural activists.[34]

THE PLACE OF ANTIPSYCHIATRY AND RADICAL THERAPY

At least as important to feminist assessments of psychological expertise were the movements known as "antipsychiatry" and "radical therapy," which distilled general criticisms of experts as antidemocratic schemers and servants of power into specific indictments of clinical practices and professionals.[35] Centered around the theoretical writing of Thomas Szasz and R. D. Laing, antipsychiatry erased any remaining distinctions between psychological knowledge and politics by holding that the former merely presented the latter in mystified form.[36] Antipsychiatry suggested that psychiatry *was* politics—not medicine, humanitarian assistance, or anything else. Mental health and illness were thus labels convenient for protecting existing social arrangements and shielding political repression from effective resistance.

Antipsychiatry turned the historic rhetoric of the "helping professions" entirely on its head. Instead of leaders in the cause of humanitarian progress, psychiatrists and other psychological experts were malevolent conspirators who scapegoated people unfortunate enough to be labeled socially different due to their (nonwhite) race, (female) gender, (homo) sexual orientation, or (impoverished) economic status. Instead of an enviable state of health, sanity designated a pitiful state of adjustment to the alienated conditions of modern existence. Instead of helpless and tormented sufferers, patients were people whose social circumstances placed them at odds with the status quo. However socially unacceptable and personally calamitous, "freaking out" was a way of speaking out.

Indistinguishable from deviance, mental anguish evaporated as a reality and became, in Szasz's famous phrase, a "myth." Much of this critique rested on a conventional, severe distinction between body and mind, between medicine and the healing of souls. Szasz, for example, held that psychiatric work bore no resemblance at all to that of other physicians, who treated actual bodily illnesses. In sharp contrast to the medical challenges of genuine disease, psychiatric clinicians encountered rage, fear, stupidity, poverty, and a variety of other problems in living. Confusing existential quandaries with sickness disguised moral and ethical dilemmas as medical problems and undermined personal responsibility by leading people to believe that they did not control their own behavior when, to a large degree, they did, at least according to Szasz. "It behooves us," he wrote, "to discriminate intelligently and to describe honestly the things doctors do to cure the sick and the things they do to control the deviant." [37]

Szasz was unequivocally hostile to all forms of involuntary intervention (i.e., commitment procedures) and to the growing power of psychiatry in the legal system (i.e., insanity pleas). He warned that measures equating criminality with mental illness would "convert our society from a political democracy to a psychiatric autocracy." [38] Such views led him to oppose all welfare state programs on the grounds that they eroded individual freedoms. For example, Szasz called the policy of community mental health "moral Fascism" and argued that liberty was an absolute value, whereas mental health (whatever it was) was not. [39] Except for these libertarian strands of his thought, which endeared him to right-wing ideologues and organizations, much of Szasz's critique was shared by leftists, and it was on the Left that most of antipsychiatry's support was located.

In the view of British countercultural psychiatrist R. D. Laing, psychiatry appeared to be as controlling as it was for Szasz, but madness was much less wicked. In fact, breakdown dissolved into breakthrough in the more extreme statements of Laing's antipsychiatric position toward the end of the 1960s. Early in the decade, he had claimed that psychosis resulted from two things: first, a rupture between self and social (especially familial) context and, second, a perception of the resulting abnormality by a psychiatric expert assumed to be capable of making such judgments. *"Sanity or psychosis is tested by the degree of conjunction or disjunction between two persons where the one is sane by common consent."* [40] In spite of his desire to offer a theoretical explanation for schizophrenia, Laing stressed the ultimate incomprehensibility of madness, the lonely gulf necessarily separating the experience of one human being from the next. By the end of the decade, Laing turned away from the effort to grasp what was really a tragic existential distinctiveness and instead promoted a highly romanticized version of that difference in subjective experience. The reinterpretation converted schizophrenia into a mode of prophetic transcendence and healing in a society gone haywire, "one of the forms in which, often through quite ordinary people, the light began to break through the cracks in our all-too-closed minds." [41]

The central theoretical works of antipsychiatry were not intended as feminist statements and all of the movement's major thinkers were men. It is nevertheless easy to see the exquisite fit between feminist denunciations of conventional gender expectations and the antipsychiatric assumption that what passed for mental anguish was a product of exploitation and alienation. [42] The emerging outlines of feminist social thought dovetailed neatly with the core propositions of antipsychiatry: that the medical establishment had inappropriately usurped authority over vital social issues, including gender and sexuality; that psychotherapeutic practice harmed women by teaching that their problems were personal and intrapsychic rather than social and relational; that the neutral language of testing, diagnosis, and treatment concealed clinicians' complicity with male domination and their determination to make women adjust to sexism; that "mental health" was nothing but shorthand for gender conformity; that faith in experts (especially male experts) was counterproductive because experience—not expertise—imparted deserved authority. Only women could liberate themselves.

Radical therapy was an activist analogue to antipsychiatric theory. It consisted of a loose alliance between Left-leaning professionals, former mental patients, and radicals interested in psychotherapy. It appealed to large numbers of women (just as conventional psychotherapy had) and frequently addressed issues being debated within feminist circles, from sexuality to self-defense.[43] It emphasized that while mental disturbance was fictive, sexism, and other types of oppression, were quite genuine. In his 1969 "Radical Psychiatry Manifesto," Claude Steiner wrote,

PARANOIA IS A STATE OF HEIGHTENED AWARENESS. MOST PEOPLE ARE PERSECUTED BEYOND THEIR WILDEST DELUSIONS. THOSE WHO ARE AT EASE ARE INSENSITIVE.[44]

Based on a thoroughly negative appraisal of psychotherapy's political function and worth, radical therapy nevertheless retained a kernel of hope that therapeutic practice could, if revolutionized, expedite both personal liberation and social change.[45] This coincided with the majority view among feminist critics, such as Bart and Chesler, that while psychotherapy as it existed was bad, abolishing it entirely might be worse.[46] "Feminist therapy," they agreed, was preferable, even if it was difficult to define beyond the obvious: it would be emptied of objectionable sexist biases but still capable of offering help and insight to women in pain.

FEMINIST ACTIVISTS CHALLENGE THE PSYCHOLOGICAL ESTABLISHMENT

The proposition that illegitimate (male) experts had fabricated mental disturbances like "hysteria" and "depression" in order to keep patriarchy insulated from effective opposition was the theoretical rationale behind the activist campaign feminists mounted against the psychological establishment in the late 1960s and early 1970s. Antipsychiatry permeated the style, as well as the substance, of feminist protest. Dramatic zap actions were organized at conventions of the American Psychiatric Association and other institutional strongholds of psychological expertise, sometimes in conjunction with gay men and lesbians.[47] Typically, activists would interrupt the proceedings, shout slogans like "The Psychiatric Profession Is Built on the Slavery of Women," and present a set of demands. Among other things, feminists called for an end to mother-blaming, freedom for the "political prisoners" living in mental institutions, assistance in filing legal claims against abusive clinicians, and a ban on sexist advertisements in professional journals and offensive exhibits at professional meetings. One typical communication, from San Francisco Redstockings to the American Psychiatric Association in 1970, offered the following suggestions to sympathetic clinicians:

1. Begin compiling a list of psychiatrists in every city who are willing to back women filing malpractice suits against psychiatrists who have fucked them over. . . .

2. Begin dealing with the treatment of women under welfare and the conditions of women in the state hospitals across the nation. . . .

3. Stop helping your male patients develop "healthy" male egos. . . .

4. Mother is not public enemy number one. Start looking for the real enemy. . . .

5. There are some exhibits at this convention that are oppressive to women. Trash them.[48]

Feminists denounced the racist, sexist, and homophobic prejudices of psychological expertise and appealed for open discussion. Not infrequently, their bold actions were jeered by the (overwhelmingly male) professionals in attendance, who sometimes greeted the unwelcome feminists with "You're a paranoid fool, you stupid bitch!" and "Why don't you idiot girls shut up!"[49] On the other hand, radicals within the professions, many of whom were seeking to eliminate "psychiatric atrocities" such as lobotomy and electroshock or put their professions on record against the Vietnam War, functioned as important allies.[50] Cooperation between movement activists and dissident professionals was often the key to effective publicity and change.[51] At the 1970 meeting of the American Psychiatric Association, for example, the Radical Caucus distributed literature to those attending the conference in a compilation titled "Psychic Tension" and presented a series of documents to the association's annual business meeting. One leaflet simply confronted the assembled masses with the question: "ARE YOU A MALE CHAUVINIST?"[52] Another, "A Credo for Psychiatrists," embodied many of the themes of the feminist critique, reviewed above.

At least get off our backs. . . . It's not penis envy or inner space or maternal urges or natural passivity or hormone-caused emotionality that determines our lives. It's an uptight, repressive male supremists [*sic*] social structure and set of social attitudes that prevents us from seeing ourselves as full human beings struggling to live out our potential. . . . The only legitimate role for therapists is to catalyse our struggles. Psychiatry that tries to adjust to a bad situation is not help. It is betrayl [*sic*] in the guise of benevolence. Psychiatrists, heal thyselves. . . . Help *us* become our own psychiatrists, to write our own theories, to define our own natures. If you can't do that then get out of the way. We don't want your crazy trips laid on us. We want LIBERATION NOW.[53]

Feminist professionals also worked tirelessly to reform their colleagues' theories and practices and to advance the professional interests of women, usually through the formation of women's caucuses, radical caucuses, and autonomous professional organizations. For example, the Association for Women Psychologists (AWP) was founded in 1969 during the annual APA meeting in Washington, D.C., which was marked by protest from other dissident groups on the Left: Psychologists for Social Action, Psychologists for a Democratic Society, the Association of Black Psychologists, and the Association of Black Psychology Students.[54] In response, the APA passed an abortion rights resolution and agreed to eliminate sex designations in its own job listings after women threatened to shut down the offending job placement booths themselves and sue the APA for sex discrimination.[55] (The Women's Equity Action League filed suit in April 1970 anyway.)

At its inception and during its early years, AWP clearly represented the prevailing mood of radical feminist anger and adhered to the leaderless organizational style common among radical women's liberation groups. Phyllis Chesler, speaking on behalf of the new organization, demanded monetary "reparations" to be used to release women from mental hospitals and psychotherapy, a suggestion that, however heartfelt, was not taken very seriously.[56] Nancy Henley, another founding mother of the organization, reflected in disgust that "talking to psychologists about action is like talking to Spiro Agnew about engaging in civil disobedience."[57] Early structural decisions decentralized AWP authority by eliminating all elected officers, making all organizational roles voluntary, and warning members against "the creation of 'stars' by forces outside our organization."[58]

Steeped in the politics of protest, the founding documents of the AWP nevertheless disclosed the positive role its authors hoped psychology might play. The statement of purpose declared that "AWP is dedicated to . . . exploring the contributions which psychology can, does and should make to the definition, investigation, and modification of current sex role stereotypes."[59] In ensuing years, the AWP called repeatedly on the APA to make good on that organization's founding promise "to advance psychology as a means of promoting human welfare" and to assist "the realization of full human potential in all persons."[60]

Psychology Constructs the Feminist

Feminists in the late 1960s and early 1970s doggedly pursued the insight that "psychology constructs the female" and campaigned publicly against the psychological establishment, as we have seen. At the same time, psychology was also helping to construct the feminist, a process that has received comparatively little attention. The remainder of this chapter will illustrate how intellectual and clinical traditions rooted in the career of postwar psychological expertise inspired early feminist theory and mobilized feminist activism, even as they served as targets of protest. Examples discussed in the following pages include Betty Friedan's early adaptation of humanistic personality theory, the central place of "identity" (a concept affiliated with Erik Erikson) in the cultural reorganization feminists envisioned, and the assimilation of the psychotherapeutic sensibility into feminism through consciousness raising and feminist therapy.

BETTY FRIEDAN AND THE FORFEITED FEMALE SELF

Years before a mass women's movement materialized, Betty Friedan anticipated Weisstein's analysis and blamed the "new psychological religion" of adjustment for endowing a self-destructive femininity with social and scientific authority.[61] Friedan, a Smith College graduate and middle-class housewife who had once aspired to a career in psychology herself, launched a journalistic attack on psychological experts in her best-selling *The Feminine Mystique* (1963). Freudian theories about femininity, she claimed, were "an obstacle to truth for women in America today, and a major cause of the pervasive problem that has no name."[62] Her survey of stories in women's magazines like *Redbook* and *Good Housekeeping* (publications for which she had written herself during the 1950s) convinced Friedan that after 1945, "Freudian and pseudo-Freudian theories settled everywhere, like fine volcanic ash."[63] Because the gospel according to Freud allowed women to derive true happiness only from their relationships to husbands and children, popularizers made housewives feel neurotic for hungering after any independent self at all. Convinced that something was deeply wrong with their mental and emotional health, middle-class housewives lined up in psychotherapists' offices, seeking yet more expert help in their quest for feminine adjustment.

These were certainly harsh criticisms, coming as they did at a moment of widespread enthusiasm about psychoanalytic ideas. But Friedan was also careful to note the "basic genius of Freud's discoveries" and insisted there was no conspiracy against women among the experts.[64] Most important, she saw the liberating possibilities of harnessing psychological theory to feminist purposes. She emphasized the notion of "some positive growth tendency within the organism," advanced by Gordon Allport, Carl Rogers, Karen Horney, and Rollo May, among others.[65] Their humanistic formulations, and especially Abraham Maslow's motivational theory, could be used as ammunition to argue that the tragedy of the (middle-class) female condition was due to "the forfeited self."[66] Maslow's theory suggested that people moved progressively through a series of human motivations, from lower, material needs to higher, nonmaterial needs. When their needs for food and housing were assured, in other words, people could be expected to attend to their desires for creative experience and accomplishment. The most popular feature of his theory was Maslow's portrait of "self-actualizing" individuals, a term he used to designate those people who had climbed to the top of the motivational ladder in order to explore their humanity through exciting, "peak experiences."

Friedan was alarmed at the almost complete absence of women on Maslow's list of peakers. (The only two exceptions were historical figures Eleanor Roosevelt and Jane Addams.) She turned women's relative exclusion from the ultimate in psychological integration, at least according to Maslow, into an appeal for feminism. She treated the scarcity of female peakers as powerful evidence that cultural prescriptions requiring middle-class housewives to devote themselves exclusively to the needs of husbands and children also doomed them to a psychological hell, or at least a decidedly second-class emotional existence. The core of the feminine mystique, Friedan wrote, was that "our culture does not permit women to accept or gratify their basic need to grow and fulfill their potentialities as human beings."[67] Why, she asked, should women be expected to renounce their natural tendencies toward individuality and creativity? Were they not entitled to equal psychological opportunities?

If the ideology of femininity directly contradicted the process of self-actualization, as Friedan maintained, then psychology could provide real support to feminist arguments. Women deserved rights and opportunities, not only to employment and equal pay, but to the less tangible rewards of living as whole human beings. That her commitment to the value of psychological knowledge was not an abstract exercise is evident in the National Organization for Women's 1966 statement of purpose, which explicitly incorporated the humanistic refrain: "NOW is dedicated to the proposition that women first and foremost are human beings, who, like all other people in our society, must have the chance to develop their fullest human potential."[68]

"IDENTITY"

Feminists' discovery that "identity" was politically serviceable did not end with Friedan's book. Subsequent feminist efforts illustrated even more broadly than Friedan's partiality to Maslovian theory how the language and theoretical tools of psychology could be made relevant and usable to the women's movement. Before the 1960s, discussions of "identity" were confined mainly to the literature on developmental psychology. During the 1960s and after, the term served as a clue to who had power, who did not, and why. It became so central to feminists, in fact, that the term "identity politics" circulated widely as a shorthand reference to a particular political position. In an abbreviated fashion, it alluded to the constellation of ideas that held the building blocks of individuality—gender, age, race, class, sexual orientation, among others—to be an efficient means of both understanding and dismantling the structure of social and political inequality. It offered, in other words, a way of tying individual experience to social context.

Throughout the postwar era, the concept of identity was closely identified with the work of German emigré psychoanalyst Erik Erikson.[69] Erikson dated its origin to his clinical work with World War II veterans, who had reported an eerie loss of feelings related to personal uniqueness and historical continuity.[70] It was during the 1950s that "identity crisis" entered the language as a common term for the first time. As a national panic over an epidemic of juvenile delinquency escalated, the concept seemed a convenient way to think about the dangers posed by adolescent male development. During the 1960s, Erikson suggested that young people had also lost their place in history, just like the veterans he had treated. In Erikson's psychosocial ideas, many young people found confirmation (or at least an explanation) of their own commitment to radical politics. Numerous social scientists also used Erikson's work as an aid in exploring the origins of the period's social movements.[71] Erikson repeatedly assented to such sociological applications.[72]

A 1964 article, "Inner and Outer Space: Reflections on Womanhood," brought Erikson to the attention of feminists.[73] Based on Erikson's work in a two-year University of California child study (which had not been intended as an investigation of gender identity or development), the article explored the gender differences in special relationships that Erikson had observed in children's play. Boys, he found, emphasized outer spaces, protrusions, and people and animals in (sometimes destructive) motion. Girls, on the other hand, emphasized inner spaces and peaceful enclosures containing people and animals at rest.

To Erikson, it was obvious that such differences indicated that "a profound difference exists between the sexes in the experience of the ground plan of the human body."[74] He explained that his concern with women's reproductive biology was not "a renewed male attempt to 'doom' every woman to perpetual motherhood and to deny her the equivalence of individuality and the equality of citizenship."[75] He nevertheless concluded that "women have found their identities in the care suggested by their bodies and in the needs of their issue, and seem to have taken it for granted that the outer world space belongs to the men."[76]

Erikson came under fierce feminist fire.[77] Kate Millett, in her widely read *Sexual Politics,* accused him of reducing sexist social arrangements to biological inevitabilities and denying women the freedom he automatically granted to men: to forge identities not circumscribed by "somatic design."[78] In part, what irked his feminist critics was also that Erikson's analysis sounded benign, at least in comparison to vulgar biological determinism. His sympathy for women, and his willingness to accord them ethical superiority in their presumed fidelity to peacefulness and nurturance, struck Millett as a clever way of leaving unquestioned the "clear understanding that civilization is a male department."[79]

Wounded and angry, Erikson defended himself. He pointed out that the essay was intended as an alternative to orthodox psychoanalytic theory, a direct challenge to the objectionable notion that female psychological development revolved around the absence of a penis. Erikson, who considered himself a friend to women, was dismayed that his ideas had been interpreted as a mockery of women's human potential, and suggested that the unfortunate misunderstanding had occurred because his ideas had been ripped from the context that made them intelligible.[80] Their lack of appreciation for his prowoman stance prompted Erikson to attribute to feminists a "moralistic projection of erstwhile negative self-images upon men as representing evil oppressors and exploiters," a statement that feminists doubtlessly perceived as both a slur and yet another example of how easily experts could dismiss feminist demands by resorting to psychological analysis.[81]

Whatever their differences with and attitude toward Erikson, feminists proceeded to use "identity" in their own way and for their own purposes. Theorists at various points on the political spectrum of feminism quickly latched onto the process of female socialization as the preferred explanation for feminine thought and behavior. It was an explanation that necessarily favored nurture over nature, history and culture over biology. Because socialization was a social process by definition, highlighting it highlighted the power of deliberate social arrangements in the manufacture of gender's meaning. In comparison, most feminists believed, biological sex was purely accidental and altogether trivial.

Kate Millett proclaimed "socialization" to be the ideological foundation of patriarchal power. Without "the formation of human personality along stereotyped lines of sexual category," she argued, consent for a system of male-dominated "sexual politics" would be impossible to obtain.[82] Such uncompromising emphasis upon the social dimensions of subjective experience was a common theme in the early years of the women's movement. Socialist-feminist Meredith Tax, for example, wrote,

We didn't get this way by heredity or accident. We have been *molded* into these deformed postures, *pushed* into these service jobs, *made* to apologize for existing, *taught* to be unable to do anything requiring any strength at all, like opening doors or bottles. We have been told to be stupid, to be silly. We have had our mental and emotional feet bound for thousands of years. And the fact that some of the pieces that have been cut out of us are ones we can never replace or reconstruct—an ego, self-confidence, an ability to make choices—is the most difficult of all to deal with.[83]

Tax expressed the rage and pain many women felt about "the pieces that have been cut out of us." But the argument that female identity had been distorted by sexist social programming and interpersonal relationships had a very bright side. Identity could be changed through social decisions and actions.

Over the long term, alterations in childrearing practices appeared especially promising as a method of reforming gender socialization. Bringing children up differently held out the possibility of eliminating polarized roles, traits, and behaviors and encouraging girls and boys alike to explore a wider range of human possibilities. Nancy Chodorow, a graduate student in sociology during the late 1960s, was interested in how the division of childrearing labor reproduced gendered personalities. Inspired by the work of culture and personality anthropologists, she noticed that although wide cross-cultural variation existed in behaviors and traits categorized as either masculine or feminine, women were always the primary socializers of infants and young children. Female caretaking was an apparent "cultural universal."[84] She hypothesized that a developmental process requiring both girls and boys to separate from their mothers in order to gain an independent psychological identity was at the root of problematic gender differentiation.

In hers, as in the other feminist critiques reviewed above, a central theme was that most psychologists, anthropologists, and other social and behavioral experts had done a terrible disservice by transposing malleable feats of culture into supposedly ironclad facts of nature. Chodorow's analysis offered an alternative. The sharp division of socializing labor between men and women because of the alleged fit between childbearing and childrearing was revealed to be a thoroughly cultural construct with profound implications for the production of gendered personalities and the maintenance of male supremacy. Chodorow tried to illustrate how the construction of gender identity might be treated as a social process while still conserving the psychoanalytic tradition's close attention to the significance of early childhood and the familial environment.

Shocked to learn they were different from their female caretakers, she speculated, boys had to actually *do* something in order to achieve masculinity, and that something often involved distancing themselves from the feminine by attributing power and prestige to whatever activities were culturally defined in masculine terms. Girls' development was smoother, but the results were more self-destructive. Because they were not different from their female caretakers, their identity did not have to be earned through activity distinguishing them from their mothers. Feminine identity simply *was*. Ascribed as a product of nature, women's identity was readily internalized by girls as a given, only to be re-created through the next generational cycle of childrearing. "Until male 'identity' does not depend on men's proving themselves, their 'doing' will be a reaction to insecurity, not a creative exercise of their humanity, and woman's 'being,' far from being an easy and positive acceptance of self, will be a resignation to inferiority."[85]

Chodorow was neither the only theorist impressed by women's exclusive responsibility for child care nor the only one to stress that girls and boys alike would benefit from growing up around men and women whose creativity managed to encompass child nurture and a wider range of other activities than were typically allowed by either masculinity or femininity. An equal division of domestic labor between men and women, from dishes to diapers, became one of the movement's central demands. Organizing projects were formed to draft men into child care, to promote nonsexist educational materials, and to ease women's domestic responsibilities. Practical equality, feminists maintained, was a simple matter of social justice for women. But it was also, as Chodorow had suggested, a matter of everyone's mental health. If men and women were equally represented as socializers, and if children were exposed to a diversity of adult possibilities, the result might be a new, and improved, experience of self. Girls and boys alike would grow to be more integrated, secure, and fully human women and men.

THE PSYCHOTHERAPEUTIC SENSIBILITY IN FEMINISM

Imagining cultural rearrangements durable enough to produce nongendered personalities in future generations was both a radical project and a very optimistic one, since it simultaneously required a great deal of patience and men's cooperation. The women's movement also advocated short-term approaches less dependent on reaching cultural consensus. Women, for example, could simply jettison the niceties of gender expectations. If enough women refused to make their behavior conform, then getting angry would amount to an effective political strategy. "A woman should be proud to declare she is a Bitch," one typical statement pointed out, because "bitches seek their identity strictly through themselves and what they do. They are subjects, not objects."[86]

Bitches are aggressive, assertive, domineering, overbearing, strong-minded, spiteful, hostile, direct, blunt, candid, obnoxious, thick-skinned, hard-headed, vicious, dogmatic, competent, competitive, pushy, loud-mouthed, independent, stubborn, demanding, manipulative, egoistic, driven, achieving, overwhelming, threatening, scary, ambitious, tough, brassy, masculine, boisterous, and turbulent. Among other things, a Bitch occupies a lot of psychological space. You always know she is around. A Bitch takes shit from no one. You may not like her, but you cannot ignore her.[87]

Being a bitch, many women discovered, was easier to appreciate in theory than to realize in practice. Layers of female socialization could not be shed so easily or comfortably, and acts of feminist willpower, no matter how resolute, were inadequate to the task. Those who did succeed found that their defiance, whether expressed at home or in public, met with swift and certain reaction, not infrequently in the form of punitive psychological intervention, as Weisstein, Chesler, Bart, and others had painstakingly shown. On the one hand, this frustrating state of affairs made the paternalism of psychological experts ever more galling to feminists. On the other hand, it confirmed the centrality of both "psychological oppression" to women's subordinated status and "psychological liberation" to a vision of sexual equality. In its early years, the women's movement addressed women's subjective experience explicitly and continually, making it the building block of movement organization, the foundation of feminist theory, and the justification for reforming the psychotherapeutic enterprise.

Consciousness raising (CR) groups, not coincidentally, were sometimes called "bitch sessions."[88] The practice of group discussion and support which formed the organizational nucleus of the movement's radical wing during its early years embodied a respectful attention to emotion and a desire to communicate the subjective feel of women's everyday lives, which ran the gamut from anger to anguish. CR groups originated with New York Radical Women (NYRW), a radical feminist group formed in the fall of 1967. After a meeting during which the women experimented with going around the room to describe their own feelings of oppression, NYRW member Kathie Sarachild coined the term "consciousness raising" to describe both the practice and the resulting insights. As a veteran of the civil rights movement and the student Left, Sarachild understood that this quintessentially feminist practice was inspired by recent civil rights activism, as well as more distant models among Chinese revolutionaries and Guatemalan guerrillas (fig. 19).[89]

Figure 19. Consciousness raising group. Photo: Women's Movement Archives, Women's Educational Center, Cambridge, Massachusetts.

CR groups were small, met regularly, and often recruited members through friendship networks as well as feminist organizations. They emphasized introspection, emotional self-exposure, and the sharing of personal, experiential testimony. Pamela Allen's "Free Space," one of the best-known statements about CR, outlined four stages in the feminist group process. "Opening up" in a nonjudgmental context was the first, followed by "sharing, "analyzing," and "abstracting." "It is imperative for our understanding of ourselves and for our mental health," she explained, "that we maintain and deepen our contact with our feelings. Our first concern must not be with whether these feelings are good or bad, but what they are. Feelings are a reality."[90] The egalitarian practice of encouraging each woman to speak, the refrain of unconditional emotional acceptance, and the value placed on emotional awareness and mental health made CR reminiscent of humanistic psychotherapeutic trends such as Carl Rogers's client-centered psychotherapy. "We always stay in touch with our feelings," began one of Sarachild's descriptions of the place of CR within feminism.[91]

But the stated goals of CR—to develop feminist theory and build a women's movement—sharply distinguished it from psychotherapy, as many feminists were at pains to point out. That the distinction was crucial is evident in numerous, repeated warnings against "thinking that women's liberation is therapy" and "thinking that male supremacy is only a psychological privilege."[92] "Our oppression is not in our heads," Jennifer Gardner vehemently declared.[93] "Therapy assumes that someone is sick and that there is a cure," Carol Hanisch retorted.[94] Psychotherapy insulted women by appeasing them, whereas CR sessions "are a form of political action."[95] "Consciousness raising is not a form of encounter group or psychotherapy," Barbara Susan reflected. "I've been involved in both and I can tell you they are very different."[96]

Still, questions persisted. "Is women's liberation a therapy group?"[97] At all points on the feminist political spectrum, women answered with a resounding no. Reducing women's status to the psychological obstructed individual consciousness and social change by trivializing the possibility that women could act collectively on the basis of a politics of gender. Dangling the illusion of a "personal solution" before women was a futile form of "go-it-alonism," according to radical feminist Kathie Sarachild, whose influential guidelines for running small feminist groups included a list of classic forms of resistance under the heading, "How to Avoid the Awful Truth."[98] Leftists interested in the radical potential of cultural politics also tried to remain alert to the difference between "life-style revolution" and "cultural revolution." In her article on this topic, Gail Kelly cautioned, "We have gotten so bogged down in the way we live that we lose the possibility of becoming relevant to the way others live."[99] For her part, Betty Friedan worried that feminist groups might deteriorate into "navel-gazing and consciousness-raising that doesn't go anywhere."[100] CR may have begun with feeling, but it was supposed to lead to thinking and acting.

The passion of feminist qualifications made it apparent that the differences between CR and psychotherapy were as elusive as they were important. There was just no way to sidestep the pressing psychological problems women brought with them into CR groups, and, for the most part, movement activists did not try. The healing spirit and communal support system CR offered were among the new movement's most conspicuous and attractive features.

Feminism's rapid growth through the vehicle of small groups was not lost on practicing psychotherapists either, especially psychotherapists with feminist sympathies. A flurry of research studies attempted to systematically analyze the group process of feminist CR.[101] Some clinicians and clinical researchers went so far as to suggest that women's liberation was really a misnomer, disguising a movement dedicated to self-help and personal sustenance with fraudulent political rhetoric.[102] Many others, however, were sensitive to the differences between feminism and psychotherapy, as well as the striking similarities. The expert guide, symbol of unwelcome authority, had been banished from the group, but CR still had therapeutic results and was "ideally suited to the exploration of personal identity issues."[103] It was possible to see the feminist practice as simultaneously a challenge and an alternative to conventional psychotherapy.

Annoyed by all the talk about psychotherapy, which they found dismissive, many feminists redoubled their efforts to convey the urgency of their political goals. But the confusion between psychological and political change endured. Feminists themselves were partially responsible. Practically every woman who spoke or wrote about CR mentioned its therapeutic results because it was obvious that collective sharing reduced the burden of self-blame and made women feel a lot better. In our groups, Pamela Allen wrote, "we begin to build (and to some extent, experience) a vision of our human potential."[104] Even feminists who worried that CR groups would "never get beyond the level of therapy sessions" to realize their "revolutionary potential" had to admit that "the rigid dichotomy between material oppression and psychological oppression fails to hold."[105] Carol Payne was one of many to describe how her own group wrestled with the perplexing relationship between individual needs and collective action.

We argued about this [the purpose of the CR group]. A women's group shouldn't be group therapy, we decided. But there were elements of group therapy in what we were trying to do, to help each other deal with personal problems. . . . We never resolved the question of what a women's liberation group was supposed to do. There was always a conflict between those who favored the personal, psychological approach and those who felt that a women's group should be building a bridge between the personal insight gained by being in a small group and political action with a larger body of women.[106]

It was simply impossible to separate women's complaints about their lives and aspirations for change from an overall assessment of women's status as a gender category and, in the end, this was precisely the point. Feminists faced this dilemma because they treated women's experience as raw data, refusing to wall off "the personal" from "the political." Barbara Susan put it simply: "Consciousness raising is a way of forming a political analysis on information we can trust is true. That information is our experience."[107]

Surely this twin belief that experience was truthful and deserved a prominent place in comprehending public issues was one of feminism's most enlightening contributions. It was also deeply flawed, as Alice Echols has argued in her history of early radical feminist groups and ideas. Echols documents the internal factionalism that grew logically out of the erroneous assumption that most radical feminists made about the nature of that experience—namely, that women constituted a cohesive sex/gender class.[108] Kathie Sarachild, one of CR's architects, pointed out that the movement's group practice and the idea that gender necessarily unified women were inseparable. CR assumed "that most women were like ourselves—not different," by which she meant white, well-educated, and middle-class.[109]

When movement organizations came face-to-face with the major internal challenges raised by working-class women and lesbians, many simply crumbled, as Echols has shown, unable to digest the fact of "differences" among women. A feminism based on the assumption of common experience could not long survive after that assumption was exposed as false. "The dream of a common language" was exchanged for "lies, secrets, and silence," and the very divisions and conflicts that (white, middle-class) feminists feared most came to the fore.[110]

Although the notion of a sex/gender class became suspect in later years, faith in the truth of experience remained at the heart of the women's movement. The conviction that "experience" was "information we can trust" continued to inspire the production of theory and the direction of activism in the late 1970s and 1980s, as a chorus of new feminist voices proceeded to describe how varied that experience could be and challenge the women's movement to account for the difference that "difference" made.[111]

"Feminist therapy" surfaced early in the movement as a possible alternative to the sexist practice of traditional therapies, as we have already seen. What it was exactly and how it differed from CR were notoriously difficult to determine, but the persistence of discussion about it, and the strong demand for it by potential consumers, illustrated yet again the abiding place of the psychotherapeutic sensibility within feminism.

Predictably, CR was an important model considered by feminists who were also practicing psychotherapists interested in offering sensitive services to their female clients. "The CR groups of the women's movement have implications for the treatment of identity problems of women in therapy," concluded one examination of the relationship between the two, which also noted that many members of CR groups had apparently had previous experience in psychotherapy.[112] "I prefer to view therapy as a consciousness raising process," wrote Anne Kent Rush, one of the authors of *Feminism as Therapy,* a superficial book that conflated feminism and psychotherapy and reasoned that anything that was "healing" and respectful must be both therapeutic and good for women.[113]

Most early efforts to define feminist therapy began and ended with the proposition that women's social environment, rather than their intrapsychic makeup, was the primary source of individual psychological problems. More specific, practical questions went unanswered. Was psychotherapy more likely to be feminist in individual or group forms? What could feminist therapy offer men, if anything, and could they practice it too? Did the theoretical orientation of the clinician make any difference? Were Rogerian psychotherapists more feminist than orthodox psychoanalysts? In the absence of guidelines for therapeutic form and content, the general feeling seemed to be that virtually any school or style of psychotherapy could qualify as feminist—from cognitive reprogramming to psychodrama and gestalt—as long as a feminist practiced it.[114]

This muddled thinking did little to interfere with the growing popular interest in therapeutic services with a feminist slant. One of the AWP's early projects, for example, was to compile a national Feminist Therapy Roster as a service to the larger feminist community.[115] A brief comment in the AWP newsletter about who should be included reflected the nebulousness of feminist therapy itself: "If they don't know what that [feminist therapy] is, then we don't want them."[116] In order to be listed, the AWP asked psychotherapists to specify their credentials, describe their services, and write up a "statement of your position on feminism."[117] The first edition of the roster was a mere twelve pages long and included only forty-five resource listings in the entire country, a very modest effort indeed compared to the thriving industry in feminist therapy that would appear in the late 1970s and 1980s.[118]

While feminists declared war on the sexism of psychological experts, they were also willing to appropriate those aspects of psychological theory and practice perceived as potentially liberating for women or strategically useful to the women's movement. I have tried to show that the culture of psychology is not adequately understood as a competitor for women's hearts and minds, peddling adjustment while feminism pledged genuine change. Psychological expertise functioned as friend and foe, with both roles facilitating feminist mobilization and lending credence to feminist thought.

That feminists quietly welcomed certain aspects of psychology while loudly denouncing others produced a paradox—but perhaps it was merely wisdom in paradoxical form—at the heart of feminism. Psychological knowledge could be feminist or antifeminist. It could promote feminist consciousness and inspire social change. It could instill self-hatred and vindicate the status quo. At times this state of affairs was extremely perplexing. Should the women's movement actively support personal growth strategies, or insist that women's only hope was in eliminating systemic barriers such as legal inequalities and discrimination? What would it matter if women achieved institutional gains, only to have their subjective experience remain mired in dependence and powerlessness? Could a line even be reasonably drawn between psychological and social experience?

The curious courtship of psychology and women's liberation thus recapitulated the ambivalent political dynamic that earlier chapters have demonstrated was so crucial to the overall historical direction of psychological expertise after World War II. Capable of soothing and exacerbating social and political ruptures, psychological experts were technologists of pacification one moment and prophets of renewal the next. For feminists, who understood keenly the danger of reducing women's social status to the psyche, the challenge was to link the dots between self and society, between the personal and the political, without making either appear to be a by-product of the other.

"Experience" was what the women's movement offered as connecting tissue. To grasp it was to anchor truth, probe the validity of theoretical formulations, and test the effectiveness of collective action against the inescapable measure of subjectivity. Historically rooted yet in constant motion, experience was feminism's ultimate evidence. It certified that psychology was a trap for women, but it also hinted that psychology might offer a way out of the trap. Experience was slippery and useful, demoralizing, liberating, and terribly confusing. Little wonder that women seeking to comprehend their past, chart their future, and realize their own humanity would sometimes long for some clearer, more reassuring way of understanding their lives. They did not find one.

11

Toward a Larger Jurisdiction for Psychology

"I can imagine nothing we could do that would be more relevant to human welfare, and nothing that could pose a greater challenge to the next generation of psychologists, than to discover how best to give psychology away."[1] Thus concluded George Miller's presidential address to the American Psychological Association (APA) in 1969. Intended to stir the souls of his professional colleagues, Miller's confidence that "scientific psychology is potentially one of the most revolutionary intellectual enterprises ever conceived by the mind of man" drew sustenance from the historical record.[2] "I believe that the real impact of psychology will be felt," he concluded, "not through the technological products it places in the hands of powerful men, but through its effects on the public at large, through a new and different public conception of what is humanly possible and what is humanly desirable."[3]

At the dawn of the 1970s, psychological experts had reason to feel satisfied with what they had accomplished since World War II. They had become players in far-flung areas of public policy and public culture, bringing their theories and research to bear on the major issues of their day. It is telling that even those critics who denounced the delivery of psychotechnologies to the military—and there were many in attendance at the 1969 APA meetings who opposed the Vietnam War—were likely to share Miller's pride that psychology had revealed positive new ways of conceiving the human experience.[4]

For better or worse, psychology's rise to power during the postwar decades changed ordinary Americans' expectations of their lives by publicizing the pertinence of emotion, the virtues of insight, and the unavoidability of subjectivity in the conduct of private and public affairs. These feats earned experts high status and permanently transformed the way war, racial conflict, gender equality, and the responsibilities and possibilities of democratic self-government were understood.

The Benefits of War

Psychology's political progress was founded, first and foremost, on the ever-present militarism of the war and postwar years. World War II had been generous to psychological experts. Because of it, they gained abundant training opportunities, professionally beneficial contacts, and a stockpile of theoretical leads to pursue when the fighting ended in 1945. They understood that helping to win the war was their first obligation, but experts never hesitated to experiment in the laboratory of international military conflict with an eye toward enhancing their scientific standing and improving the effectiveness and marketability of their technological talents.

A fixation on "morale" unified projects as diverse as running internment camps, destroying enemy morale, monitoring public opinion, procuring intelligence, and ensuring compliance and fighting spirit among soldiers and civilians. Committed to a vision of war that placed the feelings and attitudes of populations at center stage, psychological experts turned to theories that postulated fundamental parallels and intersections between individual and mass behavior. Frustration and aggression, they pointed out, were as sociologically convincing as they were psychologically sensitive. Dissatisfied people were prone to intolerance and authoritarianism, so it stood to reason that dissatisfied nations were prone to demagoguery and war.

From such comparisons, behavioral experts extracted a number of key propositions. First, psychology could and should operate as a weapon system, at least as significant, if not more so, than any other in the rapidly expanding U.S. arsenal. The real threats to global peace and national security, they believed, were epidemics of irrational emotion and flawed national characters in need of containment and reconstruction. Second, war was a fundamentally psychological conflict in which the psyche was a battlefield, persuasion was a key military strategy, and victory was measured in the capture of enemy minds. Third, no important distinctions existed between patriotic service, social responsibility, and government employment. The highest professional calling was to be of official use. Finally, the experts learned that the progress of psychology was an accurate index of democratic freedom, the public status of its practitioners a barometer of the wisdom of government policy and the soundness of society at large.

These lessons, which bonded psychological knowledge to political power, were not in the least abstract. Psychological experts toiled in the school of immediate experience. Immersed in the problems facing public organizations at war, they rapidly coordinated their skills with urgent policy needs to keep the domestic economy producing, the armed forces fighting, the melting pot from boiling over, and public opinion in line. If these jobs sometimes frustrated them, if they had to jump many hurdles before psychology could bring order and enlightenment to the policy-making process, it was also the case that World War II firmly oriented psychological experts toward policy elites and gave them a heady sense of their own potential for informing and altering the exercise of power.

Beyond the practical education World War II offered experts about the bureaucratic realities of government and the obstacles and inducements it placed in their path, world war shaped the lives and ideas of an entire generation of psychologically oriented intellectuals. What they absorbed about their own potential, their responsibilities and relationship to government, and the very changed shape of the world would guide this generation into the 1950s and 1960s.

The World War II model had stamina. For years afterward, it inspired psychological experts to bring their theories and research efforts to bear directly on issues of public importance. Social experts in a democracy were not only equipped, they believed, but positively obligated to immerse themselves in public projects—the more ambitious, the better. With their knowledge linked to progress, maturity, enlightenment, and peace—as well as power—psychological experts conceived of their future in very ambitious terms. Their postwar duty was to help construct a comprehensive "science of human behavior" that would be theoretically sophisticated yet practically equipped for the tasks of "prediction and control." They aimed at nothing less than to "fashion a new civilization" and "restructure the culture of the world."

Psychology as Public Policy

On the heels of war, a variety of psychological experts moved decisively to influence public policy. In return for their record of military service, they were accorded new prestige and greatly expanded authority. Supported by huge infusions of public funds, largely justified by psychology's military record and scientific claims, policy-oriented experts during the 1950s and 1960s contributed their research and theories to agencies of the state.

The conception of war that emerged from World War II—a "minds race" in which the quality of "mental materiel" could determine eventual victory or final defeat—was tailor-made for the Cold War era. So too, experts believed, was their knowledge of the psychology of revolutionary upheaval. Helping emerging states navigate the dangerous waters of capitalist modernization with policies geared to the design and manufacture of personalities suitable for development would surely enable the United States to conquer the territory most contested in the Cold War—the emotional loyalty residing in Third World psyches— and simultaneously ensure national security and global political stability.

From policy-makers' point of view, preventing upheaval in the first place was even more attractive than helping Third World identities mature, and the aspiration to "predict and influence" social change energized psychology's Cold War career, including the failed Project Camelot. In the aftermath of the scandal, no consensus was reached on whether Camelot was virtuous, socially engaged research, underhanded espionage, or merely proof that many intellectuals were extremely naive. Camelot revealed that the lessons of World War II remained sturdy and psychology's historical direction remained steady. The Cold War made behavioral science appear to be "one of the vital tools in the arsenal of the free societies." Waging "peacefare" in order to avoid direct superpower confrontation guaranteed a global arena in which behavioral theories could be formulated and tested. Psychological expertise continued to be applied to politically explicit goals effectively and without significant opposition. Public service and professional advance proceeded together unabated.

And so it was on the home front as well. A generation of experts whose practical techniques and analytical perspectives were shaped by military directives during World War II and the early Cold War brought their talents to bear on an array of nonmilitary concerns in later years. Racial conflict was one. During World War II, riots and a racist Nazi enemy had compelled numerous explorations of "intergroup conflict." These studies proliferated after 1945, becoming especially visible and germane upon the appearance of a mass-based civil rights movement in the 1950s, which captured the sympathies of a majority of psychological experts even as it rudely interrupted the celebration of postwar affluence and consensus.

Just as political instability in the Third World required constant attention and preventive measures, so too did threatening levels of racial hostility within U.S. borders. Their investigations into the psychology of race led experts to insist that the relevant variables were pretty much the same on the domestic scene as they were on the frontiers of the Cold War: frustration and aggression, the logic of personality formation, and, in particular, the gender dynamics involved in the production of either healthy or damaged (masculine) self-esteem. During the 1950s and 1960s, evidence of the harm prejudice and racism caused the developing personality was accorded a central place in law, government policy, and programs devoted to attaining equal opportunity and civil rights.

The Kerner Commission's deliberations, research, and policy recommendations provide evidence that official explanations of urban unrest during the 1960s had been deeply influenced by the work of psychological experts. As they analyzed the past errors and charted the future course of local police forces and municipal administrations, the commission's experts leaned heavily on the postwar themes of personality damage, wounded masculinity, and social disorganization within black ghetto communities. They recalled World War II–era investigations of irrationally prejudiced attitudes among soldiers and civilians and applied counterinsurgency models to the unrest in U.S. cities.

That the benefits of war were so flexible and far-reaching underlines the mutually reinforcing relationships between the growth of the U.S. welfare state in the twentieth century, the professionalization of the social and behavioral sciences and their recruitment into state service, and the extraordinary expansion in accepted notions of government, its proper spheres of operation, and its techniques of control. It is accurate enough to point out that wartime developments during the early 1940s had ancestors in Progressive Era reform and the depression-inspired programs of the New Deal and descendants in the Great Society of the 1960s. In each period of reform, experts supplied technical assistance in many different areas of domestic policy, from poverty and criminal justice to education and employment. While important details differed, the larger question—what role would experts play in ambitious government schemes for rational economic planning and conscious social engineering?—surfaced repeatedly over many decades.

The growth of the welfare state certainly offered psychological experts numerous opportunities to gather data, reach conclusions, and thereby test the practical validity of their theoretical hypotheses. The appearance of the warfare state and the constant military emergencies of the postwar years were at least as hospitable. The emphasis in this book on war and militarism is not intended to suggest that the growth of the state's domestically oriented concerns and bureaucracies have been insignificant to psychology's history during or after World War II. Quite the contrary. One of the most significant political developments of the postwar period is the growing convergence between the requirements of welfare and warfare, and the belief that ensuring national security in a dangerous world and constructing a just and decent society for U.S. citizens at home were necessarily part of the same project.

At times, welfare and warfare appeared as a stark choice: welfare *or* warfare? This was the case, for example, when the Kerner Commission's recommendations for expanded social programs in U.S. cities collided with the fiscal requirements of waging war in Vietnam. At other times, the warfare state assumed the functions of the welfare state. Policymakers like Daniel Patrick Moynihan utilized military behavioral research as a blueprint for 1960s social programs and insisted that the Department of Defense offer soldiers opportunities for education and training that would lift them out of the civilian underclass. Perhaps it is only now, as we look back on the Cold War as history, that this intimate relationship between welfare and warfare can finally come into focus.

Whether they were offering advice on managing the Cold War or prescribing a reduction in racial tensions in U.S. cities, psychological experts brought their considerable talents to bear on the design and administration of postwar public policy. Their mission was to enlighten approaches to the most decisive and divisive matters of their day and, in doing so, to enlarge the responsibilities and appropriate subjects of government while broadening psychology's reach and influence.

Psychology as Public Culture

The career of clinical experts was animated by the wartime normalization of psychotherapy, the evolution of mental health into a national public policy priority, and the migration of the therapeutic sensibility into the political culture of the 1960s. Far more than their policy-oriented colleagues, clinicians were concerned about individual human beings, practices like psychotherapy, and concepts like normality and mental health. But psychological experts of all types shared basic assumptions that placed them on similar historical trajectories. The belief that psychology might systematically expose universal laws of human behavior and motivation won the loyalty and captured the imaginations of psychotherapists and behavioral scientists alike.

World War II was as momentous for clinicians as it was for social and behavioral scientists. Because exposure to military conflict, especially combat, was stressful to the point of precipitating mass breakdown in otherwise normal men, clinicians accorded new prominence to social context in their estimations of what caused (and what might alleviate) symptoms of mental trouble. The job definition of clinical experts subsequently shifted from identifying individuals predisposed to emotional disturbance to treating masses of men made neurotic by war and regulating the military environment so as to prevent the same thing from happening to others. War bound professional helpers to normal human fears and anxieties, completely reversing the old association between clinical expertise and madness.

Convinced by war that their insights and practices could and should be brought to bear on a wide range of social problems in the name of mental health, clinicians pursued an ambitious strategy that fundamentally transformed the nature of their authority. Clinical practices and theories, previously considered methods of treating and understanding gross mental abnormalities and deviations from the average, gradually earned a reputation as best suited to comprehending mild forms of psychological maladjustment as well as entirely normal psychological experiences. In the case of psychiatry, a change in geographic location corresponded to this radical shift in emphasis. On the assumption that severe mental illness could be prevented, the majority of the profession moved aggressively away from isolated asylums and into the heart of U.S. communities.

As a result, psychological help was defined so broadly that everyone needed it. Because mental health became a prerequisite to social welfare and economic prosperity, and not merely a state of individual well-being, virtually no aspect of U.S. life, private or public, remained out of clinicians' reach. Neurotic emotional disturbance was gradually accepted as a fact and product of modern existence rather than as the shameful secret it had been just a few decades earlier. Clinicians, the madness specialists of an earlier era, evolved into empathetic guides whose job it was to assist their fellow humans in navigating the emotional quicksand of modern life. When mental health was accepted as a relative and unstable social resource, rather than as a property permanently belonging to (or absent in) given individuals, psychotherapeutic encounters were enshrined as precious experiences and clinical assistance and social activism became difficult to tell apart. To seek self-understanding and help became an emblem of emotional courage, a means to growth and happiness, and a step toward responsible, self-controlled citizenship. Therapeutic need began to lose its stigmatizing sting.

Mental health itself became an important concern among policy-makers after 1945, a direct result of the exposure of millions of American men—soldiers and veterans—to programs of clinical testing and treatment. Historic legislation like the National Mental Health Act of 1946 and the Community Mental Health Centers Act of 1963 reflected vigorous demand for postwar services emanating from veterans, their families, and, of course, clinical professionals themselves. Community psychology and psychiatry, the most innovative trends in the postwar clinical fields, displayed the tenacity of wartime lessons about the importance of managing emotional disturbance with methods geared to preventing it in the first place. By definition, community-sensitive methods embodied the idea that psychological fitness was inseparable from public policy devised and implemented by wise and compassionate social engineers.

In spite of the concerns they shared with social and behavioral scientists, most clinicians remained obligated to helping individuals or small groups like families, and they held fast to a correspondingly personal vision of mental health during this period. Yet the popularization of clinical work had major public consequences during the 1960s. During that decade, a diversity of political movements added to conventional political agendas demands for a drastically changed type of political participation and subjectivity. To civil rights guarantees for members of racial minority groups and an end to military involvement in Southeast Asia were added calls for participatory democracy, a feeling of "somebodiness," and a personally meaningful civic life.

These developments illustrated how politically enriching and liberating psychological perspectives could be and were. By the 1960s, psychological experts had expanded both the subjects of official government action and extended citizens' expectations of their public lives. If alienation and frustration nourished such developments, they also produced new and dynamic levels of citizen engagement, expressing desires that political responsibility, social welfare, and public activity be rejuvenated and made worthwhile for masses of disenfranchised people.

Psychology's public face did not always appear so benevolent. Clinical expertise itself became the subject of political protest during the 1960s, as if to underscore that its pernicious potential was at least as obvious as its more salutary consequences. Antipsychiatry was inspired by the critical writings of such thinkers as Thomas Szasz and R. D. Laing, and grassroots groups like the Mental Patients Liberation Front built alliances between ex-patients and leftist clinicians. Together, they elaborated a radical critique of clinical work. Even within antipsychiatry, however, which assumed that the psychological worldview was little more than a cover for the mystification and rationalization of political oppression and hierarchy, there existed liberating possibilities for the practice of "radical therapy."

The case of feminism is illustrative because it recapitulates the divergent possibilities demonstrated throughout this book: psychology could be both politically liberating and oppressive. To the extent that feminists protested the sexism of experts but utilized psychological ideas and practices for distinctly feminist purposes, the women's movement offers a fascinating window into that aspect of psychology's political history. It reveals some of the connections between mainstream social science, radical activism, and intellectual dissent.

The popularization and redefinition of clinical experience after 1945 was a significant, positive factor in the women's movement's emergence, mobilization, structure, demands, style, and theoretical literature. So too though was the critique mounted by antipsychiatry. Feminist activists did not merely imitate psychotherapy or reproduce humanistic theories wholesale. Neither did they echo the most simplistic antipsychiatric accusations that clinical practices were mere smokescreens for political repression. From the practice of consciousness raising to theoretical questions about the origin of male supremacy, feminists—at all points on the movement's political spectrum—vigorously debated the place of psychology in women's oppression and liberation. Was it part of the problem or part of the solution? The lack of consensus exposed the fundamental political legacy of postwar psychological expertise: it was neither and it was both. Feminism's dual identity as a public campaign for formal equality and a cultural revolution in the subjective experience of gender demonstrates very clearly how much the direction of postwar political activism depended upon the hallmarks of psychological expertise during this period: the merging of public and private, the political and the psychological. Psychology may have constructed the female, but it also helped to construct the feminist.

"A Larger Jurisdiction for Psychology"

Wherever they were located and whatever their immediate concerns, diverse psychological experts sought "a larger jurisdiction for psychology" during the years after 1940.[5] I have tried to show that, to a remarkable degree, they achieved it. Delighted that psychology had finally attained some of the visibility and power they thought it deserved, they contemplated the happy prospect of "giving psychology away," consolidating their gains by making psychology an inextricable element of contemporary civilization rather than a factor dependent upon the fickle fortunes of one professional group or another.

The eager exchange of ideas between clinicians and behavioral scientists nourished this broad jurisdiction. Techniques of individual diagnosis were eagerly applied to the study of national character and international relationships during World War II by such figures as Lawrence K. Frank and Alexander Leighton. Their recommendation that society be treated as "a patient" was but a single instance of a widely accepted view: namely that clinical insights could and should be adapted to the requirements of foreign and military policy. Delicate challenges in the sphere of domestic policy elicited similar perspectives on cities and urban disturbances more than twenty years later. The Kerner Commission's research effort included analyses of cities as diseased entities and riots as psychopathological symptoms which, not surprisingly, concluded with recommendations for urban treatment.

For their part, many clinicians during this period came to believe that their professional commitment to cultivating individual mental health required them to become social planners and political activists engaged in the policy-making process. This belief was the essence of community mental health, a movement spearheaded by professional organizations like the Group for the Advancement of Psychiatry, known for championing an array of activist, liberal solutions in the name of clinical social responsibility. Numerous individual careers progressed from rescuing troubled individuals to mapping public policy, a move that appeared logical and necessary in a society showing symptoms of social strain and even sickness. For example, psychiatrist John Spiegel, a clinician involved in the treatment of war neurosis during World War II and an active proponent of family therapy in the 1950s, could be found in the 1960s directing the Lemberg Center for the Study of Violence at Brandeis University, a hub of policy-oriented investigations into the causes of civil disturbance. What could be done, after all, about individual or family well-being in ghettos if one ignored dilapidated housing, wretched schools, and a climate of material impoverishment and spiritual despair?

The historical chronologies of clinical and policy-oriented experts also paralleled each other during this period. Clinicians derived long-lasting benefits from World War II, when their fervent efforts to maintain the military's mental balance underscored yet again the salience of morale. Programs that screened, diagnosed, and treated millions of individual soldiers helped to turn subjectivity into an essential ingredient of successful war making, just as psychological warfare and attitude research, designed for application to entire populations, had done. All of their wartime accomplishments were lavishly rewarded after 1945, in the tangible form of public financial support for professional training and research and in the less tangible form of enhanced popular prestige, which increased private demand for services and advice.

In sum, this book has described a metamorphosis in ideas about change: how it was to be most effectively conceived, planned, and administered. It has also attempted to illuminate a number of the historical circumstances that produced that metamorphosis. As they gained public stature and ambition in the years after 1940, psychological experts claimed increasingly broad authority to understand and alter the conditions of human behavior and experience. Some occupations gravitated toward persons, others toward populations. Enveloped in world war and Cold War, determined to reveal the sources of racial hostility and the logic of gender identity, it is hardly surprising that almost all of them concentrated on the intersections between self and society.

Experts charged with managing populations felt they had no choice but to navigate the murky depths of the interior psyche in order to accomplish their goals. Experts moved to aid suffering individuals resolved that only social alterations could alleviate pain and facilitate growth. Thus did the concerns of behavioral science and clinical healing merge, complicating the meaning of social engineering and personal liberation alike. Adding the individual psyche to the targets of public policy expanded policy's reach and redefined government as a process in which subjectivity was implicated and altered. Making clinicians accountable for environments conducive to mental health and happiness drastically extended the psychotherapeutic frontier by implying that society itself was in dire need of emotional help.

Developments such as these offer fresh vantage points from which to view postwar history in the United States and provide insights into some of its characteristic features: the blurring of public and private boundaries, the overlap between political culture and cultural politics, the anxious standoff between self and society. Psychological experts not only linked personal and social change. They suggested that the points of contact merited political scrutiny and government action, a proposition that transformed subjectivity into a potential resource and obstacle in public life. Because human psychology was an enigma—amenable to probing investigation one moment but allergic to it the next—experts with the authority to fathom and guide it were indispensable to the future of democracy.

Does the rise of psychology herald a new chapter in the evolution of humanism or merely indicate that Big Brother is bright enough to arrive cloaked in the rhetoric of enlightenment and health? If differentiating these possibilities appears a perplexing task, that only suggests that the relationship of psychological knowledge to power, which has had varied and paradoxical consequences in the past, will likely continue to present a host of thorny contradictions. The romance of American psychology in the postwar era is consequential not because it offers reassurance that freedom and control are entirely different things, but because it shows that they are not.

Notes

Key to Abbreviations in the Notes

Because they recur frequently, the following sources have been abbreviated in the notes. Other archival sources and public documents are not abbreviated, and full citations can be found in the notes. Many thanks to the librarians and archivists who granted me permission to use their materials and who guided me through the research process.

Archival Sources

GA PapersGordon Allport Papers

EB PapersEdwin Boring Papers

SS PapersSamuel Andrew Stouffer Papers
    All of the above are located in the Harvard University Archives and material is used by permission of the Harvard University Archives, Cambridge, Massachusetts.

KC ArchivesMany of the Kerner Commission's records, located in the Johnson Library in Austin, Texas, are reproduced in August Meier and John H. Bracey, Jr., eds., *Black Studies Research Sources: Microfilms from Major Archival and Manuscript Collections, Civil Rights Under the Johnson Administration, 1963–1969* (Frederick, Md.: University Publications of America,

1984–1987). Part 5 of this microfilm collection is titled "Records of the National Advisory Commission on Civil Disorder (Kerner Commission)." All references to Kerner Commission Archives in the notes are to part 5 of this collection, unless otherwise noted. Page numbers refer to microfilm pages.

RF ArchivesRockefeller Foundation Archives, located in the Rockefeller Archive Center, North Tarrytown, New York.

WHWomen's History Research Center, microfilm collection on "Women and/in Health," July 1974. All page numbers in the notes refer to microfilm pages.

Congressional Hearings and Reports

U.S. HOUSE OF REPRESENTATIVES

BSNSU.S. House of Representatives, Committee on Foreign Affairs, Subcommittee on International Organizations and Movements, "Behavioral Sciences and the National Security," Report No. 4, Together with Part IX of the Hearings on "Winning the Cold War: The U.S. Ideological Offensive," July–August 1965, 89th Cong., 2nd sess., H.R. Report 1224.

WCWU.S. House of Representatives, Committee on Foreign Affairs, Subcommittee on International Organizations and Movements, Hearings on "Winning the Cold War: The U.S. Ideological Offensive," March 1963–January 1964, 88th Cong., 1st sess., pts. 1–8.

U.S. SENATE

DDSFARU.S. Senate, Committee on Foreign Relations, Hearings on "Defense Department Sponsored Foreign Affairs Research," May 1968, pts. 1–2, 90th Cong., 2nd sess.

FSISSBRU.S. Senate, Committee on Government Operations, Subcommittee on Government Research, Hearings on "Federal Support of International Social Science and Behavioral Research," June–July 1966, 89th Cong., 2nd sess.

NNIAU.S. Senate, National Neuropsychiatric Institute Act, Hearings Before a Subcommittee of the Committee on Education and Labor, 79th Cong., 2nd sess., March 6–8, 1946.

PAFPU.S. Senate, Committee on Foreign Relations, Hearings on "Psychological Aspects of Foreign Policy," June 1969, 91st Cong., 1st sess.

PAIRU.S. Senate, Committee on Foreign Relations, Hearings on "Psychological Aspects of International Relations," May 25, 1966, 89th Cong., 2nd sess.

1: In the Name of Enlightenment

1. "American Psychological Association Membership Totals, 1892–Present" (Washington, D.C.: American Psychological Association Membership Department, 1992).

2. "American Psychiatric Association Membership Figures, 1873–Present" (Washington, D.C.: American Psychiatric Association, 1994).

3. Most of the statistics in this paragraph are drawn from National Science Foundation, *Profiles—Psychology: Human Resources and Funding* (NSF 88–325, Washington, D.C., 1988), 3, 70 (table 4), and 127–128 (table 24). Comparative historical statistics presented by James Capshew, "Constructing Subjects, Reconstructing Psychology" (paper delivered at the Twenty-third Annual Meeting of Cheiron, Slippery Rock, Pennsylvania, 22 June 1991).

4. Daniel Goleman, "New Paths to Mental Health Put Strains on Some Healers," *New York Times,* 17 May 1990, A1, B12.

5. In spite of its increasingly clinical orientation, psychology has recently been classified as one of the "behavioral sciences." The "behavioral" orientation of a new type of social expert was, in large measure, the product of large-scale philanthropy and foundations' support for research that government policy-makers could use to ameliorate the ever-worsening social problems of modern industrial capitalist society. This quest for practical modes of social engineering began in earnest after World War I. The golden years of "behavioral science," however, were to come in the 1950s, when the generosity of the Ford Foundation made "behavioral science" into shorthand for a subset of the more general category "social sciences." The "behavioral sciences" were defined so as to include psychology, anthropology, sociology, and those aspects of economics and political science devoted to the analysis of individual and group behavior rather than institutions.

6. C. Wright Mills, *White Collar: The American Middle Classes* (New York: Oxford University Press, 1951), 160.

7. Ibid., xx.

8. B. F. Skinner, audio interview by Dennis Trumble, 23 April 1985, B. F. Skinner Papers, Harvard University Archives, Cambridge, Massachusetts.

9. Edwin G. Boring to Ruth S. Tolman, 3 January 1946, Correspondence, 1919–1956, box 54, folder 1318, EB Papers.

10. Letter from Clarence Cheyney to Douglas Thom, 28 November 1947, quoted in Gerald N. Grob, *From Asylum to Community: Mental Health Policy in Modern America* (Princeton: Princeton University Press, 1991), 34.

11. Noam Chomsky, "The Responsibility of Intellectuals," in *American*

Power and the New Mandarins (New York: Vintage Books, 1967), 325, 358–359.

12. For an extensive discussion of recent historiographical trends, see my "Psychology as Politics: How Psychological Experts Transformed Public Life in the United States, 1940–1970" (Ph.D. diss., Brandeis University, 1993), chap. 2.

13. For sophisticated treatments of these issues as they relate to historians' use of "experience," psychology's epistemological foundations, and radical undercurrents in the history of philosophy itself, see Joan Scott, "The Evidence of Experience," *Critical Inquiry* 17 (Summer 1991):773–797; Jill Morawski, "Toward the Unimagined: Feminism and Epistemology in Psychology," in *Making a Difference: Psychology and the Construction of Gender*, ed. Rachel T. Hare-Mustin and Jeanne Marecek (Yale University Press, 1990), 150–183; James T. Kloppenberg, *Uncertain Victory: Social Democracy and Progressivism in European and American Thought, 1870–1920* (New York: Oxford University Press, 1986), chaps. 2 and 3.

2: War on the Enemy Mind

1. The best general secondary source on psychology in world war is James Herbert Capshew, "Psychology on the March: American Psychologists and World War II" (Ph.D. diss., University of Pennsylvania, 1986). Other useful overviews are Peter Buck, "Adjusting to Military Life: The Social Sciences Go to War, 1941–1950," in *Military Enterprise and Technological Change*, ed. Merritt Roe Smith (Cambridge: MIT Press, 1985), 203–252, and Nikolas Rose, *Governing the Soul: The Shaping of the Private Self* (London: Routledge, 1990), pt. 1.

2. J. McKeen Cattell, "Retrospect: Psychology as a Profession," *Journal of Consulting Psychology* 1 (January–February 1937):1.

3. For a discussion of how World War I advanced the professionalization efforts of psychologists, see Thomas M. Camfield, "Psychologists at War: The History of American Psychology and the First World War" (Ph.D. diss., University of Texas, 1969); Franz Samelson, "Putting Psychology on the Map: Ideology and Intelligence Testing," in *Psychology in Social Context*, ed. Allan R. Buss (New York: Irvington Publishers, 1979), 103–168; and Franz Samelson, "World War I Intelligence Testing and the Development of Psychology," *Journal of the History of the Behavioral Sciences* 13 (July 1977):274–282. For a consideration of World War I testing that focuses specifically on the negotiating process between psychological experts and the military, see John Carson, "Army Alpha, Army Brass, and the Search for Army Intelligence," *Isis* 84 (1993):278–309.

4. For background on Yerkes's work, see Donna Haraway, "A Pilot Plant for Human Engineering: Robert Yerkes and the Yale Laboratories of Primate

Biology, 1924–1942," in *Primate Visions: Gender, Race, and Nature in the World of Modern Science* (New York: Routledge, 1989,) 59–83.

5. Karl M. Dallenbach, "The Emergency Committee in Psychology, National Research Council," *American Journal of Psychology* 59 (October 1946):497.

6. "War cabinet" was Leonard Carmichael's phrase. See Capshew, "Psychology on the March," 40 n. 52.

7. Robert M. Yerkes, "Psychology and Defense," *Proceedings of the American Philosophical Society* 84 (June 1941):536.

8. Ibid.

9. Ibid., 541.

10. Capshew, "Psychology on the March," 45.

11. Gordon W. Allport, "Psychological Service for Civilian Morale," *Journal of Consulting Psychology* 5 (September–October 1941):235.

12. Ibid.

13. Ibid., 238.

14. Gordon Allport to Alice Bryan, 5 April 1941, HUG 4118.10, folder: "1938–48, Bro-Bz," GA Papers.

15. Charles William Bray, *Psychology and Military Proficiency: A History of the Applied Psychology Panel of the National Defense Research Committee* (Princeton: Princeton University Press, 1948), v. This glowing assessment was made by the navy representative to the National Defense Resource Council, Captain Lybrand Palmer Smith.

16. "Some Notes on the History of the American Psychological Association, Remarks on the Occasion of the Seventy-fifth Anniversary of the Association, September 3, 1967," Correspondence 1919–1965, box 80, folder 1679, EB Papers. For a useful summary of the war's impact on the American Psychological Association, see James H. Capshew and Ernest R. Hilgard, "The Power of Service: World War II and Professional Reform in the American Psychological Association," in *The American Psychological Association: A Historical Perspective,* ed. Rand B. Evans, Virginia S. Sexton, and Thomas C. Cadwallader (Washington, D.C.: American Psychological Association, 1992), 149–175.

17. For more on the screening of immigrants and its important connection to psychiatry's work in World War I, see Rebecca Schwartz Greene, "The Role of the Psychiatrist in World War II" (Ph.D. diss., Columbia University, 1977), 16–30.

18. "American Psychiatric Association Membership Figures, 1873–Present."

19. Ibid.

20. "American Psychological Association Membership Totals, 1892–Present."

21. Gladys C. Schwesinger, "Wartime Organizational Activities of Women Psychologists, II. The National Council of Women Psychologists," *Journal of Consulting Psychology* 7 (November–December 1943):300. For a discussion of the experience of female psychologists during World War II, see James H. Capshew and Alejandra C. Laszlo, " 'We would not take no for an answer': Women Psychologists and Gender Politics During World War II," *Journal of Social*

Issues 42 (1986):157–180, followed by comments by Alice I. Bryan and Cynthia P. Deutsch.

22. While the population increased by 57 percent between the mid-1940s and the mid-1970s, American Psychological Association membership shot up 850 percent. For a statistical overview of the growth of the psychological profession during these years, see Albert R. Gilgen, *American Psychology Since World War II: A Profile of the Discipline* (Westport, Conn.: Greenwood Press, 1982), 21, table 1.

23. For more on the work of psychological experimentalists, see Bray, *Psychology and Military Proficiency*. For more on Skinner's Project Pigeon, see B. F. Skinner, "Pigeons in a Pelican," in *Theories of Personality: Primary Sources and Research*, 2nd ed., ed. Gradner Lindzey, Calvin S. Hall, and Martin Manosevitz (New York: John Wiley and Sons, 1973), 399–413, and Capshew, "Psychology on the March," 135–150.

24. Letters by Gregory Bateson and Harold Lasswell quoted in Virginia Yans-McLaughlin, "Science, Democracy, and Ethics: Mobilizing Culture and Personality for World War II," *History of Anthropology* 4 (1986):196–197.

25. For examples, see Eli Ginzberg, *Breakdown and Recovery*, vol. 2 of *The Ineffective Soldier: Lessons for Management and the Nation* (New York: Columbia University Press, 1959), 3; Alexander H. Leighton, *The Governing of Men: General Principles and Recommendations Based on Experience at a Japanese Relocation Camp* (Princeton: Princeton University Press, 1945), 358; Daniel Lerner, *Sykewar: Psychological Warfare Against Germany, D-Day to VE-Day* (New York: George W. Stewart, 1949), 324; Samuel A. Stouffer et al., *The American Soldier: Adjustment During Army Life*, vol. 1 of *Studies in Social Psychology in World War II* (Princeton: Princeton University Press, 1949), vii.

26. See, for example, "Memorandum for the Chief of Special Services, Subject: Some Reflections on the Program of the Research Division," 3 June 1942, HUG (FP) 31.8, box 2, folder: "Research Problems," SS Papers.

27. "The Psychiatric Approach in Problems of Community Management," *American Journal of Psychiatry* 100 (November 1946):328–333.

28. Samuel Stouffer to Paul Lazarsfeld, 30 November 1945, HUG (FP) 31.8, box 1, folder: "Columbia University," SS Papers. Stouffer's 1930 doctoral dissertation, which compared statistical and life history techniques in attitude research, was typical of the interwar effort to advance and legitimate social science by making it conform to the perceived objectivity of methodological standards including quantitative measurement, value neutrality, and emotional detachment from the subject. For a discussion of this era in the University of Chicago sociology department, where Stouffer was a student, see Dorothy Ross, *The Origins of American Social Science* (New York: Cambridge University Press, 1991), 428–437.

29. Walter Lippmann, *Public Opinion* (New York: Macmillan, 1922), chap. 1.

30. For an extended discussion of the contradiction between scientific and democratic ideals in the history of academic political science, see David Ricci, *The Tragedy of Political Science: Politics, Scholarship, and Democracy* (New Ha-

ven: Yale University Press, 1984). Ricci's chapter 3 touches on the World War I experience.

31. An overview of the early intellectual history of crowd psychology can be found in Jaap van Ginneken, *Crowds, Psychology, and Politics, 1871–1899* (New York: Oxford University Press, 1992).

32. William McDougall, *Group Mind: A Sketch of the Principles of Collective Psychology, With Some Attempt to Apply Them to the Interpretation of National Life and Character* (New York: G. P. Putnam's Sons, 1920); Everett Dean Martin, *The Behavior of Crowds: A Psychological Study* (New York: Harper & Brothers Publishers, 1920). A general discussion of the importation of crowd psychology into U.S. social science can be found in Eugene E. Leach, " 'Mental Epidemics': Crowd Psychology and American Culture, 1890–1940," *American Studies* 33 (Spring 1992):5–29.

33. For useful treatments of Freudian social thought, see Louise E. Hoffman, "From Instinct to Identity: Implications of Changing Psychoanalytic Concepts of Social Life from Freud to Erikson," *Journal of the History of the Behavioral Sciences* 18 (April 1982):130–146; and "The Ideological Significance of Freud's Social Thought," in *Psychology in Twentieth-Century Thought and Society,* ed. Mitchell G. Ash and William R. Woodward (New York: Cambridge University Press, 1987), 253–269.

34. Reba N. Soffer, *Ethics and Society in England: The Revolution in the Social Sciences, 1870–1914* (Berkeley: University of California Press, 1978), esp. chap. 10. Soffer singles out social psychology as the single "revisionist" and counterrevolutionary intellectual tradition in an era of otherwise "revolutionary" and progressive social science.

35. Herbert Hoover, *American Individualism* (New York: Garland Publishing, 1922), 24–25.

36. Harold D. Lasswell, *Psychopathology and Politics* (New York: Viking Press, 1930).

37. Harold D. Lasswell, "What Psychiatrists and Political Scientists Can Learn from One Another," *Psychiatry* 1 (February 1938):37.

38. For examples of how an orientation toward "prevention" opened a plethora of new opportunities, see William Menninger, "The Role of Psychiatry in the World Today," in *A Psychiatrist for a Troubled World: Selected Papers of William C. Menninger, M.D.,* ed. Bernard H. Hall (New York: Viking, 1967), 568–581, originally published in *American Journal of Psychiatry* 104 (September 1947):155–163; William C. Menninger, *Psychiatry in a Troubled World: Yesterday's War and Today's Challenge* (New York: Macmillan, 1948), pt. 2.

39. Barbara Sicherman, "The Quest for Mental Health in America, 1880–1917," Ph.D. dissertation, Columbia University, 1967 (New York: Arno Press, 1980).

40. Lasswell, *Psychopathology and Politics,* 198.

41. Leighton, *The Governing of Men,* viii.

42. The formal title of the project was the Bureau of Sociological Research. For details on the background and evolution of the project, see Leighton, *The Governing of Men,* especially the appendix titled "Applied Anthropology in a

Dislocated Community" by Alexander Leighton and Edward Spicer. Other sources include "The Psychiatric Approach in Problems of Community Management," 328–333; and Edward H. Spicer, "The Use of Social Scientists by the War Relocation Authority," *Applied Anthropology* 5 (Spring 1946): 16–36.

43. Leighton's team was not alone in attempting to bring psychological insight to the challenge of military occupation. Kurt Lewin put his leadership and group training skills and theories to use in this area. See "Training of Social Administrators in the Field of Leadership and Social Management," n.d., c. 1943. This document specified the human management tasks involved in military occupation. HUG 4118.10, folder: "Lewin, Kurt, 1944–45," GA Papers.

44. Leighton, *The Governing of Men*, 377.

45. Tom Sasaki, Chica Sugino, Hisako Fujii, Misao Furuta, Iwao Ishino, Mary Kinoshita, June Kushino, Yoshiharu Matsumoto, Florence Mohri, Akiko Nishimoto, Jyuichi Sato, James Sera, Gene Sogioka, George Yamaguchi, and Toshio Yatsushiro were among the project's staff members.

46. Leighton, *The Governing of Men*, 44.

47. Ibid., 366.

48. Ibid., 315.

49. Ibid., 362.

50. For an example of this typical view of morale, see John Rawlings Rees, *The Shaping of Psychiatry by War* (New York: W. W. Norton, 1945), 82–88.

51. Leonard Carmichael in *A History of Psychology in Autobiography*, vol. 5, ed. Edwin G. Boring and Gardner Lindzey (New York: Appleton-Century-Crofts, 1967), 49.

52. Harold D. Lasswell, "Political and Psychological Warfare," in *Propaganda in War and Crisis: Materials for American Policy*, ed. Daniel Lerner (New York: George W. Stewart, 1951), 264.

53. Ibid., 261–266.

54. For example, military intelligence agencies wanted to know how U.S. citizens felt about martial law, the loyalty of various racial and ethnic groups, and how far military policy-makers could go with security restrictions before overstepping the bounds of democracy. For obvious reasons, they could not make these needs public, but were creative in obtaining this information from other government agencies, or private organizations. See letter from unnamed official in Honolulu's 14 ND Intelligence Office to Elmo Wilson, 16 August 1942, HUG (FP) 31.8, box 1, folder: "Miscellaneous (2 of 2)," SS Papers.

55. Brett Gary, personal communication, 17 October 1991.

56. Brett Gary, "Mass Communications Research, the Rockefeller Foundation, and the Imperatives of War, 1939–1945," *Research Reports from the Rockefeller Archive Center*, Spring 1991 (North Tarrytown, N.Y.: Rockefeller Archive Center), 3–5.

57. Hadley Cantril to John Marshall, 1 May 1947, Record Group 1.1, series 200R, box 271, folder 3226, RF Archives.

58. For a sympathetic overview of the concept, including its historical development and application during World War II, see Margaret Mead, "The Study of National Character," in *The Policy Sciences: Recent Developments in*

Scope and Method, ed. Daniel Lerner and Harold D. Lasswell (Stanford: Stanford University Press, 1951), 70–85.

59. Franz Alexander, *Our Age of Unreason: A Study of the Irrational Forces in Social Life,* rev. ed. (Philadelphia: J. B. Lippincott, 1951, originally published 1942); Erich Fromm, *Escape from Freedom* (New York: Avon Books, 1941); Karen Horney, *The Neurotic Personality of Our Time* (New York: W. W. Norton, 1937). Harry Stack Sullivan's books were not published until after World War II, but as president of the William Alanson White Foundation, editor of its journal, *Psychiatry,* and key figure in World War II psychiatry, Sullivan's "culture and personality" perspective and his commitment to making psychiatry useful during the wartime emergency, were widely known. For an unsympathetic treatment of the neo-Freudians as an example of "conformist psychology," see Russell Jacoby, *Social Amnesia: A Critique of Conformist Psychology from Adler to Laing* (Boston: Beacon Press, 1975), esp. chap. 3.

60. An excellent overview of their wartime efforts can be found in Yans-McLaughlin, "Science, Democracy, and Ethics," 184–217. An overview of the culture and personality school over several decades is Milton Singer, "A Survey of Culture and Personality Theory and Research," in *Studying Personality Cross-Culturally,* ed. Bert Kaplan (New York: Harper & Row, 1961), 9–90.

61. Edward Sapir, "Why Cultural Anthropology Needs the Psychiatrist," *Psychiatry* 1 (February 1938):10.

62. Gregory Bateson, "Morale and National Character," in *Civilian Morale,* ed. Goodwin Watson (New York: Reynal & Hitchcock, 1942), 84–85.

63. Geoffrey Gorer, "The Scientific Study of National Character," unpublished paper, quoted in H. V. Dicks, "Some Psychological Studies of the German Character," in *Psychological Factors of Peace and War,* ed. T. H. Pear (New York: The Philosophical Society, 1950), 197–198.

64. Lawrence K. Frank, "Society as the Patient," *American Journal of Sociology* 42 (November 1936):335. This and numerous other articles by Frank advocating the "psychocultural approach" were reprinted in Lawrence K. Frank, *Society as the Patient: Essays on Culture and Personality* (New Brunswick: Rutgers University Press, 1948). Twenty years later, Frank noted that psychology's incredible progress was indebted to the idea of "society as patient." Lawrence K. Frank, "Psychology and Social Order," in *The Human Meaning of the Social Sciences,* ed. Daniel Lerner (New York: Meridian Books, 1959), 214–241.

65. Edward A. Strecker, *Beyond the Clinical Frontiers: A Psychiatrist Views Crowd Behavior* (New York: W. W. Norton, 1940), 84, 180.

66. Richard M. Brickner, *Is Germany Incurable?* (Philadelphia: J. B. Lippincott, 1943), 30, 45.

67. Ibid., 307.

68. Margaret Mead, *And Keep Your Powder Dry: An Anthropologist Looks at America* (New York: William Morrow, 1942), 261. See also Mead's introduction to Brickner's *Is Germany Curable?* for another typical statement about the great wartime responsibilities and capabilities of social scientists.

69. Bruno Bettelheim to Gordon Allport, 16 August 1943, HUG 4118.20, box 4, folder 109, GA Papers.

70. Otto Klineberg, "A Science of National Character," *Journal of Social Psychology* 19 (1944):147–162. For a methodological critique of the concept following the war, see Maurice L. Farber, "The Problem of National Character: A Methodological Analysis," *Journal of Psychology* 30 (October 1950):307–316, reprinted in *Social Scientists and International Affairs: A Case for a Sociology of Social Science,* ed. Elisabeth T. Crawford and Albert D. Biderman (New York: John Wiley & Sons, 1969), 207–213.

71. For an overview of the work of the Yale Institute of Human Relations, see Mark A. May, *Toward a Science of Human Behavior: A Survey of the Work of the Institute of Human Relations Through Two Decades, 1929–1949* (New Haven: Yale University, 1950); and J. G. Morawski, "Organizing Knowledge and Behavior at Yale's Institute of Human Relations," *Isis* 77 (1986):219–242. Many human links connected the "culture and personality" school with the Yale Institute. Geoffrey Gorer, for example, had been a member of the faculty at the Yale Institute of Human Relations.

72. John Dollard et al., *Frustration and Aggression* (New Haven: Yale University Press, 1939).

73. Ibid., 1, emphasis in original; May, *Toward a Science of Human Behavior,* 20.

74. Sigmund Freud, *Civilization and Its Discontents,* trans. James Strachey (1930; reprint, New York: W. W. Norton, 1961).

75. Sigmund Freud, "Why War?" in *Collected Papers of Sigmund Freud,* ed. James Strachey (New York: Basic Books, 1959), 5:283, 286–287.

76. Mr. Frank to Mr. Edmund Day, 14 June 1932, Rockefeller Foundation internal memorandum, Record Group 1.1, series 200, box 67, folder 807, RF Archives.

77. Alan Gregg, diary excerpt, 15 December 1941, Record Group 1.1, series 200, box 68, folder 812, RF Archives.

78. "Memoranda for the Study of the Social Effects of War," 10 March 1942, Record Group 1.1, series 200, box 68, folder 813, RF Archives. Several members of the Yale faculty also consulted to the Research Branch of the army's Morale Division (later called the Information and Education Division), and brought to this work a conviction that the business of army researchers was to "perform an important function in checking up continually on the *frustrations* which arise from Army life. We want to know exactly what they are and their real as well as apparent causes are. We want to know also the results in the form of aggression, open or devious, attempts to escape, passivity, and the like. In connection with aggression, it is particularly important to know under what circumstances it is directed in a socially serviceable way, i.e., against the enemy." "Notes on Research Discussions of Carl I. Hovland and John Dollard," 25–26 April 1942, pp. 5–6, HUG (FP) 31.8, box 2, folder: "Yale University," SS Papers.

79. May, *Toward a Science of Human Behavior,* 31–32.

80. Gardner Murphy, ed., *Human Nature and Enduring Peace* (Boston: Houghton Mifflin, 1945), 21.

81. For other examples of frustration-aggression theory applied to war, see H. J. Eysenck, "War and Aggressiveness: A Survey of Social Attitude Studies," and Hilde Himmelweit, "Frustration and Aggression: A Review of Recent Ex-

perimental Work," in *Psychological Factors in Peace and War*, 49–81, 161–191. For a less sophisticated, but emphatically psychological analysis, see C. S. Bluemel, *War, Politics, and Insanity: In Which the Psychiatrist Looks at the Politician* (Denver: The World Press, 1950). Bluemel considered political leadership as practically equivalent to mental illness and war as the direct product of leaders' sick personalities, especially their characteristic obsessiveness and need for dominance.

82. John Dollard, "Yale's Institute of Human Relations: What Was It?" *Ventures* (Winter 1964), 32, Record Group 1.1, series 200, box 67, folder 804, RF Archives. This article is also quoted in Morawski, "Organizing Knowledge and Behavior at Yale's Institute of Human Relations," 241.

83. Lerner, *Sykewar*, 43; and also the Psychological Warfare Division "Standing Directive for Psychological Warfare," 403–417.

84. Lerner, *Sykewar*, 69–70, 91 n. 1.

85. In addition to the "culture and personality" school, this approach to Germany in particular found inspiration in the work of Kurt Lewin. See, for example, the 1936 article "Some Social-Psychological Differences Between the United States and Germany," in Kurt Lewin, *Resolving Social Conflicts: Selected Papers on Group Dynamics* (New York: Harper & Brothers, 1948), 3–33.

86. Lerner, *Sykewar*, 121–124. Dicks developed the typology with the assistance of University of Chicago sociologist Edward Shils.

87. Lerner, *Sykewar*, 138.

88. Henry V. Dicks, "German Personality Traits and National Socialist Ideology: A War-Time Study of German Prisoners of War," in *Propaganda in War and Crisis*, 102–104.

89. Eisenhower letter to Psychological Warfare Division Brigadier General, Robert A. McClure, quoted in Lerner, *Sykewar*, 286.

90. Lerner, *Sykewar*, chap. 11.

91. Alexander H. Leighton and Morris Edward Opler, "Psychiatry and Applied Anthropology in Psychological Warfare Against Japan," *American Journal of Psychoanalysis* 6 (1946):25.

92. Even Leighton himself conceded this point. See Alexander H. Leighton, *Human Relations in a Changing World: Observations on the Use of the Social Sciences* (New York: E. P. Dutton, 1949), 55, 117. He notes too the utter failure of the Foreign Morale Analysis Division to effect the most momentous of all decisions in the war against Japan: dropping the atomic bomb on Hiroshima and Nagasaki. According to their evidence of morale decline, such a drastic option was clearly unnecessary. See page 126. See also Carleton Mabee, "Margaret Mead and Behavioral Scientists in World War II: Problems in Responsibility, Truth, and Effectiveness," *Journal of the History of the Behavioral Sciences* 23 (January 1987):8–9.

93. Hermann Spitzer, "Psychoanalytic Approaches to the Japanese Character," *Psychoanalysis and the Social Sciences* 1 (1947):131–156. Hermann Spitzer and Ruth Benedict were responsible for compiling a comprehensive *Bibliography of Articles and Books Relating to Japanese Psychology* for the Office of War Information. See also Ruth F. Benedict, *The Chrysanthemum and the Sword: Patterns of Japanese Culture* (Boston: Houghton Mifflin, 1946).

94. Leighton, *Human Relations in a Changing World,* app. C.

95. Jerome S. Bruner in *A History of Psychology in Autobiography,* vol. 7, ed. Gardner Lindzey (San Francisco: W. H. Freeman and Company, 1980), 93. For a general discussion of the U.S. Department of Agriculture Division of Program Surveys, see Jean M. Converse, *Survey Research in the United States: Roots and Emergence 1890–1960* (Berkeley: University of California Press, 1987), 157–161. For a discussion of the administrative challenges that the morale experts faced in the U.S. Strategic Bombing Survey in Japan, see George H. H. Huey, "Some Principles of Field Administration in Large-Scale Surveys," *Public Opinion Quarterly* 11 (Summer 1947):254–263.

96. For background on the Society for the Psychological Study of Social Issues and its role in World War II, see Dorwin Cartwright, "Social Psychology in the United States During the Second World War," *Human Relations* 1 (1948):332–352; and Lorenz J. Finison, "The Psychological Insurgency: 1936–1945," *Journal of Social Issues* 42 (1986):21–33.

97. See, for example, Helen Peak, "Observations on the Characteristics and Distribution of German Nazis," *Psychological Monographs* 59, no. 276 (1945), whole issue. This study had much in common with the Dicks's breakdown of the German population according to its psychological responses to Nazism. The final reports were: U.S. Strategic Bombing Survey, Morale Division, *The Effects of Strategic Bombing on German Morale,* 2 vols. (Washington, D.C.: USSBS, 1946–47); and U.S. Strategic Bombing Survey, Morale Division, *The Effects of Strategic Bombing on Japanese Morale* (Washington, D.C.: USSBS, 1947). "The Morale Index" is described in detail in *The Effects of Strategic Bombing on Japanese Morale,* app. K, 201–204.

98. Leighton, *Human Relations in a Changing World,* 74.

99. For a brief summary of the Office of War Information mission, see Elmer Davis, "War Information," in *Propaganda in War and Crisis,* 274–277.

100. This experience was a common one among wartime psychological experts. Jerome S. Bruner, a psychologist who worked in the Office of War Information Bureau of Overseas Intelligence as well as the Federal Communication Commission's Foreign Broadcast Monitoring (later Intelligence) Service and the Department of Agriculture's Division of Program Surveys, commented that no feedback was ever received about the mountains of research reports conscientiously sent to policy-makers in the War Department, the State Department, or the Office of Strategic Services. "We had the sense of sending our daily offering into the void," he noted. "The relation between research and policy at times seemed more political than practical." Jerome S. Bruner in *A History of Psychology in Autobiography,* 7:93, 95.

101. Leonard Doob, "The Utilization of Social Scientists in the Overseas Branch of the Office of War Information," *American Political Science Review* 41 (August 1947):666.

102. Very little is known about the Office of Strategic Services Psychological Division. The only discussion I could find in the secondary literature is in Carol Cina, "Social Science for Whom? A Structural History of Social Psychology" (Ph.D. diss., State University of New York, Stony Brook, 1981), 188–

208. Cina's Appendix C, on pages 368–393, includes the text of the "OSS Generic Country Outline for Psychological Warfare."

103. Far more information is available on the Office of Strategic Services Research and Analysis Branch, headed by historian William A. Langer from 1942 to 1946. Langer's operation was grand, involving around a thousand researchers in Washington and another five hundred around the world by the end of the war: mainly historians with a sprinkling of social scientists. In the postwar period Langer maintained his involvement with the newly founded Central Intelligence Agency and became a vocal proponent of having academic experts involved in the business of intelligence because, according to Langer, "the R and A Branch of the organization was the oldest and largest part of the OSS and proved to have the most lasting value." William Langer to R. Harris Smith, 12 January 1973, HUG (FP) 19.46, folder: "OSS 1967–72," William W. Langer Papers, Harvard University Archives, Cambridge, Massachusetts. See also William L. Langer, *Up from the Ranks: The Autobiography of William L. Langer,* typescript, 1975, chap. 9, later published with minor revisions as *In and Out of the Ivory Tower: The Autobiography of William L. Langer* (New York: Neale Watson Academic Publications, 1977); and William L. Langer, "Scholarship and the Intelligence Problem," *Proceedings of the American Philosophical Society* 92 (8 March 1948):43–45.

104. Robert MacLeod letter to Gordon Allport, 9 October 1942, quoted in Cina, "Social Science for Whom?" 223. See also Gordon Allport to R. C. Tryon, 18 November 1942, and Gordon Allport to R. C. Tryon, 28 December 1942, HUG 4118.10, folder: "T, 1938–43," GA Papers.

105. Robert Yerkes, "Man-Power and Military Effectiveness: The Case for Human Engineering," *Journal of Consulting Psychology* 5 (September–October 1941):206. For more on German psychology, see Ulfried Geuter, "German Psychology During the Nazi Period," in *Psychology in Twentieth-Century Thought and Society,* 166, 170, 174. For an extended discussion, see Geuter's *The Professionalization of Psychology in Nazi Germany,* trans. Richard Holmes (New York: Oxford University Press, 1992), esp. chap. 3. The study of German psychological experts was an area of major initial effort for the Emergency Committee in Psychology which produced a confidential study in 1940 on the testing methods used by psychologists in the German army. See Dallenbach, "The Emergency Committee in Psychology," 572. Several other surveys and bibliographies about German psychological warfare and military psychology followed. See H. L. Ansbacher, "German Military Psychology," *Psychological Bulletin* 38 (June 1941):370–392; and Ladislas Farago, ed., *German Psychological Warfare* (New York: Committee on National Morale, 1941).

106. Farago, ed., *German Psychological Warfare,* 79.

107. For a description, see Capshew, "Psychology on the March," 87–94. Samples of the many different psychological tests that were utilized can be found in "History of the Assessment Schools in the United States"; Files 63–65; Entry 99, OSS History Office Collection; Record Group 226, Records of the Office of Strategic Services, National Archives, Washington, D.C.

108. Quoted in Capshew, "Psychology on the March," 114 n. 37.

109. Office of Strategic Services Assessment Staff, "The Assessment of

Men," in *Propaganda in War and Crisis,* 287. See also Office of Strategic Services, *Assessment of Men: Selection of Personnel for the Office of Strategic Services* (New York: Rinehart, 1948).

110. Eugene Taylor, personal communication, 23 June 1991. See also Henry A. Murray in *A History of Psychology in Autobiography,* 5:306–307.

111. Excerpt from Trustees' Confidential Report, May 1952, "Picking the Personality that Will Succeed," Record Group 1.2, series 205, box 3, folder 19, RF Archives.

112. Subcommittee of the Senate Committee on Military Affairs, "Hearings on Science Legislation," October 1945–March 1946, pts. 1–6, 79th Cong., 1st sess., testimony of Brigadier General John Magruder, 899–901.

3: The Dilemmas of Democratic Morale

1. Gordon Allport, "The Nature of Democratic Morale," in *Civilian Morale,* 18, emphasis in original.

2. Farago, ed., *German Psychological Warfare.*

3. Committee for National Morale letterhead, HUG 4118.10, folder: "1941–43, Co-Cz," GA Papers. A list of early members can also be found in Farago, ed., *German Psychological Warfare.* See also Mabee, "Margaret Mead and Behavioral Scientists in World War II," 4; and PAFP, testimony of Margaret Mead, 98–99.

4. Farago, ed., *German Psychological Warfare.*

5. Erik H. Erikson, *Identity: Youth and Crisis* (New York: W. W. Norton, 1968) 52.

6. Erik Erikson, "On Nazi Mentality," in *A Way of Looking at Things: Selected Papers from 1930 to 1980, Erik H. Erikson,* ed. Stephen Schlein (New York: W. W. Norton, 1987), 342.

7. Dallenbach, "The Emergency Committee in Psychology," 541.

8. Gordon Allport in *A History of Psychology in Autobiography,* 5:16.

9. Dallenbach, "The Emergency Committee in Psychology," 521–523.

10. Watson, ed., *Civilian Morale,* vi.

11. Mead, *And Keep Your Powder Dry,* 20–21, emphasis in original.

12. Ibid., 24.

13. Ibid., 25.

14. Margaret Mead in *A History of Psychology in Autobiography,* vol. 6, ed. Gardner Lindzey (Englewood Cliffs, N.J.: Prentice-Hall, 1974), 295. Mead's inclusion in this highly selective series is itself evidence of how significant her contributions to psychology were.

15. A draft of *Blackberry Winter,* quoted in Yans-McLaughlin, "Science, Democracy, and Ethics," 194.

16. Yans-McLaughlin, "Science, Democracy, and Ethics," 194.

17. Margaret Mead, "On Methods of Implementing a National Morale Program," *Applied Anthropology* 1 (October–December 1941):20–24.

18. For discussions of *And Keep Your Powder Dry,* see Richard Handler, "Boasian Anthropology and the Critique of American Culture," *American Quarterly* 42 (June 1990):252–273, and Yans-McLaughlin, "Science, Democracy, and Ethics," 204–207.

19. Mead, *And Keep Your Powder Dry,* 261.

20. Yans-McLaughlin, "Science, Democracy, and Ethics," 197.

21. For more on Mead's World War II work, see Mabee, "Margaret Mead and Behavioral Scientists in World War II," 3–13; and Yans-McLaughlin, "Science, Democracy, and Ethics," 184–217.

22. Gordon Allport, "Morale, American Style," 2, 5, HUG 4118.50, box 1, folder 2, GA Papers.

23. Gordon Allport, "Evidence for the State of National Morale," lecture given 29 October 1941, HUG 4118.50, box 1, folder 3, GA Papers.

24. Gordon Allport, "Vision of the Democratic Personality," lecture at Cleveland College, 12 December 1951, HUG 4118.50, box 5, folder 176, GA Papers.

25. Gordon Allport to Archibald MacLeish, 2 December 1941, HUG 4118.10, folder: "1941–43 Ma-Md," GA Papers. Allport was not alone in communicating findings about civilian morale to MacLeish's Office of Facts and Figures. Franz Alexander's Chicago Institute of Psychoanalysis did the same thing with the results of its morale studies. While such studies were a "special activity" for the Chicago Institute, strapped for researchers and clinicians due to the wartime personnel shortage, Alexander also acknowledged that the war had "certain stimulating effects, adding new lines to our regular work." See Franz Alexander to Alan Gregg, 4 February 1942, Record Group 1.1, series 216A, box 4, folder 40, RF Archives.

26. Ralph Barton Perry to Gordon Allport, 14 March 1944; Gordon Allport to Ralph Barton Perry, 15 March 1944; Ralph Barton Perry to Gordon Allport, 10 April 1945; HUG 4118.10, folder: "American Defense Harvard Group, 1944–45," GA Papers.

27. The advertising industry, whose profiteering image placed it in jeopardy during the war years, made its own dramatic and very successful effort to stay on the right side of public opinion, consumer loyalty, and tax laws by demonstrating "the politics of sacrifice" in the patriotic ad campaigns run by the War Advertising Council in cooperation with the government's war mobilization agencies. See Mark H. Leff, "The Politics of Sacrifice on the American Home Front in World War II," *Journal of American History* 77 (March 1991):1307–1312.

28. Crawford and Biderman, eds., *Social Scientists and International Affairs,* 7. For a useful overview of survey research and its place in the federal government, both before and after World War II, see Converse, *Survey Research in the United States.*

29. Tracy B. Kittredge memorandum, 6 August 1940, Record Group 2, series 717, box 204, folder 1440, RF Archives. Psychological experts were highly sensitive to the work of their German counterparts and, especially early in the war, looked to them as a model of what mobilized expertise could do. Robert Yerkes's important call to arms, for example, suggested that "with suffi-

cient determination and good fortune, we might succeed in compressing the worthwhile progress of a Nazi decade into a year of American effort." Yerkes, "Psychology and Defense," 533.

Christopher Simpson has pointed out that the term "psychological warfare" itself first entered the English vocabulary in 1941 as a translation of the Nazi concept *Weltanschauungskrieg*, which literally meant worldview warfare. See Christopher Simpson, "U.S. Mass Communications Research and Counter-insurgency After 1945: An Investigation of the Construction of Scientific 'Reality' " (paper delivered at conference on "Rethinking the Cold War," Madison, Wisconsin, October 1991), 10.

30. Hadley Cantril to John Marshall, 13 March 1940, Record Group 1.1, series 200R, box 270, folder 3217, RF Archives.

31. "Utilization of Project Data by Government Agencies," 24 December 1941, Record Group 1.1, series 200R, box 270, folder 3221; Hadley Cantril to John Marshall, 4 October 1943, Record Group 1.1, series 200R, box 270, folder 3225; John Marshall memorandum, 16 December 1943, Record Group 1.1, series 200R, box 270, folder 3225, RF Archives.

32. "Some Suggestions for Gauging Public Opinion in Foreign Countries: A Confidential Guide Prepared by H. C. for O.W.I. Outpost Men," 13 January 1943, HUG 4118.60, box 3, folder 61, GA Papers. In the postwar period, under Cold War pressure, Cantril's Office of Public Opinion Research became one of the Central Intelligence Agency's two wholly owned polling organizations. See Donald Freed with Dr. Fred Simon Landis, *Death in Washington: The Murder of Orlando Letelier* (Westport, Conn.: Lawrence Hill, 1980), 34.

33. For example, Allen Edwards, a Society for the Psychological Study of Social Issues member, was contacted by the War Relocation Authority about how to measure attitudes toward Japanese-Americans and other minority group members, without letting subjects know what was being investigated or why. His response was that "disguised attitude measurement" constituted a real challenge for researchers. See Allen Edwards to Gordon Allport, 27 February 1944, HUG 4118.10, folder: "SPSSI correspondence, 1944–45," GA Papers.

34. Jerome S. Bruner in *A History of Psychology in Autobiography*, 7:95.

35. "Confidential Report to the Rockefeller Foundation on Work of the Office of Public Opinion Research," n.d., see esp. "Confidential Reports for Government Agencies and Departments," 9–11, Record Group 1.1, series 200R, box 271, folder 3229, RF Archives.

36. Hadley Cantril to John Marshall, 16 April 1943, Record Group 1.1, series 200R, box 270, folder 3225, RF Archives.

37. James McKeen Cattell, quoted in J. G. Morawski, "Psychologists for Society and Societies for Psychologists: SPSSI's Place Among Professional Organizations," *Journal of Social Issues* 42 (Spring 1986):118.

38. E. W. Scripps, founding letter of the American Society for the Dissemination of Science, quoted in Morawski, "Psychologists for Society and Societies for Psychologists," 116.

39. Lasswell, *Psychopathology and Politics*, 191–192.

40. Gordon Allport in *A History of Psychology in Autobiography*, 5:14.

"Group Mind" was also the title of an important treatise on crowd psychology. See McDougall, *Group Mind.*

41. Strecker, *Beyond the Clinical Frontiers,* 79.

42. Ibid., 180.

43. Jerome S. Bruner, a psychologist who worked with Cantril at the Princeton Office of Public Opinion Research, as well as for the Office of War Information, the Division of Program Surveys of the Department of Agriculture, and the Psychological Warfare Division of Supreme Headquarters, Allied Expeditionary Force, remembers that he "was shocked at how poorly informed they [U.S. citizens] were." Jerome S. Bruner in *A History of Psychology in Autobiography,* 7:93.

44. Bluemel, *War, Politics, and Insanity,* 107.

45. Murphy, ed., *Human Nature and Enduring Peace,* 372. Chapter 20, from which this quotation is drawn, was authored by Jerome Bruner with Hadley Cantril.

46. Richard H. S. Crossman, "Supplementary Essay," in *Sykewar,* 345.

47. Gordon W. Allport, *ABC's of Scapegoating,* rev. ed. (New York: Anti-Defamation League of B'Nai B'Rith, 1948), 7.

48. Such rumors were also a major concern of military morale managers and experts in propaganda agencies. See, for example, Samuel Stouffer to R. Keith Kane, 30 May 1942, HUG (FP) 31.8, box 1, folder: "Kane, R. Keith"; Gordon Allport to Samuel Stouffer, 23 September 1942, box 1, folder: "Harvard University"; "OWI confidential memo on Rumors and Rumor Columns," 19 November 1942, box 1, folder: "Miscellaneous (2 or 2)," SS Papers.

49. Harold P. Lasswell, "The Psychology of Hitlerism," *Political Quarterly* 4 (July–September 1933):380.

50. Wilhelm Reich, *The Mass Psychology of Fascism* (1933 in German, 1946 in English; reprint, New York: Farrar, Straus, & Giroux, 1970); Fromm, *Escape from Freedom.*

51. See, for example, Dollard et al., *Frustration and Aggression,* 43–44, 89–90, 151–156.

52. Bruno Bettelheim, "Behavior in Extreme Situations," *Politics* (August 1944):209, emphasis in original, reprinted in shorter form from the *Journal of Abnormal and Social Psychology,* October 1943, where it was published as "Individual and Mass Behavior in Extreme Situations."

53. Murphy, ed., *Human Nature and Enduring Peace,* esp. chaps. 7, 11–14, 16. See also Bruno Bettelheim to Gordon Allport, 16 August 1943, HUG 4118.20, box 4, folder 109, GA Papers. The evolution of "reeducation" analysis was heavily indebted to Kurt Lewin's work. See especially Lewin's "Cultural Reconstruction," "The Special Case of German," and "Conduct, Knowledge, and Acceptance of New Values," in *Resolving Social Conflicts,* 34–68.

54. A useful overview of the historical context and importance of *The Authoritarian Personality* can be found in Franz Samelson, "Authoritarianism from Berlin to Berkeley: On Social Psychology and History," *Journal of Social Issues* 42 (Spring 1986):191–208 (followed by comment by Nevitt Sanford).

55. T. W. Adorno et al., *The Authoritarian Personality* (New York: W. W. Norton, 1950), 16.

56. Ibid., 5, emphasis in original.

57. An early study of U.S. anti-Semitism and antiblack prejudice found that 80 percent of its subjects had seriously prejudiced attitudes. See Gordon W. Allport and Bernard M. Kramer, "Some Roots of Prejudice," *Journal of Psychology* 22 (July 1946):9–39.

58. "Survey of Intelligence Materials, Supplement to Survey No. 25," 14 July 1942, HUG (FP) 31.8, box 1, folder: "Negro in America," SS Papers.

59. Alfred McClung Lee and Norman Daymond Humphrey, *Race Riot* (New York: The Dryden Press, 1943), ix, 87.

60. Kenneth Clark, "Morale among Negroes," in *Civilian Morale*, 228–248.

61. These are the titles of the final two chapters in Lee and Humphrey, *Race Riot*. They illustrate not only the impulse to be practically useful but the pervasiveness of the therapeutic and medically oriented language of diagnosis and treatment.

62. Gordon Allport to Lillian Wald Kay, 8 March 1945, HUG 4118.10, folder: "SPSSI, miscellaneous, 1944–45," GA Papers.

63. Among those who acknowledged debts to Allport's work in this area was Alfred McClung Lee, the coauthor of an important analysis of the 1943 race riot in Detroit. See Alfred McClung Lee to Gordon Allport, 23 February 1942, HUG 4118.10, folder: "La-Lh, 1941–43," GA Papers.

64. Gordon W. Allport, "Catharsis and the Reduction of Prejudice," *Journal of Social Issues* 1 (August 1945):3.

65. Lee and Humphrey, *Race Riot*, 13.

66. Ibid., 103, emphasis in original.

67. Ibid., 128.

68. Ibid., 97.

69. Franz Samelson argues that the momentous transition from a psychology that proved objective racial differences to one that proved subjective racial emotions occurred during the interwar period, the result of developments such as restrictive immigration legislation during the 1920s, the slow but steady ethnic diversification of the psychological profession itself, and its leftward tilt during the depression. He considers World War II a dramatic confirmation of the validity of psychology's change of focus, rather than a "cause." See Franz Samelson, "From 'Race Psychology' to 'Studies in Prejudice': Some Observations on the Thematic Reversal in Social Psychology," *Journal of the History of the Behavioral Sciences* 14 (July 1978):265–278.

70. Richard Sterba, "Some Psychological Factors in Negro Race Hatred and in Anti-Negro Riots," *Psychoanalysis and the Social Sciences* 1 (1947):419.

71. Menninger, *Psychiatry in a Troubled World*, 422. See also Menninger, "The Role of Psychiatry in the World Today," 572.

72. Military Mobilization Committee of the American Psychiatric Association, *Psychiatric Aspects of Civilian Morale* (New York: Family Welfare Association of America, 1942), 11–14.

73. Robert Castel, Françoise Castel, and Anne Lovell, *The Psychiatric Soci-*

ety, trans. Arthur Goldhammer (New York: Columbia University Press, 1982), chaps. 3–5; Gerald N. Grob, "World War II and American Psychiatry," *Psychohistory Review* 19 (Fall 1990):41–69; Grob, *From Asylum to Community,* chap. 1; Peter Miller and Nikolas Rose, eds., *The Power of Psychiatry* (Cambridge: Polity Press, 1986), 1–11, 43–84. For an argument that the "community" orientation originated during the Progressive Era, see Sicherman, "The Quest for Mental Health in America, 1880–1917."

74. S. Harvard Kaufman, "The Problem of Human Difference and Prejudice," *American Journal of Orthopsychiatry* 17 (April 1947):352, 356.

75. Helen V. McLean, "Psychodynamic Factors in Racial Relations," *Annals of the American Academy of Political and Social Science* 244 (March 1946):162.

76. Lecture notes for Brandeis Institute, 11 August 1960, HUG 4118.60, box 7, folder 151: "Prejudice" GA Papers. Richard I. Evans, *Gordon Allport: The Man and His Ideas,* vol. 6 in *Dialogues with Notable Contributors to Personality Theory* (New York: E. P. Dutton & Co., 1971), 61–62. See also Kenneth Clark to Gordon Allport, 4 October 1944, HUG 4118.10, folder: "Ca-Cn, 1944–45," GA Papers.

77. The two were not, of course, always easy to distinguish in practice. See, for example, the correspondence between Gordon Allport and Cornelius Golightly, an analyst for the Fair Employment Practices Committee (FEPC). Golightly approvingly reported to Allport the FEPC's promotion of an "educational persuasion campaign" to supplement its more formal, legal functions. Cornelius Golightly to Gordon Allport, 28 December 1943, HUG 4118.10, folder: "1938–45, Go-Gz," GA Papers.

78. Quoted in Russell Marks, "Legitimating Industrial Capitalism: Philanthropy and Individual Differences," in *Philanthropy and Cultural Imperialism: The Foundations at Home and Abroad,* ed. Robert F. Arnove (Boston: G. K. Hall, 1980), 105. Yerkes chaired the National Research Council's postwar Committee on Scientific Problems of Human Migration, appointed in 1922.

79. For more on the relationship between World War I intelligence testing and eugenics, as well as for a good overview of World War I psychology, see Samelson, "Putting Psychology on the Map," 103–168; and Samelson, "World War I Intelligence Testing and the Development of Psychology," 274–282. For a general historical overview of the role psychological technologies—especially testing—have played in racist and nativist movements, see Robert V. Guthrie, *Even the Rat Was White: A Historical View of Psychology* (New York: Harper & Row, 1976).

80. Yerkes, "Psychology and Defense," 540.

81. Edward A. Strecker, "Presidential Address," *American Journal of Psychiatry* 101 (July 1944):2.

82. There were dissidents, of course, even during the 1950s and 1960s, although they were rare. Psychological testing continued to provide much of the ammunition for a new-fashioned school of scientific racism, whose advocates never tired of the example offered by World War I intelligence tests. For a discussion of how heavily advocates of school segregation relied on analysis

of psychological tests in the post-*Brown* era, as well as for fascinating commentaries by some of these advocates, see I. A. Newby, *Challenge to the Court: Social Scientists and the Defense of Segregation, 1954–1966* (Baton Rouge: Louisiana State University Press, 1967), chap. 4 and commentaries.

83. Edward L. Bernays, "Morale: First Line of Defense," *Infantry Journal* 48 (May 1941):32.

84. Samuel Stouffer, "Social Science and the Soldier," HUG (FP) 31.45, box 2, folder: "1943," SS Papers. This was subsequently published in William Fielding Ogburn, ed., *American Society in Wartime* (Chicago: University of Chicago Press, 1943), 105–117.

85. W. R. Bion, "The 'War of Nerves': Civilian Reaction, Morale and Prophylaxis," in *The Neuroses in War,* ed. Emanuel Miller (New York: Macmillan, 1943), 180–200.

86. Stouffer et al., *The American Soldier: Adjustment During Army Life,* 27.

87. For a general discussion of the army's Research Branch, see Converse, *Survey Research in the United States,* 165–171, 217–224.

88. "Basic Record," HUG (FP) 31.8, box 1, SS Papers.

89. "Some Afterthoughts of a Contributor to *The American Soldier,*" quoted in Converse, *Survey Research in the United States,* 218.

90. Samuel A. Stouffer, "Studying the Attitudes of Soldiers," *Proceedings of the American Philosophical Society* 92 (12 November 1948):336.

91. "Objectives of Demobilization Study," HUG (FP) 31.8, box 1, folder: "Demobilization Process," SS Papers.

92. For example, see Russell Sage Foundation, *Effective Use of Social Science Research in the Federal Services* (New York, 1950), 14–16. Officers of the Rockefeller Foundation also thought that Stouffer's Research Branch in the army and William Langer's Research and Analysis Branch in the Office of Strategic Services were clear examples of how behavioral experts "helped the top command to wiser policies." See *Social Sciences Program, Brief Review, 1939–1949, and Future Targets,* by Joseph H. Willits, prepared for Trustees' Meeting, 7 December 1949, Record Group 3.1, series 910, box 3, folder 18, item PRO-38, RF Archives.

93. Stouffer et al., *The American Soldier,* 433.

94. Ibid., 436 (table 2), 438.

95. Ibid., 449, emphasis in original.

96. Ibid., 461.

97. Greene, "The Role of the Psychiatrist in World War II," 453–455. See also Leland Sitwell and Julius Schreiber, "Neuropsychiatric Program for a Replacement Training Center," *War Medicine* 3 (January 1943):20–29.

98. Stouffer et al., *The American Soldier,* 465.

99. Ibid., chap. 8.

100. For an interesting, revisionist interpretation of the Hawthorne experiments, see Richard Gillespie, *Manufacturing Knowledge: A History of the Hawthorne Experiments* (New York: Cambridge University Press, 1991). A shorter version is Richard Gillespie, "The Hawthorne Experiments and the Politics of

Experimentation," in *The Rise of Experimentation in American Psychology,* ed. Jill G. Morawski (New Haven: Yale University Press, 1988), 114–137.

101. Hadley Cantril to Joseph Willits, 13 May 1947, Record Group 1.1, series 200S, box 388, folder 4596; Hadley Cantril to Eric Hodgin, 27 November 1940, Record Group 1.1, series 200R, box 270, folder 3219; "The Changing Attitude Toward War," grant summary, January 1941, Record Group 1.1, series 200R, box 270, folder 3219, RF Archive.

102. The consequences of Lewin's theory are much debated. For the critical perspective that Lewin advanced an antidemocratic style of social engineering, see Peter Emanuel Franks, "A Social History of American Social Psychology Up to the Second World War" (Ph.D. diss., State University of New York, Stony Brook, 1975), pt. 3, chap. 4; and Cina, "Social Science for Whom?" chap. 4. For a celebratory perspective on Lewin as the champion of democracy and individual integrity, see Edward A. Shils, "Social Inquiry and the Autonomy of the Individual," in *The Human Meaning of the Social Sciences,* 114–157. For an interpretation somewhere between these two poles, which considers Lewin very critically as a democratic social engineer but without the simplistic, sinister overtones of Franks and Cina, see William Graebner, "The Small Group and Democratic Social Engineering, 1900–1950," *Journal of Social Issues* 42 (Spring 1986):137–154. For a discussion of Lewin's legacy in the field of prejudice reduction, see Walter A. Jackson, *Gunnar Myrdal and America's Conscience: Social Engineering and Racial Liberalism, 1938–1987* (Chapel Hill: University of North Carolina Press, 1990), 282.

103. Stouffer et al., *The American Soldier,* chap. 10. Almost all of the other surveys conducted by the Research Branch were limited to white soldiers.

104. Quoted in Gunnar Myrdal, *An American Dilemma: The Negro Problem and Modern Democracy* (New York: Harper & Brothers, 1944), 1006.

105. Malcolm X with the assistance of Alex Haley, *The Autobiography of Malcolm X* (New York: Grove Press, Inc., 1964), 104–107.

106. Greene, "The Role of the Psychiatrist in World War II," 277–298; Rutherford B. Stevens, "Racial Aspects of Emotional Problems of Negro Soldiers," *American Journal of Psychiatry* (January 1947):493–498.

107. U.S. Department of War, "The Negro Soldier," directed by Frank Capra, 1943.

108. "Some Notes on Research Methods," 13 October 1944, emphasis in original, HUG (FP) 31.8, box 2, folder: "Research Problems," SS Papers.

109. "Embarrassing Questions," n.d. (c. January 1945), HUG (FP) 31.8, box 2, folder: "Research Problems," SS Papers.

110. Stouffer et al., *The American Soldier,* 37.

111. Gordon Allport to Dwight Chapman, 5 November 1943, HUG 4118,10, folder: "1944–45, SPSSI misc," GA Papers.

112. Kurt Danziger, *Constructing the Subject: Historical Origins of Psychological Research* (New York: Cambridge University Press, 1990), esp. chap. 7; Nikolas Rose, "Calculable Minds and Manageable Individuals," *History of the Human Sciences* 1 (October 1988):181–200; Samelson, "Putting Psychology on the Map," 103–168; Samelson, "World War I Intelligence Testing and the

Development of Psychology," 274–282; Robert I. Watson, "A Brief History of Clinical Psychology," *Psychological Bulletin* 50 (September 1953):321–346.

113. "A Barometer of International Security," n.d. (c. July 1944), HUG (FP) 31.8, box 1, folder: "Dodd, Stuart C.," SS Papers.

114. Leighton, *Human Relations in a Changing World*, 190.

115. Stouffer, "Studying the Attitudes of Soldiers," 340.

116. Paul F. Lazarsfeld, "*The American Soldier*—An Expository Review," *Public Opinion Quarterly* 13 (Fall 1949):404.

117. Gordon Allport to All Members of Congress, 5 April 1945, HUG 4118.50, box 1, folder 10, GA Papers.

118. "Human Nature and the Peace: A Statement by Psychologists," HUG 4118.50, box 1, folder 10, GA Papers. The statement is also reprinted in Murphy, ed., *Human Nature and Enduring Peace*, 455–457.

119. Ibid., emphasis in original.

120. See the extensive correspondence related to publicity and key contacts among policy-makers in HUG 4118.10, folders: "SPSSI correspondence, 1944–45" and "SPSSI miscellaneous, 1944–45"; HUG 4118.10, box 1, folder 10, GA Papers.

121. Robert Yerkes to Secretaries of War and Navy, 18 December 1944 and "Recommendations Concerning Post-War Psychological Services in the Armed Forces," Records of the American Psychological Association, box G-8, folder: "Psychology and the Military, Yerkes Committee: Misc. Reports," Library of Congress, Washington, D.C.

122. William Ogburn, a University of Chicago sociologist who directed Hoover's famous Research Committee on Social Trends, is credited with coining the term "cultural lag" to designate the distance between rapid technological advance and slow cultural adjustment. "Cultural lag" was among the most fundamental presumptions animating the history of U.S. social scientists during the late nineteenth and early twentieth centuries; it indicated that Americans were not responding all that well, personally and socially, to the massive changes occurring around them in the economy, the world of science, and elsewhere. See William F. Ogburn, *Social Change, with Respect to Culture and Original Nature* (New York: B. W. Buebsch, 1922).

123. Murphy, ed., *Human Nature and Enduring Peace*, 271, emphasis in original.

124. "Social Engineering," 1–2, HUG 4118.10, folder: "SPSSI miscellaneous, 1944–45," GA Papers.

125. Fromm, *Escape from Freedom*, xiv.

126. Edwin Boring, "Psychology for the Common Man," Summer 1945, 20, HUG 4229.80, folder: "Personal Mss, unpublished," EB Papers.

127. Edward A. Purcell, *The Crisis of Democratic Theory: Scientific Naturalism & the Problem of Value* (Lexington: University Press of Kentucky, 1973). Purcell suggests that World War II resolved "the crisis of democratic theory" that had generated by the model of scientific naturalism and decades of evidence that the scientific truth about human behavior undermined the very basis of liberal democratic institutions. Beginning early in the century, the pessimistic findings of psychological science about mental inequalities and mass irrational-

ity had contributed directly to causing the crisis. World War II managed to resolve it, at least temporarily, by producing a consensus among intellectuals that the normative state of U.S. institutions and policy was equivalent to U.S. democratic ideals. The experiences of psychological experts offer a useful illustration of this equation. For a discussion of this development within political science, see Ricci, *The Tragedy of Political Science,* chap. 4.

128. Quoted in Yans-McLaughlin, "Science, Democracy, and Ethics," 195.

129. Ibid., 209.

130. Murphy, ed., *Human Nature and Enduring Peace,* 442, emphasis in original.

131. For a general discussion of the appeal and spread of "scientism" within the social sciences after World War I, see Ross, *The Origins of American Social Science,* chap. 10.

4: Nervous in the Service

1. Edward A. Strecker and Kenneth E. Appel, "Morale," *American Journal of Psychiatry* 99 (September 1942):159.

2. Ibid., 160.

3. The best general secondary source on psychiatry in World War II is Greene, "The Role of the Psychiatrist in World War II." Another useful summary is Grob, *From Asylum to Community,* chap. 1. Key primary sources are Menninger, *Psychiatry in a Troubled World,* and U.S. Army, Medical Department, *Neuropsychiatry in World War II,* 2 vols., ed. Albert J. Glass (Washington, D.C.: Office of the Surgeon General, Department of the Army, 1966). In different ways, each of these sources offers evidence that World War II precipitated a radical shift in the concerns of clinicians: from mental illness to health, from prediction to prevention, from the individual to the environment.

4. Donald S. Napoli, *Architects of Adjustment: The History of the Psychological Profession in the United States* (Port Washington, N.Y.: National University Publications, 1981), 103.

5. Sol L. Garfield, "Psychotherapy: A 40-Year Appraisal," *American Psychologist* 36 (February 1981):174.

6. Steuart Henderson Britt and Jane D. Morgan, "Military Psychologists in World War II," *American Psychologist* 1 (October 1946):427 (tables 6 and 8), 428; Watson, "A Brief History of Clinical Psychology," 339–340.

7. Quoted in Menninger, *Psychiatry in a Troubled World,* xiv.

8. Ibid., xiv.

9. Comparative statistics on World War I and II psychiatry can be found in Menninger, *Psychiatry in a Troubled World,* chap. 23.

10. Castel, Castel, and Lovell, *The Psychiatric Society,* 45; Purcell, *The Crisis of Democratic Theory,* 98–99; Samelson, "Putting Psychology on the Map,"

123; Samelson, "World War I Intelligence Testing and the Development of Psychology," 277–278.

11. Menninger, *Psychiatry in a Troubled World*, 17, 254.

12. Ibid., 7.

13. Southern Psychiatric Association, "Report of Its Committee on Psychiatry and the National Defense," *Psychiatry* 3 (1940):619.

14. Ibid., 620.

15. William C. Menninger, "A Condensed Neuropsychiatric Examination for Use by Selective Service Boards," *War Medicine* 2 (November 1941):851.

16. Martin Cooley, "The Economic Aspect of Psychiatric Examination of Registrants," *War Medicine* 2 (May 1941):376–378.

17. Southern Psychiatric Association, "Report of Its Committee on Psychiatry and the National Defense," 619.

18. Menninger, "A Condensed Neuropsychiatric Examination for Use by Selective Service Boards," 843–853.

19. Selective Service System, Medical Circular No. 1, "Minimum Psychiatric Inspection," revised, May 1941, *Journal of the American Medical Association* 116 (3 May 1941):2060.

20. Ibid., 2061.

21. Medical Bulletin No. 58, issued in April 1941, quoted in Greene, "The Role of the Psychiatrist in World War II," 66.

22. Arthur Weider, Keeve Brodman, Bela Mittelmann, David Wechsler, and Harold G. Wolff with the technical assistance of Margaret Meixner, "Cornell Service Index: A Method for Quickly Assaying Personality and Psychosomatic Disturbances in Men in the Armed Forces," *War Medicine* 7 (April 1945):209–213.

23. For a chart contrasting the psychiatric screening program as it was designed with how it was actually conducted, see Greene, "The Role of the Psychiatrist in World War II," 171. See also Harry Stack Sullivan, "Psychiatry, the Army, and the War," Record Group 1.1, series 200A, box 117, folder 1444, RF Archives.

24. Albert Deutsh, "Military Psychiatry: World War II, 1941–1943," in *One Hundred Years of American Psychiatry* (New York: Columbia University Press, 1944), 426.

25. Ibid.

26. All statistics in this paragraph are from Menninger, *Psychiatry in a Troubled World*, 341–343, app. D. Just as the four-volume work *The American Soldier* (1949) presented and analyzed the survey data gathered by the Research Branch of the army's Morale Division on soldiers' attitudes, another postwar multivolume work interpreted military personnel and medical records in order to discover why 2.5 million individuals had been rejected or discharged for psychological reasons. See Ginzberg, *The Ineffective Soldier*, 3 vols.

27. Statistics in this paragraph are from Menninger, *Psychiatry in a Troubled World*, 114, chap. 23, app. D, 587–588; Greene, "The Role of the Psychiatrist in World War II," 187–191, 253, 277.

28. Greene, "The Role of the Psychiatrist in World War II," 210–211, 282–284; Menninger, *Psychiatry in a Troubled World*, 39–40. For an example

in which such statistics could not be cited, see Roy R. Grinker and John P. Spiegel, *Men Under Stress* (Philadelphia: Blakiston, 1945), viii.

29. Gordon Allport, for example, wrote the following about a former student of his who had just been drafted: "Although I am not a psychiatrist and should not like to be quoted as diagnosing a case, I should way [*sic*] that he is hysterical, sexually compulsive, lacks self control and breaks down in minor crises. He seems to me to be exactly the type of psycho-neurotic who will hinder rather than help national defense. The case is of interest because the same newspaper [that mentioned the student] featured the fact that 1/5 of the draftees were being rejected for physical reasons by army doctors. I suspect that only a small per cent of these physical defects were in fact as serious a liability as my former student's neurosis." Gordon Allport to Lawrence K. Frank, 30 November 1940, HUG 4118.10, folder: "1944–45 Frank, Lawrence K.," GA Papers.

30. Menninger, *Psychiatry in a Troubled World*, 293.

31. Ibid., 460.

32. Alan Gregg, "Lessons to Learn: Psychiatry in World War II," *American Journal of Psychiatry* 104 (October 1947):219. For data on the incomes of neuropsychiatrists, relative to other physicians during the 1930s and early 1940s, see Menninger, *Psychiatry in a Troubled World*, 433 n. 34.

33. Alan Gregg to Franklin Ebaugh, 28 September 1943, Record Group 1.1, series 200A, box 109, folder 1345, RF Archives.

34. For example, see William C. Porter, "The School of Military Neuropsychiatry," *American Journal of Psychiatry* 100 (July 1943):25–27.

35. The term "visiting fireman" is from Franklin Ebaugh to Alan Gregg, 28 February 1944, Record Group 1.1, series 200A, box 109, folder 1346, RF Archives. For other documents related to this program, see Walter Bauer to Alan Gregg, 4 January 1944, Record Group 1.1, series 200A, box 109, folder 1346; William Menninger to Robert Morison, 11 April 1946; RF grant action 46073, Record Group 1.1, series 200A, box 110, folder 1355, RF Archives.

36. Alan Gregg, "A Critique of Psychiatry," *American Journal of Psychiatry* 101 (November 1944):291.

37. Grob, *From Asylum to Community*, 17; and Gary R. Vandenbos, Nicholas A. Cummings, and Patrick H. Deleon, "A Century of Psychotherapy: Economic and Environmental Influences," in *History of Psychotherapy: A Century of Change*, ed. Donald K. Freedheim (Washington, D.C.: American Psychological Association, 1992), 76.

38. Menninger, *Psychiatry in a Troubled World*, 459.

39. Lawrence J. Friedman, *Menninger: The Family and the Clinic* (New York: Alfred A. Knopf, 1990), esp. chaps. 7 and 9.

40. Lewis Terman, quoted in Samelson, "Putting Psychology on the Map," 105.

41. Napoli, *Architects of Adjustment*, 90.

42. Bray, *Psychology and Military Proficiency*, 49.

43. Gilgen, *American Psychology Since World War II*, 173.

44. Capshew, "Psychology on the March," 73–75.

45. Walter V. Bingham with James Rorty, "How the Army Sorts Its Man Power," *Infantry Journal* 51 (October 1942):28–29.

46. For example, see Carleton W. Leverenz, "Minnesota Multiphasic Personality Inventory," *War Medicine* 4 (December 1943):618–629.

47. Menninger, *Psychiatry in a Troubled World,* app. D, 592, 597.

48. Capshew, "Psychology on the March," 102. For an enthusiastic description by a psychologist of "a patient-directed 'talking-out session' on the Carl Rogers model" near the German front lines, see Stephen T. Boggs to Gordon Allport, 24 March 1945, HUG 4118.10, folder: "Boggs, Stephen T. 1958–61," GA Papers.

49. James G. Miller, "Clinical Psychology in the Veterans Administration," *American Psychologist* 1 (June 1946):182.

50. Britt and Morgan, "Military Psychologists in World War II," 423–437, see esp. tables 6, 8, and 21.

51. Sullivan, "Psychiatry, the Army, and the War."

52. Roy R. Grinker and John P. Spiegel, *War Neuroses* (Philadelphia: Blakiston, 1945), 115, emphasis in original.

53. Menninger, "The Role of Psychiatry in the World Today," 570.

54. Menninger, *Psychiatry in a Troubled World,* 340. The term "everyman" is used in Grinker and Spiegel, *Men Under Stress,* vii.

55. Menninger, *Psychiatry in a Troubled World,* 55, emphasis in original.

56. Ibid., 352.

57. Grinker and Spiegel, *Men Under Stress,* 411.

58. Menninger, *Psychiatry in a Troubled World,* 38, 344.

59. Technical nosologies were radically altered by the war. For detailed comparison and definition of various types of war neuroses, see Grinker and Spiegel, *Men Under Stress,* and Menninger, *Psychiatry in a Troubled World,* app. B. See also Gerald N. Grob, "Origins of *DSM-I:* A Study in Appearance and Reality," *American Journal of Psychiatry* 148 (April 1991):427–430.

60. Menninger, *Psychiatry in a Troubled World,* app. B, 557. In appendix D, Menninger placed the following note under a chart documenting the percentages of neuropsychiatric admissions in various diagnostic categories: "Stress Often So Severe in Army That Psychiatric Reactions Develop in Normal Men."

61. Not enough time remained in the war to determine whether or not this policy prevented or reduced mental trouble. Years later, some evidence from the Vietnam War indicated that fixed one-year tours of duty may have contributed to dramatically lower rates of psychiatric disorder. See Robert E. Huffman, "Which Soldiers Break Down: A Survey of 610 Psychiatric Patients in Vietnam," *Bulletin of the Menninger Clinic* 34 (November 1970):346–347.

62. Menninger, *Psychiatry in a Troubled World,* 84.

63. Grinker and Spiegel, *Men Under Stress,* 181.

64. Ibid., 39.

65. Strecker and Appel, "Morale," 162.

66. Kenneth Appel, report to Eighth Service Command, June 1944, 4a–4b, Record Group 1.1, series 200A, box 110, folder 1348, RF Archives. For descriptions of one such effort that integrated lectures about adjustment with visual material, see R. Robert Cohen, "Factors in Adjustment to Army Life: A Plan for Preventive Psychiatry by Mass Psychotherapy," *War Medicine* 5 (February 1944):83–91, and "Visual Aids in Preventive Psychiatry," *War Medicine* 6 (July 1944):18–23.

67. Edwin Boring, "Psychology for the Common Man," 30, presidential address written in summer 1945 for the Eastern Psychological Association, HUG 4229.80, EB Papers.

68. Ibid., 36.

69. "Sell" was the word Edwin Boring used, in quotation marks. See Edwin Boring to T. D. Stamps, 27 February 1943, HUG 4229.5, box 48, folder 1065, EB Papers. For a summary of the book project, see the description of the Subcommittee on a Textbook in Military Psychology in Dallenbach, "The Emergency Committee in Psychology," 526–530. A general discussion of the effort can be found in Capshew, "Psychology on the March," chap. 5.

70. National Research Council, *Psychology for the Fighting Man* (Washington: The Infantry Journal, 1943), 300–301, 410–412.

71. Edwin Boring to Alice Bryan, 27 January 1943; and Mildred Atwood to Boring, 15 December 1942, HUG 4229.5, box 8, folder 168 and box 44, folder 949, EB Papers.

72. National Research Council, *Psychology for the Fighting Man*, 12.

73. Ibid., 339.

74. Ibid., 336.

75. The best source on homosexuality during World War II, which gives a starring role to military psychiatrists, is Allan Bérubé, *Coming Out Under Fire: The History of Gay Men and Women in World War Two* (New York: The Free Press, 1990), esp. chaps. 1, and 5–6.

76. "Neuropsychiatry in the Army," *Journal of the American Medical Association* 121 (3 April 1943):1155.

77. National Research Council, *Psychology for the Fighting Man*, 340.

78. Ibid., 304.

79. Roy R. Grinker, Sr., *Fifty Years in Psychiatry: A Living History* (Springfield, Ill.: Charles C. Thomas, 1979), 81.

80. John Dollard, *Fear in Battle* (Washington, D.C.: The Infantry Journal, 1944), and "Twelve Rules on Meeting Battle Fear," *Infantry Journal* 54 (May 1944):36–38. *Fear in Battle*, which incorporated results of research done with three hundred veterans of the Abraham Lincoln Brigade of the Spanish Civil War, was originally published in 1943 by the Yale Institute of Human Relations. It was funded by the Rockefeller Foundation but used by the army. See, for example, John Dollard to Samuel Stouffer, 28 April 1943, and John Dollard to Samuel Stouffer, 25 May 1943, HUG (FP) 31.8, box 2, folder: "Yale University," SS Papers.

81. Dollard, "Twelve Rules on Meeting Battle Fear," 38.

82. Ibid., 37.

83. Ibid., 38.

84. Strecker, "Presidential Address," 2.

85. Ibid.

86. Roy D. Halloran and Malcolm J. Farrell, "The Function of Neuropsychiatry in the Army," *American Journal of Psychiatry* 100 (July 1943): 17.

87. This delayed delivery of on-site mental health services was avoided entirely in Vietnam, where clinicians relied heavily on the World War II learning curve in spite of the many important differences between the conflict in South-

east Asia and the earlier world war. Clinicians accompanied troops into the field from the very beginning of military escalation in 1965 and focused their efforts on environmental manipulation and preventive techniques. Lower psychiatric casualty rates, at least until late 1969, led leaders of the clinical effort to conclude that "the American soldier in Vietnam has generally been psychologically healthier than his counterpart in previous wars." Edward M. Colbach and Matthew D. Parrish, "Army Mental Health Activities in Vietnam, 1965–1970," *Bulletin of the Menninger Clinic* 34 (November 1970):339.

88. Grinker and Spiegel, *War Neuroses*, 70.

89. Grinker and Spiegel estimated that the drug was used on 50 percent of all their psychotherapeutic patients. See Grinker and Spiegel, *Men Under Stress*, chap. 17. For another general discussion of "narcosynthesis," see Grinker and Spiegel, *War Neuroses*, 78–86. Essentially, the idea behind narcosynthesis was that by inducing semiconsciousness, sedatives would prompt patients to reexperience the traumatic events in a therapeutic setting, bring repressed anxieties to consciousness, and allow the damaged ego to gather strength and heal.

90. Menninger, *Psychiatry in a Troubled World*, 305–307.

91. Grinker and Spiegel, *Men Under Stress*, 348, emphasis in original.

92. Ibid., 218.

93. Ibid., 158.

94. Ibid., 368.

95. Menninger, *Psychiatry in a Troubled World*, 451.

96. Grinker and Spiegel, *Men Under Stress*, 149.

97. Menninger, *Psychiatry in a Troubled World*, 451, emphasis in original.

98. Henry W. Brosin, "The Army Has Learned These Lessons," quoted in Grob, *From Asylum to Community*, 18, emphasis in original.

99. Menninger, *Psychiatry in a Troubled World*, 410.

100. The term "pensionitis" is taken from B. M. Baruch's report to Gen. Omar Bradley, director of the Veterans Administration, on 16 August 1945, quoted in Menninger, *Psychiatry in a Troubled World*, 391. The cost of pensions based on psychiatric discharges was a significant concern among policymakers. In 1946, 60 percent of all cases in Veterans Administration hospitals were psychiatric and they cost $40,000 or more per case. As of June 1947, all the neuropsychiatrically disabled vets from World War I and World War II combined were receiving pensions costing the government $20 million each month. Jeanne L. Brand, "The National Mental Health Act of 1946: A Retrospective," *Bulletin of the History of Medicine* 39 (May–June 1965):236–237; and Menninger, *Psychiatry in a Troubled World*, 380.

101. Daniel Blain, "Programs of the Veterans Administration for the Physical and Mental Health of Veterans," *Bulletin of the Menninger Clinic* 10 (March 1946) 34.

102. Gregg, "A Critique of Psychiatry," 291.

103. Franz Alexander, "What Can Psychiatry Contribute to the Alleviation of National and International Difficulties? A Symposium," *American Journal of Orthopsychiatry* (October 1941):619.

104. Alexander, *Our Age of Unreason*, 235.

105. Strecker, *Beyond the Clinical Frontiers*, 199.

106. Lawrence K. Frank, "Freedom for the Personality," *Psychiatry* 3 (August 1940):349.

5: The Career of Cold War Psychology

1. John G. Darley, "Contract Support of Research in Psychology," *American Psychologist* 7 (December 1952):719.

2. Department of the Army, "Psychological Operations," Department of the Army Field Manual, FM 33–5 (Washington, D.C.: Dept. of the Army, January 1962), i.

3. Even decades later, this was still considered the most significant lesson of the World War II experience. See National Academy of Sciences, *Behavioral and Social Science Research in the Department of Defense: A Framework for Management*, Report of the Advisory Committee on the Management of Behavioral Science Research in the Department of Defense, Division of Behavioral Sciences, National Research Council (Washington, D.C., 1971), 6.

4. This phrase was used by Theodore Vallance, the director of Project Camelot's sponsoring organization, the Special Operations Research Office (SORO) at the American University. See Theodore R. Vallance, "Psychological Aspects of Social Change Mediated Through the Interaction of Military Systems of Two Cultures," in U.S. Army Behavioral Science Research Laboratory, *Technical Report S-1, Psychological Research in National Defense Today* (June 1967), 314. Although not published until 1967, Vallance presented this material as a talk at the September 1964 meetings of the American Psychological Association, before Camelot was canceled.

5. Darley, "Contract Support of Research in Psychology," 720. On the institutionalization and scope of psychological research for the military in the immediate postwar period, and articulation of the idea that defense research was an example of psychological professionals' public service in a democratic society, see Lyle H. Lanier, "The Psychological and Social Sciences in the National Military Establishment," *American Psychologist* 4 (May 1949), 127–147.

The critical postwar role of Department of Defense funding has been more widely acknowledged by historians of the physical sciences than by historians of psychology, probably because the sums involved and absence of other public sources of support were even more dramatic. By the early 1950s, 70 percent of all work conducted in academic physics departments was for the DOD, and university campuses were inundated with classified scientific research contracts. See, for example, Paul Forman, "Behind Quantum Electronics: National Security as Basis for Physical Research in the United States, 1940–1960," *Historical Studies in the Physical and Biological Sciences* 18 (1987):149–229.

6. National Science Foundation, *Federal Funds for Science*, 1950–51 and 1951–52 (Washington, D.C.):39–40, table F.

7. Quoted in Simpson, "U.S. Mass Communications Research and Counterinsurgency After 1945," 12–13.

8. Frank A. Geldard, "Military Psychology: Science or Technology?" *American Journal of Psychology* 66 (July 1953):335–348.

9. See Talcott Parsons, "Social Science: A Basic National Resource," in *The Nationalization of the Social Sciences*, ed. Samuel Z. Klausner and Victor M. Lidz (Philadelphia: University of Pennsylvania Press, 1986), 41–112. This important document, although not published until 1986, was commissioned by the Social Science Research Council as part of its effort to persuade politicians that National Science Foundation funding for social science should be mandated from the outset. (The NSF was finally "allowed" but not "required" to support social research.) Although Parsons's report was thought ill-suited for its purpose because it considered philosophical issues as well as cataloging the practical effectiveness of government-supported social science, it does illustrate how thoroughly arguments for social science's inclusion in the government's expanded postwar science effort relied upon World War II successes. For a general discussion of the initial campaign to include social science in the NSF, see Otto N. Larsen, *Milestones and Millstones: Social Science at the National Science Foundation, 1945–1991* (New Brunswick, N.J.: Transaction Publishers, 1992), chap. 1.

10. Barton Meyers, "The Effects of Funding on Psychology in the United States after World War II" (unpublished paper, n.d.), 20.

11. Lerner and Lasswell, eds., *The Policy Sciences*.

12. Parsons, "Social Science," 107.

13. For one such prophetic warning, see E. A. Shils, "Social Science and Social Policy," *Philosophy of Science* 16 (July 1949):219–242, reprinted in *Social Scientists and International Affairs*, 35–49.

14. Henry W. Riecken, Assistant Director for Social Sciences, National Science Foundation, "National Resources in the Social Sciences," in *Symposium Proceedings: The U.S. Army's Limited-War Mission and Social Science Research*, 26–28 March 1962, ed. William A. Lybrand (Washington, D.C.: Special Operations Research Office, 1962), 300. In 1938 the entire budget for military research and development was $14 million. See Crawford and Biderman, eds., *Social Scientists and International Affairs*, 10.

15. Good sources for data on levels of military funding for psychological and social science research include: DDSFAR; Irving Louis Horowitz, "Social Science and Public Policy: Implications of Modern Research," in *The Rise and Fall of Project Camelot: Studies in the Relationship Between Social Science and Practical Politics*, ed. Irving Louis Horowitz (Cambridge: MIT Press, 1967), 339–376; Michael T. Klare, *War Without End: American Planning for the Next Vietnams* (New York: Alfred A. Knopf, 1972), apps. For a comparison with recent Department of Defense expenditures, see James E. Driskell and Beckett Olmstead, "Psychology and the Military: Research Applications and Trends," *American Psychologist* 44 (January 1989):43–54. This review is also useful for illustrating how little the perspective of military psychologists has changed over the fifty-year period since World War II. Driskell and Olmstead summarize the current relationship between psychology and the military as one of "reciprocal

exchange" and conclude that "the 'growth potential' for military psychology is great."

For comparative data on levels of funding by the Defense Department and the Department of Health, Education and Welfare (and other domestically oriented agencies), see National Science Foundation, *Federal Funds for Science, 1950–62* (Washington, D.C.), followed by *Federal Funds for Research, Development, and Other Scientific Activities, 1962–70* (Washington, D.C.). According to the statistics provided in these volumes, fiscal year 1961 was the first during which total HEW spending on psychological sciences surpassed total DOD funding. HEW spent $20.4 million during that year, fully half of the federal government's total for such research. The DOD, in comparison, spent only $15.7 million. See National Science Foundation, *Federal Funds for Science, 1960, 1961, 1962* (Washington, D.C.), 102, table 16.

16. Arthur W. Melton, "Military Requirements for the Systematic Study of Psychological Variables," in *Psychology in the World Emergency,* John C. Flanagan et. al. (Pittsburgh: University of Pittsburgh Press, 1952), 136.

17. John G. Darley, "Psychology and the Office of Naval Research: A Decade of Development," *American Psychologist* 12 (June 1957):305.

18. Psychologists, such as McGill University's Donald Hebb, whose work on sensory deprivation for the Canadian Defense Research Board emerged directly out of war-inspired concerns with "brainwashing" were not permitted to say as much in their published studies. See Gilgen, *American Psychology Since World War II,* 122. For a general discussion among psychiatrists of the issues raised by the Korean War controversy, see "Factors Used to Increase the Susceptibility of Individuals to Forceful Indoctrination: Observations and Experiments" and "Methods of Forceful Indoctrination: Observations and Interviews," in *Psychiatry and Public Affairs: Reports and Symposia of the Group for the Advancement of Psychiatry* (Chicago: Aldine Publishing Company, 1966, originally published as GAP symposia #3 and #4), 205–311.

19. For a general discussion of this development, see Simpson, "U.S. Mass Communications Research and Counterinsurgency After 1945."

20. The most important Central Intelligence Agency experiments of these kinds occurred from approximately 1945 to 1965, and included 149 projects, 80 institutions, 183 researchers (many of them academics), and $25 million. Known as MK/ULTRA and MK/DELTA, details of their existence were not exposed until the late 1970s. Much of the research involved laboratories at home, but the CIA also sent teams comprised of a psychiatrist, a hypnotist, and an interrogator to Communist countries to try out their scientific techniques. See John Marks, *The Search for the "Manchurian Candidate": The CIA and Mind Control* (New York: Times Books, 1979).

There is evidence that the American Psychological Association continued its World War II practice of helping the government's secret agencies recruit psychological experts after 1945, although such covert activities were never publicly acknowledged. See, for example, Matthew W. Baird to Robert R. Sears, 26 March 1951, quoted in Napoli, *Architects of Adjustment,* 146.

CIA recruitment, as well as operations, required help from psychological experts. Aside from performing strenuous batteries of tests, CIA psychological experts developed profiles of individuals, analyzed audio and video tapes, and aided case officers with a variety of human management problems. John Stockwell, personal communication, 23 October 1990.

One congressional estimate in the 1960s was that the CIA employed 13 percent of all the social scientists working for the federal government, but the actual number was never public information. See "The Case for a National Social Science Foundation," in *Social Science and National Policy,* 2nd ed., ed. Fred R. Harris (New Brunswick, N.J.: Transaction Books, 1973), 221.

21. Quoted in John Marks and Patricia Greenfield, "How the CIA Assesses Weaknesses: The Gittinger Personality Assessment System," in *The Power of Psychology,* ed. David Cohen (London: Croom Helm, 1987), 25.

The extent of the CIA's nontherapeutic approach to personality assessment was illustrated when the architect of the agency's "personality assessment system," psychologist John Gittinger, was rushed to the White House during the Cuban Missile Crisis to advise the Kennedy administration on Khrushchev's probable responses to a variety of moves (p. 13).

22. George W. Croker, "Some Principles Regarding the Utilization of Social Science Research within the Military," in *Social Scientists and International Affairs,* 189–192; Peter Watson, *War on the Mind: The Military Uses and Abuses of Psychology* (New York: Penguin, 1980), 216–223.

23. Proposed Consultant Panels, Records of the Psychological Strategy Board, quoted in Simpson, "U.S. Mass Communications Research and Counterinsurgency After 1945," 13a–13b.

24. Don K. Price, *Government and Science: Their Dynamic Relation in American Democracy* (1954; reprint, New York: Oxford University Press, 1962), 89, 96.

25. DDSFAR, testimony of Vice Admiral Hyman G. Rickover, pt. 2, 28 May 1968, 25.

26. Ibid., 26.

27. Earlier indications existed that social and psychological expertise was associated with gender nonconformity as well as sheer silliness. Consider, for example, the following statement from Ohio congressional representative Clarence Brown, during the 1946 debate over establishment of a national science foundation: "The average American just does not want some expert running around prying into his life and his personal affairs and deciding for him how he should live, and if the impression becomes prevalent in the Congress that this legislation is to establish some sort of an organization in which there would be a lot of short-haired women and long-haired men messing into everybody's personal affairs and lives, inquiring whether they love their wives or do not love them and so forth, you are not going to get your legislation." Quoted in Mark Solovey, "Shattered Dreams and Unfulfilled Promises: The Wisconsin Social Systems Research Institute and Interdisciplinary Social Science Research, 1945–1965" (M.A. thesis, University of Wisconsin, Madison, 1990), 12.

28. Investigating the validity of this accusation was the 1953 mandate of the Cox Committee. It was joined by the Reece Committee in 1954, which denounced the "socialism" and "un-Americanism" of the social sciences. The Cox Committee is quoted in Gene M. Lyons, *The Uneasy Partnership: Social*

Science and the Federal Government in the Twentieth Century (New York: Russell Sage Foundation, 1969), 278. For the records of the congressional hearings, see House Select Committee to Investigate Tax-Exempt Foundations and Comparable Organizations, November, December 1952, 82nd Cong., and House Special Committee to Investigate Tax-Exempt Foundations and Comparable Organizations, May–July 1954, 83rd Cong.

For contemporary analyses of changes in congressional attitudes toward the social sciences during the 1950s, see Harry Alpert, "Congressmen, Social Scientists, and Attitudes Toward Federal Support of Social Science Research," *American Sociological Review* 23 (December 1958):682–686, and Harry Alpert, "The Government's Growing Recognition of Social Science," *Annals of the American Academy of Political and Social Science* 327 (January 1960):59–67. The best recent discussion can be found in Mark Solovey, "Shaping the Social Sciences: Private and Public Patronage Since World War II (Ph.D. diss., University of Wisconsin, in progress).

Although mainly a product of the McCarthy years, the socialist taint remained an undercurrent in many different areas of psychology's history. In the late 1960s, Fred Harris blamed the failure of the campaign for a National Social Science Foundation on the long-lasting confusion of social science and socialism. See "The Case for a National Social Science Foundation," 222.

29. The support of the Behavioral Science Division of the Ford Foundation in the 1950s (one of the private foundations suspected of left-wing inclinations) also did a great deal to promote the term. "Behavioral science" became shorthand for a subset of the more general category "social sciences." The term included psychology, anthropology, sociology, and those aspects of economics and political science devoted to the analysis of individual and group behavior rather than institutions or processes. Although the Ford Foundation's division was disbanded in 1957, the term stuck. See Peter J. Seybold, "The Ford Foundation and the Triumph of Behavioralism in American Political Science," in *Philanthropy and Cultural Imperialism*, 269–303.

For a review of McCarthy-era attacks on social psychologists, see S. Stansfeld Sargent and Benjamin Harris, "Academic Freedom, Civil Liberties, and SPSSI," *Journal of Social Issues* 42 (Spring 1986):43–67. The best general overview of academic McCarthyism is Ellen W. Schrecker, *No Ivory Tower: McCarthyism and the Universities* (New York: Oxford University Press, 1986). Interestingly, she finds that physical scientists (especially physicists) were most likely to be the first targets of congressional investigation because of their collective reputation for radicalism and their actual participation in or connection to the Manhattan Project. Much of the House Un-American Activities Committee's interest in higher education in the late 1940s was inspired by its hunt for atomic spies.

30. Gordon Allport, "Social Science and Human Values/Wellesley Address," 17 May 1955, 1, emphasis in original, HUG 4118.50, box 3, folder 79, GA Papers. This lecture was actually delivered on 17 March 1955. The folder is dated incorrectly.

31. In the late 1960s, Jerome Wiesner, who had been John F. Kennedy's science advisor and an advocate for government support of behavioral science, was still warning professional colleagues that misgivings lurked in Congress.

See Jerome B. Wiesner, "The Need for Social Engineering," in *Psychology and the Problems of Society,* ed. Frances F. Korten, Stuart W. Cook, and John I. Lacey (Washington, D.C.: American Psychological Association, 1970), 85. Even in the early 1980s, Tom Foley (then Speaker of the House), made the following comment about congressional attitudes toward social science: "Do the media respond, do your colleagues give a damn? Members of Congress can easily vote with the representative from Ohio [John Ashbrook] against social science because they gain credit with constituents for opposing nonsense and for saving money. Nobody else seems to care." Quoted in Larsen, *Milestones and Millstones,* xiii.

32. WCW, pt. 8, 15–16 January 1964, 1028.

33. How little military psychologists actually knew (as well as how much the military could do for psychology) was a refrain in virtually all the essays written for Flanagan et al., *Psychology in the World Emergency.*

34. Franz Samelson, personal communication, 23 June 1991. For another glowing report about how much World War II did for psychology, see John G. Jenkins, "New Opportunities and New Responsibilities for the Psychologist," *Science* 103 (11 January 1946):33–38. See also Edwin Boring to Helen Peak, 10 June 1946, HUG 4229.5, box 46, folder 1017, EB Papers.

35. Melton, "Military Requirements for the Systematic Study of Psychological Variables," 134.

36. Dwight D. Eisenhower, 31 May 1954 address at Columbia University Bicentennial Dinner, reprinted in "The Use of Social Research in Federal Domestic Programs," A Staff Study for the Research and Technical Programs Subcommittee of the House Committee on Government Operations, 90th Cong., 1st sess., pts. 1–4, April 1967, 164.

37. Ibid., 169.

38. For lists and descriptions of psychological think tanks founded in the postwar period, see DDSFAR, 38; Horowitz, "Social Science and Public Policy," 346, table 1; *Federal Funds for Research, Development, and Other Scientific Activities,* 1962, 1963, and 1964 (Washington, D.C.), 101–102; Watson, *War on the Mind,* app. 2.

39. Crawford and Biderman, eds., *Social Scientists and International Affairs,* 11 n. 1.

40. Ibid., 2.

41. In addition to Federal Contract Research Centers like RAND and the Special Operations Research Office, there were literally thousands of private research businesses contracting with the military by the late 1960s. See DDSFAR, 39.

42. Crawford and Biderman, eds., *Social Scientists and International Affairs,* 156. For a methodological critique of the concept following World War II, see Farber, "The Problem of National Character."

43. Report of Carl I. Hovland, 13 May 1946, Record Group 3.1, series 910, box 3, folder 10, RF Archives.

44. Leonard W. Doob, *Becoming More Civilized: A Psychological Explanation* (New Haven: Yale University Press, 1960).

45. Ibid., 225–226, emphasis in original.

46. Ibid., 3.

47. Ibid., app. C. This appendix includes a brief summary of all the hypotheses about "civilized" and "uncivilized" personalities discussed, in detail, throughout the book.

48. Ibid., 60–66, app. B. For a discussion of the appeal of projective testing techniques in postwar cross-cultural research, see Gardner Lindzey, *Projective Techniques and Cross-Cultural Research* (New York: Appleton-Century-Crofts, 1961).

49. William Henry, "Projective Tests in Cross-Cultural Research," in *Studying Personality Cross-Culturally*, ed. Bert Kaplan (New York: Harper & Row, 1961), 587.

50. David C. McClelland, *The Achieving Society* (Princeton: D. Van Nostrand Company, 1961), 337, 429.

51. Ibid., 387.

52. Ibid., 105.

53. Ibid., 437, emphasis in original.

54. Ibid., 424.

55. Subcommittee on International Organizations and Movements of the House Committee on Foreign Affairs, "Modern Communications and Foreign Policy." Part 10 of *Winning the Cold War: The U.S. Ideological Offensive*, 90th Cong., 1st sess., 8–9 February 1967, David McClelland testimony, 86.

56. McClelland, *The Achieving Society*, 427.

57. PAFP and PAIR.

58. PAFP, 1.

59. Ibid., 2.

60. PAIR, Jerome Frank testimony, 15.

61. Evidence of the seriousness with which nonpsychologists took psychological research can be seen, for example, in the activities of the Harvard University Center for International Affairs in the early 1960s. During the 1960–61 academic year, it sponsored a Faculty Seminar on Social and Cultural Aspects of Development whose purpose was to identify areas deserving of intensive future research. David McClelland was an invited seminar speaker and the report which summarized the seminar's conclusions identified "personality traits" as a top priority. See "Summary Report on Research Problems," 10 July 1961, HUG (FP) 42.25, box 1, folder: "International Affairs Seminar: 1961, vol. II," Talcott Parsons Papers, Harvard University Archives, Cambridge, Massachusetts.

62. Robert Staughton Lynd, *Knowledge for What? The Place of Social Science in American Culture* (Princeton: Princeton University Press, 1939), 160.

63. Walt W. Rostow, *The Stages of Economic Growth: A Non-Communist Manifesto* (Cambridge: Cambridge University Press, 1960). Chapter 10 includes the most explicit discussion of Rostow's psychological assumptions.

64. WCW, pt. 6, 13–14 January 1964 and 20 February 1964, 751.

65. Gabriel A. Almond, *The Civic Culture: Political Attitudes and Democracy in Five Nations* (Boston: Little, Brown & Company, 1963), 13, emphasis in original. For the origin of the "political culture" concept, see Gabriel Almond, "Comparative Political Systems," *Journal of Politics* 18 (August

1956):391–409. For elaborations, see also Lucian W. Pye and Sidney Verba, eds., *Political Culture and Political Development* (Princeton: Princeton University Press, 1965).

66. Almond, *The Civic Culture*, 11–12.

67. Lucian W. Pye, "Political Culture and Political Development," in *Political Culture and Political Development*, 7–8.

68. Gertrude Blanck and Rubin Blanck, *Ego Psychology: Theory & Practice* (New York: Columbia University Press, 1974), chap. 1.

69. Sidney Verba, "Comparative Political Culture," in *Political Culture and Political Development*, 516.

70. Almond, *The Civic Culture*, 30–35.

71. Pye and Verba, eds., *Political Culture and Political Development*, vii.

72. Lucian W. Pye was the chairman of the Social Science Research Council (SSRC) Committee on Comparative Politics. Members included: Gabriel A. Almond, Leonard Binder, R. Taylor Cole, James S. Coleman, Herbert Hyman, Joseph LaPalombara, Sidney Verba, Robert E. Wood, and Myron Weiner. For a summary of the work of the Committee on Comparative Politics, see Seybold, "The Ford Foundation and the Triumph of Behavioralism in American Political Science," 286–292. For an overview of the political development literature during this period, see Jean Hardisty Dose, "A Social and Political Explanation of Social Science Trends: The Case of Political Development Research" (Ph.D. diss., Northwestern University, 1976).

73. Lucian W. Pye, *Politics, Personality, and Nation Building: Burma's Search for Identity* (New Haven: Yale University Press, 1962), xv.

74. Verba, "Comparative Political Culture," 529–535.

75. Rex D. Hopper, "The Revolutionary Process: A Frame of Reference for the Study of Revolutionary Movements," *Social Forces* 28 (March 1950):270–279.

76. Ibid., 270.

77. Ibid.

78. Rex D. Hopper, "Cybernation, Marginality, and Revolution," in *The New Sociology: Essays in Social Science and Social Theory in Honor of C. Wright Mills*, ed. Irving Louis Horowitz (New York: Oxford University Press, 1964), 328.

79. See HUG (FP) 42.25, box 1, folder: "Princeton Symposium on Internal War, 1961," Talcott Parsons Papers. Papers from the Princeton Symposium were eventually published as Harry Eckstein, ed., *Internal War: Problems and Approaches* (1964; reprint, Westport, Conn.: Greenwood Press, 1980).

80. Cina, "Social Science for Whom?" 302, 399.

81. Edward A. Tiryakian, "A Model of Societal Change and Its Lead Indicators," in *The Study of Total Societies*, ed. Samuel Z. Klausner (New York: Frederick A. Praeger, 1967), 69–97. This book collects pieces from a conference connected with the just canceled Project Camelot. It was held on 28–29 July 1965 in Washington, D.C., sponsored by the army through the Special Operations Research Office "as part of SORO's long-term research interests in the problems of analyzing societies." Samuel Klausner, the editor, had been a Camelot consultant.

82. Paul Fitts et al., *Report of the Ad Hoc Advisory Group on Psychology and*

the Social Sciences, 19 December 1957, p. 8, Record Group 179, Research Group in Psychology and the Social Sciences, 1957–63, box 2, folder: "Director of Defense Research and Engineering," Smithsonian Institution, Washington, D.C.

83. Ibid., 3.

84. Ibid., 12.

85. Remarks of Dr. John W. Riley, Jr., Second Vice-President and Director of Social Research, Equitable Life Insurance Society, in *Symposium Proceedings,* 155.

86. E. K. Karcher, Jr., Office Chief, Research and Development, "Army Social Science Programs and Plans," in *Symposium Proceedings,* 348.

87. Lybrand, ed., *Symposium Proceedings,* x, emphasis in original.

88. The term "technology of human behavior" was used to describe the Smithsonian Group's work by Dr. Carroll L. Shartle, Chief, Psychology and Social Science Division, Office of Science, Office of the Director of Defense Research and Engineering, Office of the Secretary of Defense. See *Symposium Proceedings,* 336. It was also the title of an article Bray published right after the conference. See Charles W. Bray, "Toward a Technology of Human Behavior for Defense Use," *American Psychologist* 17 (August 1962):527–541.

On the importance of leaving one's political philosophy at home, see Guy J. Pauker, RAND Corporation, "Sources of Turbulence in the New Nations," and E. K. Karcher, Jr., "Army Social Science Programs and Plans," in *Symposium Proceedings,* 178–179, 359.

89. Lieutenant General Arthur G. Trudeau, Chief of Research and Development, Department of the Army, "Welcoming Address," in *Symposium Proceedings,* 11–12.

90. Lybrand, ed., *Symposium Proceedings,* vii.

91. For one example, see the remarks of Elmo C. Wilson, President, International Research Associates, in *Symposium Proceedings,* 193–199. Wilson himself had been chief of the Office of War Information Surveys Division.

92. Frederick T. C. Yu, "Images, Ideology and Identity in Asian Politics and Communication," in *Symposium Proceedings,* 214.

93. Ibid., 218.

94. Ibid., 215.

95. Lucian W. Pye, "The Role of the Military in Political Development," in *Symposium Proceedings,* 167.

96. Vallance, "Psychological Aspects of Social Change Mediated Through the Interaction of Military Systems of Two Cultures," 315.

6: Project Camelot and Its Aftermath

1. Ralph Beals, *Politics of Social Research: An Inquiry Into the Ethics and Responsibilities of Social Scientists* (Chicago: Aldine Publishing Company, 1969), 18.

2. Horowitz, ed., *The Rise and Fall of Project Camelot,* 47.

3. Excerpt from Theodore Vallance's congressional testimony, reprinted in "Testimony Before House Subcommittee on International Organizations and Movements of the Committee on Foreign Affairs, July 8, 1965," *American Psychologist* 21 (May 1966):469.

4. BSNS, testimony of Lt. Gen. W. W. Dick, Jr., Chief of Research and Development, Department of the Army, 28.

5. Bray, *Psychology and Military Proficiency,* 171.

6. Charles Windle and T. R. Vallance, "The Future of Military Psychology: Paramilitary Psychology," *American Psychologist* 19 (February 1964):128. See also Theodore R. Vallance and Charles D. Windle, "Cultural Engineering," *Military Review* 42 (December 1962):60–64.

7. Theodore Vallance, "Project Camelot: An Interim Postlude," *American Psychologist* 21 (May 1966):441, emphasis in original.

8. For a detailed chronology of Camelot's projected research, see BSNS, testimony of Lt. Gen. W. W. Dick, Jr., Chief of Research and Development, Department of the Army, 30–32.

9. Ibid., 32.

10. Irving Louis Horowitz, "The Life and Death of Project Camelot," *American Psychologist* 21 (May 1966):452; Horowitz, ed., *The Rise and Fall of Project Camelot,* 27.

11. Aniceto Rodriguez, "A Socialist Commentary on Camelot," in *The Rise and Fall of Project Camelot,* 229.

12. See the review of federally sponsored research in the year immediately after Camelot's exposure in FSISSBR. In these hearings, Thomas L. Hughes, Director of Intelligence and Research, Department of State, noted that many projects similar to Camelot had in fact been classified and these, obviously, never came to public attention. For a list of classified projects in military psychology during this period, see Watson, *War on the Mind,* 30. Later, Hughes declared that the futility of structural reform, such as that mandated by Johnson's memo, was an inevitable product of the confusing relationship between objective expertise and policy-making, unequal experts and policy-makers, and the unpredictability of human personality in general. "It is the human variables that defy the jurisdictional reforms, mock the machinery of government and frustrate the organizational tinkering. These are the phenomena that help assure that no rejuggling of administrative charts can finally surmount the uneven qualities of the men who inhabit the institutions. The human material, much as the institutional framework, will in the end determine whether intelligence and policy, either or both, have feet of clay." Thomas L. Hughes, "The Fate of Facts in a World of Men: Foreign Policy and Intelligence-Making," *Headline Series* no. 233 (New York: Foreign Policy Association, December 1976), 60.

13. Howard Margolis, "McNamara Ax Dooms Camelot," *Washington Post,* 9 July 1965, B6.

14. December 4, 1964, description sent by the Special Operations Research Office to scholars in Camelot, quoted in *The Rise and Fall of Project Camelot,* 48.

15. The term "feasibility" was used in Camelot's own documents and the project was described as a "feasibility study" by Special Operations Research Office Director Theodore Vallance in his "Project Camelot," 442.

16. The total Department of Defense budget for behavioral and social science research was $27.3 million in 1965, when Camelot was exposed. In 1966 the figure had reached $34 million and it was almost $50 million in 1970. See BSNS, 97, and Klare, *War Without End*, 373, app. C.

17. BSNS, 5R.

18. Ibid., 6R, and testimony of Dean Rusk, Secretary of State, 108.

19. The most useful single source on the response to Camelot among social and behavioral scientists is Horowitz, ed., *The Rise and Fall of Project Camelot*. See also his "The Life and Death of Project Camelot," 445–454, reprinted from *Trans-action* (1965):3–7, 44–47.

20. Robert A. Nisbet, "Project Camelot and the Science of Man," in *The Rise and Fall of Project Camelot*, 316, 323. See also Nisbet's "Project Camelot: An Autopsy," in *On Intellectuals: Theoretical Studies/Case Studies*, ed. Philip Rieff (New York: Anchor Books, 1970), 307–339.

21. Horowitz, "The Life and Death of Project Camelot," 448. See also Robert Boguslaw, "Ethics and the Social Scientist," in *The Rise and Fall of Project Camelot*, 107–127. Of all the experts involved in Camelot, Boguslaw defended most strongly the noble motive—"to find nonmilitary and nonviolent solutions to international problems."

22. "Feedback from Our Readers," *Trans-action* 3 (January-February 1966):2. For another statement of the view that the U.S. military's patronage of behavioral science demonstrated more enlightenment than was evident in civilian government agencies, see George E. Lowe, "The Camelot Affair," *Bulletin of the Atomic Scientists* 22 (May 1966):48.

23. FSISSBR, testimony of Gabriel Almond, 27 June 1966, 114.

24. Walt Rostow, quoted in Allan A. Needell, " 'Truth Is Our Weapon': Project TROY, Political Warfare, and Government-Academic Relations in the National Security State," *Diplomatic History* 17 (Summer 1993):417. According to Needell, the center was a direct outgrowth of a top-secret State Department program, Project TROY, which mobilized an impressive group of social and physical scientists (including a number of psychologists with experience in World War II) in the area of anti-Communist political and psychological warfare. For more on the center's CIA ties, and for the role of the new intelligence community in supporting research on mass communication, see Simpson, "U.S. Mass Communications Research and Counterinsurgency after 1945," 21–29.

25. Ithiel de Sola Pool, "The Necessity for Social Scientists Doing Research for Governments," in *The Rise and Fall of Project Camelot*, 267–268.

26. Ibid., 277.

27. Horowitz, ed., *The Rise and Fall of Project Camelot*, 7.

28. Horowitz, "Social Science and Public Policy," 341.

29. Kurt Lewin, "Action Research and Minority Group Problems," in *Resolving Social Conflicts*, 213.

30. Alpert, "Congressmen, Social Scientists, and Attitudes Toward Federal Support of Social Science Research," 685.

31. Daniel Lerner, "Social Science: Whence and Whither?" in *The Human Meaning of the Social Sciences*, 30.

32. Horowitz, "The Life and Death of Project Camelot," 454; Irving Louis

Horowitz, "The Rise and Fall of Project Camelot," in *The Rise and Fall of Project Camelot*, 40–41.

33. Herbert C. Kelman, "Manipulation of Human Behavior: An Ethical Dilemma," in *A Time To Speak: On Human Values and Social Research* (San Francisco: Jossey-Bass, Inc., 1968), 16.

34. Herbert C. Kelman, "The Social Consequences of Social Research," in *A Time To Speak*, 32–33.

35. Franz Boas, "Scientists as Spies" (1919 letter to *The Nation*), in *The Shaping of American Anthropology, 1883–1911: A Franz Boas Reader*, ed. George W. Stocking, Jr. (New York: Basic Books, 1974), 336. See also the reference to this episode in Beals, *Politics of Social Research*, 51.

36. "Statement on Problems of Anthropological Research and Ethics," in Beals, *Politics of Social Research*, 193, 195–196. Beals's *Politics of Social Research* was based in large part on the report he did under American Anthropological Association auspices in the aftermath of Camelot. For the original text of the report, see "Background Information on Problems of Anthropological Research and Ethics," *American Anthropological Association Newsletter* 8 (January 1967). See also Stephen T. Boggs's and Ralph L. Beals's testimony in FSISSBR, 72–93; and Bryce Nelson, "Anthropologists' Debate: Concern Over Future of Foreign Research," *Science* 154 (December 23, 1966):1525–1527.

37. Beals, *Politics of Social Research*, 78.

38. See for example, the testimony of Stephen T. Boggs, Executive Secretary, American Anthropological Association, in FSISSBR, 72–77. He discusses, among other things, anthropologists' deep concerns over the revelations of a CIA-funded project on Vietnam at Michigan State University. For more on the CIA-MSU connection, see Max Frankl, "University Project Cloaked C.I.A. Role in Saigon, 1955–59," *New York Times*, 14 April 1966, 1–2; and Warren Hinkle, "The University on the Make," *Ramparts* 4 (April 1966):11–22.

39. Martin Diskin, personal communication, 26 October 1990.

40. Eric R. Wolf and Joseph G. Jorgensen, "Anthropology on the Warpath in Thailand," *The New York Review of Books* 15 (19 November 1970):26–35. For additional insight into the debate within anthropology, see "Social Responsibilities Forum," *Current Anthropology* 9 (December 1968).

41. There were, predictably, far more restrictions erected in Latin America than in Asia or Africa, but repercussions were felt by researchers working in Burma, Nepal, Afghanistan, Iran, Pakistan, Iraq, Yemen, Saudi Arabia, Sudan, Egypt, and South Africa, among other countries. See Beals, *Politics of Social Research*, 20–25. Accounts of research directly and negatively effected by Project Camelot can be found in *American Anthropological Association Fellow Newsletter* 6 (December 1965):2–3; Elinor Langer, "Foreign Research: CIA Plus Camelot Equals Troubles for U.S. Scholars," *Science* 156 (23 June 1967):1583–1584; letter to the editor by Dale L. Johnson, *American Anthropologist* 68 (August 1966):1016–1017; Kalman H. Silvert, "American Academic Ethics and Social Research Abroad: The Lesson of Project Camelot," in *The Rise and Fall of Project Camelot*, 81–82.

42. Gabriel Almond, at an American Political Science Association forum on

Project Camelot in September 1965, quoted in Lowe, "The Camelot Affair," 47.

43. Horowitz, ed., *The Rise and Fall of Project Camelot*, 20; FSISSBR, 20; Dose, "A Social and Political Explanation of Social Science Trends," 197. For a senior Special Operations Research Office researcher's defense of Project Task as "a most uncynical and unsinister project," and his complaint that the debate surrounding Camelot's demise had been dishonest and shrill, see Milton Jacobs, "L'Affaire Camelot," letter to the editor, *American Anthropologist* 69 (June–August 1967):364–366.

44. On Project Agile, see Lyons, *The Uneasy Partnership*, 197; Watson, *War on the Mind*, 319. On post-Camelot research aimed at preventing revolution in Latin America, see DDSFAR, 64–65.

45. Memo from Director of Defense Research and Engineering to Assistant Secretaries for Research and Development of the Army, Navy, Air Force, and the Director, Advanced Research Projects Agency, 18 August 1965, 1–2, "NAS Archives Central Policy Files: DNRC: Behavioral Sciences: Com on Govt Programs in Behavioral Sc: Adv: General: 1965," National Academy of Sciences, Washington, D.C. I am indebted to Mark Solovey for sharing this document with me.

46. DDSFAR, testimony of John S. Foster, Jr., Director of Defense Research and Engineering, 93.

47. FSISSBR, testimony of Arthur Brayfield, Executive Officer, American Psychological Association, 66.

48. Mark Solovey, "Social Science and the State during the 1960s: Senator Fred Harris's Effort to Create a National Social Science Foundation" (paper presented at "Toward a History of the 1960s," Madison, Wisconsin, 30 April 1993).

49. Subcommittee on Government Research of the Senate Committee on Government Operations, Hearings on "National Foundation for Social Sciences," February, June, July 1967, 90th Cong., 1st sess., pts. 1–3. For excerpts of the hearing testimony, see "The Case for a National Social Science Foundation," 219–252. For a general discussion of the effort to establish a separate social science foundation, and changes within the NSF during the 1960s, see Larsen, *Milestones and Millstones*, chap. 4.

50. DDSFAR, pt. 1, 52–55.

51. A clear statement of this equation was offered by Milton Jacobs, a senior researcher at the Special Operations Research Office during the Camelot era, who noted several years later from a perch in academia that "working for the United States Government should not suddenly become sinful. . . . I am sure that most university professors and intellectuals, in and out of government, feel responsibility to their society as well as to their chosen field of endeavor. I doubt that these responsibilities need be contradictory. If they are, our nation is in deep trouble." Jacobs, "L'Affaire Camelot," 366.

52. Quoted in DDSFAR, 16, and in Klare, *War Without End*, 98. For a critical analysis of the Defense Science Board's *Report of the Panel on Defense Social and Behavioral Sciences,* which treats it as evidence of "the ominous conversion of social science into a service industry of the Pentagon," see Irving

Louis Horowitz, "Social Science Yogis & Military Commissars," *Trans-action* 5 (May 1968):29–38.

53. Watson, *War on the Mind*, 307.

54. DDSFAR, pt. 1, testimony of John S. Foster, Jr., Director of Defense Research and Engineering, 10, 18. See also BSNS, testimony of Maj. Gen. John W. Vogt, Director, Policy Planning Staff, Office of the Assistant Secretary of Defense for International Security Affairs, 81–82.

55. For a general discussion of the evolution of these morale studies, and their relationship to the conduct of the Vietnam War, see Watson, *War on the Mind*, 27–28, 265–267, 299–300, 326; and "The RAND Papers," *Ramparts* 11 (November 1972):25–42, 52–62.

56. The source of this oft-repeated phrase appears to be Alexander Leighton, who wrote that "the administrator uses social science the way a drunk uses a lamppost, for support rather than illumination." See Leighton, *Human Relations in a Changing World*, 128. That this phrase had become conventional wisdom among experts and bureaucrats is illustrated by the fact that Thomas L. Hughes, Director of Intelligence and Research, Department of State, from 1963 to 1969, used it, without attribution, almost thirty years later in his "The Fate of Facts in a World of Men," 24. Leighton was a psychiatrist who worked in the Postan, Arizona, Japanese-American relocation center and then headed the Office of War Information's Foreign Morale Analysis Division, set up by the Military Intelligence Service of the War Department in 1944. Leighton and his group of behavioral scientists studied Japanese-Americans, and then Japanese citizens, by taking a "psychiatric approach in problems of community management."

57. Project head Leon Goure, for example, regularly briefed most of the war's top policy-makers—Bundy, McNamara, Rostow, and Westmoreland—and the Viet-Cong Motivation and Morale Project office in Saigon was a central gathering place for high-level bureaucrats passing through South Vietnam. Carl Rowar, former head of the U.S. Information Service, also wrote in 1966 that the VC M&M "lies at the heart of President Johnson's strategy." "The RAND Papers," 60–61.

58. Anthony Russo, "Looking Backward: RAND and Vietnam in Retrospect," *Ramparts* 11 (November 1972):56.

59. D. M. Condit, Bert H. Cooper, Jr., et al., *Challenge and Response in Internal Conflict,* 3 vols. (Washington, D.C.: American University, Center for Research in Social Systems, 1968), xxi–xxii.

60. See *Annotated Bibliography of SORO Publications* (Washington, D.C.: American University, Special Operations Research Office, February 1966); *Annotated Bibliography of CRESS Publications* (Washington, D.C.: American University, Special Operations Research Office, August 1966); *Annotated Bibliography of CRESS Publications* (Washington, D.C.: American University, Special Operations Research Office, April 1969).

61. The study refers repeatedly to World War II attitude investigations like Samuel Stouffer's *The American Soldier.* For an example, see Andrew R. Molnar with Jerry M. Tinker and John D. LeNoir, *Human Factors Considerations of Undergrounds in Insurgencies* (Washington, D.C.: American University, Center for Research in Social Systems, 1966), 80.

62. Hopper, "The Revolutionary Process," 270–279.

63. Molnar with Tinker and LeNoir, *Human Factors Considerations of Undergrounds in Insurgencies,* 270, 274–275.

64. Ted Gurr with Charles Ruttenberg, *Cross-National Studies in Civil Violence* (Washington, D.C.: American University, Center for Research in Social Systems, May 1969), 11–12.

65. M. Gordon et al., "COCON—Counterinsurgency (POLITICA): The Development of a Simulation Model of Internal Conflict under Revolutionary Conflict Conditions," quoted in Cina, "Social Science for Whom?" 326.

66. Cina, "Social Science for Whom?" 331.

67. This comment was made by Iowa congressional representative H. R. Gross during the Camelot hearings. See BSNS, 94.

68. For an example of an ambitious, apolitical vision for psycho-technological aid to defense organizations and policy-making, see Bray, "Toward a Technology of Human Behavior for Defense Use," 527–541. For a spirited critique of this postwar trend in the social sciences, see C. Wright Mills, *The Sociological Imagination* (New York: Oxford University Press, 1959). For an even earlier critique that anticipated these trends, see Lynd, *Knowledge for What?*

69. George A. Lundberg, *Can Science Save Us?* (New York: Longmans, Green and Co., 1947), 38.

70. Horowitz, ed., *The Rise and Fall of Project Camelot,* 48. For some interesting comments on the language of Camelot documents, see Marshall Sahlins, "The Established Order: Do Not Fold, Spindle, or Mutilate," in *The Rise and Fall of Project Camelot,* 77–78.

71. For a portrait of these and other individuals, whose commitments to a military policy informed by behavioral expertise decisively shaped the Vietnam War, see David Halberstam, *The Best and the Brightest* (New York: Penguin Books, 1969).

72. Rensis Likert, "Behavioural Research: A Guide for Effective Action," in *Some Applications of Behavioural Research,* ed. Rensis Likert and Samuel P. Hayes (Paris: UNESCO, 1957), 11.

73. B. F. Skinner, *Beyond Freedom and Dignity* (New York: Alfred A. Knopf, 1971), 67. *Beyond Freedom and Dignity* analyzed the political function of psychology and made explicit recommendations for the public roles of psychological experts. See also B. F. Skinner, "Freedom and the Control of Men," *American Scholar* 25 (Winter 1955–56):47–65.

74. For the argument that, in spite of such challenges, "the military uses of psychology have been pursued with ever more energy and increasing imagination" since the early 1960s, see Watson, *War on the Mind.*

75. Harold D. Lasswell, "Must Science Serve Political Power?" *American Psychologist* 25 (February 1970):119.

76. For comparative data on levels of funding by the DOD and HEW (and other domestically oriented agencies), see National Science Foundation, *Federal Funds for Science,* 1950–62, followed by *Federal Funds for Research, Development, and Other Scientific Activities,* 1962–70.

77. National Science Foundation, *Federal Funds for Science,* 1960, 1961, 1962, p. 100, table 15; *Federal Funds for Research, Development, and Other Scientific Activities: Fiscal Years 1965, 1966, and 1967* 15:102, table C-13.

78. Noam Chomsky, "Intellectuals and the State," in *Towards a New Cold War: Essays on the Current Crisis and How We Got There* (New York: Pantheon Books, 1982), 65.

79. For more of Chomsky's work on the political consequences of social scientific scholarship and the responsibilities of intellectuals, see *American Power and the New Mandarins* (New York: Vintage Books, 1967); *Deterring Democracy* (New York: Hill and Wang, 1991); *For Reasons of State* (New York: Vintage Books, 1970); *Towards a New Cold War: Essays on the Current Crisis and How We Got There* (New York: Pantheon Books, 1982); *Necessary Illusions: Thought Control in Democratic Societies* (Boston: South End Press, 1989). For Chomsky's well-known critique of B. F. Skinner's behaviorism and its political implications, see his review of *Verbal Behavior* by B. F. Skinner, *Language* 35 (January–March 1959):26–58, and "The Case Against B. F. Skinner," *New York Review of Books* 17 (30 December 1971):18–24.

80. 1972 draft of *Blackberry Winter,* quoted in Yans-McLaughlin, "Science, Democracy, and Ethics, 214.

81. For a description of the conference action, see "Psychology and Campus Issues," in Korten, Cook, and Lacey, eds., *Psychology and the Problems of Society,* 366–376. In this instance, protest was leveled not against the foreign area research activities of psychologists, but against a research project being conducted on the student New Left itself by Alexander W. Astin and the American Council on Education.

7: The Damaging Psychology of Race

1. Charles E. Hendry in 1947, quoted in Jackson, *Gunnar Myrdal and America's Conscience,* 281–282. Hendry was the director of the American Jewish Congress's Commission on Community Interrelations, a key source of support and funding for behavioral research on prejudice in the postwar era.

2. The definitive recent work on Myrdal is Jackson, *Gunnar Myrdal and America's Conscience.* Jackson's excellent analysis illuminates not only important biographical issues but *An American Dilemma* itself and its central role in the development of a lasting liberal orthodoxy on race and race relations in the United States. Although not intended to illuminate the history of psychological experts, Jackson's treatment of the origins, course, and eventual failure of racial liberalism shares important characteristics with my description of the World War II worldview and the challenges eventually directed against it.

3. Jackson, *Gunnar Myrdal and America's Conscience,* 32–33.

4. Henry Murray in Milton Senn, "Insights on the Child Development Movement in the United States," quoted in Steve Joshua Heims, *The Cybernetics Group* (Cambridge: MIT Press, 1991), 65. For more on Lawrence K. Frank's life and career, see Margaret Mead's obituary in *American Sociologist* 4 (February 1969):57–58.

5. Walter A. Jackson, "The 'American Creed' from a Swedish Perspective:

The Wartime Context of Gunnar Myrdal's *An American Dilemma*," in *The Estate of Social Knowledge*, ed. Joanne Brown and David K. van Keuren (Baltimore: Johns Hopkins University Press, 1991), 209–227; Jackson, *Gunnar Myrdal and America's Conscience*, chap. 4.

6. Jackson, "The 'American Creed' from a Swedish Perspective," 222; Jackson, *Gunnar Myrdal and America's Conscience*, 163.

7. Gunnar Myrdal to Gustav Cassel, 5 March 1940, quoted in Jackson, "The 'American Creed' from a Swedish Perspective," 214; Jackson, *Gunnar Myrdal and America's Conscience*, 139.

8. Myrdal, *An American Dilemma*, 1022–1024.

9. *To Secure These Rights: The Report of the President's Committee on Civil Rights* (Washington, D.C.: Government Printing Office, 1947), 139.

10. Ibid., 145–146.

11. Myrdal drew scores of U.S. social and behavioral scientists into the project. Of the individuals whose postwar work is addressed at length in this chapter, Kenneth Clark and E. Franklin Frazier were directly involved.

12. Myrdal, *An American Dilemma*, 928, emphasis in original. For amplification, see the section titled "The Negro Community as a Pathological Form of an American Community" in chap. 43.

13. Otto Klineberg, ed., *Characteristics of the American Negro* (New York: Harper & Row, 1944).

14. For a discussion of Klineberg's importance in the debate about race and intelligence during the late 1920s and 1930s, see Carl N. Degler, *In Search of Human Nature: The Decline and Revival of Darwinism in American Social Thought* (New York: Oxford University Press, 1991), 179–186.

15. This is one of Jackson's major conclusions as well. See Jackson, *Gunnar Myrdal and America's Conscience*, esp. chap. 7.

16. Myrdal, *An American Dilemma*, xlvii–xlviii, emphasis in original.

17. See the photograph in Jackson, *Gunnar Myrdal and America's Conscience*, 84.

18. Sissela Bok, *Alva Myrdal: A Daughter's Memoir* (Reading, Mass.: Addison-Wesley, 1991), 159.

19. On the couple's collaborative work and on Alva's wartime views, see Jackson, *Gunnar Myrdal and America's Conscience*, chaps. 2 and 4. During the Myrdals' temporary return to Sweden in 1940–41, they coauthored a book about the United States designed to stiffen the anti-Nazi resolve of the Swedish population. In this book, *Kontakt med Amerika* (Contact with America), they dwelled on the virtues of democratic morale and formulated the outlines of the "American Creed," which would become the central theme in *An American Dilemma*.

20. Myrdal, *An American Dilemma*, 31.

21. The argument of *An American Dilemma* did not face its first serious challenges until the 1960s, when fresh behavioral research suggested that white Americans might not have such guilty consciences after all, and the "American Creed" might not be nearly as powerful a force in shaping white attitudes as Myrdal had hoped. See also Jackson, "The 'American Creed' from a Swedish Perspective," 209–227. Jackson argues that it was Myrdal's own guilty response

to the dilemma of Swedish neutrality that led him to distort and romanticize the "American Creed."

22. Otto Klineberg, "Tests of Negro Intelligence," in *Characteristics of the American Negro*, 23–96. See also his review of personality test studies, on pages 97–138. Carl Degler and Franz Samelson have both suggested that the shift away from a psychology of objective racial differences was largely completed by the time of World War II, perhaps as early as the early 1930s. See Degler, *In Search of Human Nature*, esp. chap. 7; and Samelson, "From 'Race Psychology' to 'Studies in Prejudice,'" 265–278.

23. Rapport also emerged as a significant concern among World War II, and then among Veterans Administration, clinicians, especially white psychiatrists and psychologists who were treating black patients. See, for example, Jerome D. Frank, "Adjustment Problems in Selected Negro Soldiers," *Journal of Nervous and Mental Disease* 105 (January–June 1947):647–660; Ralph W. Heine, "The Negro Patient in Psychotherapy," *Journal of Clinical Psychology* 6 (October 1950):373–376; Harvey R. St. Clair, "Psychiatric Interview Experiences with Negroes," *American Journal of Psychiatry* 108 (August 1951):113–119.

Not surprisingly, the work of black psychologists during World War II also displayed concern with "rapport" between experts and their subjects, even in nonclinical fields. See, for example, Kenneth B. Clark, "Group Violence: A Preliminary Study of the Attitudinal Pattern of Its Acceptance and Rejection: A Study of the 1943 Harlem Riot," *Journal of Social Psychology* 19 (May 1944):320.

Interestingly, the issue of gender rapport, in both clinical treatment and psychological research, was initially overlooked, probably because the vast majority of both wartime experts and subjects were male. As more and more women filled the professional ranks of clinical psychology and social work, however, and as women became more frequent subjects of psychological expertise, conflicting assumptions were sometimes made about the gender dynamics between experts and subjects.

The Bettelheim and Janowitz study, *Dynamics of Prejudice*, discussed below, assumed that female interviewers always had better rapport with male subjects. See Bruno Bettelheim and Morris Janowitz, *Social Change and Prejudice, Including Dynamics of Prejudice* (New York: Free Press of Glencoe, 1964), 114–116. In contrast, the research design of *The Authoritarian Personality* incorporated the view that male subjects would achieve better rapport with male interviewers and female subjects would do better with female interviewers. See Adorno et al., *The Authoritarian Personality*, 301.

24. For an analysis that suggests the early civil rights movement anticipated much of the "new consciousness" of the counterculture, see Robert N. Bellah, "The New Consciousness and the Berkeley New Left," in *The New Religious Consciousness*, ed. Charles Y. Glock and Robert N. Bellah (Berkeley: University of California Press, 1976), 77–92.

25. Walter Jackson points out that Myrdal's analysis of religion in the black community led him to make a very serious error in the otherwise prophetic *An American Dilemma*. Rather than seeing the church as the source of civil rights

activism it would become, he discounted black Americans' religious convictions as overly emotional, a view doubtlessly shaped by his own emphatic secularism. After a field trip to Father Divine's Kingdom in Harlem, he even suggested that the tools of abnormal psychology be applied to the subject! See Jackson, *Gunnar Myrdal and America's Conscience,* 107, 223–224.

26. Myrdal, *An American Dilemma,* 1023.

27. Jackson, *Gunnar Myrdal and America's Conscience,* 281.

28. Gordon W. Allport, *The Nature of Prejudice,* abbr. ed. (Garden City, N.Y.: Doubleday, 1958), chap. 9.

29. Although the view that minority group members were necessarily victimized by their status was adopted as a fundamental assumption of the U.S. legal and educational systems in the postwar decades, this was a new development. For a perspective on important historical shifts in the understanding of the term "minority," see Philip Gleason, "Minorities (Almost) All: The Minority Group Concept in American Social Thought," *American Quarterly* 43 (September 1991):392–424.

30. C. H. Thompson, "The Conclusions of Scientists Relative to Racial Differences," quoted in Otto Klineberg, "Tests of Negro Intelligence," 95.

31. Max Deutscher and Isidor Chein, "The Psychological Effects of Enforced Segregation: A Survey of Social Science Opinion," quoted in Helen Leland Witmer and Ruth Kotinsky, "The Effects of Prejudice and Discrimination," in *Personality in the Making: The Fact-Finding Report of the Midcentury White House Conference on Children and Youth* (New York: Harper & Brothers, 1952), 139.

32. Exceptions to this rule are documented in Newby, *Challenge to the Court.*

33. It was reprinted, along with a number of follow-up essays, in Bettelheim and Janowitz, *Social Change and Prejudice, Including Dynamics of Prejudice.*

34. Ibid., 105.

35. This application of frustration-aggression theory to racial prejudice was not, of course, new after World War II. It had been an essential part of psychoanalytically oriented theoretical works such as John Dollard et al., *Frustration and Aggression.*

36. Bettelheim and Janowitz, *Social Change and Prejudice, Including Dynamics of Prejudice,* 106–107.

37. Ibid., 278.

38. Ibid., 285.

39. Ibid., 289.

40. The epidemic of national destruction supposedly being caused by "momism" was, in large part, a product of the fears that clinical work during World War II produced about the precarious mental state of male soldiers and the decidedly defective mental state of the 1.8 million men who had been rejected from the military for psychiatric reasons. After the war, as clinicians' client base shifted from male veterans to their female kin, "momism" came to denote the notion that mothers were responsible for male neurosis, which was, in turn, responsible for social and political problems ranging from McCarthyite

hysteria to labor strife, political corruption, alcoholism, sexual perversion, and war. See Philip Wylie, "Common Women," in *Generation of Vipers* (New York: Pocket Books, 1942), 184–206. Wylie coined the term "momism." For a general discussion of the importance of postwar gender and family ideology, see Elaine Tyler May, *Homeward Bound: American Families in the Cold War Era* (New York: Basic Books, 1988).

41. There is good reason to wonder whether "matriarchy" existed at any point in the history of black American families. For example, even at the height of the "black matriarchy" debate during the mid-1960s, approximately 75 percent of black families included male breadwinners, conforming to the patriarchal nuclear norm. I nevertheless include the term "matriarchy" in my discussion because it was the term used at the time.

42. Julius Horwitz, "The Arithmetic of Delinquency," *New York Times Magazine* (31 January 1965):52.

43. Ibid., 54–55.

44. The major statement on this issue was, of course, Friedrich Engels's *The Origin of the Family, Private Property and the State* (1891). While this work, and the historical specificity of the relationship between women's subordination and capitalism, would become a major theoretical preoccupation within the socialist-feminist wing of the second wave of feminism, it was typically treated as an ahistorical and universal truth—a fact to be asserted rather than explained—at the time Frazier's study was published. That Frazier took pains to make the connection between capitalism and patriarchy explicit recalled elements of Engels's analysis (although Engels was not cited anywhere) and made his book something of an exception to the rule. See especially the treatments of family economy and property rights in E. Franklin Frazier, *The Negro Family in the United States* (Chicago: University of Chicago Press, 1939), chaps. 9 and 10. On Frazier's complex amalgam of left-wing politics, see Walter A. Jackson, "Between Socialism and Nationalism," *Reconstruction* 1 (1991): 124–134.

45. "Motherhood in Bondage" is the title of chapter 3 in Frazier, *The Negro Family in the United States.*

46. "Roving Men and Homeless Women" is the title of chapter 13 in Frazier, *The Negro Family in the United States.* "In the City of Destruction" is the title of part 4 of the book.

47. "Social engineering" was a term used by Kardiner and Ovesey themselves. See Abram Kardiner and Lionel Ovesey, *The Mark of Oppression: Explorations in the Personality of the American Negro* (Cleveland: World Publishing Company, 1951), xiii.

48. Ibid., 54.

49. Ibid., 65.

50. Ibid., 297.

51. Ibid., 387, emphasis in original.

52. Ibid., 310.

53. Kenneth B. Clark, *Dark Ghetto: Dilemmas of Social Power* (New York: Harper & Row, 1965), 47–50.

54. Ibid., 70.

55. Ibid., 70–74, section titled "The Negro Matriarchy and the Distorted Masculine Image."

56. Although they published several articles in 1939 and 1940 on the topic of segregation, racial identification, and sense of self in young black children, two later articles seem to have made the deepest impression on policy-makers, if published references to them are any indication. These were Kenneth B. Clark and Mamie P. Clark, "Racial Identification and Preference in Negro Children," in Theodore M. Newcomb and Eugene L. Hartley, eds., *Readings in Social Psychology*, rev. ed. (New York: Holt, 1952), 551–560, and "Emotional Factors in Racial Identification and Preference in Negro Children," *Journal of Negro Education* 19 (1950):341–350.

57. Clark and Clark, "Emotional Factors in Racial Identification and Preference in Negro Children," 342.

58. Ibid., 350.

59. Ibid.

60. Witmer and Kotinsky, "The Effects of Prejudice and Discrimination," 135–158. This document can also be found, in somewhat revised form, in Kenneth B. Clark, *Prejudice and Your Child*, 2nd ed. (Boston: Beacon Press, 1963), pts. 1 and 2.

61. Clark, *Prejudice and Your Child*, 61, 63.

62. Quoted in Richard Kluger, *Simple Justice: The History of* Brown v. Board of Education *and Black America's Struggle for Equality* (New York: Alfred A. Knopf, 1987), 316. The state of South Carolina apparently tried to line up some expert testimony too, but was unable to find a single, well-known figure willing to testify in favor of segregation, more evidence of how overwhelming the civil rights consensus was among social and behavioral scientists by the early 1950s.

63. It is probable that Kenneth Clark took on this job because of Mamie Clark's connections to a number of the professionals involved in the state-level cases. After graduating from college, she had worked as a secretary in the law office of William Houston, a "hub" of National Association for the Advancement of Colored People's Legal Defense Fund activity. See Mamie Clark's autobiography in Agnes N. O'Connell and Nancy Felipe Russo, eds., *Models of Achievement: Reflections on Eminent Women in Psychology* (New York: Columbia University Press, 1983), 266–277.

64. *Briggs V. Elliott*, quoted in Newby, *Challenge to the Court*, 29–30.

65. Kenneth Clark to Gordon Allport, 30 July 1953, HUG 4118.10, folder: "1951–53, Ca-Cn," GA Papers. A summary of these events is offered in Otto Klineberg, "SPSSI and Race Relations, in the 1950s and After," *Journal of Social Issues* 42 (Winter 1986):53–59. For Kenneth Clark's description, see "The Role of the Social Sciences in Desegregation," in Clark, *Prejudice and Your Child*, 210–214, app. 5. For a general discussion of the role of social-scientific experts in *Brown*, see Jackson, *Gunnar Myrdal and America's Conscience*, 292–293.

66. "The Effects of Segregation and the Consequences of Desegregation: A Social Science Statement," *Minnesota Law Review* 37 (1952–53):427–429. Also reprinted in Clark, *Prejudice and Your Child*, app. 3.

67. "The Effects of Segregation and the Consequences of Desegregation: A Social Science Statement," 438, 429.

68. Gordon Allport to Kenneth Clark, 4 August 1953, HUG 4118.10, folder: "1951–53, Ca-Cn," GA Papers. See also Gordon Allport, "Backgrounds—Radio Talk on the Supreme Court Ruling," HUG 4118.10, folder: "Supreme Court Ruling, May 1954," GA Papers.

69. *Brown v. Board of Education*, 34 U.S. 494. The full text of this opinion is also reprinted in Clark, *Prejudice and Your Child*, app. 2.

70. *Brown v. Board of Education*, 34 U.S. 494–495.

71. For more on segregationist social science, see Newby, *Challenge to the Court*. For McCarthyite equations between racial liberalism and socialism, see Jackson, *Gunnar Myrdal and America's Conscience*, 292–293. Because *Brown* cited his work, Gunnar Myrdal was denounced by Mississippi Senator James Eastland as a "Swedish socialist" and editorialists across the South accused him of membership in the international Communist conspiracy.

72. For mention of one such effort, see "The Desegregation Cases: Criticism of the Social Scientist's Role," in Clark, *Prejudice and Your Child*, 206, app. 4, n. 12.

73. Kenneth Clark to Gordon Allport, 7 June 1954, HUG 4118.10, folder: "1954–57, Ca-Cn," GA Papers.

74. Stuart W. Cook, "The 1954 Social Science Statement and School Desegregation: A Reply to Gerard," *American Psychologist* 39 (August 1984):830. Cook was responding to the criticisms expressed in Harold B. Gerard, "School Desegregation: the Social Science Role," *American Psychologist* 38 (August 1983):869–877.

Kenneth Clark never gave in to criticisms of experts' role in *Brown*. In the face of early criticism, in the late 1950s and early 1960s, Clark insisted that "the collaboration between psychologists and other social scientists which culminated in the *Brown* decision will continue in spite of criticism" because the goals of law, government, and social science were identical, "to secure for man personal fulfillment in a just, stable, and viable society." See "The Desegregation Cases: Criticism of the Social Scientist's Role," 205, app. 4. A decade later, Clark still forcefully defended the effort he had spearheaded in the early 1950s. "This citation [footnote no. 11] demonstrated dramatically that the theories and research findings of social scientists could influence public policy decisions on educational and other problems." Kenneth B. Clark, "Social Policy, Power, and Social Science Research," *Harvard Educational Review* 43 (February 1973):113–121.

75. Such questions remain the subject of intense debate. See, for example, J. G. Morawski, "Psychology and the Shaping of Policy," *Berkshire Review* 18 (1983):92–117, and the response to Morawski by Saul Kassin, which mentions *Brown*, among other examples.

76. Robert Lindner, *The Fifty-Minute Hour* (New York: Bantam Books, 1955). See especially the case of Mac, the Communist party member whom Lindner met at a civil rights meeting. This case is also a useful illustration of how readily political commitments of any sort—integrationist, socialist, whatever—were interpreted in psychological terms, even by a sympathetic psychoanalyst.

77. For an interesting discussion of how psychological research and theory shaped the various responses of policy-makers to rising rates of nonmarital pregnancy among both black and white women after 1945, a social problem with dimensions that were explicitly sexual as well as racial, see Rickie Solinger, *Wake Up Little Susie: Single Pregnancy and Race Before Roe v. Wade* (New York: Routledge, 1992), esp. chaps. 3 and 6.

78. One of the best overviews of the Moynihan Report is Lee Rainwater and William L. Yancey, *The Moynihan Report and the Politics of Controversy* (Cambridge: MIT Press, 1967). It includes the entire text of the report itself, a number of important contemporary responses to the report, and a comprehensive analysis of the controversy. A discussion of the continuing salience of Moynihan's ideas about the black family during the neoconservative revival of the 1970s and 1980s, which stressed "family values" and "self-help" as goals in welfare reform, can be found in Carl Ginsburg, *Race and Media: The Enduring Life of the Moynihan Report* (New York: Institute for Media Analysis, 1989).

79. The term "social scientist-politico" is from Rainwater and Yancey, *The Moynihan Report and the Politics of Controversy,* 18, 262. Other terms included "idea broker," "scientific diagnostician," and "scholar-politician." See "Light in the Frightening Corners," *Time* 90 (28 July 1967):10–15; Fred Powledge, "Idea Broker in the Race Crisis," *Life* 63 (3 November 1967):72–80; Thomas Meehan, "Moynihan of the Moynihan Report," *New York Times Magazine,* 31 July 1966, 5.

80. Daniel Patrick Moynihan, *Family and Nation* (New York: Harcourt, Brace, Jovanovich, 1987), 18.

81. Lisa Hsiao, "Project 100,000: The Great Society's Answer to Military Manpower Needs in Vietnam," *Vietnam Generation* 1 (Summer 1989):14. Hsiao uses Project 100,000 to argue that, even during the War on Poverty, a high point in the history of the U.S. welfare state, the government's prosecution of the Vietnam War was used as a critically important institutional vehicle of domestic social welfare goals. Further, the government officially recognized the social welfare and gender socialization functions of the Department of Defense and some of the goals of the War on Poverty were transferred, at least in theory, to the military. In less than three years (the program lasted five years and was officially terminated in 1972), approximately 250,000 men had been recruited under the program, most from low-income, female-headed families. The vast majority were high school dropouts with very poor literacy skills. Close to 40 percent were black, compared to 8 percent of the military population overall. Although the stated purpose of the program was to provide education and training, over 40 percent received combat assignments in Vietnam and only 7.5 percent received extra benefits.

82. Among professional historians, Stanley Elkins offered the personality-destroying portrait of slavery that was most compatible with E. Franklin Frazier's thesis in *The Negro Family in the United States.* Elkins's book *Slavery,* published in 1959, was also one of Moynihan's major sources for his report on the black family.

83. Daniel Patrick Moynihan, *The Negro Family: The Case for National Action* (Washington, D.C.: Office of Policy Planning and Research, United States Department of Labor, March 1965), 5, 29, 42–43.

84. Nathan Glazer and Daniel Patrick Moynihan, *Beyond the Melting Pot: The Negroes, Puerto Ricans, Jews, Italians, and Irish of New York City* (Cambridge: MIT and Harvard University Press, 1963).

85. "Light in the Frightening Corners," 12.

86. Daniel P. Moynihan, "The President & the Negro: The Moment Lost," *Commentary* 43 (February 1967):31–45.

87. Bayard Rustin and Daniel Patrick Moynihan, *Which Way? A Discussion of Racial Tensions* (New York: The America Press, 1966), 23–24.

88. Mary Dublin Keyserling, "The Negro Woman at Work: Gains and Problems," 3, speech given 11 November 1965 to the Conference on the Negro Woman in the U.S.A., in Mary Dublin Keyserling Papers, Schlesinger Library, Radcliffe College, Cambridge, Massachusetts.

89. Tracey A. Fitzgerald, *The National Council of Negro Women and the Feminist Movement, 1935–1975* (Washington, D.C.: Georgetown University Press, 1985), 42.

90. Important feminist responses to the ideas of the Moynihan Report included Angela Davis, "Reflections on the Black Woman's Role in the Community of Slaves," *Black Scholar* 3 (December 1971):2–15.

91. William Ryan, "Mammy Observed: Fixing the Black Family," in *Blaming the Victim* (New York: Vintage Books, 1971), 76–77. This was based on Ryan's 1965 critique. See William Ryan, "Savage Discovery: The Moynihan Report," *The Nation* 201 (22 November 1965):380–384. Another prominent civil rights movement critic was Rev. Benjamin Payton. See Benjamin Payton, "New Trends in Civil Rights," *Christianity in Crisis* (13 December 1965), reprinted in Rainwater and Yancey, *The Moynihan Report and the Politics of Controversy*, 395–402.

92. This phrase was William Ryan's. See his *Blaming the Victim* (New York: Vintage Books, 1971). Two notable exceptions to the rule that civil rights activists and leaders took positions critical of Moynihan were Bayard Rustin and Kenneth Clark, although Clark later changed his mind and went so far as to support Moynihan's Republican opponent in his first run for the Senate in 1976. See Bayard Rustin, "A Way Out of the Exploding Ghetto," in *Down the Line: The Collected Writings of Bayard Rustin*, ed. C. Vann Woodward (Chicago: Quadrangle Books, 1971), 178–186, originally published in the *New York Times Magazine*, 13 August 1967; Rustin and Moynihan, *Which Way?*; Douglas Schoen, *Pat: A Biography of Daniel Patrick Moynihan* (New York: Harper & Row, 1979), 166, 258.

93. Interestingly, Moynihan seems to have been deeply influenced by Alva Myrdal's and Gunnar Myrdal's ideas about family policy and inspired by their successful example of turning conservative fears of population decline and family disorganization to the progressive purpose of constructing a comprehensive welfare state. One of Moynihan's recent books, *Family and Nation* (1987), recalls the title of Alva Myrdal's *Nation and Family* (1941). Moynihan wrote the introduction to the 1968 MIT Press paperback reissue.

94. For his analysis of this failure, see Moynihan, *Family and Nation;* Daniel Patrick Moynihan, *Maximum Feasible Misunderstanding: Community Action in the War on Poverty* (New York: The Free Press, 1969); Moynihan, "The President & the Negro," 31–45.

95. Daniel P. Moynihan, "Text of 'Benign Neglect' Memorandum on the Status of Negroes," *New York Times*, 1 March 1970, 69.

96. Moynihan, "The President & the Negro," 35.

97. Moynihan, *Family and Nation*, 26.

98. Rainwater and Yancey, *The Moynihan Report and the Politics of Controversy*, 26.

99. On the numbers of copies printed and circulated, see Rainwater and Yancey, *The Moynihan Report and the Politics of Controversy*, 26, 151–152, 158.

100. *Wall Street Journal*, 16 August 1965; *Washington Post*, 23 August 1965. For a discussion of the role played by the establishment press in publicizing and perpetuating Moynihan's ideas, see Ginsburg, *Race and Media*.

101. Moynihan, "The President & the Negro," 38–39.

102. Powledge, "Idea Broker in the Race Crisis," 72.

103. "Light in the Frightening Corners," 12.

8: The Kerner Commission and the Experts

1. "Mass treatment programs" was the term used by Bettelheim and Janowitz to describe community-based social welfare programs in their 1964 follow-up to *Dynamics of Prejudice*. See Bettelheim and Janowitz, *Social Change and Prejudice, Including Dynamics of Prejudice*, 92.

2. Joint Commission on Mental Illness and Health, *Annual Report*, 1956, quoted in Grob, *From Asylum to Community*, 197.

3. Kenneth B. Clark, "Problems of Power and Social Change: Toward a Relevant Social Psychology," *Journal of Social Issues* 21 (July 1965):11.

4. Three other presidential commissions investigated crime and civil disturbance and published reports. They were the President's Commission on Law Enforcement and the Administration of Justice (*The Challenge of Crime in a Free Society*, 1967); the National Commission on the Causes and Prevention of Violence (*To Establish Justice, To Insure Domestic Tranquility*, 1969); the President's Commission on Campus Unrest (*Report of the President's Commission on Campus Unrest*, 1970, also known as the Scranton Report).

5. "Excerpts from President Lyndon B. Johnson's Address to the Nation on Civil Disorder, July 27, 1967," in *Report of the National Advisory Commission on Civil Disorders* (New York: Bantam Books, 1968), app. C, 539. The full text of this broadcast can also be found in the KC Archives, reel 18, pp. 673–677.

6. "Remarks of the President Upon Issuing an Executive Order Establishing a National Advisory Commission on Civil Disorders, July 29, 1967," in *Report of the National Advisory Commission on Civil Disorders*, app. B, 536–537.

7. Ibid., app. B, 537.

8. Robert Shellow, "Social Scientists and Social Action from within the Establishment," *Journal of Social Issues* 26 (Winter 1970):207–208.

9. Ibid., 208.

10. Ibid., 208–209.

11. "Review Symposium," *American Political Science Review* 63 (December 1969):1281.

12. Erik H. Erikson, "A Memorandum on Identity and Negro Youth," in *A Way of Looking at Things,* 650. This piece was originally published in the *Journal of Social Issues* in 1964. See also Erik H. Erikson, "The Concept of Identity in Race Relations: Notes and Queries," *Daedalus* 95 (Winter 1966):145–171.

One interesting example of how difficult Erikson found it to understand black nationalism in anything but negative psychological terms is his published dialogue with Huey Newton. See Erik H. Erikson and Huey P. Newton, *In Search of Common Ground: Conversations with Erik H. Erikson & Huey P. Newton* (New York: W. W. Norton, 1973). Rather than an exchange of ideas, one has the impression that Erikson and Newton did not understand each other at all: Newton kept trying to explain the Black Panther party's ideology while Erikson offered a psychohistorical interpretation of military symbolism in Newton's life and its resonance with U.S. historical themes of westward expansion and conquest.

13. James P. Comer, "Individual Development and Black Rebellion: Some Parallels," *Midway* 9 (Summer 1968):33–48.

14. Alvin F. Poussaint, "A Negro Psychiatrist Explains the Negro Psyche," in *Being Black: Psychological-Sociological Dilemmas,* ed. Robert V. Guthrie (San Francisco: Canfield Press, 1970), 15–25. This piece was reprinted from the *New York Times Magazine,* 20 August 1967. See also Alvin F. Poussaint, "The Negro American: His Self-Image and Integration," in *The Black Power Revolt: A Collection of Essays,* ed. Floyd B. Barbour (Boston: Porter Sargent, 1968), 94–102. For another example from two other black psychiatrists, see William H. Grier and Price M. Cobbs, *Black Rage* (New York: Bantam Books, 1968).

Interestingly, Abram Kardiner, one of the authors of *The Mark of Oppression,* contributed an article to a collection compiled in the wake of Project Camelot about the monitoring and prediction of global revolution and upheaval. Kardiner argued that the extreme rage and self-hatred among black Americans qualified them as a population armed with tremendous amounts of aggression, and therefore revolutionary potential. See Abram Kardiner, "Models for the Study of Collapse of Social Homeostasis in a Society," in *The Study of Total Societies,* 177–190.

15. Martin Luther King, Jr., "Letter from Birmingham Jail," in *Why We Can't Wait* (New York: New American Library, 1963), 82, 81.

16. For example, see the important 1966 transitional document, "Position of the Student Nonviolent Coordinating Committee," in *A History of Our Time,* ed. William H. Chafe and Harvard Sitkoff, 3rd ed. (New York: Oxford University Press, 1991), 198–202.

17. Eldridge Cleaver, "On Becoming," in *Soul on Ice* (New York: Delta, 1968), 3–17.

18. Walter Truett Anderson, *The Upstart Spring: Esalen and the American Awakening* (Reading, Mass.: Addison-Wesley, 1983), 162–164, 195–199.

19. Quoted in Garry Wills, "The Second Civil War," *Esquire* 69 (March 1968):142.

20. Jesse Jackson to Mayor Richard J. Daley, 2 August 1967, KC Archives, reel 13, p. 1018.

21. The eleven commissioners were Illinois governor Otto Kerner (chairman), New York mayor John Lindsay (vice-chairman), Oklahoma senator Fred Harris, Massachusetts senator Edward Brooke, California representative James Corman, Ohio representative William McCulloch, United Steelworkers of America president I. W. Abel, Litton Industries CEO Charles Thornton, NAACP executive director Roy Wilkins, former Kentucky commissioner of commerce Katherine Graham Peden, and Atlanta chief of police Herbert Jenkins.

22. Andrew Kopkind, "White on Black: The Riot Commission and the Rhetoric of Reform," in *The Politics of Riot Commissions, 1917–1970: A Collection of Official Reports and Critical Essays,* ed. Anthony Platt (New York: Macmillan, 1971), 381. This article was originally published in *Hard Times*, 15–22 September 1969.

23. Jerome H. Skolnick, "Violence Commission Violence," *Trans-action* 7 (October 1970):33. Menninger was appointed to the National Commission on the Causes and Prevention of Violence.

24. *Report of the National Advisory Commission on Civil Disorders,* 1.

25. Michael Lipsky and David J. Olson, *Commission Politics: The Processing of Racial Crisis in America* (New Brunswick: Transaction Books, 1977), 135.

26. Ibid., 137 n. 37.

27. Arthur Brayfield to Fred Harris, 14 August 1967, KC Archives, reel 14, p. 371. In his letter to Harris, Brayfield praised the credentials of a number of other psychological experts as well, some of whom—Rensis Likert and David McClelland, to mention only two—were important figures in World War II and Cold War psychology, reviewed in earlier chapters.

28. *Supplemental Studies for the National Advisory Commission on Civil Disorders* (New York: Frederick A. Praeger, 1968).

29. Lipsky and Olson, *Commission Politics,* 203–204 n. 57.

30. Kopkind, "White on Black," 382; Lipsky and Olson, *Commission Politics,* 120.

31. I could find only a single mention of the Vietnam War in the text of the final report, and the gist of it was that the country had enough money to conduct the war *and* eliminate social problems at home, a conclusion disputed, in 1967, by antiwar and civil rights activists alike. See *Report of the National Advisory Commission on Civil Disorders,* 411.

32. Descriptive material on ten cities ended up in the final report, concentrated in chapter 1, "Profiles of Disorder."

33. Memo from Robert Shellow to David Ginsburg, 17 January 1968, KC Archives, reel 18, pp. 346–349.

34. Angus Campbell and Howard Schuman, "Racial Attitudes in Fifteen American Cities," in *Supplemental Studies for the National Advisory Commission on Civil Disorders,* 1–67.

35. For a brief, general description of the National Institute of Mental Health "mass violence" studies, see John Gardner's statement to the Kerner Commission, 1 August 1967, KC Archives, reel 1, p. 371.

36. "Is Mass Violence an Epidemic Disease?" *Medical World News* 8 (1 September 1967):38–48, in KC Archives, reel 16, pp. 293–296; Elliot Luby et al., "The Detroit Riot: Some Characteristics of Those on the Street," *Psychiatric Opinion* 5 (June 1968):29–35; Richard D. Lyons, "Riots Laid to Old Hates," *New York Times,* 6 August 1967, 1, 51; United Press International summary of Detroit Study, KC Archives, reel 16, p. 152.

37. "Summary of October 27 Meeting of Survey Research Scientists Active in Studies of Negro-White Attitudes," KC Archives, reel 7, pp. 394–402; memo from Henry B. Taliaferro, Jr., to Arnold Sagalyn, Milan Miskovsky, and Victor Palmieri, 27 October 1967, KC Archives, reel 11, pp. 45–46; D. P. Gerlach, "The U.S.A. and Revolutionary Social Movements," 26 October 1967, KC Archives, reel 11, pp. 58–61. The design of an "Index of Negro Dissatisfaction" was an old project of the Lemberg Center for the Study of Violence at Brandeis University, a research center whose work was widely used by Kerner Commission experts. See, for example, Lemberg Center for the Study of Violence, Brandeis University, *Annual Report to the Board of Overseers* (1968), 13.

38. Memo from Louise Sagalyn to Victor Palmieri, 11 October 1967, KC Archives, reel 22, pp. 622–626; Charles A. Pinderhughes, "Pathogenic Social Structure: A Prime Target for Preventive Psychiatric Intervention," *Journal of the National Medical Association* 58 (November 1966):424–429; Charles A. Pinderhughes and Herbert O. Levine, "The Psychology of Adolescents in a Peaceful Protest and in an Urban Riot," 6 November 1967, KC Archives, reel 27, pp. 511–549.

39. Kopkind, "White on Black," 379; Lipsky and Olson, *Commission Politics,* 169; Skolnick, "Violence Commission Violence," 33. At its peak strength, the Kerner Commission staff numbered 191.

40. The term "social science input" was part of the work culture of the Kerner Commission itself, and can be found frequently in its records.

41. Shellow, "Social Scientists and Social Action from within the Establishment," 213. This anecdote is reported by another member of the Kerner Commission social science staff in Gary T. Marx, "Two Cheers for the National Riot Commission," in *Black America,* ed. John F. Szwed (New York: Basic Books, 1970), 96 n. 24.

42. David Burnham, "New Urban Riots Foreseen in U.S.," *New York Times,* 30 December 1967, 21.

43. Ibid.

44. "The Secretary of Health, Education, and Welfare," *American Psychologist* 20 (October 1965):811–814.

45. Draft of John Gardner's statement to the Kerner Commission, 1 August 1967, KC Archives, reel 1, pp. 87–88.

46. *Report of the National Advisory Commission on Civil Disorders,* 483.

47. Kenneth Clark statement to the Kerner Commission, 13 September 1967, KC Archives, reel 3, pp. 139–140.

48. Elliot Liebow, *Tally's Corner: A Study of Streetcorner Men* (Boston: Little, Brown and Company, 1967).

49. Ibid., 214.

50. Elliot Liebow statement to the Kerner Commission, 9 November 1967, KC Archives, reel 5, pp. 967–968.

51. Matthew P. Dumont, "The Role of Youth Groups in the Minority Community," in *The Absurd Healer: Perspectives of a Community Psychiatrist* (New York: Viking, 1968), 149–155.

52. Ibid., 154.

53. One of the very few examples I could find of commission experts asking questions about the gender of rioters was in Robert H. Fogelson and Robert Hill, "Who Riots? A Study of Participation in the 1967 Riots," in *Supplemental Studies for the National Advisory Commission on Civil Disorders,* 234–235. Fogelson and Hill at least speculated about whether police were less likely to arrest women, therefore making female rioters less visible rather than nonexistent. They concluded, however, that rioters were, overwhelmingly, male and young.

54. Grob, *From Asylum to Community;* Miller and Rose, eds., *The Power of Psychiatry,* 1–42.

55. For example, see Leigh M. Roberts, Seymour L. Halleck, and Martin B. Loeb, eds., *Community Psychiatry* (New York: Anchor Books, 1966), 3, 7.

56. Leonard J. Duhl and Robert L. Leopold, "Relationship of Psychoanalysis with Social Agencies: Community Implications," in *Modern Psychoanalysis: New Directions and Perspectives,* ed. Judd Marmor (New York: Basic Books, 1968), 579.

57. See, for example, Judd Marmor, "Some Psychosocial Aspects of Contemporary Urban Violence," in *Psychiatry in Transition: Selected Papers* (New York: Brunner/Mazel, 1974), 406–415.

58. "The City as Patient" is the title of chapter 4, on urban riots, in Dumont, *The Absurd Healer.*

59. The most recent, comprehensive historical analysis of this significant policy shift can be found in Grob, *From Asylum to Community.* Grob is critical of the postwar shift toward community mental health policy. He argues that, because it was based on utopian hopes and untested assumptions about the nature of mental illness, it abandoned responsibility for the needs of severely and chronically mentally ill, institutionalized individuals, and did little or nothing to treat them or provide an integrated system of long-term care. Instead, it generated new demands for clinical services among healthy, or mildly maladjusted, individuals, serving mainly to extend the reach of psychological expertise to new populations who needed it least. He is careful to point out, however, that such negative consequences were not by any means the intention of malevolent policy-makers or uncaring clinicians, nor could they have been anticipated at the time. The failure of the mental health system to serve truly mentally ill people is, in this instance, simply an example of Grob's generally tragic interpretation of history, which emphasizes the predictably unpredictable effects of human action.

60. Robert Reiff, "Social Intervention and the Problem of Psychological

Analysis," Presidential Address to the Division of Community Psychology, 2 September 1967, KC Archives, reel 21, p. 876.

61. Dumont, *The Absurd Healer,* 50.

62. Fred Harris, for example, later titled a series of essays on federal urban policy, "Sick Cities . . . And the Search for a Cure." See Harris, ed., *Social Science and National Policy,* pt. 1.

63. Dumont, *The Absurd Healer,* 74–75.

64. V. H. Mark, W. H. Sweet, and F. R. Ervin, "Role of Brain Disease in Riots and Urban Violence," letter to the editor, *Journal of the American Medical Association* 201 (11 September 1967):217.

65. Robert N. McMurry, "Permissiveness and the Riot-Prone," *Psychiatric Opinion* 5 (June 1968):14.

66. Ibid., 13, emphasis in original.

67. Ibid., 18.

68. Dumont, *The Absurd Healer,* 125.

69. For an interesting early example, based largely on Allport's and Postman's efforts, see Joseph D. Lohman, *The Police and Minority Groups: A Manual Prepared for Use in the Chicago Park District Police Training School* (Chicago: Chicago Park District, 1947). For an example of 1960s police training in "preventive mental health," see Morton Bard, "Alternatives to Traditional Law Enforcement," in *Psychology and the Problems of Society,* 128–132. Bard concludes that "police departments might be structured along the lines of highly flexible service organizations without in any way compromising their basic law enforcement mission."

70. FBI director J. Edgar Hoover statement to the Kerner Commission, 1 August 1967, KC Archives, reel 1, p. 252.

71. Federal Bureau of Investigation, *Prevention and Control of Mobs and Crowds* (Washington, D.C., 1967), esp. chaps. 2–4, sections on "Crowds and Their Behavior," "The Riot Pattern," "Characteristics of a Riot," and "The Police Role in Preventing Riots."

72. For an explicit rejection of therapeutic analogies in law enforcement because of a comparison between foreign counterinsurgency and the occupation of ghettos by domestic police forces, see Howard Zinn to Kerner Commission, 4 November 1967, KC Archives, reel 11, pp. 422–423.

73. Kenneth Keniston, "How Community Mental Health Stamped Out the Riots (1968–78)," *Trans-action* 5 (July-August 1968):20–29.

74. Ibid., 28, emphasis in original.

75. Mabry Blaylock to Fred Harris, 5 August 1967, KC Archives, reel 14, pp. 82–90; Robert Jackson to the Kerner Commission, 27 August 1967, KC Archives, reel 13, pp. 861–862; Ulric Haynes, Jr., to Lyndon Johnson, 8 April 1968, in *Black Studies Research Sources: Microfilms from Major Archival Manuscript Collections,* August Meier and John H. Bracey, Jr., eds., *Civil Rights Under the Johnson Administration, 1963–1969,* pt. 1, White House Files, reel 5, pp. 2–3; Rector L. Smith to the Kerner Commission, 8 August 1967, KC Archives, reel 14, pp. 120–122.

76. Memo from Executive Director to the Commission, 22 December

1967, in *Black Studies Research Sources: Microfilms from Major Archival Manuscript Collections,* August Meier and John H. Bracey, Jr., eds., *Civil Rights Under the Johnson Administration,* 1963–1969, pt. 1, White House Files, reel 10, p. 148, emphasis in original.

77. Ted Gurr, "Urban Disorder: Perspective from the Comparative Study of Civil Strife," *American Behavioral Scientist* 11 (March-April 1968):50–55. This issue of the *American Behavioral Scientist* was edited by Kerner Commission consultant Louis H. Masotti and reported on a number of riot studies that had been sponsored by the military, or cooperatively sponsored by military and civilian bureaucracies. Gurr's study was funded by the Center for Research into Social Systems and the Department of Defense's Advanced Research Projects Agency (ARPA). William McCord's and John Howard's survey, "Negro Opinions in Three Riot Cities," to mention another example, was funded jointly by the Texas Department of Mental Health and ARPA.

78. Lipsky and Olson, *Commission Politics,* 179.

79. Memo on military's "Directly Related Experience," n.d., KC Archives, reel 11, pp. 24–31.

80. Wills, "The Second Civil War," 71–81, 136–151. For example, see Col. Rex Applegate's discussion of the indebtedness of riot experts to World War II–era military materials and his criticism of the FBI role in riot training.

81. For documentation and analysis of behavioralism in postwar political science, see Ricci, *The Tragedy of Political Science,* chap. 5; and Seybold, "The Ford Foundation and the Triumph of Behavioralism in American Political Science," 269–303.

82. Neil J. Smelser, *Theory of Collective Behavior* (New York: Free Press, 1962); Ralph H. Turner and Lewis M. Killian, *Collective Behavior* (Engelwood Cliffs, N.J.: Prentice-Hall, 1957). Smelser called collective behavior "crude," "excessive," and eccentric," the expression of impulses normally repressed. He maintained that Freudian psychology was a necessary element of its analysis. For especially clear examples of the persistence in the postwar era of ideas not unlike Gustave Le Bon's in the late nineteenth century, see Turner and Killian, chap. 4, "Social Contagion," and chap. 5, "The Forms of Crowd Behavior."

83. *Report of the National Advisory Commission on Civil Disorders,* chap. 2. Chapter 2, "Patterns of Disorder," is followed by almost fifty pages of statistical footnotes. It is an excellent example of how social and behavioral data was concentrated and presented to confer a feeling of solidity and numerical fact upon the final report.

84. These terms were lifted directly out of general theories like Turner's and Killian's. See, for example, Hans W. Mattick, "The Form and Content of Recent Riots," *Midway* 9 (Summer 1968):3–32. Mattick was a University of Chicago Law School professor who was hired by the Kerner Commission after Robert Shellow and the in-house research team members were fired. His typology also included the possibility of a "rational" riot, caused by objective grievances and characterized by clear goals.

85. Clark, "Group Violence," 319–337. Clark found that 60 percent of the

black Harlem residents interviewed one month following the riot condemned this type of group violence out of hand, but a full 30 percent were willing to justify and defend it.

86. Clark, *Dark Ghetto*, 15.

87. Kenneth B. Clark, " 'The Wonder Is There Have Been So Few Riots,' " *New York Times Magazine*, 5 September 1965, 10.

88. Gary T. Marx, "Civil Disorder and the Agents of Social Control," in *Muckraking Sociology: Research as Social Criticism*, ed. Gary T. Marx (New Brunswick: Transaction Books, 1972), 75–97. Another example of psychological tests and models applied to police can be found in David Bayley and Harold Mendelsohn, *Minorities and the Police: Confrontation in America* (New York: Free Press, 1969). Bayley and Mendelsohn administered standard measures such as the F Scale in order to understand the personalities and "perceptual world" of police officers. What they discovered was a chronically doubtful, anxious, and suspicious self-image.

89. Robert Kapsis et al., *The Reconstruction of a Riot: A Case Study of Community Tensions and Civil Disorder* (Waltham, Mass.: Brandeis University, Lemberg Center for the Study of Violence, 1970), 51–52, 58–60, 62–69.

90. Lipsky and Olson, *Commission Politics*, 38.

91. Ibid., 77, chap. 11.

92. The number of riots in 1967 was 164, according to the Kerner Commission's experts, but they admitted that definitions of "civil disorder" varied widely enough for the total to range between 51 and 217, and they settled for a rough categorization of "major," "serious," and "minor" disorders. See *Report of the National Advisory Commission on Civil Disorders*, 112–113, 158–159.

93. Quoted in Lipsky and Olson, *Commission Politics*, 16.

94. The Kerner Commission did not systematically exclude McCone-type theories, but analysis that blamed criminal "riffraff," black nationalists, or Communist agitators for civil disturbances was rare. For an exception to this rule, see J. Edgar Hoover statement to the Kerner Commission, 1 August 1967, KC Archives, reel 1, pp. 249–316. Hoover emphatically blamed black power advocates like H. Rap Brown and Stokely Carmichael for inciting violence, suggested that civil rights leaders like Martin Luther King served the evil purposes of communism, and concluded that riots were often the work of hardened criminals.

95. *Report of the National Advisory Commission on Civil Disorders*, 2.

96. Kopkind, "White on Black," 385, emphasis in original.

97. *Report of the National Advisory Commission on Civil Disorders*, chap. 7.

98. Ibid., 203, chap. 4.

99. Ibid., chap. 17.

100. Francis Keppel testimony before the Subcommittee on Government Research of the Senate Committee on Government Operations, Hearings on "Deprivation and Personality—A New Challenge to Human Resources Development," pts. 1–2, April 1968, 90th Cong., 2nd sess., 70.

101. "Review Symposium," 1275.

102. Telegram from Lester Maddox to Lyndon Johnson, 9 March 1968,

in *Black Studies Research Sources: Microfilms from Major Archival Manuscript Collections,* August Meier and John H. Bracey, Jr., eds., *Civil Rights Under the Johnson Administration, 1963–1969,* White House Files, pt. 1, reel 5, pp. 37–38.

103. An example can be found in Skolnick, "Violence Commission Violence," 32–38. Skolnick objects to the pattern of commissions distorting experts' work and exploiting their names for the purposes of legitimizing their dubious conclusions, but he also defends the value of commission expertise. At least data has been gathered, he points out, making alternative interpretations and policy recommendations possible. For other examples of the view that Kerner Commission expertise had been ignored, resisted, and even ridiculed, see Karl Menninger's testimony in PAFP, 52; and the description of Daniel Moynihan's severe criticism of the Kerner Commission in Schoen, *Pat,* 139.

104. Arthur Brayfield testimony before the Subcommittee on Government Research of the Senate Committee on Government Operations, Hearings on "Deprivation and Personality—A New Challenge to Human Resources Development," 265–266.

105. Ibid., 265, emphasis in original.

106. Shellow, "Social Scientists and Social Action from within the Establishment," 219.

9: The Growth Industry

1. William C. Menninger and Munro Leaf, *You and Psychiatry* (New York: Charles Scribner's Sons, 1948), 70. This book was one of Menninger's efforts to popularize psychodynamic personality theory, as well as convey the overwhelmingly social lessons of wartime clinical work. He called it a "war baby" (p. v).

2. John Dollard and Neal E. Miller, *Personality and Psychotherapy: An Analysis in Terms of Learning, Thinking, and Culture* (New York: McGraw-Hill Book Company, 1950), 5, emphasis in original. Dollard and Miller were associated with the important postwar effort, based at Yale's Institute of Human Relations, to put the principles of Freudian psychology to the test of behavioral verification.

3. The definitive work on post–World War II mental health policy is Grob, *From Asylum to Community.*

4. Greene, "The Role of the Psychiatrist in World War II," 499.

5. Miller, "Clinical Psychiatry in the Veterans Administration," 182. Similar statistics on the numbers of psychiatric patients in the VA can be found in Blain, "Program of the Veterans Administration for the Physical and Mental Health of Veterans," 33–46; Brand, "The National Mental Health Act of 1946," 236–237; Menninger, *Psychiatry in a Troubled World,* 380; NNIA, testimony of Dr. Daniel Blain, Chief, VA Neuropsychiatric Division, 28–30; Veterans Adminis-

tration, *Department of Medicine and Surgery Policy Memorandum Number 2* (30 January 1946):4.

6. Menninger, *Psychiatry in a Troubled World*, 380; Brand, "The National Mental Health Act of 1946," 236–237.

7. Quoted in Emanuel K. Schwartz, "Is There Need for Psychology in Psychotherapy?" in *Psychology, Psychiatry and the Public Interest*, ed. Maurice H. Krout (Minneapolis: University of Minnesota Press, 1956), 118.

8. Blain, "Programs of the Veterans Administration for the Physical and Mental Health of Veterans," 39; Nina Ridenour, *Mental Health in the United States: A Fifty-Year History* (Cambridge: Harvard University Press, 1961), 61.

9. NNIA testimony of Dr. Daniel Blain, Chief, VA Neuropsychiatric Division, 29; Blain, "Programs of the Veterans Administration for the Physical and Mental Health of Veterans," 43–44.

10. For a detailed description of this program, see Dana L. Moore, "The Veterans Administration and the Training Program in Psychology," in *History of Psychotherapy*, 786–798.

11. Miller, "Clinical Psychiatry in the Veterans Administration," 182, 189.

12. Victor C. Raimy, ed., *Training in Clinical Psychology* (New York: Prentice-Hall, 1950), 166.

13. R. C. Tryon, "Psychology in Flux: The Academic-Professional Bipolarity," *American Psychologist* 18 (March 1963):136. Tryon's analysis was based on a survey of American Psychological Association membership directories from 1940, 1959, and 1962. For additional statistical evidence, see George W. Albee, *Mental Health Manpower Trends*, Joint Commission on Mental Health and Illness Monograph Series No. 3 (New York: Basic Books, 1959), 124–125.

14. Greene, "The Role of the Psychiatrist in World War II," 530.

15. Ibid., 500–504.

16. Carl R. Rogers and John L. Wallen, *Counseling with Returned Servicemen* (New York: McGraw-Hill Book Company, 1946), 19. For an even earlier statement of his belief that counseling could help to restore the democratic ethos sacrificed, of necessity, to military goals, see Carl R. Rogers, *Counseling and Psychotherapy: Newer Concepts in Practice* (Boston: Houghton Mifflin Company, 1942), 11.

17. Rogers and Wallen, *Counseling with Returned Servicemen*, 23.

18. A very useful discussion of this legislation can be found in Grob, *From Asylum to Community*, chap. 3.

19. NNIA, testimony of General Lewis B. Hershey, Director, National Selective Service System, 47–58.

20. Ibid., testimony of Dr. S. Bernard Wortis, Chief of Bellevue Hospital's Psychiatric Division, 129.

21. There were differences of opinion among experts, but these were confined to questions of funding, organization, and other such bureaucratic details. The only real opposition to the National Mental Health Act came from quarters consistently hostile to the extension of federal power. Even here, however, support from such conservative Republicans as Senator Robert H. Taft and Representative Clarence J. Brown managed to foil what little criticism of the bill existed. See Grob, *From Asylum to Community*, 52–53.

22. NNIA, Mrs. Lee Steiner, member, American Association of Psychiatric Social Workers, 115.

23. Ibid., Captain Robert Nystrom, 100–101.

24. Brand, "The National Mental Health Act of 1946," 242.

25. NNIA, Senator Claude Pepper, opening statement, 5. J. Percy Priest (D-Tenn.) introduced the bill in the House of Representatives.

26. Menninger, *Psychiatry in a Troubled World,* 471 n. 7.

27. Quoted in Grob, *From Asylum to Community,* 55.

28. Ibid., 54–55. The origins of the community mental health movement are frequently dated to psychiatrist Erich Lindemann's World War II–era observations of soldiers' relatives and his "grief work" with the survivors of a Boston nightclub fire that killed hundreds of people. See Erich Lindemann and Stanley Cobb, "Neuropsychiatric Observations," *Annals of Surgery* 117 (June 1943):814–824; and Erich Lindemann, "Symptomatology and Management of Acute Grief," *American Journal of Psychiatry* 101 (September 1944):141–148. For an analysis dating the origin of community mental health in the Progressive Era, see Sicherman, "The Quest for Mental Health in America, 1880–1917."

29. John A. Clausen, "Social Science Research in the National Mental Health Program," *American Sociological Review* 15 (June 1950):404.

30. Statistics on National Institute of Mental Health budget and funding levels from Greene, "The Role of the Psychiatrist in World War II," 527; and Joint Commission on Mental Illness and Health, *Action for Mental Health* (New York: Basic Books, 1961), 6–7.

31. Brand, "The National Mental Health Act of 1946," 243.

32. Stella Leche Deignan and Esther Miller, "The Support of Research in Medical and Allied Fields for the Period 1946–1951," *Science* 115 (28 March 1952):330, table 7.

33. Ibid., 331, fig. 9.

34. Joint Commission on Mental Illness and Health, *Action for Mental Health,* 6–7, 210. The Joint Commission estimated that mental illness cost $3 billion annually, compared with a total research expenditure of around $70 million (from all sources) in 1958.

35. FSISSBR, testimony of Ralph L. Beals, American Anthropological Association, Committee on Research Problems and Ethics, 83. For a good example of National Institute of Mental Health–supported research devoted to tracking mass trends in the mental health of the normal U.S. population, with special attention to the influence of larger community and national developments, see Norman Bradburn and David Caplovitz, *Reports on Happiness: A Pilot Study of Behavior Related to Mental Health* (Chicago: Aldine Publishing Company, 1965).

36. Lyons, *The Uneasy Partnership,* 276.

37. Grob, *From Asylum to Community,* 66–67.

38. "Young Turks" was a frequent designation for the Group for the Advancement of Psychiatry founders. See, for example, Joint Commission on Mental Illness and Health, *Action for Mental Health,* 201. For a discussion of GAP's founding and place within postwar psychiatry, see Grob, *From Asylum*

to Community, chap. 2. Grob points out (pp. 32–34, 311–312 n. 21) that "Young Turks" was hardly an accurate description of the age of GAP members, which averaged forty-seven in 1950.

39. Group for the Advancement of Psychiatry Circular Letter 154 (16 September 1949), quoted in Grob, *From Asylum to Community,* 311 n. 16.

40. Group for the Advancement of Psychiatry, Committee on Social Issues, "The Social Responsibility of Psychiatry," originally published as GAP Report No. 13 (New York: July 1950), reprinted in *Psychiatry and Public Affairs: Reports and Symposia of the Group for the Advancement of Psychiatry* (Chicago: Aldine Publishing Company, 1966), 12.

41. Robert Yerkes in Intersociety Constitutional Convention, condensed transcript, American Psychological Association, 29–31 May 1943, quoted in Capshew, "Psychology on the March," 254; and Capshew and Hilgard, "The Power of Service," 162.

42. Group for the Advancement of Psychiatry, Committee on Social Issues, "The Social Responsibility of Psychiatry," 11.

43. Group for the Advancement of Psychiatry, "Psychiatric Aspects of School Desegregation," in *Psychiatry and Public Affairs* (originally published as GAP Report No. 37, 1957), 15–105. GAP also published an abbreviated and less technical version of this report, titled "Emotional Aspects of School Desegregation," as Report No. 37A, in 1960.

44. Grob, *From Asylum to Community,* 26, 40, 314 n. 39.

45. Group for the Advancement of Psychiatry, "Considerations Regarding the Loyalty Oath as a Manifestation of Current Social Tension and Anxiety," Symposium No. 1, 1954.

46. For a full discussion of the work of the Joint Commission on Mental Illness and Health, see Grob, *From Asylum to Community,* chaps. 8 and 9.

47. Joint Commission on Mental Illness and Health, *Action for Mental Health,* xxvii.

48. Ibid., xiv. Gerald Grob argues that to consider the general recommendations of the Joint Commission on Mental Illness and Health as the major precursor to the federal legislation of the 1960s is to perpetuate the "myth" that the JCMIH emphasized community-based over institutional services. While the specific proposal of the JCMIH for community centers catering to outpatients certainly became the centerpiece of that decade's legislation, the rest of the JCMIH work, which emphasized the care of severely and chronically mentally ill individuals, was ignored, according to Grob, since these latter populations were underserved by community mental health centers. Even Grob points out that this result was only visible in hindsight, however, Abandoning the mentally ill was not the intention of clinicians or policy-makers, who truly believed that community mental health centers would provide more humane and effective services to previously institutionalized people. See Grob, *From Asylum to Community,* 229. For an indication that the main concern of the JCMIH actually was treating severe mental illness and increasing public sensitivity to it—rather than diverting attention and money toward the more comfortable subject of mental health—see Joint Commission on Mental Illness and Health, *Action for Mental Health,* chap. 3, 242.

49. John F. Kennedy, "Special Message to the Congress on Mental Illness and Mental Retardation," 5 February 1963, in *Public Papers of the Presidents of the United States, John F. Kennedy, Containing the Public Messages, Speeches, and Statements of the President, January 1 to November 22, 1963* (Washington, D.C.: Government Printing Office, 1964), 127.

50. Ibid., 127.

51. Ibid., 128–129.

52. P.L. 88–164, Title II.

53. Alfred M. Freedman, "Historical and Political Roots of the Community Mental Health Centers Act," *American Journal of Orthopsychiatry* 37 (April 1967):493.

54. For one sample of how broadly the jurisdiction of community mental health was defined, see the table of contents in Stuart E. Colann and Carl Eisdorfer, eds., *Handbook of Community Mental Health* (New York: Appleton-Century-Crofts, 1972).

55. Roberts, Halleck, and Loeb, eds., *Community Psychiatry*, 7.

56. Chester C. Bennett, "Community Psychology: Impressions of the Boston Conference on the Education of Psychologists for Community Mental Health," *American Psychologist* 20 (October 1965):833.

57. Chaim Shatan, "Community Psychiatry—Stretcher Bearer of the Social Order?" *International Journal of Psychiatry* 7 (May 1969):319–320.

58. An account of this event at Lincoln Hospital and the Albert Einstein College of Medicine can be found in Castel, Castel, and Lovell, *The Psychiatric Society*, 156–159.

59. Ibid., 157, emphasis in original.

60. Joel Kovel, "Desiring Speech," *Zeta* (July-August 1989):140.

61. C. C. Burlingame, "Psychiatric Sense and Nonsense," *Journal of the American Medical Association* 133 (5 April 1947):971.

62. Nevitt Sanford, "Psychotherapy and the American Public," in *Psychology, Psychiatry and the Public Interest*, 3.

63. Lawrence S. Kubie, "A Doctorate in Psychotherapy: The Reasons for a New Profession," in *New Horizon for Psychotherapy: Autonomy as a Profession,* ed. Robert R. Holt (New York: International Universities Press, 1971), 14.

64. Quoted in Jack David Pressman, "Uncertain Promise: Psychosurgery and the Development of Scientific Psychiatry in America, 1935 to 1955" (Ph.D. diss., University of Pennsylvania, 1986), 318.

65. There has been considerable controversy about whether the psychoactive drug "revolution" was a significant factor in deinstitutionalization. All observers do agree that the absolute numbers of institutionalized mental patients began to decline in 1956, sharply reversing long-term trends. See Grob, *From Asylum to Community*, 260, table 10.2; William Gronfein, "Psychotropic Drugs and the Origins of Deinstitutionalization," *Social Problems* 32 (June 1985):440, table 1; Joint Commission on Mental Illness and Health, *Action for Mental Health*, 7, 21, table 3; Andrew Scull, *Decarceration: Community Treatment and the Deviant, A Radical View*, 2nd ed. (Cambridge, England: Policy Press, 1984), 68, table 4–2.

66. Grob, *From Asylum to Community*, 42.

67. Efforts to explain deinstitutionalization have been marked by disagreement, even though there is widespread agreement that the policy has failed miserably. For a sample, see Castel, Castel, and Lovell, *The Psychiatric Society*, pt. 2; Grob, *From Asylum to Community*, chap. 10; Paul Lerman, *Deinstitutionalization and the Welfare State* (New Brunswick: Rutgers University Press, 1982), esp. chap. 6; Scull, *Decarceration*, esp. chap. 8.

68. Scull, *Decarceration*, 152.

69. Gerald N. Grob, "The History of the Asylum Revisited: Personal Reflections," in *Discovering the History of Psychiatry*, ed. Mark Micale and Roy Porter (New York: Oxford University Press, 1993), 260–281.

Andrew Scull and Gerald Grob represent opposite poles in this debate. The most succinct statements of their respective historiographical and philosophical views can be found in Andrew Scull, "Humanitarianism or Control? Some Observations on the Historiography of Anglo-American Psychiatry," in *Social Control and the State: Historical and Comparative Essays*, ed. Stanley Cohen and Andrew Scull (Oxford: Martin Robertson, 1983), 118–140; and Gerald N. Grob, "Rediscovering Asylums: The Unhistorical History of the Mental Hospital," in *The Therapeutic Revolution: Essays in the Social History of American Medicine*, ed. Morris J. Vogel and Charles E. Rosenberg (Philadelphia: University of Pennsylvania Press, 1979), 135–157. See also their reviews of each other's recent work in *History of Psychiatry* 1 (1990):223–232, and *Milbank Quarterly* 70 (1992):557–579.

70. "American Psychiatric Association Membership Figures, 1873–Present"; Grob, *From Asylum to Community*, 297, table 11.1.

71. Grob, *From Asylum to Community*, 253.

72. Martin L. Gross, *The Psychological Society: A Critical Analysis of Psychiatry, Psychotherapy, Psychoanalysis and the Psychological Revolution* (New York: Simon and Schuster, 1978), 272–275; and Vandenbos, Cummings, and Deleon, "A Century of Psychotherapy: Economic and Environmental Influences," 70–71.

73. Gross, *The Psychological Society*, 7.

74. Carl R. Rogers, *Client-Centered Therapy: Its Current Practice, Implications, and Theory* (Boston: Houghton Mifflin, 1951), 14, referring to the report issued by the American Psychological Association Committee on Training in Clinical Psychology in 1947.

75. Raimy, ed., *Training in Clinical Psychology*, xix.

76. Ibid., 39, 185.

77. Ibid., 26.

78. Ibid., 96.

79. Ibid., 93.

80. H. J. Eysenck, "The Effects of Psychotherapy," *Journal of Consulting Psychology* 16 (October 1952):322.

81. A useful summary of the era's research on psychotherapy can be found in Hans H. Strupp and Kenneth I. Howard, "A Brief History of Psychotherapy Research," in *History of Psychotherapy*, 309–334.

82. A summary of the conflict between psychiatry and psychology over the independent practice of psychotherapy can be found in Grob, *From Asylum to*

Community, 102–114. Documentation of this ongoing controversy can be found in Krout, ed. *Psychology, Psychiatry and the Public Interest,* which includes arguments from both psychiatry and clinical psychology.

83. American Medical Association, American Psychiatric Association, and American Psychoanalytic Association, "Resolution on Relations of Medicine and Psychology," in *Psychology, Psychiatry and the Public Interest,* 24.

84. For evidence that this professional conflict was sometimes considered in gendered terms, see Paul E. Huston, "A Psychiatrist's Observation on the Orientation of Clinical Psychology," in *Psychology, Psychiatry and the Public Interest,* 32.

85. Sanford, "Psychotherapy and the American Public," 6.

86. "The Cold War Between Psychiatry and Psychology," *Psychiatric Opinion* 4 (June 1967, October 1967).

87. As early as 1948, for example, one review article discussed more than ten popular Hollywood films in which psychological disturbances, experts, and treatments were central themes. See Keith Sward, "Boy and Girl Meet Neurosis," *The Screen Writer* (September 1948):8–26. I am grateful to Susan Ohmer for bringing this article to my attention.

88. Arnold A. Rogow, *The Psychiatrists* (New York: G. P. Putnam's Sons, 1970), 18.

89. Janet Walker, *Couching Resistance: Women, Film, and Psychoanalytic Psychiatry* (Minneapolis: University of Minnesota, 1993), chap. 6.

90. Rogow, *The Psychiatrists,* 15–16.

91. Napoli, *Architects of Adjustment,* 142.

92. Garfield, "Psychotherapy: A 40-Year Appraisal," 174.

93. The original study was conducted by the Survey Research Center at the University of Michigan, involved 2,460 normal adults, and was published as *Americans View Their Mental Health* (1960). In 1976 the National Institute for Mental Health funded a follow-up study. It replicated the 1957 study, so that time comparisons could be made, but added some new questions, especially in regard to use of mental health professionals and resources. It was published in two volumes: Joseph Veroff, Elizabeth Douvan, and Richard A. Kulka, *The Inner American: A Self-Portrait from 1957–1976* and *Mental Health in America: Patterns of Help-seeking from 1957–1976* (New York: Basic Books, 1981). The 14 percent figure can be found in 2:79, table 5.1.

94. Veroff, Douvan, and Kulka, *Mental Health in America,* 79, table 5.1, 222, table 7.1, 231.

95. Veroff, Douvan, and Kulka, *The Inner American,* 14.

96. Ibid., 25, 20. Although the biggest demographic shift was socioeconomic and educational (many more people at the lower ends of the income and educational ladders were likely to seek help), certain demographic indicators still pointed to disproportionately high use of professional expertise. These indicators were youth, female gender, high level of education, Jewish background, West Coast residence, professional parents, and a family history that included divorce. See Veroff, Douvan, and Kulka, *Mental Health in America,* 90, 111–112, 124–125.

97. Veroff, Douvan, and Kulka, *Mental Health in America,* 271.

98. Lawrence S. Kubie, "Social Forces and the Neurotic Process," in *Explorations in Social Psychiatry*, ed. Alexander H. Leighton, John A. Clausen, and Robert N. Wilson (New York: Basic Books, 1957), 83.

99. John R. Seeley, "Psychiatry: Revolution, Reform, and 'Reaction,' " in *Modern Psychoanalysis*, 699.

100. Kubie, "A Doctorate in Psychotherapy," 16–17.

101. Gordon W. Allport, *Becoming: Basic Considerations for a Psychology of Personality* (New Haven: Yale University Press, 1955), 100–101.

102. Abraham Maslow, "Existential Psychology—What's In It for Us?" in *Existential Psychology*, ed. Rollo May, 2nd ed. (New York: Random House, 1969; 1st ed. published 1961), 57, 50.

103. Ibid., 51.

104. For a brief introduction to the ideas of five pioneers in humanistic psychology, including Rogers and Maslow, see Roy José DeCarvalho, *The Founders of Humanistic Psychology* (New York: Praeger, 1991).

105. Abraham H. Maslow, *Toward A Psychology of Being*, 2nd ed. (New York: D. Van Nostrand Company, 1968), iii; Abraham H. Maslow, *Motivation and Personality*, 2nd ed. (New York: Harper & Row, 1970; 1st ed. 1954), x.

106. "A Larger Jurisdiction for Psychology" is the title of part 1 in Maslow, *Toward a Psychology of Being*. See also Abraham H. Maslow, *The Psychology of Science* (Chicago: Henry Regnery Company, 1969), xvi.

107. The fullest statement of the client-centered approach is Rogers, *Client-Centered Therapy*.

108. See Carl R. Rogers, "A Physician-Patient or a Therapist-Client Relationship?" in *Psychology, Psychiatry and the Public Interest*, 135–145.

109. The first verbatim transcript of an entire course of psychotherapy was published by Rogers in 1942. See "The Case of Herbert Bryan," in Rogers, *Counseling and Psychotherapy*, 261–437. Rogers himself wrote prolifically about his research activities. An accessible place to begin is with a number of the essays in Carl R. Rogers, *On Becoming a Person: A Therapist's View of Psychotherapy* (Boston: Houghton Mifflin Company, 1961). This volume also includes an interesting autobiographical statement ("This Is Me") and a useful chronological bibliography of his writings from 1930 through 1960. A quick summary of Rogers's early research can be found in Laura N. Rice and Leslie S. Greenberg, "Humanistic Approaches to Psychotherapy," in *History of Psychotherapy*, 199–202.

110. See, for example, Richard L. Evans, *Carl Rogers: The Man and His Ideas*, vol. 8 in *Dialogues with Notable Contributors to Personality Theory* (New York: E. P. Dutton & Co., 1975), 24–27.

111. Carl R. Rogers, "Introduction," in *Psychotherapy and Personality Change: Co-ordinated Research Studies in the Client-Centered Approach*, ed. Carl R. Rogers and Rosalind F. Dymond (Chicago: University of Chicago Press, 1954), 4.

112. Carl R. Rogers, "Some Hypotheses Regarding the Facilitation of Personal Growth," in *On Becoming a Person*, 35, emphasis in original.

113. Rogers, *Counseling and Psychotherapy*, 29, emphasis in original.

114. Rogers, *Client-Centered Therapy*, 24.

115. R. Morison's notes on a visit with Carl Rogers, dated 5 November 1948, Record Group 1.2, series 216, box 1, folder 4, RF Archives.

116. Rogers, *Client-Centered Therapy*, 225, quoting his own earlier paper, "Divergent Trends in Methods of Improving Adjustment," *Harvard Educational Review* (1948):209–219.

117. Rogers, *Client-Centered Therapy*, 422. Rogers repeatedly linked the elements of his counseling philosophy with the elements of democracy. Other explicit examples can be found in Rogers, *Counseling and Psychotherapy*, 127; and Rogers and Wallen, *Counseling with Returned Servicemen*, 5, 22–24.

118. Carl R. Rogers, "Some of the Directions Evident in Therapy," in *On Becoming a Person*, 105. This article was originally published in O. Hobart Mowrer, ed., *Psychotherapy: Theory and Research* (1953). For another illustration of awareness that the ideas of humanistic psychology defied dominant psychological notions about human nature, see Allport, *Becoming*, 99–101.

119. See "Some Issues Concerning the Control of Human Behavior: A Symposium" in Evans, *Carl Rogers*, xliv–lxxxviii. This is the widely reprinted dialogue that first appeared in *Science* 124 (30 November 1956):1057–1066. For a less widely known dialogue between Rogers and Skinner which took place in June 1962, see Howard Kirschenbaum and Valerie Hand Henderson, eds., *Carl Rogers: Dialogues: Conversations with Martin Buber, Paul Tillich, B. F. Skinner, Gregory Bateson, Michael Polanyi, Rollo May, and Others* (Boston: Houghton Mifflin, 1989), 82–152.

120. Skinner, "Freedom and the Control of Men," 47.

121. For another, early formulation of his ideas on democracy, science, and social control, see B. F. Skinner, *Science and Human Behavior* (New York: Free Press, 1953), esp. chap. 29.

122. Carl R. Rogers, "Persons or Science? A Philosophical Question," in *On Becoming a Person*, 213.

123. Ibid., 214.

124. Rogers, *Client-Centered Therapy*, 54.

125. Evans, *Carl Rogers*, 65, 67.

126. The fullest statement of his motivational theory can be found in Maslow, *Motivation and Personality*. The term "self-actualization" first appeared in *The Organism* (1939) by German refugee physician and Gestalt psychologist Kurt Goldstein.

127. Richard J. Lowry, ed., *The Journals of A. H. Maslow*, 2 vols. (Monterey, Calif.: Brooks/Cole Publishing Company, 1979).

128. See, for example, Abraham H. Maslow, "Power Relationships and Patterns of Personal Development," in *Problems of Power in American Democracy*, ed. Arthur Kornhauser (Detroit: Wayne State University Press, 1957), 92–131. An earlier essay had equated authoritarianism with mental sickness. See A. H. Maslow, "The Authoritarian Character Structure," *Journal of Social Psychology*, S.P.S.S.I. *Bulletin* 18 (November 1943):401–411.

129. Maslow, *Motivation and Personality*, 67, emphasis in original.

130. Ibid., 99, emphasis in original.

131. Ibid., chap. 11. See also Maslow, *Toward A Psychology of Being*, 74–96.

132. Maslow, *Motivation and Personality,* 180.

133. Ibid., 58 n. 9.

134. Ibid., 38.

135. Lowry, ed., *The Journals of A. H. Maslow,* 1:51, 52.

136. Ibid., 1:631–632.

137. Abraham H. Maslow, "Eupsychia—The Good Society," *Journal of Humanistic Psychology* 1 (Fall 1961):10.

138. Lowry, ed., *The Journals of A. H. Maslow,* 2:835.

139. Ibid., 2:838.

140. Ibid., 1:262, 429, 629, emphasis in original.

141. Ibid., 2:877. The fullest statement of Maslow's political agenda can be found in 1:631–632.

142. Ibid., 1:646, 2:733, 1120.

143. Maslow, *Toward a Psychology of Being,* 8, emphasis in original. For another formulation, see Maslow, *Motivation and Personality,* 268.

144. Abbie Hoffman, *Soon to be a Major Motion Picture* (New York: Perigree, 1980), 26.

145. Ibid., 26.

146. Lowry, ed., *The Journals of A. H. Maslow,* 2:1090.

147. Ibid., 2:883.

148. Carl R. Rogers, "The Emerging Person: A New Revolution," in Evans, *Carl Rogers,* 175.

10: The Curious Courtship of Psychology and Women's Liberation

1. See, for example, Barbara Ehrenreich, *The Hearts of Men: American Dreams and the Flight from Commitment* (New York: Anchor Press/Doubleday, 1983); Todd Gitlin, *The Sixties: Years of Hope, Days of Rage* (New York: Bantam, 1987); Maurice Isserman, *If I Had a Hammer . . . The Death of the Old Left and the Birth of the New Left* (New York: Basic Books, 1987); Marty Jezer, *The Dark Ages: Life in the United States, 1945–1960* (Boston: South End Press, 1982).

2. For an interesting examination of the idea of "postindustrial society," which emphasizes that leftists were as enthusiastic about "the obsolescence of the economic" as were liberals like Daniel Bell, see Howard Brick, "Optimism of the Mind: Imagining Postindustrial Society in the 1960s and 1970s," *American Quarterly* 44 (September 1992):348–380.

3. Ellen Herman, "Being and Doing: Humanistic Psychology and the Spirit of the 1960s," in *Sights on the Sixties,* ed. Barbara Tischler (New Brunswick: Rutgers University Press, 1992), 87–101.

4. William H. Chafe, *The American Woman: Her Changing Social, Economic, and Political Roles, 1920–1970* (New York: Oxford University Press,

1972); Sara Evans, *Personal Politics: The Roots of Women's Liberation in the Civil Rights Movement & the New Left* (New York: Random House, 1979).

5. Philip Wylie, "Common Women," in *Generation of Vipers* (New York: Pocket Books, 1942), 188.

6. Ibid., 191.

7. Philip Wylie, "The Transmogrification of Mom," in *Sons and Daughters of Mom* (New York: Doubleday, 1971), 41.

8. Edward A. Strecker, *Their Mothers' Sons: The Psychiatrist Examines an American Problem* (Philadelphia: J. B. Lippincott, 1946), 30.

9. Ibid., 219–220.

10. Ferdinand Lundberg and Marynia F. Farnham, *Modern Woman: The Lost Sex* (New York: Harper & Brothers, 1947), 143, 67.

11. Ibid., 356–359.

12. Robert Coughalan, "Changing Roles in Modern Marriage," *Life* 41 (24 December 1956):110.

13. Ibid., 116.

14. Roxanne Dunbar, "Spock Sentences Women," *Helix* (11 December 1969), in WH, reel 2, p. 594.

15. "Psychology Constructs the Female" is the title of an important feminist manifesto authored by psychologist Naomi Weisstein. It is discussed in greater detail below.

16. Weisstein's piece was first published by the New England Free Press in pamphlet form under the title, "Kinder, Küche, Kirche as Scientific Law: Psychology Constructs the Female." It was subsequently revised as "Psychology Constructs the Female" and was widely reprinted in the early 1970s. The original text can be found in WH, reel 2, pp. 689–696.

17. Naomi Weisstein, "Adventures of a Woman in Science," in *Women Look at Biology Looking at Women: A Collection of Feminist Critiques,* ed. Ruth Hubbard, Mary Sue Henifin, and Barbara Fried (Boston: G. K. Hall, 1979), 188.

18. For another story about how Harvard's Psychology Department marginalized its female graduate students and faculty members, see Miriam Lewin, "The Kurt Lewin Memorial Award Presentation and Introduction," *Journal of Social Issues* 48 (1992):170.

19. Weisstein, "Adventures of a Woman in Science," 189; Naomi Weisstein, Virginia Blaisdell, and Jesse Lemisch, *The Godfathers: Freudians, Marxists, and the Scientific and Political Protection Societies* (New Haven: Belladonna Publishing, 1975), 2.

20. Weisstein, "Adventures of a Woman in Science," 200.

21. Naomi Weisstein, "Psychology Constructs the Female or The Fantasy Life of the Male Psychologist (with some attention to the fantasies of his friends, the male biologist and the male anthropologist)," in *Radical Feminism,* ed. Anne Koedt, Ellen Levine, and Anita Rapone (New York: Quadrangle, 1973), 181.

22. Ibid., 179.

23. Ibid., 195.

24. Ibid., 181.

25. Ibid., 189.

26. The phrase "ideological pollution" is from Nancy M. Henley, "Shaking the Lead Out: Action Proposals for Psychology," paper presented at the 1971 meeting of the Eastern Psychological Association, in WH, reel 3, p. 702.

27. Pauline B. Bart, "Sexism and Social Science: From the Gilded Cage to the Iron Cage, or, the Perils of Pauline," *Journal of Marriage and the Family* (November 1971):737. See also her "Depression in Middle-Aged Women," in *Woman in Sexist Society: Studies in Power and Powerlessness,* ed. Vivian Gornick and Barbara K. Moran (New York: New American Library, 1971), 163–186, and "The Myth of a Value-Free Psychotherapy," in *The Sociology of the Future: Theory, Cases, and Annotated Bibliography,* ed. Wendell Bell and James A. Mau (New York: Russell Sage Foundation, 1971), 113–159.

28. Phyllis Chesler, "Marriage and Psychotherapy," in *The Radical Therapist,* ed. Jerome Agel (New York: Ballantine Books, 1971), 175–180; "Patient and Patriarch: Women in the Psychotherapeutic Relationship," in *Woman in Sexist Society,* 362–392; "Women as Psychiatric and Psychotherapeutic Patients," *Journal of Marriage and the Family* 33 (November 1971):746–759.

29. Phyllis Chesler, *Women & Madness* (New York: Avon, 1972), 56, emphasis in original.

30. Ibid., 16, emphasis in original.

31. Chesler, "Women as Psychiatric and Psychotherapeutic Patients," 757; Chesler, "Marriage and Psychotherapy," 180; Chesler, *Women & Madness,* chap. 10.

32. An overview of feminist work to transform psychology, in these and other fields, can be found in a special issue of *Psychology of Women Quarterly* 15 (December 1991) devoted to "Women's Heritage in Psychology."

33. An early effort to discuss the class and race biases of feminist critiques of psychiatry is Judi Chamberlain, "Women's Oppression and Psychiatric Oppression," in *Women Look at Psychiatry,* ed. Dorothy E. Smith and Sara J. David (Vancouver: Press Gang, 1975), 39–46.

34. The best overview of the intellectual history of the early women's movement is Alice Echols, *Daring to Be Bad: Radical Feminism in America, 1967–1975* (Minneapolis: University of Minnesota Press, 1989). The first book to argue that feminism's most important, generative roots were in the civil rights movement and the New Left was Evans, *Personal Politics.* Another analysis, which stresses the importance of Freedom Summer in establishing continuity of key personnel, ideas, and strategies between various 1960s movements, is Doug McAdam, *Freedom Summer* (New York: Oxford University Press, 1988).

35. General overviews of antipsychiatric theory and activism can be found in Norman Dain, "Critics and Dissenters: Reflections on 'Anti-Psychiatry' in the United States," *Journal of the History of the Behavioral Sciences* 25 (January 1989):3–25; Grob, *From Asylum to Community,* 279–288; Jane M. Ussher, *Women's Madness: Misogyny or Mental Illness?* (Amherst: University of Massachusetts Press, 1991), chap. 6.

36. For example, R. D. Laing, *The Politics of Experience* (New York: Ballantine Books, 1967); Thomas S. Szasz, *The Myth of Mental Illness: Foundations of a Theory of Personal Conduct,* rev. ed. (New York: Harper & Row, 1974). One

of the best anthologies from the activist wing of the movement is Jerome Agel, ed., *The Radical Therapist.*

37. Szasz, *The Myth of Mental Illness,* 69.

38. Thomas S. Szasz, *Law, Liberty, and Psychiatry: An Inquiry into the Social Uses of Mental Health Practices* (New York: Collier Books, 1963), 106.

39. Ibid., 248, 223.

40. R. D. Laing, *The Divided Self: An Existential Study in Sanity and Madness* (Baltimore: Penguin, 1962), 36, emphasis in original.

41. Laing, *The Politics of Experience,* 129.

42. For discussions that emphasize the conflicts between antipsychiatric and feminist analysis of madness and the helping professions, see Elaine Showalter, "Women, Madness, and the Family: R. D. Laing and the Culture of Antipsychiatry," in *The Female Malady: Women, Madness, and English Culture, 1830–1980* (New York: Pantheon, 1985), 220–247; Ussher, *Women's Madness,* chap. 7.

43. See for example, Agel, ed., *The Radical Therapist,* pt. 3; Judi Chamberlain, *On Our Own: Patient-Controlled Alternatives to the Mental Health System* (New York: Hawthorn Books, 1978); K. Portland Frank, *The Anti-Psychiatry Bibliography and Resource Guide,* 2nd ed. (Vancouver: Press Gang, 1979), section on "Psychiatry and Women"; Smith and David, eds., *Women Look at Psychiatry;* Hogie Wyckoff, ed., *Love, Therapy and Politics: Issues in Radical Therapy—The First Year* (New York: Grove Press, 1976), esp. pt. 2.

44. Claude Steiner, "Radical Psychiatry Manifesto," in Claude Steiner et al., *Readings in Radical Psychiatry* (New York: Grove Press), 6. This document is reprinted in Agel, ed., *The Radical Therapist,* 280–282.

45. Partisans of radical therapy were sometimes sharply divided on the question of whether anything positive could be salvaged from psychotherapy. For example, the collective that published one of the movement's major publications, *The Radical Therapist,* split in early 1972 over this issue. The faction opposed to any type of psychotherapy moved to Cambridge, Massachusetts, where it began to publish *Rough Times,* a quarterly whose name was eventually changed to *State and Mind.* That part of the movement which continued to support the work of radical therapists was centered in the Berkeley Radical Psychiatry Center and published *Issues in Radical Therapy.*

46. A few theorists took a harder line. See, for example, Dorothy Tennov Hoffman, "Psychotherapy as an Agent of Patriarchy," typescript, talk delivered to Pittsburgh Psychological Association, 23 April 1971, in WH, reel 2, pp. 804–820. Hoffman termed psychotherapy "a monster in our midst" and "a kind of opiate." Her tone moderated somewhat over the next several years. See Dorothy Tennov, "Feminism, Psychotherapy and Professionalism," *Journal of Contemporary Psychotherapy* 5 (Summer 1973):107–111. She eventually published a book that reclassified psychotherapy from monstrous to "hazardous." See Dorothy Tennov, *Psychotherapy: The Hazardous Cure* (New York: Abelard-Schumen, 1975).

Several years later, Mary Daly also argued that "the concept of 'feminist' therapy is inherently a contradiction." Psychotherapy of any sort was, in Daly's analysis, the equivalent of "mind rape." "A woman seduced into treatment is 'inspired' with dis-ease she had never before even suspected. . . . The multiplicity of therapies feeds into this dis-ease, for they constitute an arsenal for the manufacture of the many forms of semantic bullets used to bombard the minds of women struggling to survive in the therapeutically polluted environment." Mary Daly, *Gyn/Ecology: The Metaethics of Radical Feminism* (Boston: Beacon Press, 1979), 282, 287, 276.

47. A number of documents relating to these types of actions can be found in WH.

48. San Francisco Redstockings, "Radical Psychiatrists," letter following 1970 American Psychiatric Association convention, in WH, reel 2, p. 787. This document is also reprinted in Agel, ed., *The Radical Therapist,* 173–174.

49. David Perlman, "The Psychiatrists & the Protestors," *San Francisco Sunday Examiner & Chronicle,* 24 May 1970, in WH, reel 2, p. 727.

50. Untitled document presented to business meeting, Radical Caucus of the American Psychiatric Association, documents from the May 1970 ApA convention, in WH, reel 2, p. 1149.

51. Perhaps the best illustration of this came in 1973, when a protracted campaign organized by gay liberationists, feminists, and professional supporters finally resulted in the deletion of homosexuality from the third edition of psychiatry's roster of mental illnesses, *DSM-III.* See Ronald Bayer, *Homosexuality and American Psychiatry: The Politics of Diagnosis* (Princeton: Princeton University Press, 1987), and Eric Marcus, *Making History: The Struggle for Gay and Lesbian Equal Rights, 1945–1990, An Oral History* (New York: Harper Collins, 1992), 221–225, 250–255.

52. Radical Caucus of the American Psychiatric Association, documents from the May 1970 ApA convention, in WH, reel 2, p. 1153.

53. Ibid., 1150, emphasis in original.

54. The only overview of Association for Women in Psychology history is Leonore Tiefer, "A Brief History of the Association for Women in Psychology, 1969–1991," *Psychology of Women Quarterly* 15 (December 1991):635–649. A somewhat longer version was published in pamphlet form by the AWP for its members as part of the 1992 centennial celebration of the American Psychological Association. It is this longer version that is cited in the notes below. See also Ian E. McNett, "Psychologists: One Session Taken Over Five Dissident Groups Seek Changes," *Chronicle of Higher Education* 3 (15 September 1969):7.

55. Henley, "Shaking the Lead Out," WH, reel 3, p. 702.

56. Leonore Tiefer, "A Brief History of the Association for Women in Psychology, 1969–1991" (Indiana, Pa.: Association for Women in Psychology, 1992), 9.

57. Henley, "Shaking the Lead Out," WH, reel 3, p. 700.

58. Tiefer, "A Brief History of the Association for Women in Psychology, 1969–1991," 9.

59. Ibid., 6.

60. "Psychology and the New Woman: Statement of the Association for Women Psychologists to the American Psychological Association," September 1970, Miami Beach, Florida, in WH, reel 2, pp. 1234–1235.

61. Betty Friedan, *The Feminine Mystique* (New York: Dell, 1963), 115.

62. Ibid., 96.

63. Ibid., 115.

64. Ibid., 95.

65. Ibid., 299.

66. Ibid., chap. 13.

67. Ibid., 69.

68. The National Organization for Women, "Statement of Purpose," in Betty Friedan, *It Changed My Life: Writings on the Women's Movement* (New York: Random House, 1976), 87.

69. For a brief overview of the concept's intellectual pedigree, see Hoffman, "From Instinct to Identity," 130–146.

70. Erikson, *Identity: Youth and Crisis,* 17.

71. For examples, see Fredric Solomon and Jacob R. Fishman, "Youth and Social Action: II. Action and Identity Formation in the First Student Sit-In Demonstration," *Journal of Social Issues* 20 (April 1964):36–45.

72. See, for example, Erikson, "The Concept of Identity in Race Relations," 145–171; "A Memorandum on Identity and Negro Youth," 644–659; and "Race and the Wider Identity" in *Identity: Youth and Crisis,* 295–320.

73. Erik H. Erikson, "Inner and Outer Space: Reflections on Womanhood," *Daedalus* 93 (1964):582–606. In 1968 Erikson published this article in revised form as "Womanhood and the Inner Space" in *Identity: Youth and Crisis,* 261–294.

74. Erikson, "Womanhood and the Inner Space," 273.

75. Ibid., 290.

76. Ibid., 274.

77. For example, see Elizabeth Janeway, *Man's World, Woman's Place: A Study in Social Mythology* (New York: William Morrow, 1971), 93–96.

78. Erikson, "Womanhood and the Inner Space," 266. Erikson may have grated on the radical feminist and socialist-feminist sensibilities of the late 1960s, but he clearly anticipated the cultural feminist themes of the mid-1970s: the view of women as closer to "nature" and to "life" than men, more devoted to human connection and healing, and capable of contributing a desperately needed caretaking ethic—rooted in maternalism—to public policy questions. Compare, for example, Erikson's article with Alice Echols's discussion of Jane Alpert's 1973 cultural feminist manifesto, "Mother Right: A New Feminist Theory." Echols, *Daring to Be Bad,* 247–262.

79. Kate Millett, *Sexual Politics* (New York: Avon, 1969), 294.

80. Erik H. Erikson, "Once More the Inner Space: Letter to a Former Student," in *Women & Analysis: Dialogues on Psychoanalytic Views of Femininity,* ed. Jean Strouse (New York: Grossman Publishers, 1974), 320–322.

81. Ibid., 334.

82. Kate Millett, "Sexual Politics: A Manifesto for Revolution," in *Radical Feminism,* 366.

83. Meredith Tax, "Woman and Her Mind: The Story of Everyday Life," in *Radical Feminism,* 26, emphasis in original.

84. For an early formulation of Chowdorow's thesis, see Nancy Chodorow,

"Being and Doing: A Cross-Cultural Examination of the Socialization of Males and Females," in *Woman in Sexist Society,* 259–291.

85. Ibid., 286.

86. Joreen, "The Bitch Manifesto," in *Radical Feminism,* 51.

87. Ibid., 50–51.

88. Kathie Sarachild, "A Program for Feminist 'Consciousness Raising,' " *Notes From the Second Year,* ed. Shulamith Firestone and Anne Koedt (1970), 79. Reprinted in *Voices from Women's Liberation,* ed. Leslie B. Tanner (New York: New American Library, 1970), 154–157.

89. For a more extended discussion of New York Radical Women and the origin of CR within the women's movement, see Echols, *Daring to Be Bad,* 72–92.

90. Pamela Allen, "Free Space," in *Radical Feminism,* 273. This article was originally published in *Notes from the Third Year* (1970).

91. Kathie Sarachild, "Consciousness-Raising and Intuition," in *The Radical Therapist,* 158.

92. Irene Peslikis, "Resistances to Consciousness," *Notes From the Second Year,* 81. Reprinted in *Voices from Women's Liberation,* 233–235.

93. Jennifer Gardner, "False Consciousness," in *Voices from Women's Liberation,* 232.

94. Carol Hanisch, "The Personal Is Political," *Notes From the Second Year,* 76. Also reprinted in *The Radical Therapist,* 152–157.

95. Ibid., 76.

96. Barbara Susan, "About My Consciousness Raising," in *Voices from Women's Liberation,* 240.

97. Marilyn Zweig, "Is Women's Liberation a Therapy Group?" in *The Radical Therapist,* 160–163.

98. Sarachild, "A Program for Feminist 'Consciousness Raising,' " 154–157.

99. Gail Paradise Kelly, "Women's Liberation and the Cultural Revolution," *Radical America* 4 (February 1970):24.

100. Betty Friedan, "Critique of Sexual Politics" (1970), in *It Changed My Life,* 163.

101. For reviews of this literature, see Barbara Kirsh, "Consciousness-Raising Groups as Therapy for Women," in *Women in Therapy: New Psychotherapies for a Changing Society,* ed. Violet Franks and Vasanti Burtle (New York: Brunner/Mazel, 1974), 342–350; and Diane Kravetz, "Consciousness-Raising and Self-Help," in *Women and Psychotherapy: An Assessment of Research and Practice,* ed. Annette M. Brodsky and Rachel T. Hare-Mustin (New York: Guilford Press, 1980), 270–274.

102. For two such studies claiming the success of CR had little to do with the rhetoric of women's collective action and much to do with the therapeutic benefits feminist groups offered, see Morton A. Lieberman and Gary R. Bond, "The Problem of Being a Woman: A Survey of 1700 Women in Consciousness-Raising Groups," *Journal of Applied Behavioral Science* 12 (July–August–September 1976):363–379; and Morton A. Lieberman, Nancy Solow, Gary R. Bond, and Janet Reibstein, "The Psychotherapeutic Impact of Women's Consciousness-Raising Groups," in *Women and Mental Health,* ed. Elizabeth

Howell and Marjorie Bayes (New York: Basic Books, 1981), 581–599, originally published in *Archives of General Psychiatry* 36 (February 1979):161–168. A slightly different analysis did not suggest that the movement's political aims were deceptive, but did suggest that "personal change, as opposed to political or ideological change, is the most important benefit of a consciousness-raising experience. . . . The consciousness-raising group emerges as a new form of therapy for women." Lynda W. Warren, "The Therapeutic Status of Consciousness-Raising Groups," *Professional Psychology* 7 (May 1976):139.

103. Annette M. Brodsky, "Therapeutic Aspects of Consciousness-Raising Groups," in *Psychotherapy for Women: Treatment Toward Equality,* ed. Edna I. Rawlings and Dianne K. Carter (Springfield, Ill.: Charles C. Thomas, 1977), 300. For similar perspectives, see Carol J. Barrett et al., "Implications of Women's Liberation and the Future of Psychotherapy," *Psychotherapy: Theory, Research and Practice* 11 (Spring 1974):11–15; Joy K. Rice and David G. Rice, "Implications of the Women's Liberation Movement for Psychotherapy," *American Journal of Psychiatry* 130 (February 1973): 191–196.

104. Allen, "Free Space," 278.

105. Kathy McAfee and Myrna Wood, "Bread and Roses," in *Voices from Women's Liberation,* 416, 419.

106. Carol Williams Payne, "Consciousness Raising: A Dead End?" in *Radical Feminism,* 283.

107. Susan, "About My Consciousness Raising," 242.

108. Echols, *Daring to Be Bad.*

109. Kathie Sarachild, "Consciousness-Raising: A Radical Weapon," quoted in Echols, *Daring to Be Bad,* 90.

110. These are both titles of books by feminist poet and theorist Adrienne Rich. See *The Dream of a Common Language* (New York: W. W. Norton, 1978) and *On Lies, Secrets and Silence* (New York: W. W. Norton, 1979).

111. In the late 1970s and 1980s, race became the leading edge of the "difference" discussion among feminists. See, for example, Cherríe Moraga and Gloria Anzaldúa, *This Bridge Called My Back* (Kitchen Table: Women of Color Press, 1983).

112. Annette M. Brodsky, "The Consciousness-Raising Group as a Model of Therapy for Women," in *Women and Mental Health,* 577; originally published in *Psychotherapy: Theory, Research and Practice* 10 (Spring 1973):24–29. See also the revised version of this article, "Therapeutic Aspects of Consciousness-Raising Groups," 300–309.

113. Anica Vesel Mander and Anne Kent Rush, *Feminism as Therapy* (New York and Berkeley: Random House and Bookworks, 1974), 37. For a shorter version, see Anica Vesel Mander, "Feminism as Therapy," in *Psychotherapy for Women,* 285–299.

114. Elizabeth Howell, "Psychotherapy with Women Clients: The Impact of Feminism," in *Women and Mental Health,* 509–513; Edna I. Rawlings and Dianne K. Carter, "Feminist and Nonsexist Therapies," in *Psychotherapy for Women,* 49–76.

115. Tiefer, "A Brief History of the Association for Women in Psychology, 1969–1991," 15–16.

116. *AWP Newsletter,* April 1971.

117. WH, reel 2, p. 66.
118. Ibid., 69–80.

11: Toward a Larger Jurisdiction for Psychology

1. George A. Miller, "Psychology as a Means of Promoting Human Welfare," *American Psychologist* 24 (December 1969):1074.
2. Ibid., 1065.
3. Ibid., 1066.
4. Miller's address, for example, took place during the first meeting of the American Psychology Association ever to be devoted entirely to "Psychology and the Problems of Society," a programmatic decision that resulted from the activities of the Ad Hoc Committee of Psychologists for Social Responsibility before and during the 1968 meeting in San Francisco. In 1968 the Ad Hoc Committee proposed moving the 1969 meeting out of Chicago, where it had already been scheduled, to protest the police actions against demonstrators at the Democratic National Convention. Their proposal succeeded and the APA Council of Representatives voted to move the 1969 meeting to Washington, D.C. The Ad Hoc Committee then formed a new organization, American Psychologists for Social Action, and advocated that the relationship between psychology and society be the theme of the 1969 meeting. Although they succeeded here as well, Psychologists for Social Action organized a takeover of the session on "Psychology and Campus Issues," claiming that its radical agenda had been both ignored and co-opted. In addition to Miller's address, the official record of the conference includes both harsh criticisms and visionary statements from left-wing radicals about psychologists as social change agents capable of exacerbating and ameliorating a wide range of social problems. See Korten, Cook, and Lacey, eds., *Psychology and the Problems of Society.*
5. "A Larger Jurisdiction for Psychology" is the title of part 1 in Maslow, *Toward a Psychology of Being.*

Index

Abraham Lincoln Brigade, 343 n. 80
Abt, Clark, 169
Abt Associates, 169
Academia, relationship to military and intelligence agencies, 17–19, 20–47, 48–80, 126–129, 149–152, 154–173, 329 n. 103
Achieving Society, The, 139–141
Action for Mental Health, 252
Addams, Jane, 291
Adorno, Theodor, 59
Agency for International Development, 220
Albert Einstein College of Medicine, 256
Alexander, Franz, 33, 121, 331 n. 25
Allen, Pamela, 298, 300
Allende, Salvador, 169, 170
Allport, Gordon, 18, 19, 44, 48, 49, 50, 52–53, 56, 57, 60, 61–62, 64, 77, 79, 125, 133, 180, 183, 197, 198, 226, 264, 291, 335 n. 77, 341 n. 29
Almond, Gabriel, 130, 143, 147, 160
Alpert, Harry, 161
American Anthropological Association, Committee on Research Problems and Ethics, 163–164
American Association for Humanistic Psychology, 270
American Association of Psychiatric Social Workers, 246

American Council of Learned Societies, 32
American Dilemma, An, 66, 176–181, 182, 202
American Institute of Public Opinion, 53
American Institutes for Research, 164
American Jewish Committee, Department of Scientific Research, 185
American Jewish Congress, Commission on Community Interrelations, 360 n. 1
American Psychiatric Association, 8, 66, 249, 252, 261, 278, 287, 288–289; membership figures, 2, 3, 20, 92, 257, 258, 259
American Psychological Association, 50, 77, 129, 165, 172, 173, 193, 216, 235, 250, 259, 265, 289, 290, 304, 347 n. 20, 394 n. 4; membership figures, 2, 3, 20, 84, 262, 322 n. 22
American Society for the Dissemination of Science, 55
American Soldier, The, 76–77
American University, 155
And Keep Your Powder Dry, 52
Anthropologists for Radical Political Action, 164
Antipsychiatry, 284–287, 312. *See also* Radical therapy
Anti-Semitism, 57–61, 181, 185
Appel, John, 98–99

Appel, Kenneth, 83
Arensberg, Conrad M., 28
Association for Women Psychologists, 289–290, 302
Association of Black Psychologists, 289
Association of Black Psychology Students, 289
Authoritarian Personality, The, 58–61, 182, 185, 195
Authority, psychological analysis of, 41, 58–60, 182, 282

Baby and Child Care, 277
Bart, Pauline, 282, 287, 297
Bateson, Gregory, 33, 49, 51, 80
Beals, Ralph, 154, 163–164
Behavioral science, 4, 68, 133, 156, 165–166, 170–171, 177–178, 307; defined, 319 n. 5; origin of term, 349 n. 29
Behaviorism, 8, 36, 122–123, 180, 241, 265, 269
Bell, Daniel, 147
Benedict, Ruth, 33, 49
Benjamin, Walter, 59
Bernard, Jessie, 156
Bernays, Edward, 66
Bettelheim, Bruno, 58, 184–186, 191, 281
Bingham, Walter, 49
Black community, and social pathology, 179, 182, 192, 201–207, 208, 220, 233, 308
Black family, 186–193, 199, 201–207, 233; and matriarchy, 189–193, 201–202, 205, 206, 207, 220, 364 n. 41
Black nationalism, 199, 205, 213–215, 232
Black Panther party, 214
Blain, Daniel, 120, 243
Boas, Franz, 33, 163
Boesel, David, 217
Boring, Edwin G., 8, 9, 49, 80, 100–108
Boulding, Kenneth, 147
Brandeis University, 270–274
Brando, Marlon, 216
Bray, Charles, 135, 150, 155, 161
Brayfield, Arthur, 165, 216, 234–235
Brickner, Richard, 35
Briggs. v. Elliott, 196
Brooke General Hospital, 91, 94
Brooklyn College, 28, 146, 156, 269

Brosin, Henry, 119, 120
Brown, Edmund G., 232
Brown v. Board of Education, 195–199, 208, 209, 251, 366 n. 71
Bruner, Jerome S., 328 n. 100, 333 n. 43
Buber, Martin, 265
Bundy, McGeorge, 143, 171
Burlingame, C. C., 8–9, 257

Camp Callen Training Center, 70
Cantril, Hadley, 32, 49, 54–55, 56, 67, 130, 197
Capra, Frank, 70, 74
Carmichael, Leonard, 135, 148
Carnegie Corporation, 147, 176, 220
Carter, Robert, 196
Cartwright, Dorwin, 42
Cattell, James McKeen, 17
Causes of World War Three, The, 6
Center for Research in Social Systems, 164, 168–169, 228
Center for Studies of the Person, 266
Central Intelligence Agency, 43, 46, 129–130, 158, 160, 163–164, 232, 329 n. 103, 347–348 n. 20
Challenge and Response in Internal Conflict, 168
Characteristics of the American Negro, 179
Chesler, Phyllis, 282–284, 287, 289, 297
Chicago Institute of Psychoanalysis, 331 n. 25
Chicago Women's Liberation Union, 281
Childhood and Society, 145
Childrearing, 34, 51, 140, 182, 186–188, 191, 221, 295–296
Chile, 155, 157, 164, 169–170
Chodorow, Nancy, 295–296
Chomsky, Noam, 10, 172
Civil rights movement: during World War II, 73–74, 89, 175–176; post-World War II, 174, 182, 184, 188, 193–199, 202–205, 208, 213–215, 230, 237, 273, 277, 284, 297, 308
Civilization and Its Discontents, 36
Clark, Kenneth, 187, 192–195, 196, 197, 198, 201, 202, 209–210, 220–221, 222, 224, 231
Clark, Mamie, 187, 193–195, 197, 365 n. 63
Cleage, Albert, 215
Cleaver, Eldridge, 214

Clinical professions: growth during World War II, 82–84, 91–95; growth post-World War II, 3, 243–244, 250–251, 259, 262

Cobbs, Price, 214

Coles, Robert, 218

Collective behavior, 219, 222, 229–230; riots as, 229–231. *See also* Crowd psychology

Colson, Elizabeth, 26

Columbia Broadcasting System (CBS), 67

Columbia Bureau of Applied Social Research, 67

Columbia University Teachers College, 267

Columbia University, 163, 179, 193

Coming of Age in Samoa, 51

Command of Negro Troops, 67, 74

Committee for National Morale, 48–49

Committee on Psychological Examining of Recruits, 65

Community mental health, 4, 223–224, 227–228, 242, 248, 249–258, 276, 285, 314, 379 n. 28

Community psychiatry and psychology, 63, 223–224, 225–226, 228, 240, 254–255, 310, 311

Concentration camp studies, 58, 184

Congress of Racial Equality, 175, 284

Consciousness raising, 290, 297–302, 312; photo, 298

Cook, Stuart, 199

Cornell University, 217

Coser, Lewis, 156

Cotton, John, 279

Cottrell, Leonard, 148

Counseling With Returned Servicemen, 244–245

Counterculture. *See* Human potential movement

Counterinsurgency, 125, 143, 149–152, 155–170, 210, 229, 236, 308

Cross-Cultural Survey. *See* Human Relations Area Files

Crossman, Richard, 56–57

Crowd psychology, 23, 62, 146, 213, 218, 226–227, 229–231; in relation to democracy, 23, 55–56. *See also* Collective behavior

Cultural anthropology, 163–164

Cultural interpersonal school. *See* Culture and personality

Cultural lag, 79–80, 125, 180; origin of term, 338 n. 122

Culture and personality, 4, 33–34, 36, 295, 325 n. 59, 326 n. 71, 327 n. 85

Daley, Richard, 215

Dark Ghetto, 192

Darley, John, 124

Deinstitutionalization, 200, 257–258, 381 n. 65

Del Solar, Daniel, 170

Democracy, psychology of, 50–66, 77–78, 121–123, 180, 186, 241, 252, 264–266, 268–274; role of social and behavioral experts in, 23–25, 35–38, 51–57, 79–81, 121–123, 125, 158, 160–164, 170–173, 237, 245, 252, 256, 268–269, 306, 315, 338–339 n. 127

Dewey, John, 265

Dick, W. W., 156

Dicks, Henry, 39

Dollard, John, 36, 37, 38, 67, 110–111

Dominican Republic, 156

Doob, Leonard, 31, 36, 43, 49, 127, 135, 137–138, 139, 141, 144, 151

Duke University, 147

Dumont, Matthew, 222–224, 225–226

Dungan, Ralph, 157

Dynamics of Prejudice, 185

Echols, Alice, 301

Eckstein, Harry, 147

Economic Opportunity Act of 1964, 209

Edwards, Allen, 332 n. 33

Einstein, Albert, 37, 271

Eisenhower, Dwight, 38, 40, 135

Electroshock, 112, 288

Ellis Island, 19

Emergency Committee in Psychology, 17, 49–50, 102, 329 n. 105; Special Subcommittee on War Experiences and Behavior, 50; Subcommittee on Defense Seminars, 50

Engels, Friedrich, 364 n. 44

Erikson, Erik, 36, 49, 145, 214, 281, 290, 292–294

Ervin, Frank, 225

Esalen, 214

Ethnographic Board, 32

Existentialism, 265

Experimental Division for the Study of Wartime Communications, 32
Eysenck, Hans, 260–261

F Scale, 60, 138
Fair Employment Practices Commission, 63, 64, 176, 335 n. 77
Farnham, Marynia, 278–279
Fascell, Dante, 158, 166
Fear in Battle, 100, 111, 343 n. 80
Federal Bureau of Investigation, 226–227
Federal Communications Commission, 32, 220, 328 n. 100
Federal Contract Research Centers, 135–136, 155
Felix, Robert, 246, 247–248, 259
Fellowship of Reconciliation, 175
Feminine Mystique, The, 290–292
Feminism, 188, 204, 275–303, 312–313
Feminism as Therapy, 302
Feminist therapy, 287, 290, 301–302
Fifty-Minute Hour, The, 199
Fletcher School of Law and Diplomacy, Tufts University, 200
Fogelson, Robert, 233–234
Ford Foundation, 160, 319 n. 5, 349 n. 29
Foreign Broadcast Intelligence Service. *See* Foreign Broadcast Monitoring Service
Foreign Broadcast Monitoring Service, 32, 220, 328 n. 100
Fort Bragg, 149
Fort Sam Houston, 91
Frank, Jerome, 142
Frank, Lawrence K., 35, 122, 176–177, 248, 313
Frankfurt School, 58–59
Frazier, E. Franklin, 187, 188–190, 191, 192, 198, 201, 202, 222
Frenkel-Brunswik, Else, 59, 197
Freud, Sigmund, 23, 36–37, 265, 291
Friedan, Betty, 290–292, 299
Fromm, Erich, 33, 49, 58, 59, 79, 265
Frustration and Aggression, 36–38, 94, 137
Frustration and aggression, as a theme in psychological analyses of social issues, 22, 36–38, 63, 136, 169, 174, 178, 185–186, 192, 213, 226, 228, 229, 233, 305, 308, 326 n. 78
Fulbright, J. William, 141–142

Gallup, George, 53
Gallup Poll, 53
Galtung, Johan, 157
Gardner, Jennifer, 299
Gardner, John, 220
Geldard, Frank, 135
Gender, assumptions in social and behavioral science, 140, 189, 192, 201–205, 279–280, 281–284, 286, 287–290, 293, 295. *See also* Identity; Masculinity; Motherhood
German Psychological Institute for War and Propaganda, 54
Gestalt psychology, 265
GI Bill, 75, 238
Ginsburg, David, 215, 219, 228
Ginzberg, Eli, 22
Goldberg, Louis, 217
Goldstein, Kurt, 265
Golightly, Cornelius, 335 n. 77
Goodenough Drawing Test, 138
Gorer, Geoffrey, 33, 34, 49, 191, 326 n. 71
Governing of Men, The, 28–29
Great Society, 129, 200, 205, 208–209, 211, 217, 219, 224, 234, 255, 309
Gregg, Alan, 37, 85, 91, 120–121
Grinker, Roy, 95, 99, 110, 113, 115, 116, 117, 118
Group for the Advancement of Psychiatry, 247, 249–251, 252, 253, 314; Committee on Social Issues, 249–250
Guadalcanal, 89
Gurr, Ted, 228–229
Guthrie, Edwin, 31

Hanisch, Carol, 299
Harlem Youth Opportunities Unlimited, 193
Harlow, Harry, 148
Harris, Fred, 166, 215, 216, 349 n. 28
Hartmann, Heinz, 144
Harvard University, 56, 80, 177, 281; Business School, 71; Center for International Affairs, 351 n. 61; Department of Social Relations, 68, 217; Laboratory of Social Relations, 68, 127; Sound Control Project, 20
Hawthorne experiments, Western Electric Company, 71
Henley, Nancy, 289
Hershey, Louis, 127, 200, 246

Hilgard, Ernest, 36
Hirohito, Japanese emperor, 41
Hiroshima, 41, 46, 327 n. 92
Hitler, Adolph, 39, 49, 50, 51, 57, 59, 145
Hoffman, Abbie, 274
Homosexuality, in World War II, 88, 89, 108–109
Hoover, Herbert, 24, 53, 243
Hoover, J. Edgar, 226
Hopper, Rex, 146–147, 156, 169
Horkheimer, Max, 59
Horney, Karen, 33, 265, 291
Horowitz, Irving, 160–162
Hovland, Carl, 67, 137
Howard University, 193
Hull, Clark, 36
Human factors engineering, 128, 129. See also World War II, man-machine engineering
Human potential movement, 265, 274
Human Relations Area Files, 37
Humanistic psychology, 122–123, 214, 241, 264–274, 290–292, 312
Humphrey, Norman Daymond, 61, 62
Hysteria, 110, 287

Identity, 277, 280, 290, 292–293; gender, 279, 280, 290–292, 294–296, 315; gender, as a factor in racial identity, 183, 186–193, 199–207, 308; national, 145–146, 151, 307; racial, 174, 181–184, 187–199. See also Gender; Prejudice; Racism and personality damage
Identity crisis, 292–293
Identity politics, 292
Immigration Act of 1924, 65
Immigration, psychological experts and, 19, 65
Industrial psychology, 71, 240
Institute for Living, 8, 257
Institute for Social Research, 59
Institute of Personality Assessment and Research, 46
Intelligence agencies, use of social and behavioral science, 129–130, 153, 157–158, 163–164
Interagency Task Force on Mental Health, 200
Intercultural education, 183. See also Prejudice

Intergroup conflict. See Prejudice
Irrationality, 27–29, 31, 38, 41, 43, 55, 69, 72, 99–100, 110, 171–172, 185, 200, 208, 213, 230, 305, 308
Is Germany Curable?, 35

Jackson, Jesse, 215
James, William, 271
Janowitz, Morris, 135, 151, 184–186, 191
Jefferson, Thomas, 271
Johns Hopkins University, 130, 217
Johnson, Lyndon, 14, 143, 157, 162, 166, 206, 208, 210–212, 215, 216, 217, 219, 231, 234, 252; photo, 211
Joint Commission on Mental Illness and Health, 252, 262, 380 n. 48
Jorgensen, Joseph, 164
Josiah Macy Jr. Foundation, 35, 177
Journal of Humanistic Psychology, 270

Kardiner, Abram, 187, 190–192, 370 n. 14
Katz, Daniel, 42
Kelly, Gail, 299
Kelman, Herbert, 162
Keniston, Kenneth, 227–228
Kennedy, John F., 143, 155, 200, 252–253; photo, 254
Kerner, Otto, 210
Kerner Commission, 14, 166, 207, 208–237, 308, 309; photo, 211; social and behavioral research of, 210, 212–213, 216–224, 228–236, 249, 313
Keyserling, Mary, 203–204
Khrushchev, Nikita, 155
King, Jr., Martin Luther, 182, 214, 215, 277
Kinsey reports, 277
Klineberg, Otto, 42, 179, 181, 191, 197
Kluckhohn, Clyde, 130
Korean War, 126, 127, 129–130, 133, 153, 158
Krech, David, 42
Kris, Ernst, 32
Kubie, Lawrence, 118, 246, 264

Laing, R. D., 284, 296, 312
Langer, William A., 329 n. 103, 336 n. 92
Laredo Army Air Field, 155

Lasswell, Harold, 24–25, 30–31, 32, 57–58, 60, 130, 147, 160, 172
Laura Spelman Rockefeller Memorial, 176, 177
Lawson General Hospital, 91
Lazarsfeld, Paul, 67, 76–77
Le Bon, Gustave, 23, 24, 146, 231
Leadership and the Negro Soldier, 74
Lee, Alfred McClung, 61, 62, 197
Leighton, Alexander H., 22, 26–29, 31, 40, 41, 43, 76, 130, 313, 358 n. 56
Lemberg Center for the Study of Violence, Brandeis University, 218, 231, 314
LeNoir, John, 169
Lerner, Daniel, 22, 130, 135, 161
Lerner, Eugene, 79
Lesbians, 301
Levinson, Daniel, 59
Levy, David M., 39, 49
Lewin, Kurt, 49, 52, 71–72, 161, 324 n. 43, 327 n. 85
Library of Congress, 32, 160
Liebow, Elliot, 217, 221–222, 223, 230
Likert, Rensis, 42, 127, 130, 171
Lincoln, Abraham, 271
Lincoln Hospital Mental Health Services, 256–257
Lindner, Robert, 199
Lippitt, Ronald, 248
Lippmann, Walter, 23
Lipset, Seymour Martin, 147
Lipsky, Michael, 213
Listen, Yankee, 6
Luby, Elliot, 225
Lundberg, Ferdinand, 278–279
Lundberg, George, 170
Lynd, Robert, 143

McCarthy, Joseph, 198
McCarthyism, and social, behavioral, and clinical experts, 132–133, 198, 251, 348–349 n. 28, 366 n. 71
McClelland, David, 139–141, 144, 145, 186, 351 n. 61
McClure, Robert, 40
Maccoby, Nathan, 127
McCone, John A., 232
McCone Commission, 232
McDougall, William, 23, 146
MacKinnon, Donald, 45, 46
Macleod, Robert, 45

McMurry, Robert, 225–226
McNamara, Robert, 157, 159, 171, 201
Maddox, Lester, 234
Malcolm X, 73, 74, 199
Marcuse, Herbert, 59
Mark, Vernon, 225
Mark of Oppression, The, 190–192, 195
Marshall, Thurgood, 196
Martin, Everett Dean, 23
Marx, Gary, 217, 231
Marxism, 58, 59, 133
Masculinity, 187, 189–193, 199–207, 218, 219–222, 223, 231, 233, 296, 308. *See also* Gender; Identity
Maslow, Abraham, 241, 265–266, 269–274, 291, 292
Massachusetts Institute of Technology, 145; Center for International Studies, 160, 355 n. 24; MIT Harvard Joint Center for Urban Studies, 207; Research Center for Group Dynamics, 68
May, Mark, 37
May, Rollo, 291
Mayo, Elton, 71
Mead, Margaret, 33, 35, 49, 51, 57, 60, 80, 142, 173, 180, 191, 248
Medicare and Medicaid, 258
Menninger, Karl, 49, 142
Menninger, W. Walter, 215
Menninger, William, 85, 90, 92, 95, 96, 97, 99, 118, 119, 120, 121, 215, 239, 246, 247, 249
Mental health and illness, changing definitions of, 95–98, 110, 111, 113, 119–123, 223, 242, 271–272, 274–275, 284–287, 311; policy, 200, 209, 227–228, 238–258, 310, 311. *See also* Normality and abnormality
Mental hygiene, in Progressive Era, 25
Mental institutions, 112, 242, 253, 257–258, 288, 289
Mental Patients Liberation Front, 312
Mental Retardation and Community Mental Health Centers Construction Act of 1963, 223–224, 253, 311
Meyer, Adolph, 49
Midcentury White House Conference on Children and Youth, 195, 198
Milgram, Stanley, 282
Military Intelligence Service, War Department, 40

Military psychology, 17–47, 66–81, 82–123, 126–136, 148–152, 153–173, 200–202, 309; illustration, 131
Military sponsorship of social and behavioral science, 68, 125, 126–136, 149–152, 153–173, 307, 309, 355 n. 16
Miller, George, 304
Miller, Neal, 36, 148
Millett, Kate, 293, 294
Mills, C. Wright, 6–7, 161
Modern Woman: The Lost Sex, 278
Modernization. *See* Third World development and revolution
Molnar, Andrew, 169
Montgomery bus boycott, 182
Morale. *See* World War II morale
Morison, Robert, 268
Motherhood, 137, 139, 140, 186–187, 189, 278–279, 288, 293, 363–364 n. 40
Mowrer, O. H., 36
Moynihan, Daniel Patrick, 200–207, 215, 309
Moynihan Report, 188, 199–207, 209, 215
Muller v. Oregon, 195–196
Murdock, George Peter, 37
Murphy, Gardner, 37, 49, 80
Murray, Henry, 45, 46, 49, 177
Myrdal, Alva, 180
Myrdal, Gunnar, 66, 176–181, 182, 183, 185, 193, 197, 198, 202, 222, 366 n. 71

Nagasaki, 41, 46, 327 n. 92
National Academy of Sciences, 157
National Advisory Commission on Civil Disorders. *See* Kerner Commission
National Association for the Advancement of Colored People, 198; Legal Defense Fund, 196, 365 n. 63
National character, 32–43, 59, 136–137, 143–144, 151, 171, 176, 179, 182, 191, 230, 305, 313; American, 50–53; German, 38–40, 42–43, 58, 71, 151, 184; Japanese, 40–43, 71, 151
National Defense Education Act, 259
National Defense Research Committee, Applied Psychology Panel, 135
National Institute of Mental Health, 127–128, 200, 216, 217, 218, 221, 222,

247–249, 252, 259; National Advisory Mental Health Council, 278
National Institutes of Health, 247
National Liberation Front, 165, 167, 168
National Mental Health Act of 1946, 120, 127, 240, 245–249, 253, 311, 378 n. 21
National Mental Health Study Act, 251
National Neuropsychiatric Institute Act. *See* National Mental Health Act of 1946
National Organization for Women, 292
National Research Council, 32; Committee on Food Habits, 52; Division of Anthropology and Psychology, 17, 29–30
National Science Foundation, 46, 127–128, 129, 136, 157, 161, 166, 346 n. 9; estimate of employment in psychological fields, 3
National Security Act of 1947, 43–44, 133
National Social Science Foundation, 166, 349 n. 28
Nazi-era German psychology, 45, 49, 54, 329 n. 105, 331–332 n. 29
Nazism, psychological analysis of, 32, 39, 49, 56, 57–58, 145
Negro Family in the United States, The, 188–190
Negro Family: The Case for National Action. See Moynihan Report
Negro Soldier, The, 74
Neo-Freudians, 33, 87, 265. *See also* Alexander, Franz; Fromm, Erich; Horney, Karen; Sullivan, Harry Stack
New Deal, 183, 272, 309; economists in, 5
New Frontier, 200
New Left, 161, 276, 277, 284
New School for Social Research, 32
New York Radical Women, 297
Newcomb, Ted, 42
1960s, challenge to World War II worldview, 10, 81, 230–231, 236, 255–257, 273–274, 284–285, 312
Nisbet, Robert, 159
Nixon, Richard, 133, 206
Normality and abnormality, 100–119, 238–242, 251, 264, 267, 271, 274–275, 282, 284, 310; illustrations, 101–107. *See also* Mental health and

Normality and abnormality (*continued*)
  illness, changing definitions of
Northside Center for Child Development,
  193
Nutini, Hugo, 157, 164
Nystrom, Robert, 247

Office of Economic Opportunity, 219
Office of Facts and Figures, 31, 331 n. 25
Office of Indian Affairs, 26
Office of Naval Research, 129, 133
Office of Scientific Research and Develop-
  ment, 118
Office of Strategic Services, 31, 43–46,
  53, 54, 158, 180, 220, 328 n. 100;
  photo, 44; Psychological Division, 44;
  Research and Analysis branch, 329 n.
  103, 336 n. 92
Office of War Information, 31, 53, 54,
  180, 333 no. 43; Bureau of Overseas
  Intelligence, 43, 61, 328 n. 100; For-
  eign Morale Analysis Division, 22, 40–
  43, 59, 327 n. 92
Ohio State University, 266
One-Third of a Nation, 201
Operation Breadbasket, 215
Operation Task, 165
*Origin of the Family, Private Property and
  the State, The*, 364 n. 44
Osgood, Charles, 142
Ovesey, Lionel, 187, 190–192

Parsons, Talcott, 128, 147, 346 n. 9
Payne, Carol, 300
Peak, Helen, 42
Pepper, Claude, 247
Pinderhughes, Charles, 218
Plessy v. Ferguson, 198
Police training, 61–62, 226
Policy sciences, 128
Political culture, 143–146, 171
Pope, Arthur Upham, 49
Popular psychology, 100–112, 188, 199
Postman, Leo, 61, 226
Poston Relocation Center for Japanese-
  Americans, 22; photo, 27; Sociologi-
  cal Research Project, 26–29, 40
Poussaint, Alvin, 214
Prejudice, psychology of, 57–66, 72–74,
  174–175, 177–186, 196, 197, 199–
  200, 208, 213, 219–220, 233–235,
  308, 314

President's Defense Science Board, 128
*Prevention and Control of Mobs and
  Crowds*, 226
Price, Don, 132
Princeton University, Center for Interna-
  tional Studies, 147, 169; Listening
  Center, 32, 33 (photo); Office of Pub-
  lic Opinion Research, 32, 54–55, 67,
  332 n. 32, 333 n. 43; Princeton Sym-
  posium on Internal War, 147
Prisoners of war, as subjects of military
  psychology, 39, 40, 49, 129, 167
Professional ethics, 159–168
Project 100,000, 201
Project Agile, 165
Project Camelot, 13, 76, 125, 126, 128,
  133, 134, 135, 136, 146, 147, 148–
  152, 153–173, 209–210, 212, 218,
  228, 230, 307, 352 n. 81, 370 n. 14;
  congressional investigation of, 157–
  158
Project CLEAR, 130
Project Simpatico, 165
Project Themis, 166
Psychiatry, 325 n. 59
Psychoactive drugs, 257, 381 n. 65
Psychoanalysis, 33, 36–38, 51, 55–56,
  58, 59, 60, 112, 115, 117, 138, 139,
  144, 180, 182, 184, 186, 187, 188,
  191–192, 200, 241, 247, 265, 284,
  291, 294
Psychological testing, 45, 55, 59, 64, 92–
  93, 108, 128, 129, 138, 181, 192,
  194–196, 240, 284
Psychological warfare, 124, 128, 155,
  167, 229; origin of term, 332 n. 29.
  See also World War II, psychological
  warfare
Psychological Warfare Division, Supreme
  Headquarters, Allied Expeditionary
  Force, 31, 38–40, 41, 42, 56, 59, 333
  n. 43
Psychologists for a Democratic Society,
  289
Psychologists for Social Action, 289, 394
  n. 4
Psychologists' Peace Manifesto, 77–78
Psychology for the Fighting Man, 102–110
Psychoneurosis, "normal," 95–100, 113,
  119, 244, 257, 259, 262–264, 267,
  277, 311
Psychotherapy, client-centered, 266–268,

274, 298 (*see also* Rogers, Carl); and democracy, 245, 264–266, 268; feminist critique of, 282–284, 283 (illustration), 286, 287, 288–289, 298–300; groups, 263 (photo), 298–302; hypnosis, 114 (photo); narcosynthesis, 115, 344 n. 89; popularization of, 240–241, 244, 257–264, 274, 301–302, 310, 312; professional rivalries in, 259–261, 264; psychodynamic, 117, 267; in World War II, 90, 94, 110, 112–119, 114 (photos)
Public opinion polling, 53–54, 68, 72
Pye, Lucian, 144, 145, 147, 352 n. 72

Racial differences, psychological experts on, 63, 64–66, 179, 181, 184, 335 n. 82
Racism and personality damage, 183–184, 190–199, 204–205, 208, 213, 214, 219–220, 308. *See also* Identity
Radical therapy, 255, 284, 287, 312, 389 n. 45. *See also* Antipsychiatry
RAND Corporation, 136, 167–168, 170
Reagan, Ronald, 227
Redfield, Robert, 26
Reich, Wilhelm, 58
Reiff, Robert, 224
Research Committee on Social Trends, 53
Research Project on Totalitarian Communications, 32
Rheingold, Joseph, 281
Rickover, Hyman, 132
Riesman, David, 159–160
Riots: in Chicago (1919), 232; in Detroit (1925), 232; in Detroit (1943), 60, 61, 206, 232; in Detroit (1967), 207, 210, 215; in East St. Louis (1917), 232; in Harlem (1935), 232; in Harlem (1943), 231, 232; in Los Angeles (1943), 60; psychological analysis of, 61–63, 76, 181, 207, 208–237, 308; in Washington, D.C. (1919), 232; in Watts (1965), 206–207, 209, 232
Rise and Fall of Project Camelot, The, 160
Rockefeller Foundation, 35, 37, 91, 137, 268, 336 n. 92, 343 n. 80; Communications Group, 32; Medical Science Division, 85
Rockefeller General Education Board, 177

Rogers, Carl, 62, 241, 244–245, 265–269, 274, 291
Roosevelt, Eleanor, 51, 271, 291
Roosevelt, Franklin Delano, 32, 40, 49, 54, 86
Rorschach test, 138, 191; photo, 45
Rostow, Walt, 143, 171
Ruml, Beardsley, 176
Rush, Anne Kent, 302
Rusk, Dean, 158, 159
Ryan, William, 205

San Francisco Redstockings, 288
Sanford, R. Nevitt, 59, 197
Sapir, Edward, 33, 34
Sarachild, Kathie, 297, 299, 301
Schreiber, Julius, 70
Scientific management, in Progressive Era, 25, 55
Scientific professionalism, 9–10, 22, 46–47, 74–77, 130–136, 170–171, 212–213, 235–237, 281, 305–306
Sears, Robert, 36, 94
Self, the, 16, 27, 109–110, 183, 192, 213, 251, 255, 265, 266, 267, 286, 290–292, 296, 303, 315
Self-actualization, 267, 269, 270–274, 291–292
Self-help literature, 100–112; illustrations, 105–107
Sexual Politics, 293
Shatan, Chaim, 256
Shellow, Robert, 212–213, 216, 217, 218, 219, 236
Skinner, B. F., 8, 21, 172, 268–269
Slavery, 74, 175, 184, 188–189, 192, 199, 201, 202
Smelser, Neil, 156, 218, 229
Smith College, 290
Smithsonian Institution, 32; Research Group in Psychology and the Social Sciences, 135, 147, 148–149, 150, 152, 161
Social Science Research Council, 32, 37, 76, 176, 346 n. 9; Committee on Comparative Politics, 145, 352 n. 72
Social welfare policies and programs, 193, 199–206, 208–209, 219, 224, 225, 227–228, 233–235, 250–251, 255, 258, 285, 308–309, 311
Social work, growth since 1975, 3

Society for the Psychological Study of Social Issues, 42, 44, 77, 193, 196–198, 332 n. 33; Committee on War Service and Research, 50
Sodium pentothal, 115
Sola Pool, Ithiel de, 160, 171, 228–229
Sorensen, Theodore C., 201
Special Operations Research Office, 128, 136, 149–152, 155, 157, 164, 165, 168, 352 n. 81
Special warfare. *See* Psychological warfare
Speier, Hans, 32
Spelman Memorial, 177
Spicer, Edward H., 26
Spiegel, John, 95, 99, 113, 115, 116, 118, 225, 314
Spock, Benjamin, 279
Sputnik, 128, 133
St. Elizabeth's Hospital, 247
Stages of Economic Growth, The, 143
Stanford University, 143; Center for Advanced Study in the Behavioral Sciences, 68
Stanford-Binet scale, 138
Stanton, Frank, 67
Steiner, Claude, 287
Steiner, Lee, 246
Stevens, S. Smith, 135, 148
"Story of Mack and Mike," illustrations from, 104–107
Stouffer, Samuel A., 22, 67–70, 75, 126–127, 130, 135, 177, 197, 322 n. 28, 336 n. 92
Strecker, Edward A., 35, 49, 56, 65, 83, 278
Student Mobilization Committee to End the War in Vietnam, 164
Student Nonviolent Coordinating Committee, 214, 273
Students for a Democratic Society, 284
Subjectivity, 14–15, 27–28, 144, 194, 213, 235, 237, 241, 265, 274, 275, 280, 297, 300–301, 303, 305, 311, 314, 315
Sullivan, Harry Stack, 33, 86, 87, 88, 95, 121, 265, 325 n. 59
Susan, Barbara, 299, 300
Szasz, Thomas, 284, 285–286, 312

Tally's Corner, 221–222
Tax, Meredith, 294–295

Tet Offensive, 211
Thematic Apperception Test, 59, 138, 191
Third World development and revolution, 125, 126, 135, 136–148, 150–157, 164–173, 186, 236, 239, 307, 308
Tinker, Jerry, 169
Tiryakian, Edward, 147
To Secure These Rights, 178, 195
Tomlinson, Thomas, 219
Trudeau, Arthur G., 150
Truman, Harry, 41, 130, 178, 195, 247
Tryon, Robert C., 44, 244
Turner, Ralph, 217, 218, 229

Uncommitted, The, 227
Union Theological Seminary, 267
University of Arkansas, 142
University of California: Berkeley, 217; Los Angeles, 217
University of Chicago, 24, 26, 127, 266
University of Michigan, 173; Institute for Social Research, 68, 127, 218 (Survey Research Center)
University of Pennsylvania Medical School, 278
University of Pittsburgh, 157
University of Wisconsin, 266
U.S. Air Force, Human Resources Research Institute, 130
U.S. Army: Adjutant General, 92; Neuropsychiatric Consultants Division, 90; Office of Research and Development, 154; Office of the Surgeon General, 92, 98 (Mental Hygiene Branch, Psychiatry Division); Operations Research Office, 130; Research Branch, Morale Division, 67–71, 73–76, 99, 110, 127, 130, 177, 326 n. 78, 336 n. 92
U.S. Department of Agriculture, Division of Program Surveys, Bureau of Agricultural Economics, 42, 53, 127, 328 n. 100, 333 n. 43
U.S. Department of Defense: Advanced Research Projects Agency, 169; Defense Science Board, 166; Research and Development Board, 132
U.S. Department of Health, Education, and Welfare, 159, 172, 220
U.S. Department of Justice, 54
U.S. Department of Labor, Office of Pol-

icy Planning and Research, 200; Women's Bureau, 203

U.S. Department of State, 54, 158, 160; Bureau of Intelligence and Research, Foreign Affairs Research Council, 157; Policy Planning Council, 143

U.S. House of Representatives, Committee on Foreign Affairs, Subcommittee on International Organizations and Movements, 157–158

U.S. Psychological Strategy Board, 130

U.S. Public Health Service, Division of Mental Hygiene, 246, 247

U.S. Senate, Committee on Foreign Relations, 141–142

U.S. Strategic Bombing Survey, Morale Division, 42–43, 127

U.S. Supreme Court, 178, 195–199

Vallance, Theodore, 128, 135, 151, 155, 168

Van de Water, Marjorie, 102

Verba, Sidney, 147

Veterans, 185, 240, 244–245, 292, 311; cost of psychiatric services and disability, 86, 120, 243, 344 n. 100

Veterans Administration, 94, 120, 242–245, 258, 259, 344 n. 100

Viet-Cong Motivation and Morale Project, 167, 170, 358 n. 57

Vietnam War, 81, 156, 163, 166, 167–169, 172, 211, 217, 219, 236, 273, 288, 309, 342 n. 61, 343–344 n. 87; opposition to, 10, 81, 142, 160, 161, 164, 172–173, 208, 217, 227, 277, 304

Violence and the Brain, 225

Walden Two, 8, 268

War, psychological analysis of, 17–47, 48–81, 95–112, 124–152, 153–173, 177, 305–306, 307

"War of the Worlds," 54

War on Poverty, 13, 193, 201, 205–206, 208–255

War Relocation Authority, 26, 28, 332 n. 33

Wartime Communications Research Project, 32

Watson, Goodwin, 32, 49

Weisstein, Naomi, 280–282, 284, 290, 297

Welles, Orson, 54

Wellesley College, 133, 281

West Point, 149

Western Behavioral Sciences Institute, 266

Westmoreland, William, 167, 227

What the Soldier Thinks, 67

White Collar, 6

"Why We Fight," 70

Whyte, William H., 240

William Alanson White Psychiatric Foundation, 86, 325 n. 59

Wilson, Elmo, 151

Wirtz, W. Willard, 200

Wolf, Eric, 164

Wolfe, Dael, 135, 148

Women's Army Corps, 74, 89

Women's Equity Action League, 289

Women's liberation. *See* Feminism

World War I: military mental testing, 55, 64, 85, 92, 181, 335 n. 82; propaganda, 23, 30, 55

World War II: employment of psychological experts in, 18, 84; intelligence, 29, 43–46, 305; internment of Japanese-Americans, 26–29, 27 (photo), 60, 175, 227, 305; man-machine engineering, 20, 128; military racial segregation, 72–74, 175–176; mobilization of psychological experts, 17–25, 82–95; propaganda, 21, 29–30, 32, 39, 70, 108, 135; psychiatric casualties in, 93–100, 96–97, 112–119, 116 (photo), 127, 238, 241, 242–243, 278, 310; psychiatric discharge and rejection, 87, 88–90, 109, 244, 246, 341 n. 29; psychiatric screening, psychological testing, and psychotherapeutic treatment, 68, 84–90, 92–94, 108, 110, 112–119, 114 (photos) 314; psychological warfare, 21–22, 29–31, 34, 36, 38–46, 108; public opinion, 21, 30, 31, 53–57, 305, 333 n. 43; rumor control, 50, 57; shortage of clinical professionals, 87–88, 90–91, 118, 243, 246; sykewar (*see* Psychological warfare); watershed in the history of psychological experts, 5, 19, 74–81, 82–84, 118–123

World War II morale, 29–32, 42–43, 83, 305, 314; democratic, 51–53, 69–72, 180; enemy, 29–43, 305; minority group, 61–62, 72–74, 332 n. 33; U.S. civilian, 48–66; U.S. military, 66–74, 99–100
Wortis, S. Bernard, 246
Wylie, Philip, 278

Yale University, 282; Institute of Human Relations, 36–38, 43, 67, 68, 110, 127, 326 n. 71, 343 n. 80
Yerkes, Robert, 17, 18, 36, 49, 65, 78–79, 85, 125, 148, 181, 250, 332 n. 29
Young Man Luther, 145
Young Radicals, 227
Yu, T. C., 151

Designer: U.C. Press Staff
Compositor: Maple-Vail Book Manufacturing Group
Text: 10/13 Galliard
Display: Galliard
Printer: Maple-Vail Book Manufacturing Group
Binder: Maple-Vail Book Manufacturing Group